RANDOM ACTS OF MANAGEMENT

A DILBERT® BOOK
BY SCOTT ADAMS

BOXTREE

First published 2000 by Andrews McMeel Publishing, Kansas City, Missouri

This edition published 2000 by Boxtree
an imprint of Macmillan Publishers Ltd
25 Eccleston Place London SW1W 9NF
Basingstoke and Oxford

www.macmillan.co.uk

Associated companies throughout the world

ISBN 0 7522 7174 1

9 8 7 6 5

A CIP catalogue record for this book is available from
the British Library.

Printed by Bath Press

RANDOM ACTS OF MANAGEMENT

For Smokey's favorite

Other DILBERT books from Boxtree

Dilbert Gives You the Business
ISBN: 0 7522 2394 1

Don't Step in the Leadership
ISBN: 0 7522 2389 5

Journey to Cubeville
ISBN: 0 7522 2384 4

I'm Not Anti-Business, I'm Anti-Idiot
ISBN: 0 7522 2379 8

Seven Years of Highly Defective People
ISBN: 0 7522 2407 7

Casual Day Has Gone Too Far
ISBN: 0 7522 1119 6

Fugitive from the Cubicle Police
ISBN: 0 7522 2431 X

Still Pumped from Using the Mouse
ISBN: 0 7522 2265 1

It's Obvious You Won't Survive by Your Wits Alone
ISBN: 0 7522 0201 4

Bring Me the Head of Willy the Mailboy!
ISBN: 0 7522 0136 0

Shave the Whales
ISBN: 0 7522 0849 7

Always Postpone Meetings with Time-Wasting Morons
ISBN: 0 7522 0854 3

Introduction

I keep reading stories about CEOs of large companies who make hundreds of millions of dollars in stock options. There is some debate as to whether this is appropriate. One argument is that these CEOs are visionaries, uniquely qualified to create spectacular stockholder value. Another possibility is that CEOs are just showing up and shuffling things around until something lucky happens. I'm leaning toward the "showing up and shuffling" theory.

I'm not saying CEOs are dumb. Put yourself in their shoes. When you're a CEO the only information you have is what your subordinates give you. And they're all unscrupulous sycophants. The last thing you'd ever hear is the truth. So there you are, a powerful CEO astride some mammoth enterprise, armed with no useful information whatsoever. You know you have to do something but there's no way to know what. Your only rational strategy is to do random things until something lucky happens, then take credit.

The alternative – acting nonrandomly – is a sure loser. Let's say, for example, you're a CEO and you fire everyone whose last name starts with the letter *M*. That's a clear pattern, and not a good one. Everyone would think you were a nut. You see, when you don't have a good strategy, any activity that looks like a pattern just makes you look bad.

Conversely, if you act randomly, reorganizing for no particular reason, promoting idiots, merging unrelated businesses, spinning off a few divisions – that looks like leadership. It's leadership for the simple reason that your employees never would have made those changes on their own. Later, when something lucky happens, you can take credit. If nothing lucky happens, call it a transition period.

I wonder what CEOs say to their spouses in private. Do the CEOs begin to believe that their management decisions are connected to the results? I bet they do. It probably sounds like this:

CEO: "Honey, I fired my VP of marketing because I didn't like his shirt, and our stock went up a point!"

Spouse: "Didn't the Fed lower interest rates today?"

CEO: "Try to stay on the topic."

Speaking of other topics, you can still join Dogbert's New Ruling Class (DNRC) and receive the free *Dilbert* newsletter whenever I feel like it, which turns out to be about three or four times a year. When Dogbert conquers the earth, those not on the list will become our domestic servants, except for the CEOs, who have no useful skills.

To subscribe, send a blank E-mail to dilbert-text-on@list.unitedmedia.com.
To unsubscribe, send a blank E-mail to dilbert-off@list.unitedmedia.com.
If you have problems with the automated subscription method, write to newsletter@unitedmedia.com.

You can also subscribe via snail mail:

> Dilbert Mailing List
> United Media
> 200 Madison Ave.
> New York, NY 10016

S. Adams

Scott Adams

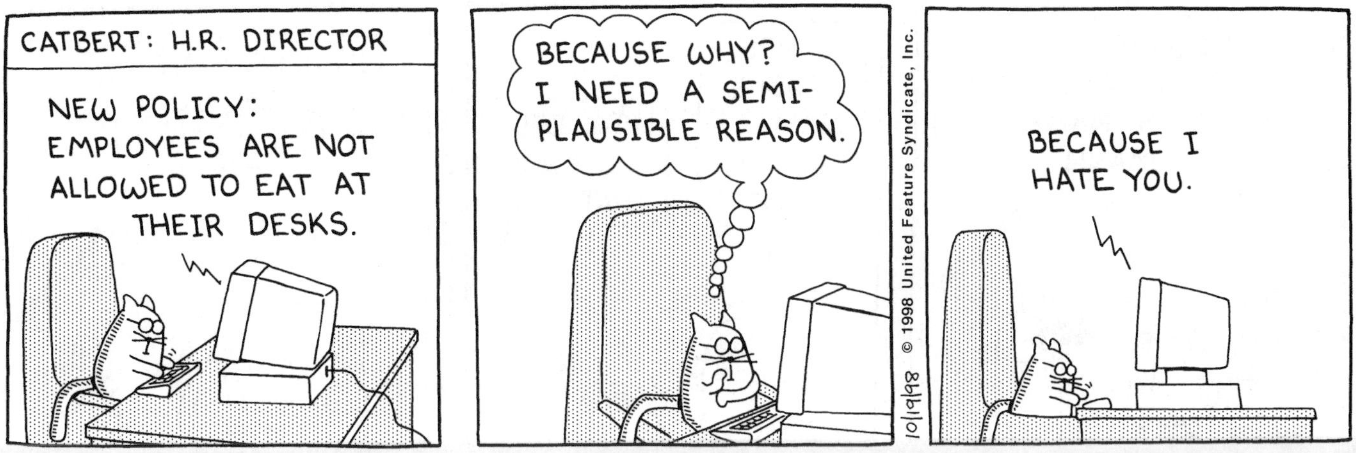
CATBERT: H.R. DIRECTOR
NEW POLICY: EMPLOYEES ARE NOT ALLOWED TO EAT AT THEIR DESKS.
BECAUSE WHY? I NEED A SEMI-PLAUSIBLE REASON.
10/19/98 © 1998 United Feature Syndicate, Inc.
BECAUSE I HATE YOU.

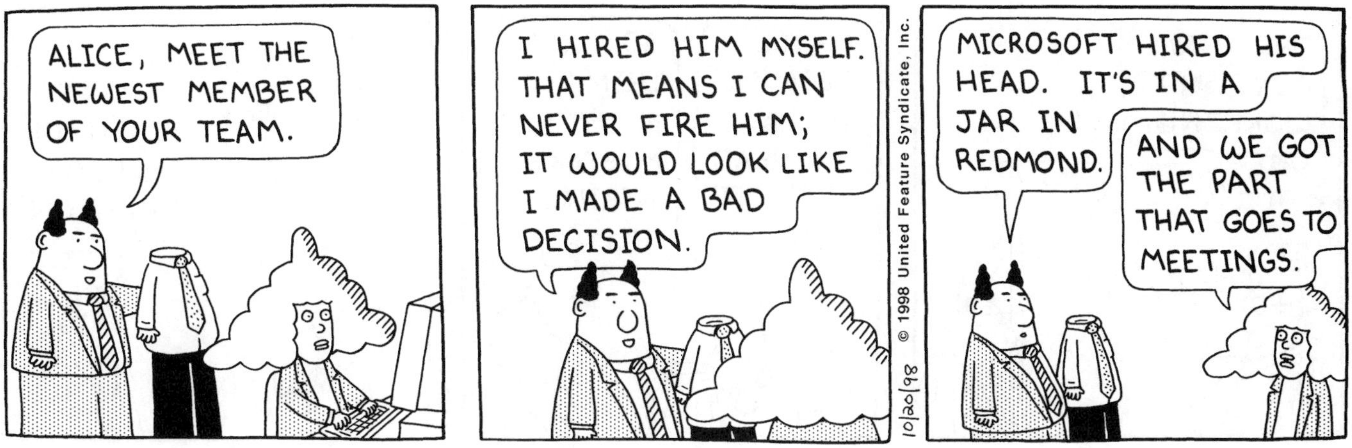
ALICE, MEET THE NEWEST MEMBER OF YOUR TEAM.
I HIRED HIM MYSELF. THAT MEANS I CAN NEVER FIRE HIM; IT WOULD LOOK LIKE I MADE A BAD DECISION.
10/20/98 © 1998 United Feature Syndicate, Inc.
MICROSOFT HIRED HIS HEAD. IT'S IN A JAR IN REDMOND.
AND WE GOT THE PART THAT GOES TO MEETINGS.

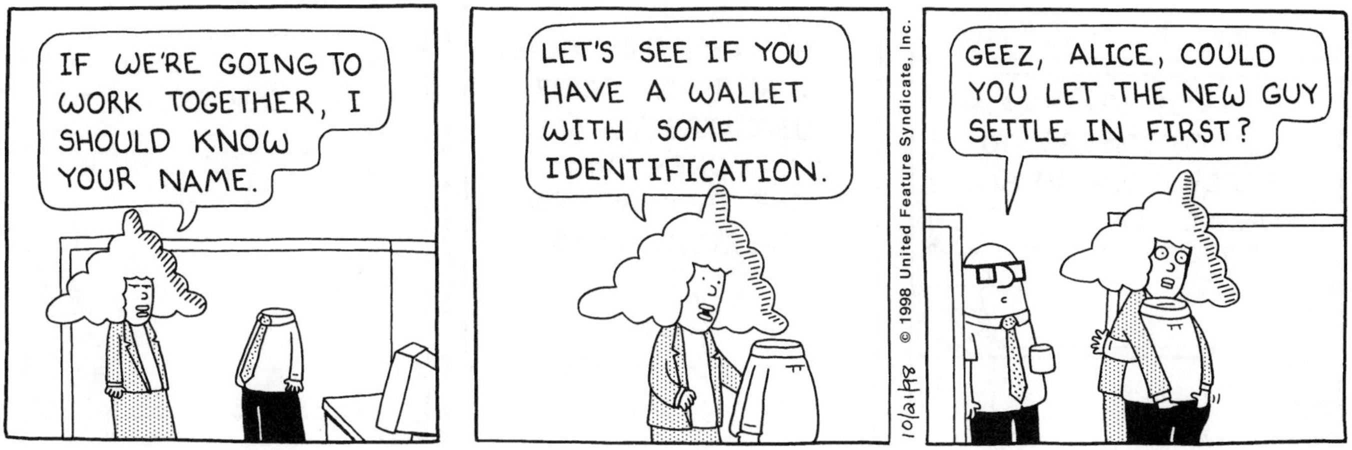
IF WE'RE GOING TO WORK TOGETHER, I SHOULD KNOW YOUR NAME.
LET'S SEE IF YOU HAVE A WALLET WITH SOME IDENTIFICATION.
10/21/98 © 1998 United Feature Syndicate, Inc.
GEEZ, ALICE, COULD YOU LET THE NEW GUY SETTLE IN FIRST?

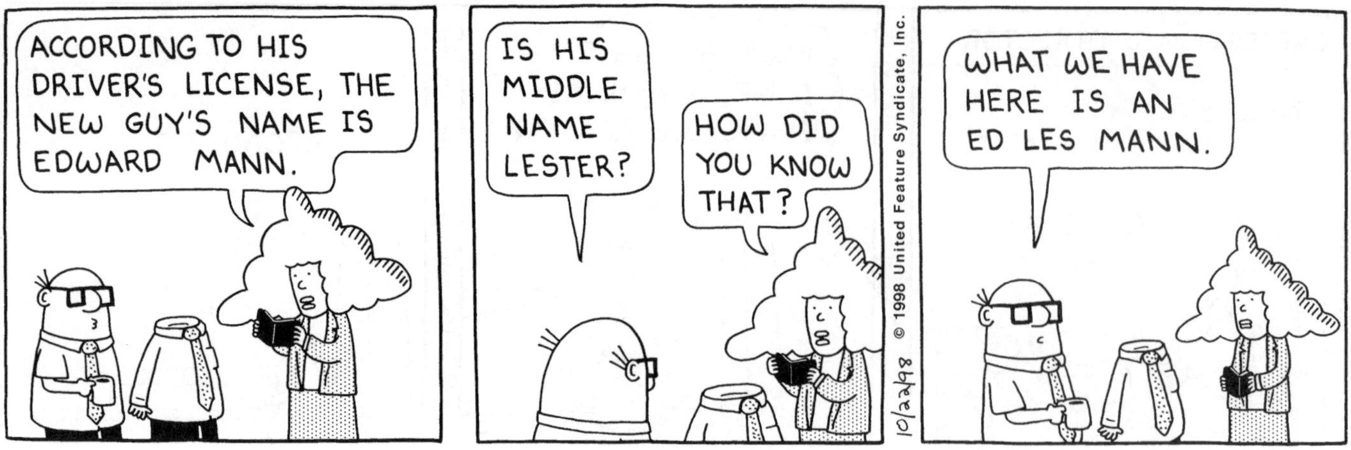
ACCORDING TO HIS DRIVER'S LICENSE, THE NEW GUY'S NAME IS EDWARD MANN.
IS HIS MIDDLE NAME LESTER?
HOW DID YOU KNOW THAT?
WHAT WE HAVE HERE IS AN ED LES MANN.
10/22/98 © 1998 United Feature Syndicate, Inc.

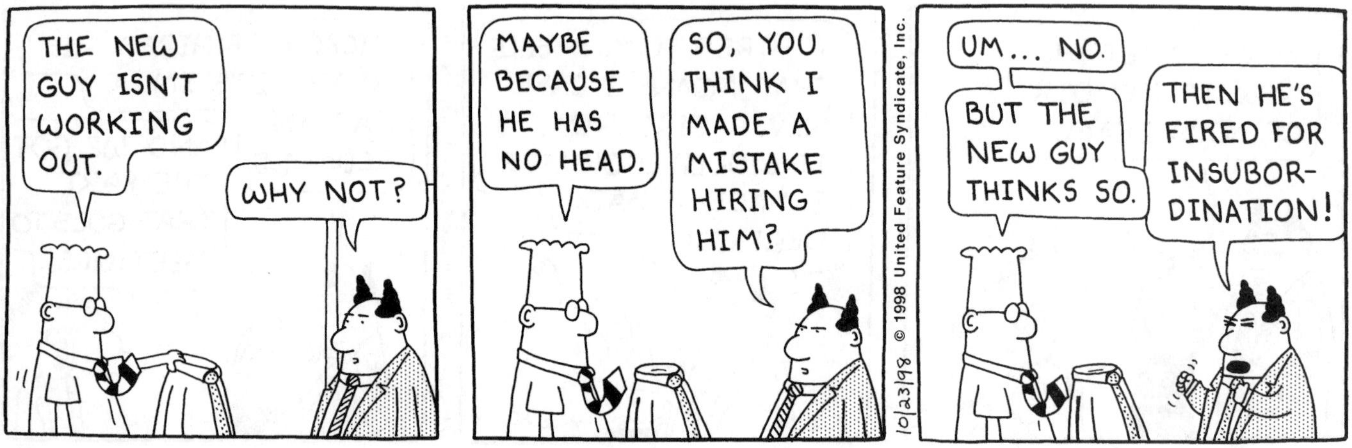
THE NEW GUY ISN'T WORKING OUT.
WHY NOT?
MAYBE BECAUSE HE HAS NO HEAD.
SO, YOU THINK I MADE A MISTAKE HIRING HIM?
UM... NO.
BUT THE NEW GUY THINKS SO.
THEN HE'S FIRED FOR INSUBORDINATION!
10/23/98 © 1998 United Feature Syndicate, Inc.

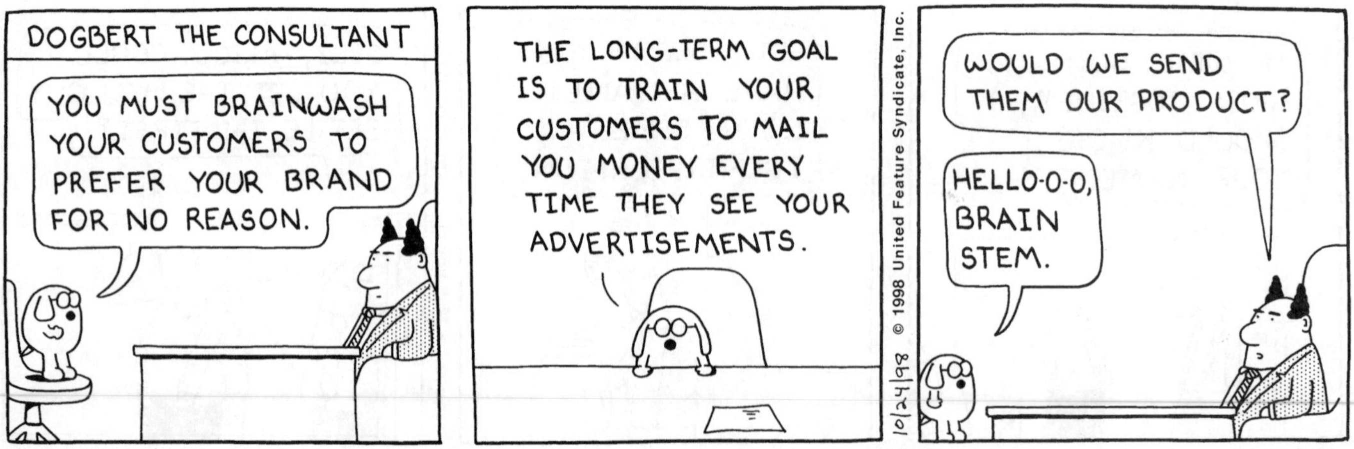
DOGBERT THE CONSULTANT
YOU MUST BRAINWASH YOUR CUSTOMERS TO PREFER YOUR BRAND FOR NO REASON.
THE LONG-TERM GOAL IS TO TRAIN YOUR CUSTOMERS TO MAIL YOU MONEY EVERY TIME THEY SEE YOUR ADVERTISEMENTS.
WOULD WE SEND THEM OUR PRODUCT?
HELLO-O-O, BRAIN STEM.
10/24/98 © 1998 United Feature Syndicate, Inc.

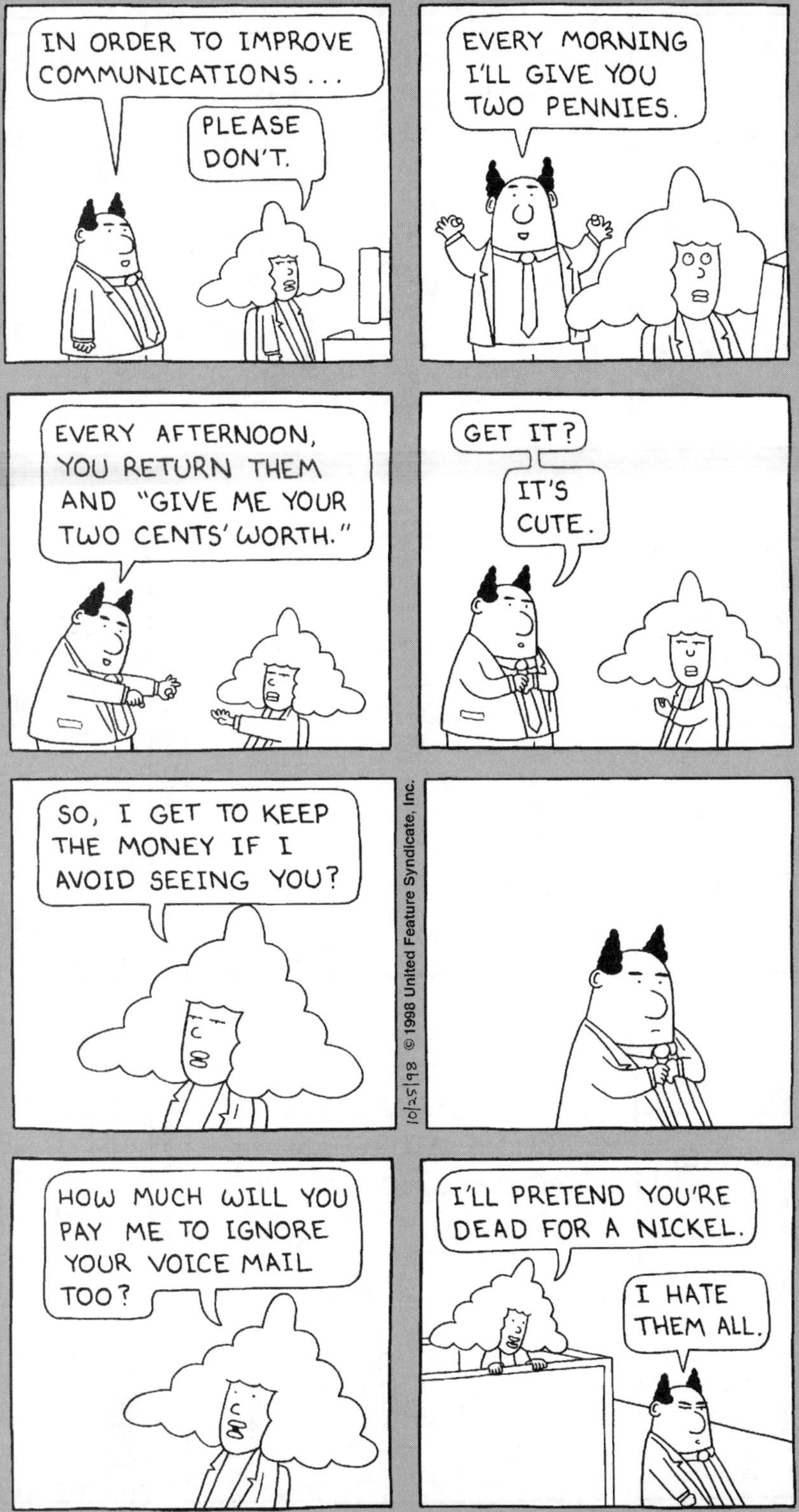
IN ORDER TO IMPROVE COMMUNICATIONS . . .
PLEASE DON'T.
EVERY MORNING I'LL GIVE YOU TWO PENNIES.
EVERY AFTERNOON, YOU RETURN THEM AND "GIVE ME YOUR TWO CENTS' WORTH."
GET IT?
IT'S CUTE.
SO, I GET TO KEEP THE MONEY IF I AVOID SEEING YOU?
HOW MUCH WILL YOU PAY ME TO IGNORE YOUR VOICE MAIL TOO?
I'LL PRETEND YOU'RE DEAD FOR A NICKEL.
I HATE THEM ALL.

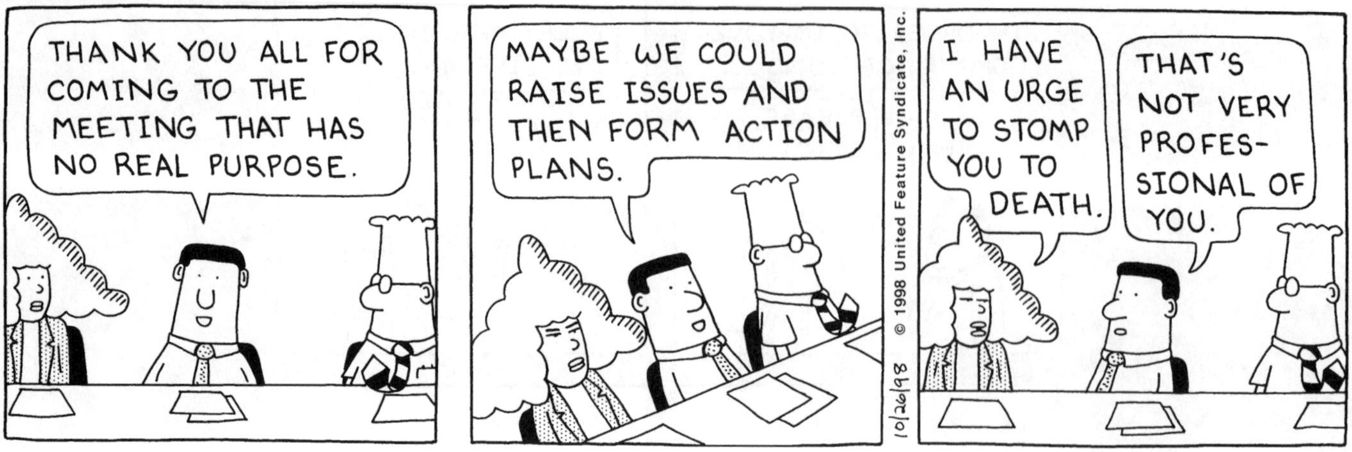
THANK YOU ALL FOR COMING TO THE MEETING THAT HAS NO REAL PURPOSE.
MAYBE WE COULD RAISE ISSUES AND THEN FORM ACTION PLANS.
10/26/98 © 1998 United Feature Syndicate, Inc.
I HAVE AN URGE TO STOMP YOU TO DEATH.
THAT'S NOT VERY PROFES-SIONAL OF YOU.

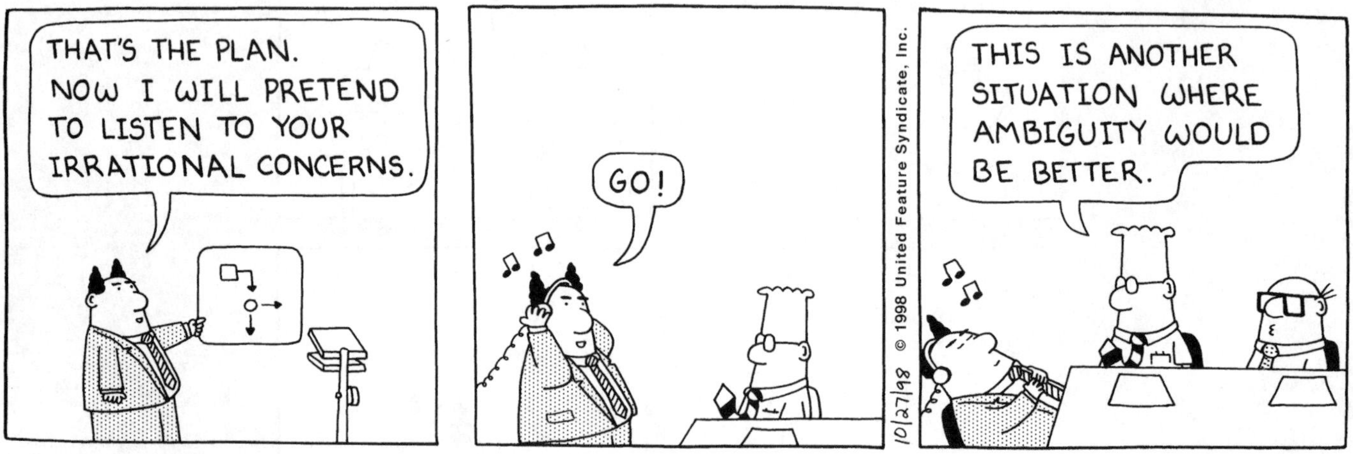
THAT'S THE PLAN. NOW I WILL PRETEND TO LISTEN TO YOUR IRRATIONAL CONCERNS.
GO!
10/27/98 © 1998 United Feature Syndicate, Inc.
THIS IS ANOTHER SITUATION WHERE AMBIGUITY WOULD BE BETTER.

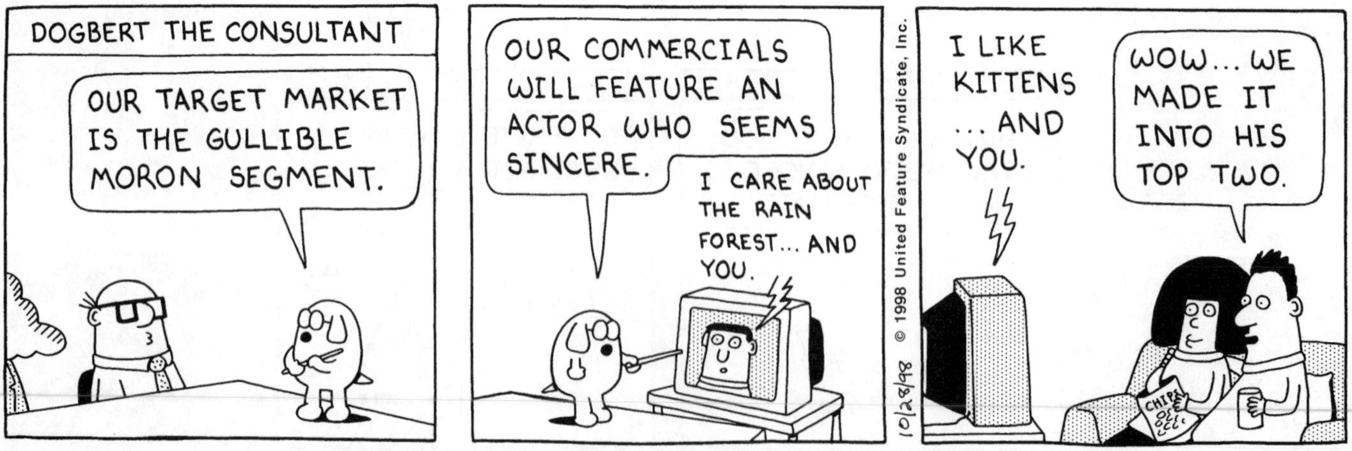
DOGBERT THE CONSULTANT
OUR TARGET MARKET IS THE GULLIBLE MORON SEGMENT.
OUR COMMERCIALS WILL FEATURE AN ACTOR WHO SEEMS SINCERE.
I CARE ABOUT THE RAIN FOREST... AND YOU.
10/28/98 © 1998 United Feature Syndicate, Inc.
I LIKE KITTENS ... AND YOU.
WOW... WE MADE IT INTO HIS TOP TWO.
CHIPS

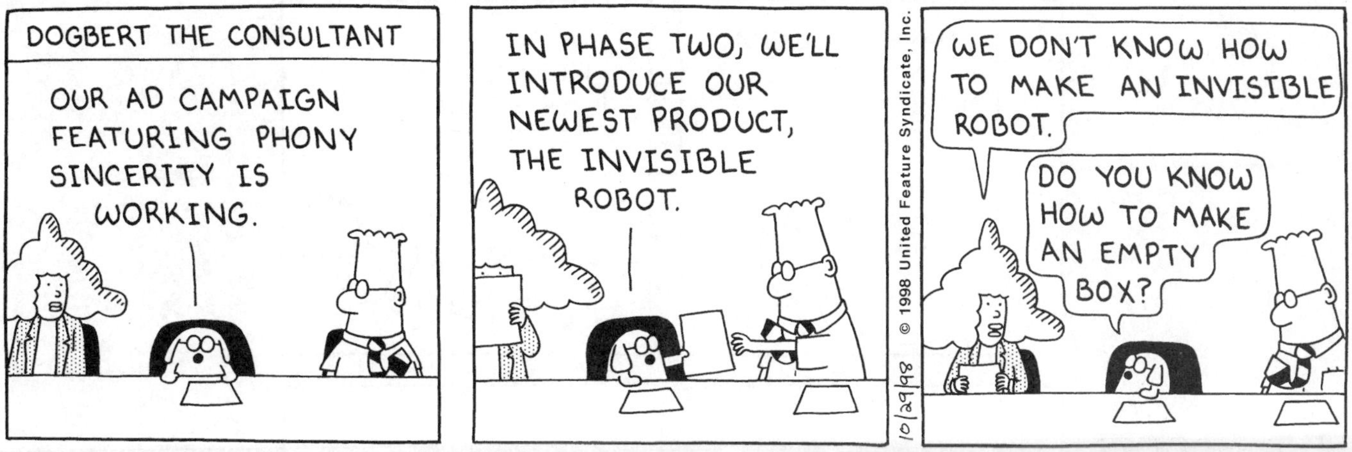
DOGBERT THE CONSULTANT
OUR AD CAMPAIGN FEATURING PHONY SINCERITY IS WORKING.
IN PHASE TWO, WE'LL INTRODUCE OUR NEWEST PRODUCT, THE INVISIBLE ROBOT.
10/29/98 © 1998 United Feature Syndicate, Inc.
WE DON'T KNOW HOW TO MAKE AN INVISIBLE ROBOT.
DO YOU KNOW HOW TO MAKE AN EMPTY BOX?

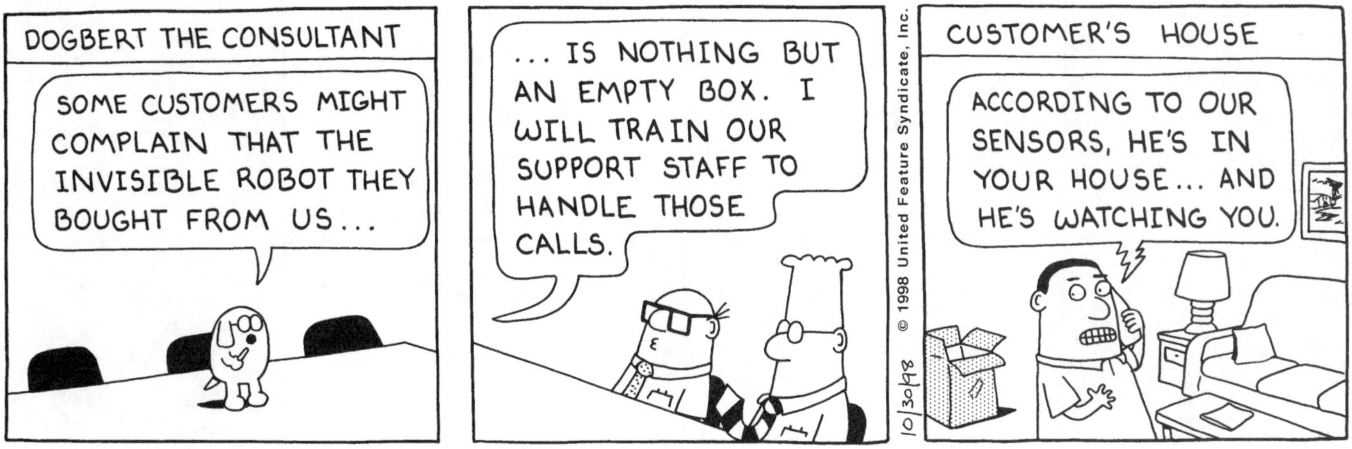
DOGBERT THE CONSULTANT
SOME CUSTOMERS MIGHT COMPLAIN THAT THE INVISIBLE ROBOT THEY BOUGHT FROM US...
... IS NOTHING BUT AN EMPTY BOX. I WILL TRAIN OUR SUPPORT STAFF TO HANDLE THOSE CALLS.
10/30/98 © 1998 United Feature Syndicate, Inc.
CUSTOMER'S HOUSE
ACCORDING TO OUR SENSORS, HE'S IN YOUR HOUSE... AND HE'S WATCHING YOU.

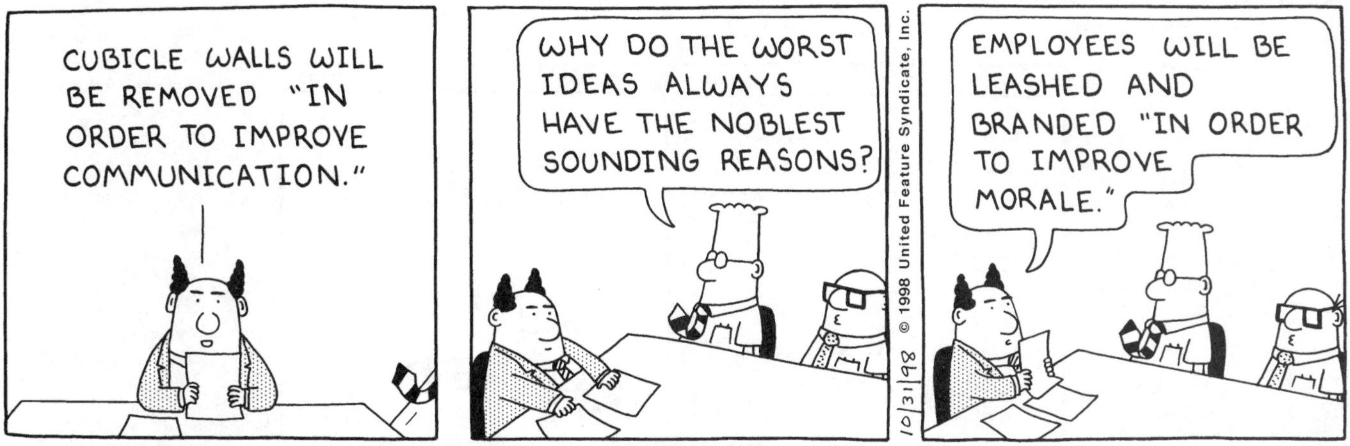
CUBICLE WALLS WILL BE REMOVED "IN ORDER TO IMPROVE COMMUNICATION."
WHY DO THE WORST IDEAS ALWAYS HAVE THE NOBLEST SOUNDING REASONS?
10/31/98 © 1998 United Feature Syndicate, Inc.
EMPLOYEES WILL BE LEASHED AND BRANDED "IN ORDER TO IMPROVE MORALE."

I HAVE A SOLUTION TO OUR MORALE PROBLEM.
Morale Problem
WE NEED A NICKNAME FOR OUR GROUP.
CAN IT BE SOMETHING SCATOLOGICAL?
UM... NO.
HOW ABOUT SOMETHING THAT INVOLVES MONKEYS?
I DON'T THINK SO.
OOH... BUT COULD IT BE SOMETHING THAT'S BOTH SCATOLOGICAL AND INVOLVES MONKEYS?
IT'S HARD TO BE OPTIMISTIC WHILE HE'S SO GRUMPY.
© 1998 United Feature Syndicate, Inc.
11/1/98

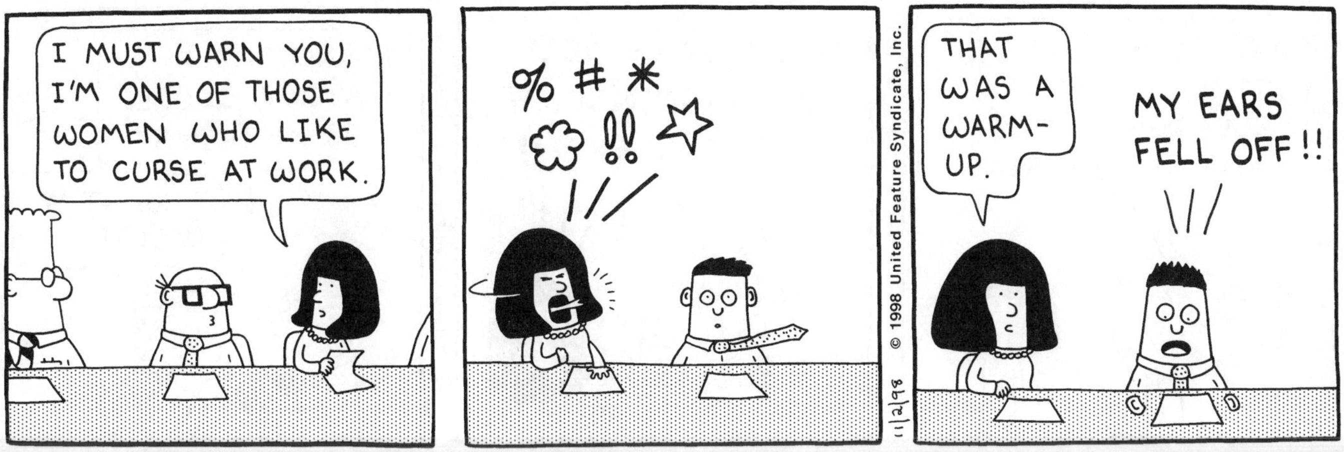
I MUST WARN YOU, I'M ONE OF THOSE WOMEN WHO LIKE TO CURSE AT WORK.
% # * !! ☆
THAT WAS A WARM-UP.
MY EARS FELL OFF!!
11/2/98

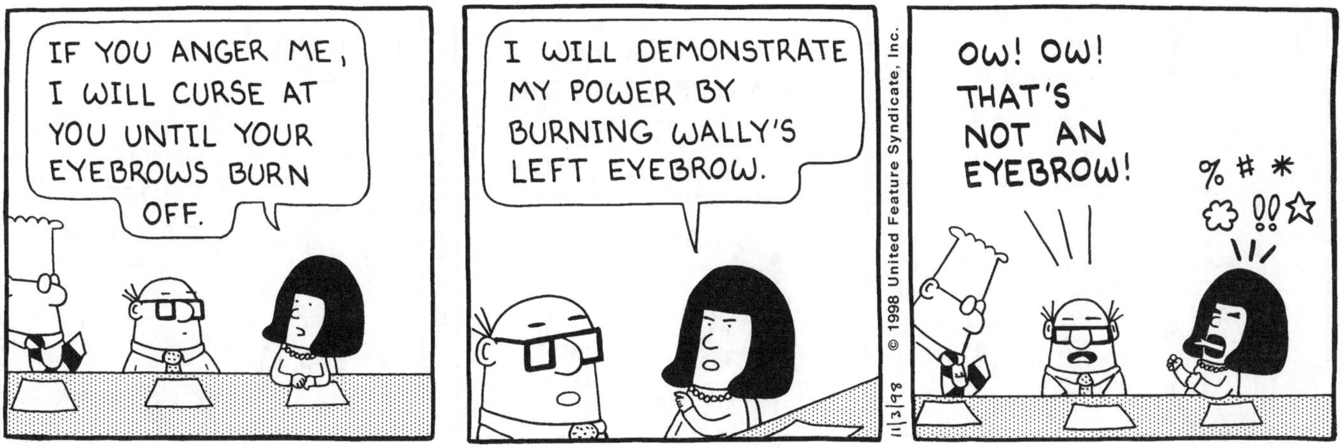
IF YOU ANGER ME, I WILL CURSE AT YOU UNTIL YOUR EYEBROWS BURN OFF.
I WILL DEMONSTRATE MY POWER BY BURNING WALLY'S LEFT EYEBROW.
OW! OW! THAT'S NOT AN EYEBROW!
% # * !! ☆
11/3/98

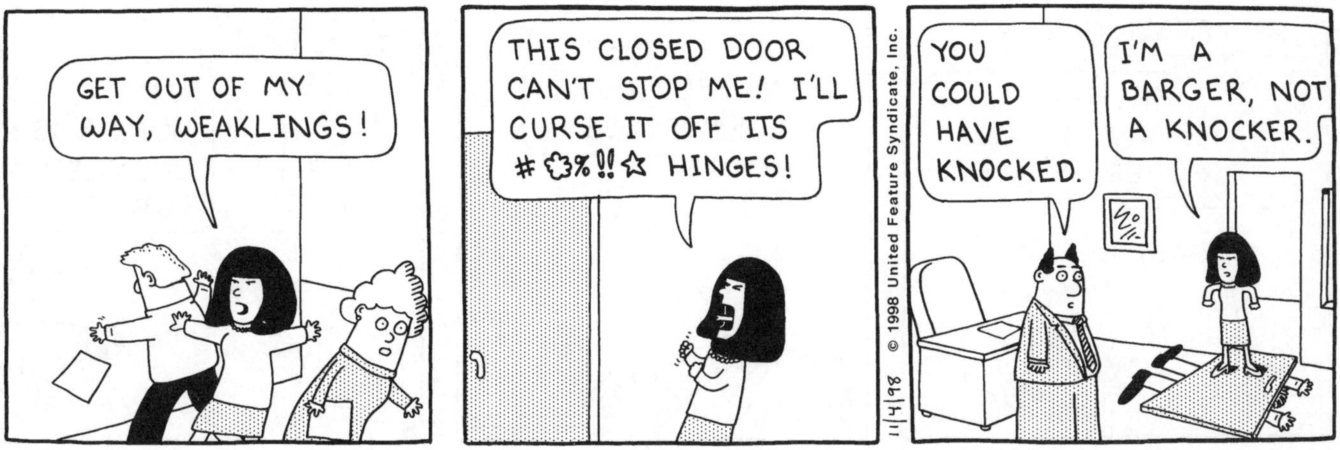
GET OUT OF MY WAY, WEAKLINGS!
THIS CLOSED DOOR CAN'T STOP ME! I'LL CURSE IT OFF ITS #%!!☆ HINGES!
YOU COULD HAVE KNOCKED.
I'M A BARGER, NOT A KNOCKER.
11/4/98

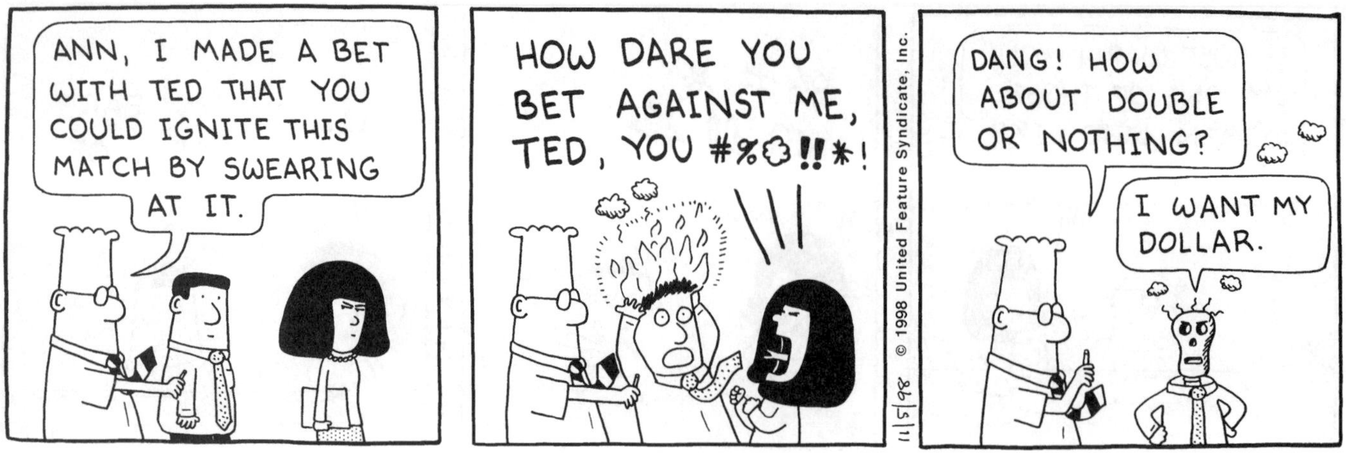
ANN, I MADE A BET WITH TED THAT YOU COULD IGNITE THIS MATCH BY SWEARING AT IT.
HOW DARE YOU BET AGAINST ME, TED, YOU #%✪!!*!
11/5/98 © 1998 United Feature Syndicate, Inc.
DANG! HOW ABOUT DOUBLE OR NOTHING?
I WANT MY DOLLAR.

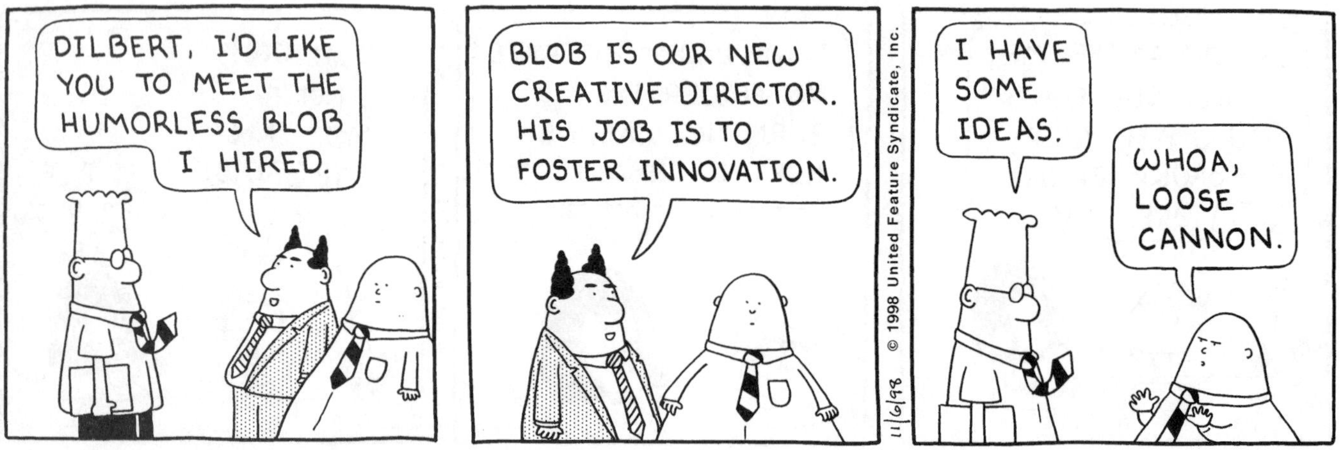
DILBERT, I'D LIKE YOU TO MEET THE HUMORLESS BLOB I HIRED.
BLOB IS OUR NEW CREATIVE DIRECTOR. HIS JOB IS TO FOSTER INNOVATION.
11/6/98 © 1998 United Feature Syndicate, Inc.
I HAVE SOME IDEAS.
WHOA, LOOSE CANNON.

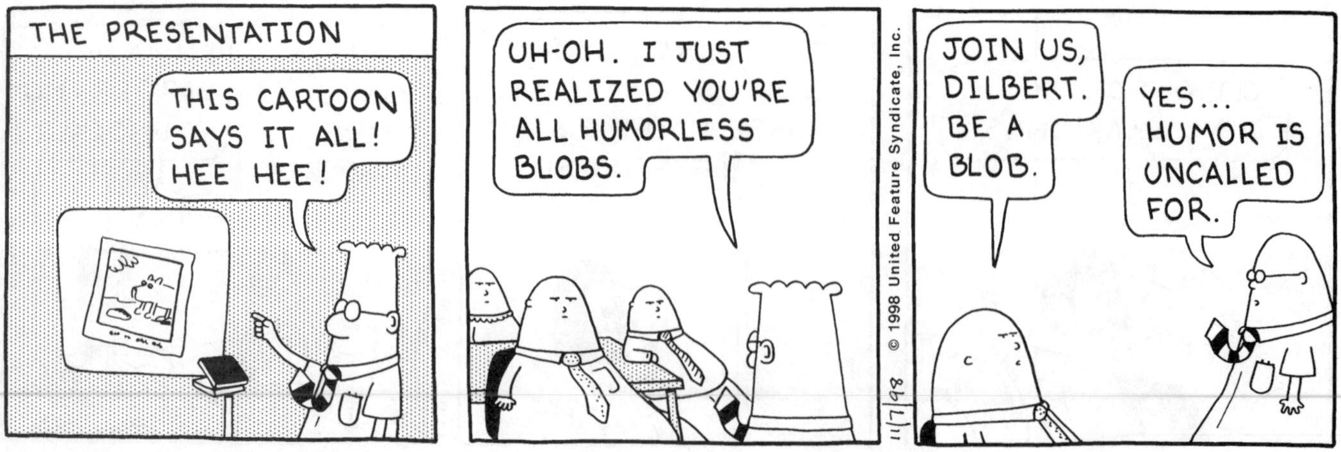
THE PRESENTATION
THIS CARTOON SAYS IT ALL! HEE HEE!
UH-OH. I JUST REALIZED YOU'RE ALL HUMORLESS BLOBS.
11/7/98 © 1998 United Feature Syndicate, Inc.
JOIN US, DILBERT. BE A BLOB.
YES... HUMOR IS UNCALLED FOR.

WALLY, YOU HAVEN'T DONE ANY ACTUAL WORK FOR YEARS, YET WE CONTINUE TO PAY YOU.
HAVE I SAID THANKS?
I'D FIRE YOU, BUT YOUR PERFORMANCE REVIEWS ARE ALL "EXCELLENTS."
SO, MY PLAN IS TO MAKE YOUR JOB A LIVING HELL UNTIL YOU QUIT.
YOU'LL NEVER WIN! MY STANDARDS ARE LOWER THAN YOU CAN IMAGINE!
I'LL START BY MOVING YOU TO A SMALLER CUBICLE.
IS THAT THE BEST YOU GOT? HA HA HA!!!
MOM, GUESS WHO GOT AN OFFICE WITH A DOOR!
11/8/98 © 1998 United Feature Syndicate, Inc.

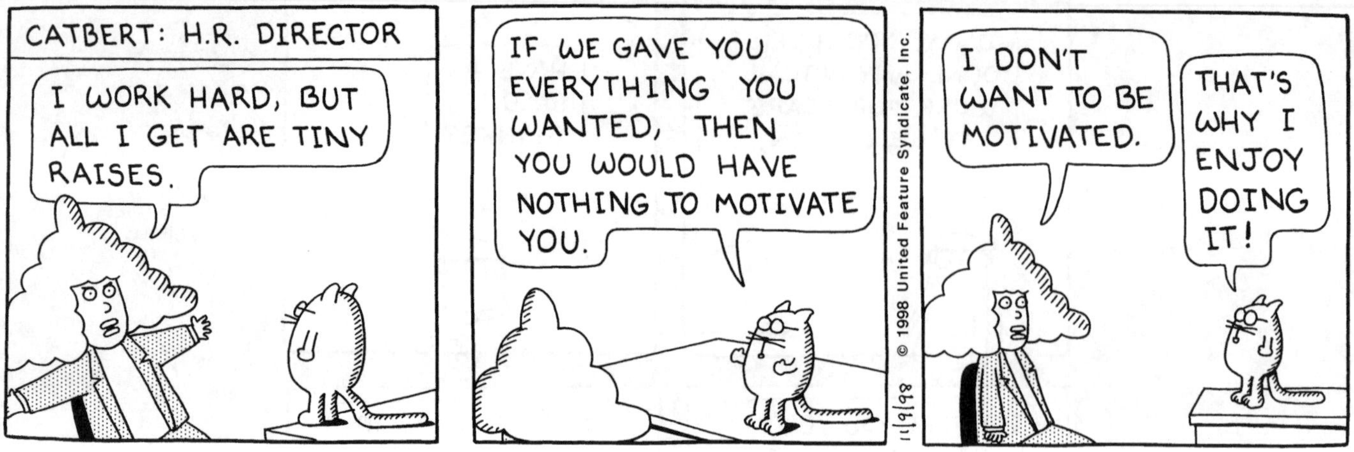
CATBERT: H.R. DIRECTOR
I WORK HARD, BUT ALL I GET ARE TINY RAISES.
IF WE GAVE YOU EVERYTHING YOU WANTED, THEN YOU WOULD HAVE NOTHING TO MOTIVATE YOU.
11/9/98 © 1998 United Feature Syndicate, Inc.
I DON'T WANT TO BE MOTIVATED.
THAT'S WHY I ENJOY DOING IT!

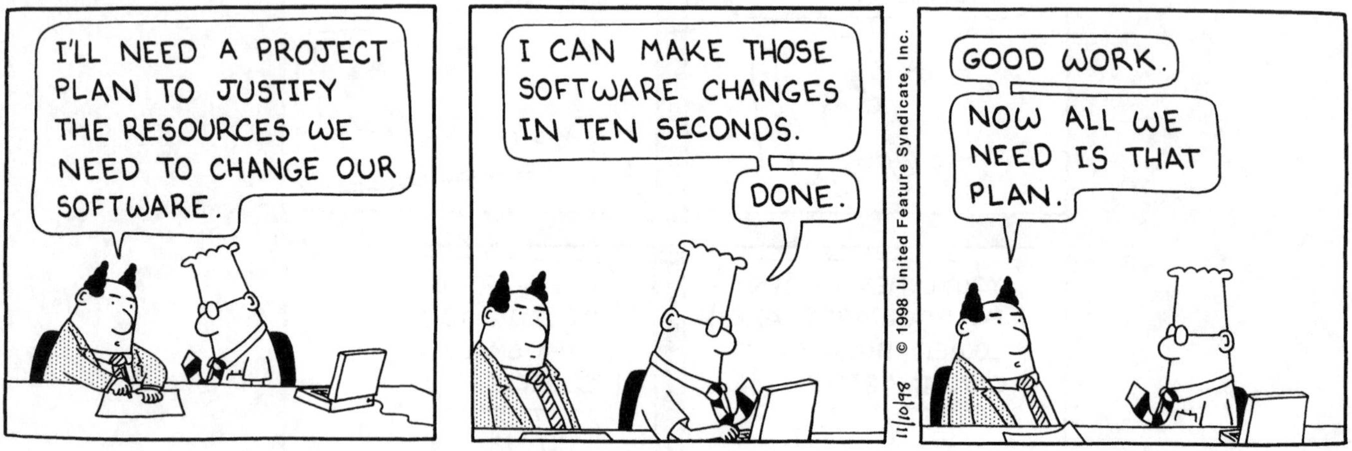
I'LL NEED A PROJECT PLAN TO JUSTIFY THE RESOURCES WE NEED TO CHANGE OUR SOFTWARE.
I CAN MAKE THOSE SOFTWARE CHANGES IN TEN SECONDS.
DONE.
11/10/98 © 1998 United Feature Syndicate, Inc.
GOOD WORK.
NOW ALL WE NEED IS THAT PLAN.

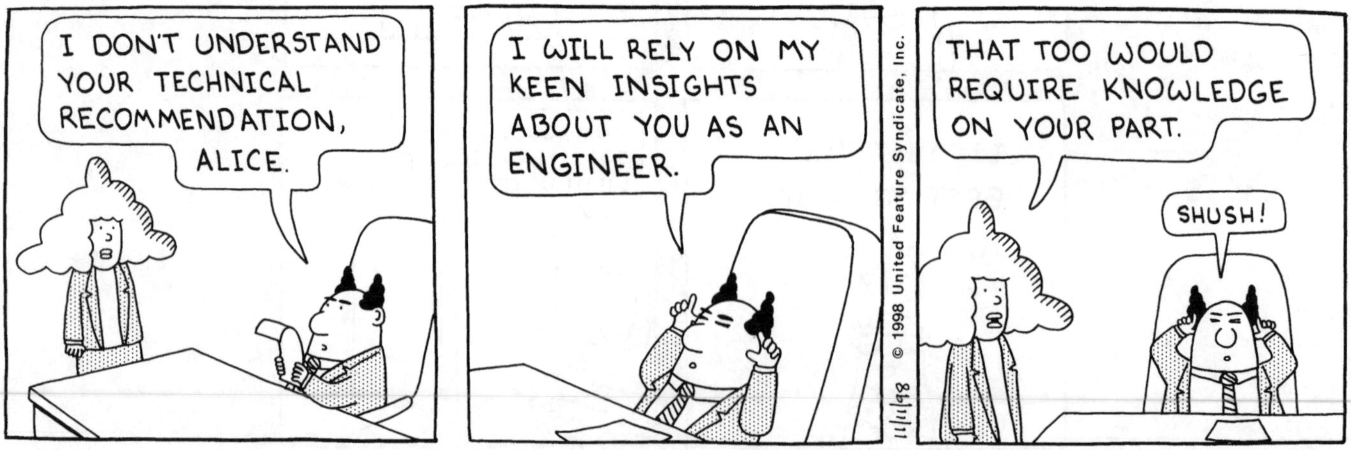
I DON'T UNDERSTAND YOUR TECHNICAL RECOMMENDATION, ALICE.
I WILL RELY ON MY KEEN INSIGHTS ABOUT YOU AS AN ENGINEER.
11/11/98 © 1998 United Feature Syndicate, Inc.
THAT TOO WOULD REQUIRE KNOWLEDGE ON YOUR PART.
SHUSH!

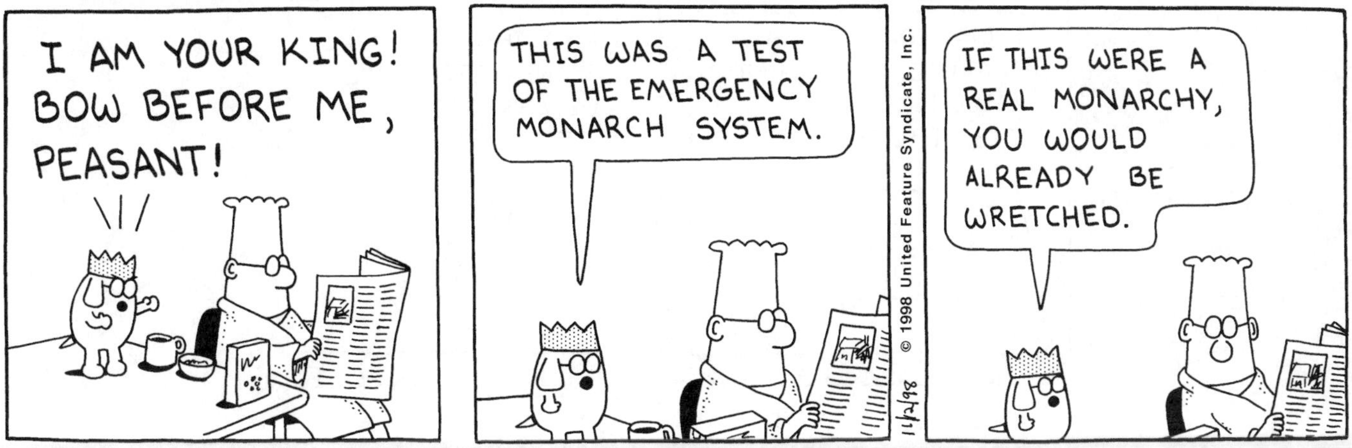
I AM YOUR KING! BOW BEFORE ME, PEASANT!
THIS WAS A TEST OF THE EMERGENCY MONARCH SYSTEM.
11/2/98
© 1998 United Feature Syndicate, Inc.
IF THIS WERE A REAL MONARCHY, YOU WOULD ALREADY BE WRETCHED.

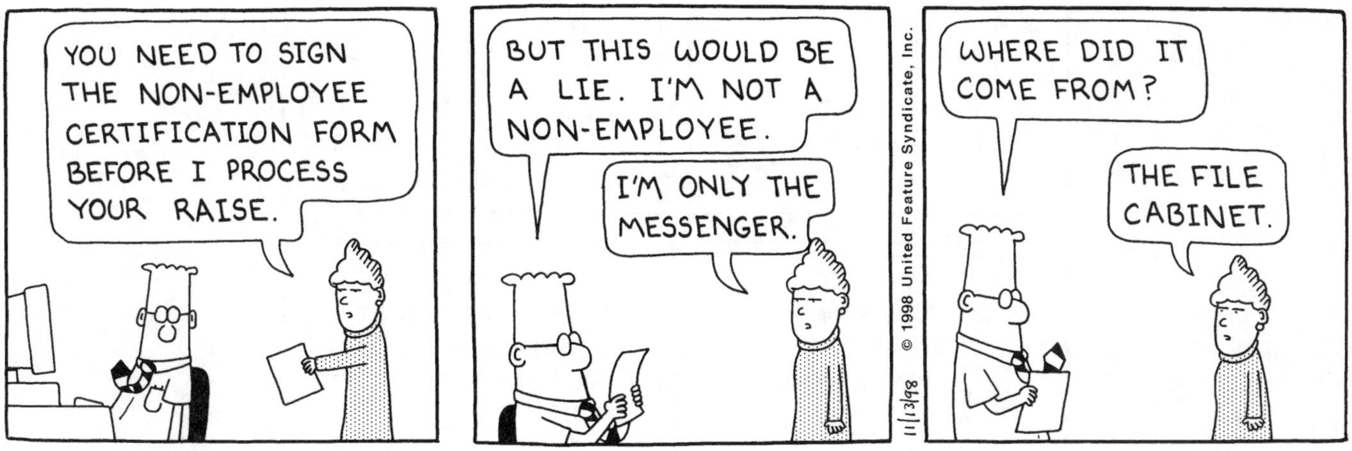
YOU NEED TO SIGN THE NON-EMPLOYEE CERTIFICATION FORM BEFORE I PROCESS YOUR RAISE.
BUT THIS WOULD BE A LIE. I'M NOT A NON-EMPLOYEE.
I'M ONLY THE MESSENGER.
11/13/98
© 1998 United Feature Syndicate, Inc.
WHERE DID IT COME FROM?
THE FILE CABINET.

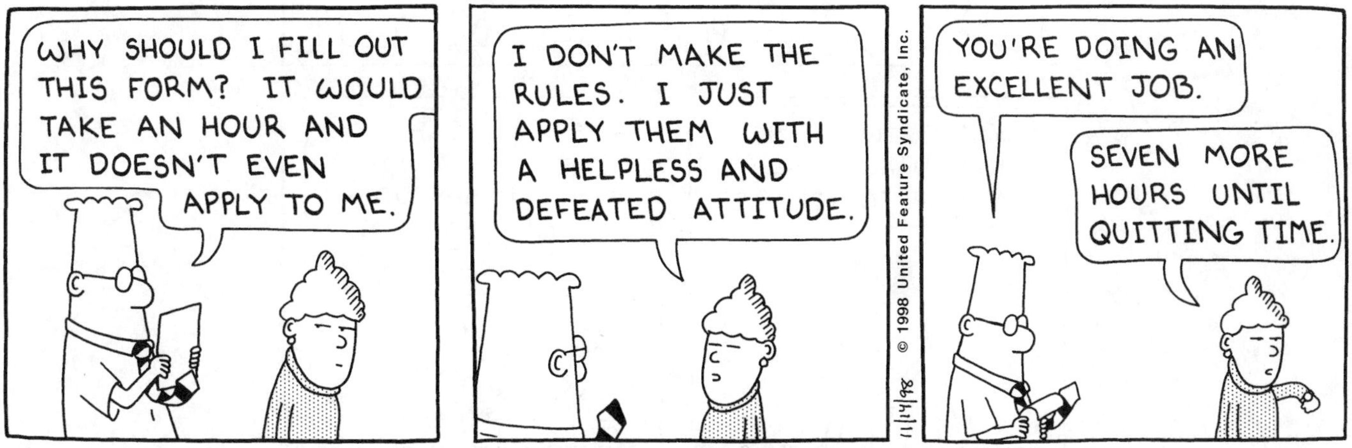
WHY SHOULD I FILL OUT THIS FORM? IT WOULD TAKE AN HOUR AND IT DOESN'T EVEN APPLY TO ME.
I DON'T MAKE THE RULES. I JUST APPLY THEM WITH A HELPLESS AND DEFEATED ATTITUDE.
11/14/98
© 1998 United Feature Syndicate, Inc.
YOU'RE DOING AN EXCELLENT JOB.
SEVEN MORE HOURS UNTIL QUITTING TIME.

FROM NOW ON, THE ORGANIZATION CHART WILL NOT BE DISTRIBUTED.

AND THE INTERNAL PHONE LISTS WILL BE SHREDDED.

CRUMPLE

THIS WILL PREVENT HEADHUNTERS FROM EASILY PICKING US CLEAN.

WHY WOULD HEADHUNTERS CALL US?

THEY WANT TO STEAL YOU AWAY AND DOUBLE YOUR PAY AT ANOTHER COMPANY.

© 1998 United Feature Syndicate, Inc.

11/5/98

WHAT MAKES YOU THINK WE WON'T LEAVE ON OUR OWN ANYWAY?

BECAUSE WORKING HERE DRAINS ALL OF YOUR INITIATIVE.

LET'S PROVE HIM WRONG!

YEAH! I'M NOT SHREDDING MY PHONE LIST!

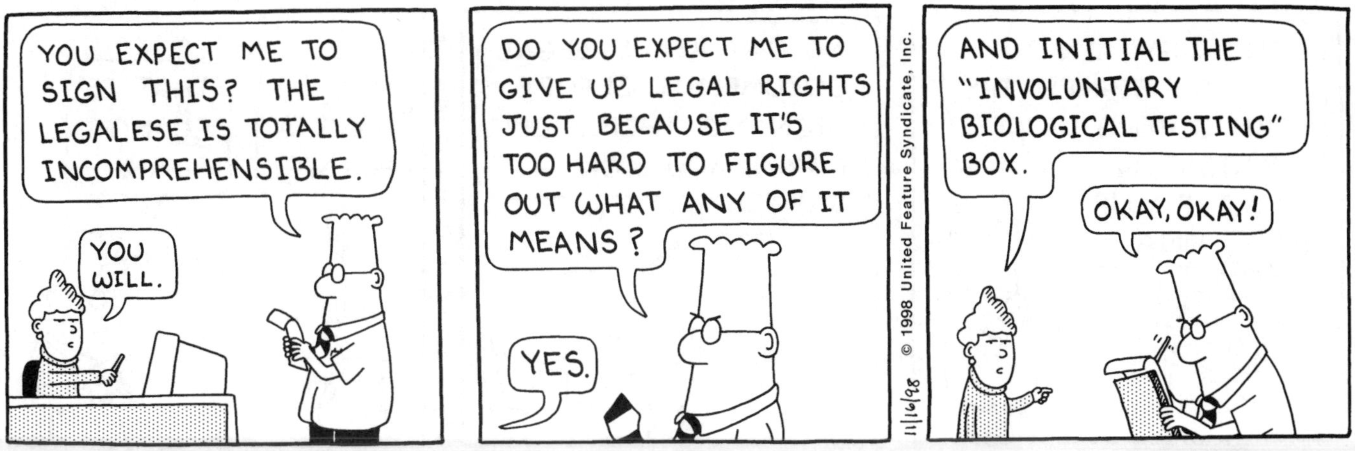
YOU EXPECT ME TO SIGN THIS? THE LEGALESE IS TOTALLY INCOMPREHENSIBLE.
YOU WILL.
DO YOU EXPECT ME TO GIVE UP LEGAL RIGHTS JUST BECAUSE IT'S TOO HARD TO FIGURE OUT WHAT ANY OF IT MEANS?
YES.
11/16/98 © 1998 United Feature Syndicate, Inc.
AND INITIAL THE "INVOLUNTARY BIOLOGICAL TESTING" BOX.
OKAY, OKAY!

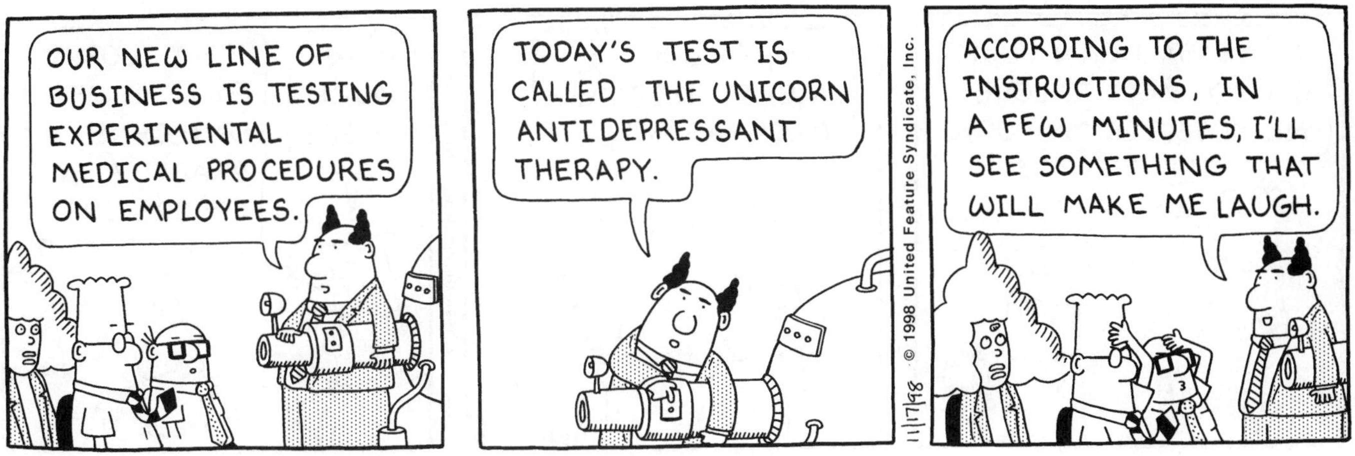
OUR NEW LINE OF BUSINESS IS TESTING EXPERIMENTAL MEDICAL PROCEDURES ON EMPLOYEES.
TODAY'S TEST IS CALLED THE UNICORN ANTIDEPRESSANT THERAPY.
11/17/98 © 1998 United Feature Syndicate, Inc.
ACCORDING TO THE INSTRUCTIONS, IN A FEW MINUTES, I'LL SEE SOMETHING THAT WILL MAKE ME LAUGH.

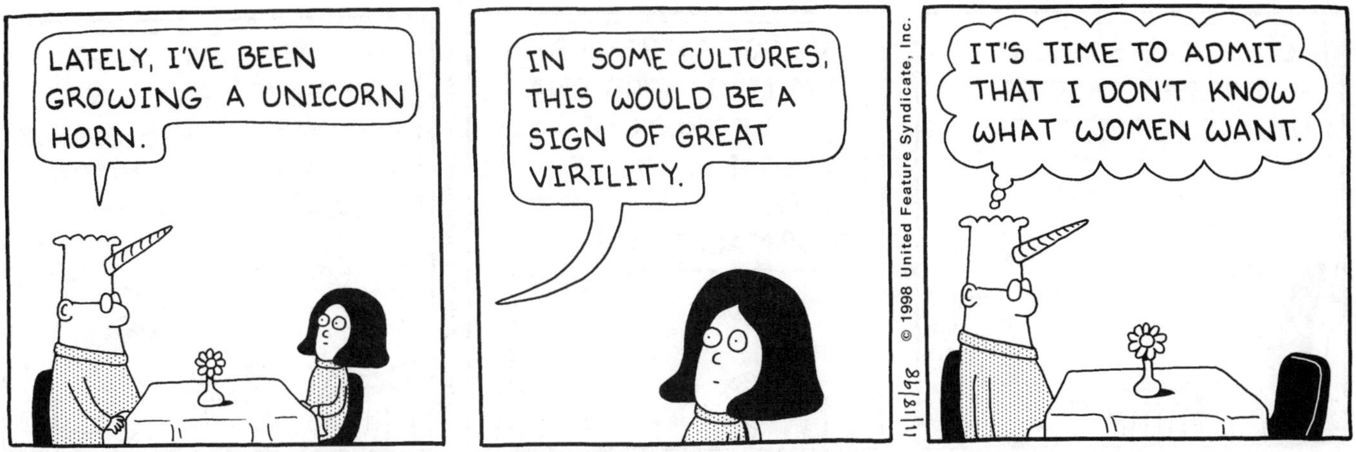
LATELY, I'VE BEEN GROWING A UNICORN HORN.
IN SOME CULTURES, THIS WOULD BE A SIGN OF GREAT VIRILITY.
11/18/98 © 1998 United Feature Syndicate, Inc.
IT'S TIME TO ADMIT THAT I DON'T KNOW WHAT WOMEN WANT.

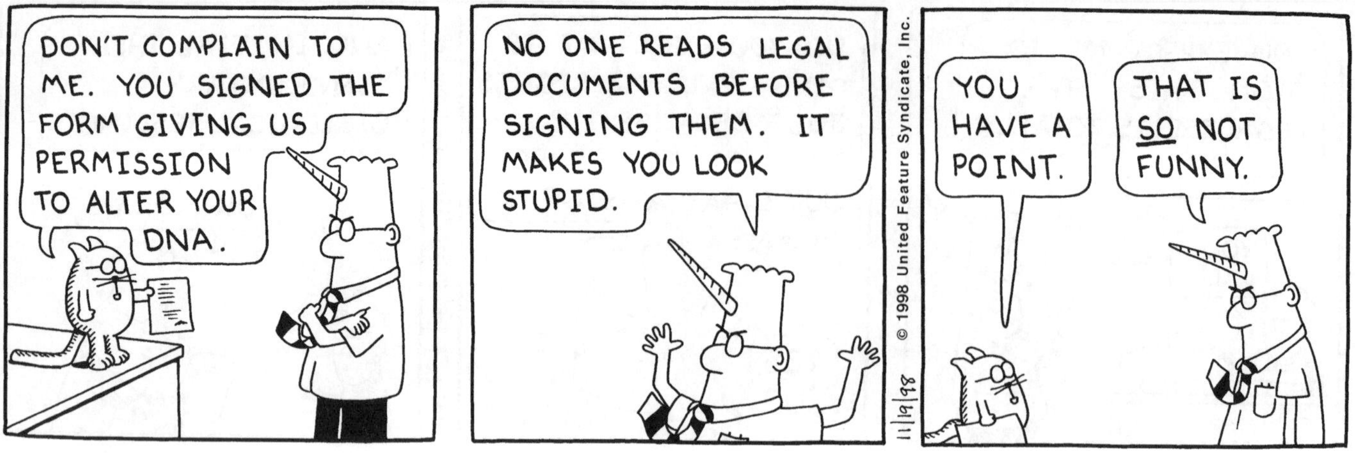
DON'T COMPLAIN TO ME. YOU SIGNED THE FORM GIVING US PERMISSION TO ALTER YOUR DNA.
NO ONE READS LEGAL DOCUMENTS BEFORE SIGNING THEM. IT MAKES YOU LOOK STUPID.
© 1998 United Feature Syndicate, Inc.
11/19/98
YOU HAVE A POINT.
THAT IS SO NOT FUNNY.

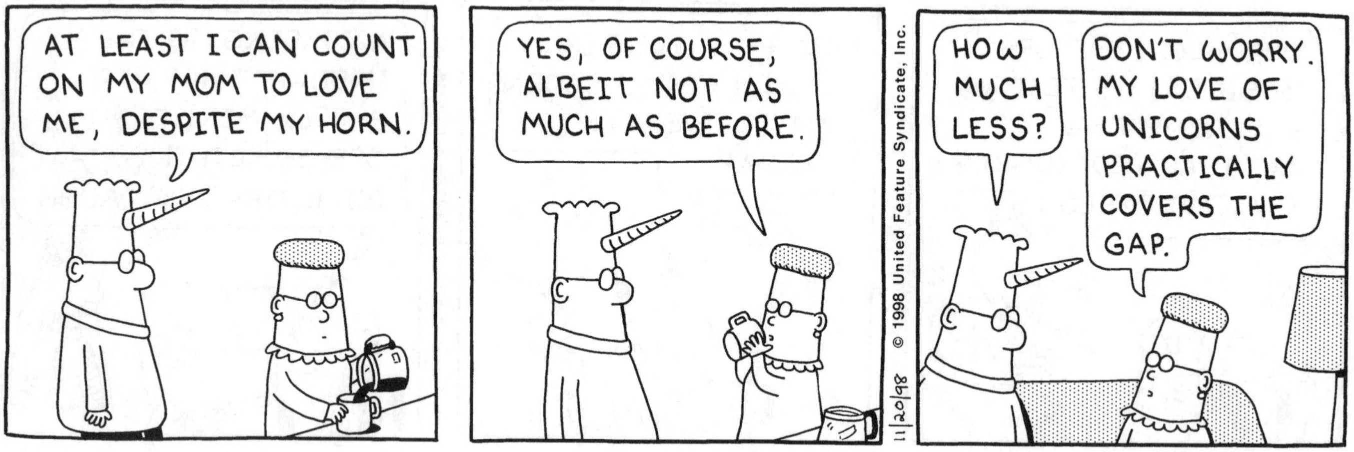
AT LEAST I CAN COUNT ON MY MOM TO LOVE ME, DESPITE MY HORN.
YES, OF COURSE, ALBEIT NOT AS MUCH AS BEFORE.
© 1998 United Feature Syndicate, Inc.
11/20/98
HOW MUCH LESS?
DON'T WORRY. MY LOVE OF UNICORNS PRACTICALLY COVERS THE GAP.

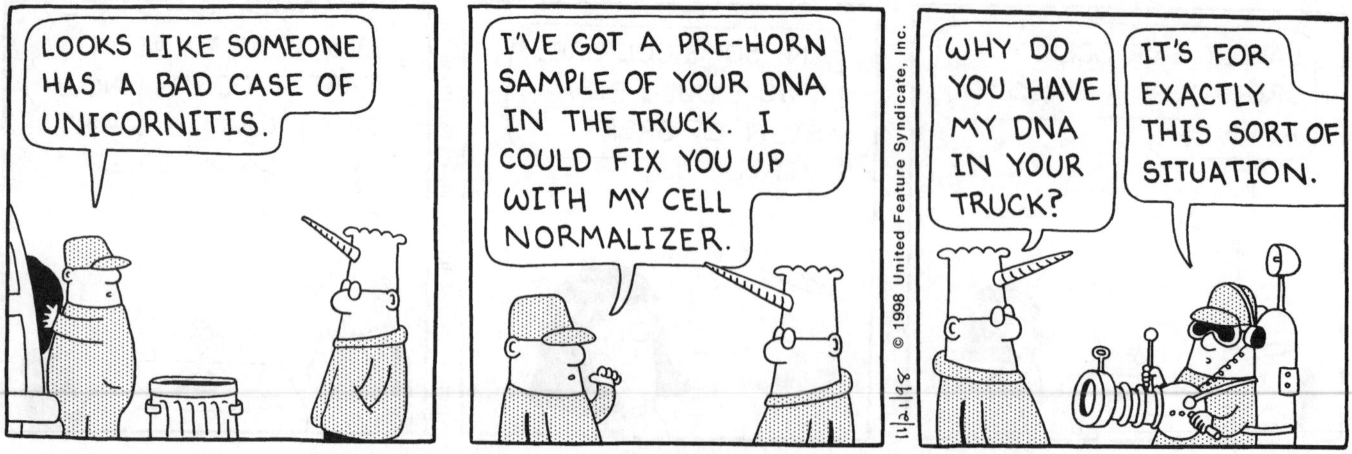
LOOKS LIKE SOMEONE HAS A BAD CASE OF UNICORNITIS.
I'VE GOT A PRE-HORN SAMPLE OF YOUR DNA IN THE TRUCK. I COULD FIX YOU UP WITH MY CELL NORMALIZER.
© 1998 United Feature Syndicate, Inc.
11/21/98
WHY DO YOU HAVE MY DNA IN YOUR TRUCK?
IT'S FOR EXACTLY THIS SORT OF SITUATION.

OUR GOAL THIS YEAR IS ZERO DISABLING INJURIES.
INJURIES
0
LAST YEAR OUR GOAL WAS TWENTY-SIX DISABLING INJURIES.
IN RETROSPECT, THAT WAS A MISTAKE.
26
WE HAD TO INJURE NINE EMPLOYEES TO MEET THE GOAL.
IF YOU HAVE AN INJURY, FILL OUT THESE FORMS IMMEDIATELY.
11/22/98 © 1998 United Feature Syndicate, Inc.
THESE ARE RESIGNATION FORMS.
IF YOU COVER THE WORD "RESIGNATION" WITH YOUR THUMB, IT'S AN INJURY REPORT.
THIS PLACE MAKES ME SICK.
WE'LL MISS YOU.

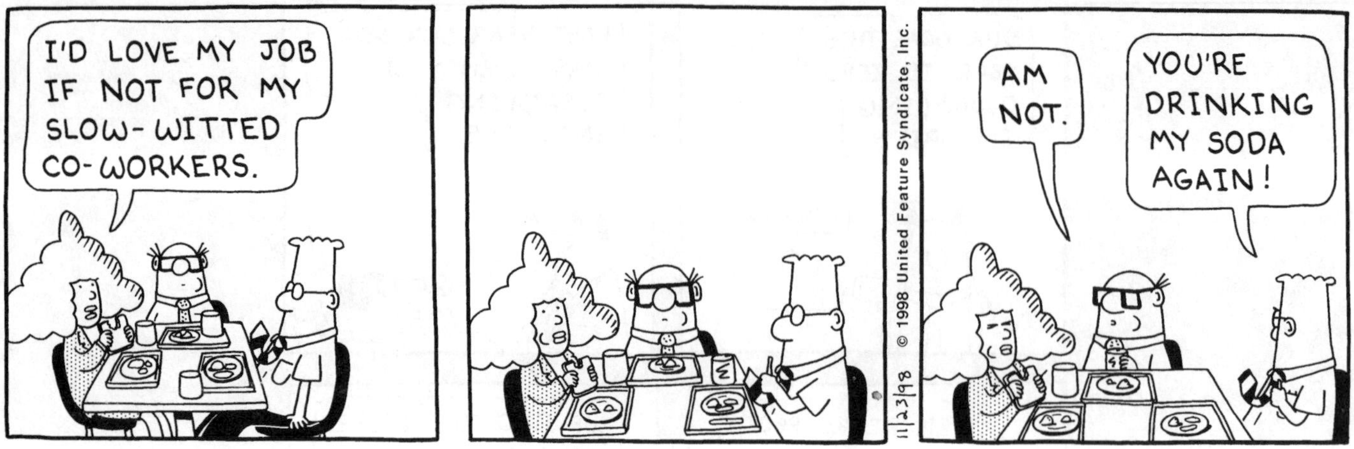
I'D LOVE MY JOB IF NOT FOR MY SLOW-WITTED CO-WORKERS.
11/23/98 © 1998 United Feature Syndicate, Inc.
AM NOT.
YOU'RE DRINKING MY SODA AGAIN!

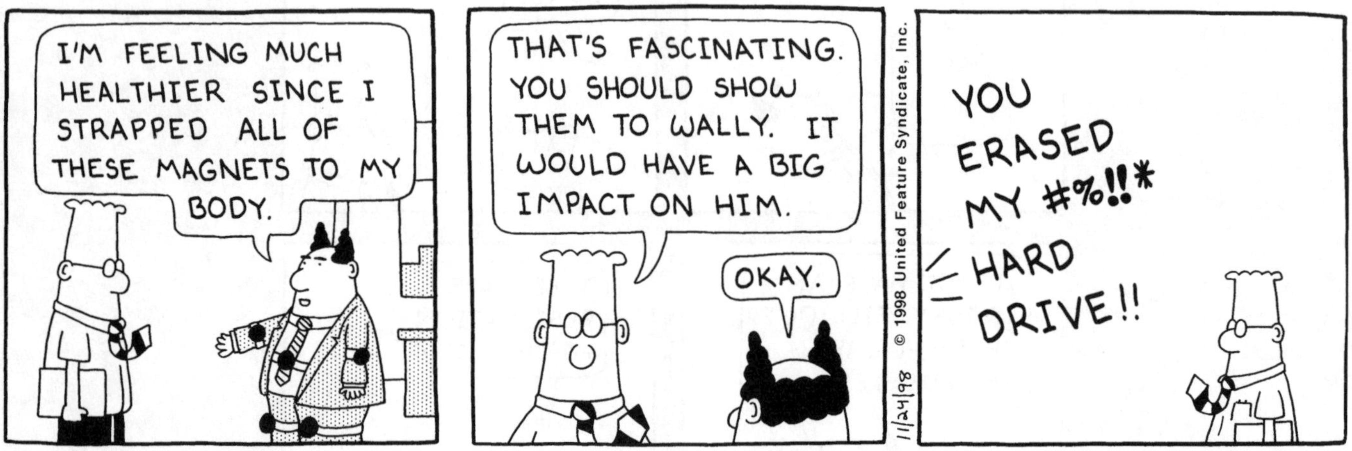
I'M FEELING MUCH HEALTHIER SINCE I STRAPPED ALL OF THESE MAGNETS TO MY BODY.
THAT'S FASCINATING. YOU SHOULD SHOW THEM TO WALLY. IT WOULD HAVE A BIG IMPACT ON HIM.
OKAY.
11/24/98 © 1998 United Feature Syndicate, Inc.
YOU ERASED MY #%!!* HARD DRIVE!!

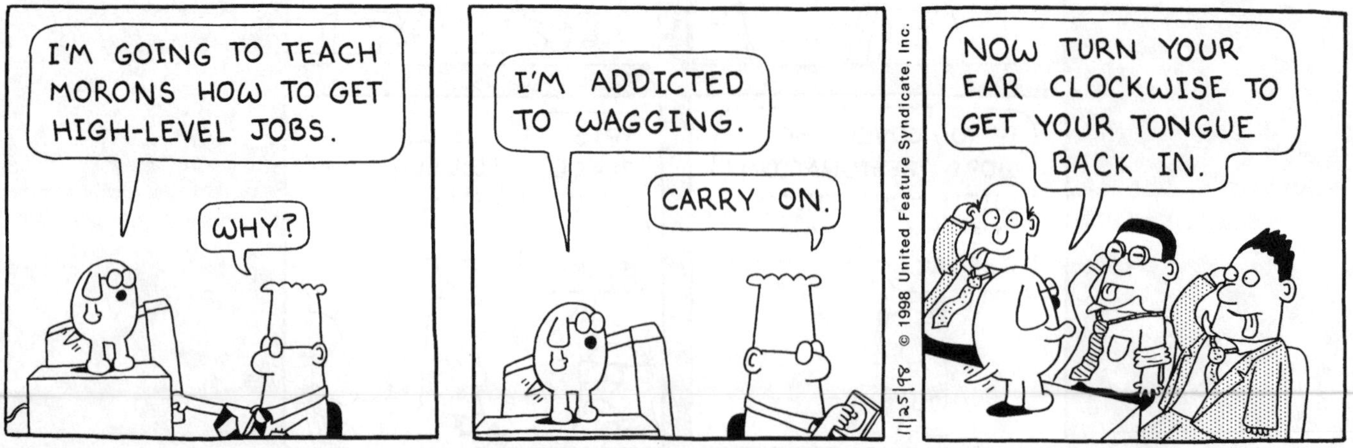
I'M GOING TO TEACH MORONS HOW TO GET HIGH-LEVEL JOBS.
WHY?
I'M ADDICTED TO WAGGING.
CARRY ON.
11/25/98 © 1998 United Feature Syndicate, Inc.
NOW TURN YOUR EAR CLOCKWISE TO GET YOUR TONGUE BACK IN.

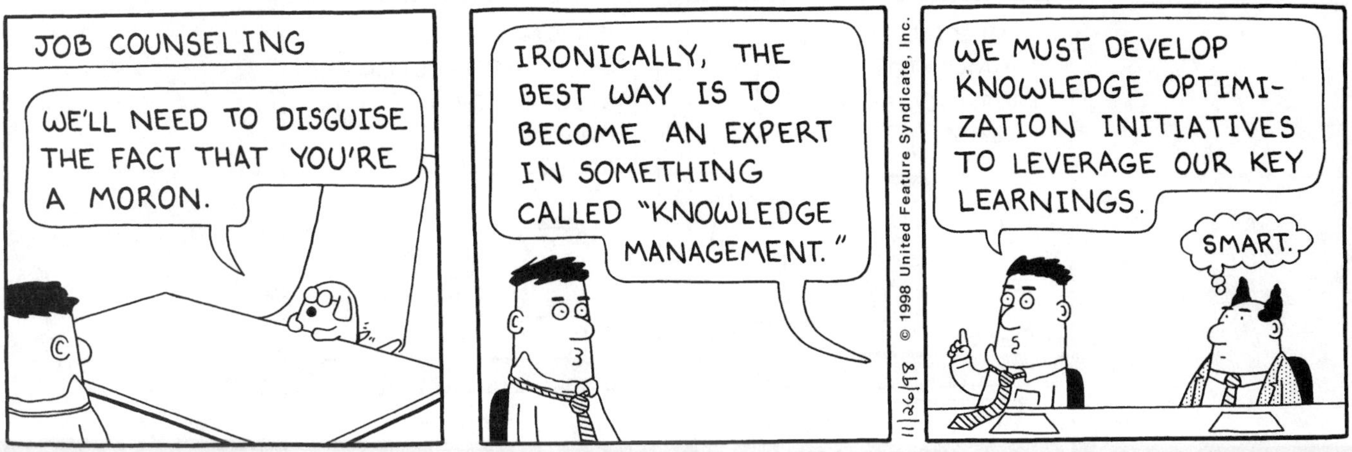
JOB COUNSELING
WE'LL NEED TO DISGUISE THE FACT THAT YOU'RE A MORON.
IRONICALLY, THE BEST WAY IS TO BECOME AN EXPERT IN SOMETHING CALLED "KNOWLEDGE MANAGEMENT."
11/26/98 © 1998 United Feature Syndicate, Inc.
WE MUST DEVELOP KNOWLEDGE OPTIMI-ZATION INITIATIVES TO LEVERAGE OUR KEY LEARNINGS.
SMART.

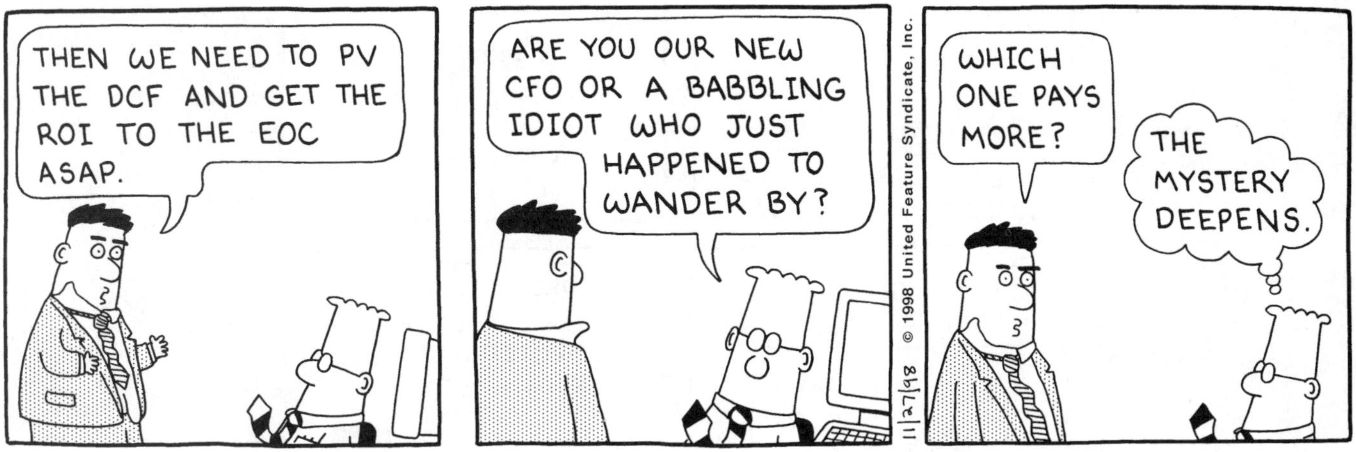
THEN WE NEED TO PV THE DCF AND GET THE ROI TO THE EOC ASAP.
ARE YOU OUR NEW CFO OR A BABBLING IDIOT WHO JUST HAPPENED TO WANDER BY?
11/27/98 © 1998 United Feature Syndicate, Inc.
WHICH ONE PAYS MORE?
THE MYSTERY DEEPENS.

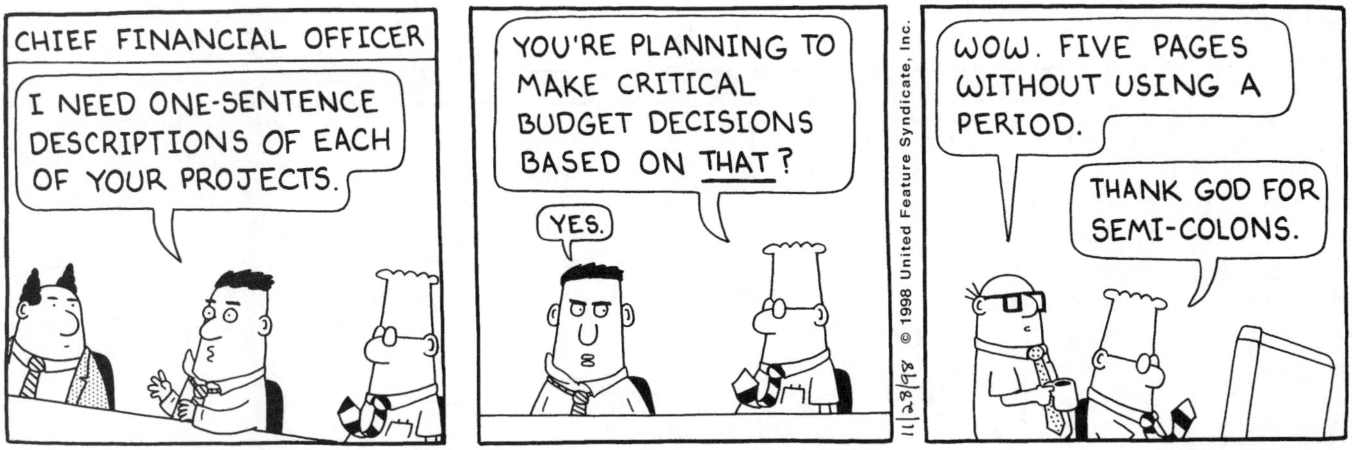
CHIEF FINANCIAL OFFICER
I NEED ONE-SENTENCE DESCRIPTIONS OF EACH OF YOUR PROJECTS.
YOU'RE PLANNING TO MAKE CRITICAL BUDGET DECISIONS BASED ON THAT?
YES.
11/28/98 © 1998 United Feature Syndicate, Inc.
WOW. FIVE PAGES WITHOUT USING A PERIOD.
THANK GOD FOR SEMI-COLONS.

WELCOME TO THE MANDATORY WINDOWS NT™ CLASS.
PERSONALLY, I'VE ONLY BEEN USING A COMPUTER FOR... HOW LONG? ANYONE?
2 WEEKS
BUT A GOOD TRAINER CAN TEACH ANY SUBJECT.
OKAY, EVERYONE STAND UP AND STRETCH!
OR SIT THERE AND GLARE AT ME.
THAT'S GOOD TOO.
I FORGOT TO RESERVE THE ROOM WITH THE COMPUTERS, SO I'LL USE THIS BOX.
... AND LET'S SAY THIS ERASER IS THE MOOSE.
I LEFT WHEN HE TOLD US TO USE OUR TEETH AS A KEYBOARD.
OOH-YAH.

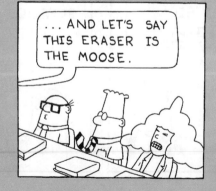

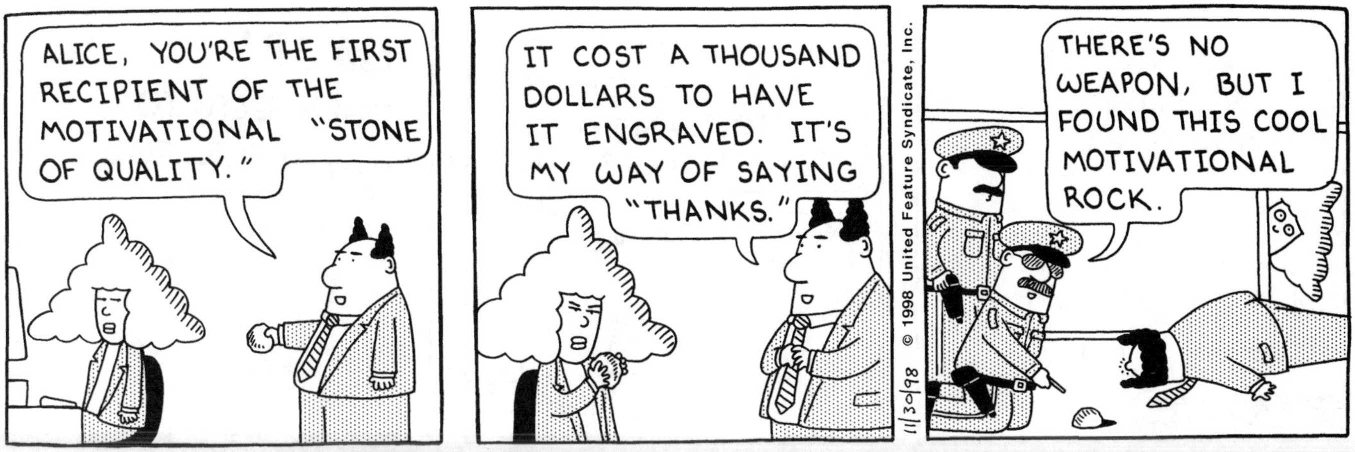
ALICE, YOU'RE THE FIRST RECIPIENT OF THE MOTIVATIONAL "STONE OF QUALITY."
IT COST A THOUSAND DOLLARS TO HAVE IT ENGRAVED. IT'S MY WAY OF SAYING "THANKS."
11/30/98 © 1998 United Feature Syndicate, Inc.
THERE'S NO WEAPON, BUT I FOUND THIS COOL MOTIVATIONAL ROCK.

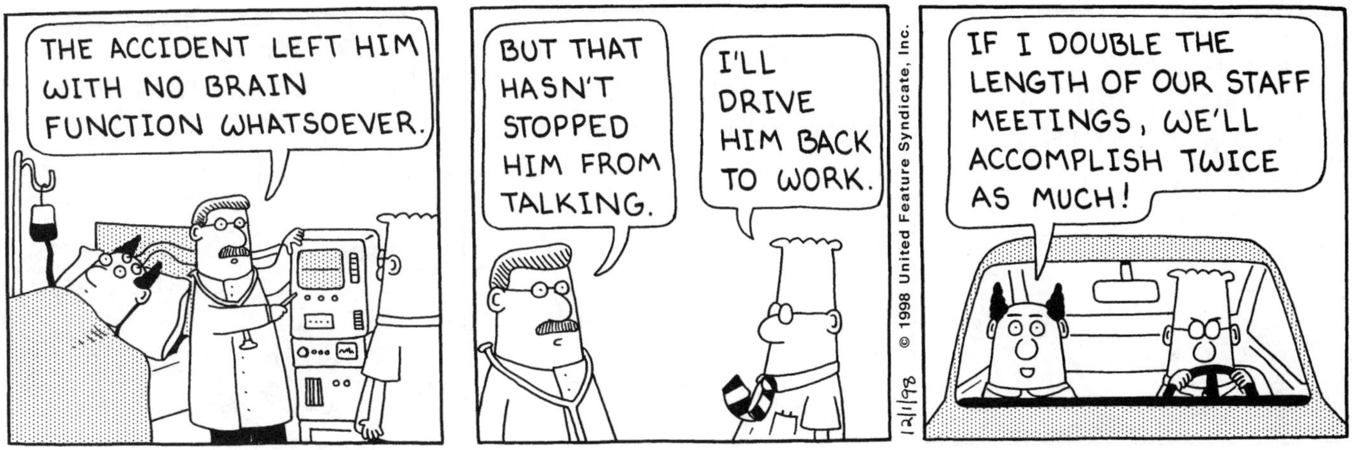
THE ACCIDENT LEFT HIM WITH NO BRAIN FUNCTION WHATSOEVER.
BUT THAT HASN'T STOPPED HIM FROM TALKING.
I'LL DRIVE HIM BACK TO WORK.
12/1/98 © 1998 United Feature Syndicate, Inc.
IF I DOUBLE THE LENGTH OF OUR STAFF MEETINGS, WE'LL ACCOMPLISH TWICE AS MUCH!

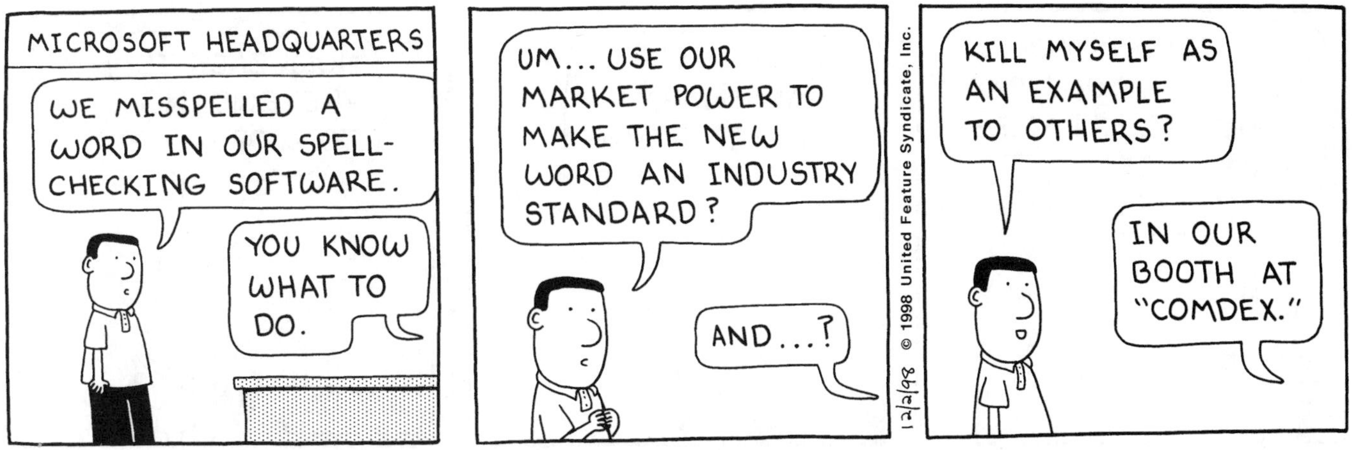
MICROSOFT HEADQUARTERS
WE MISSPELLED A WORD IN OUR SPELL-CHECKING SOFTWARE.
YOU KNOW WHAT TO DO.
UM... USE OUR MARKET POWER TO MAKE THE NEW WORD AN INDUSTRY STANDARD?
AND...?
12/2/98 © 1998 United Feature Syndicate, Inc.
KILL MYSELF AS AN EXAMPLE TO OTHERS?
IN OUR BOOTH AT "COMDEX."

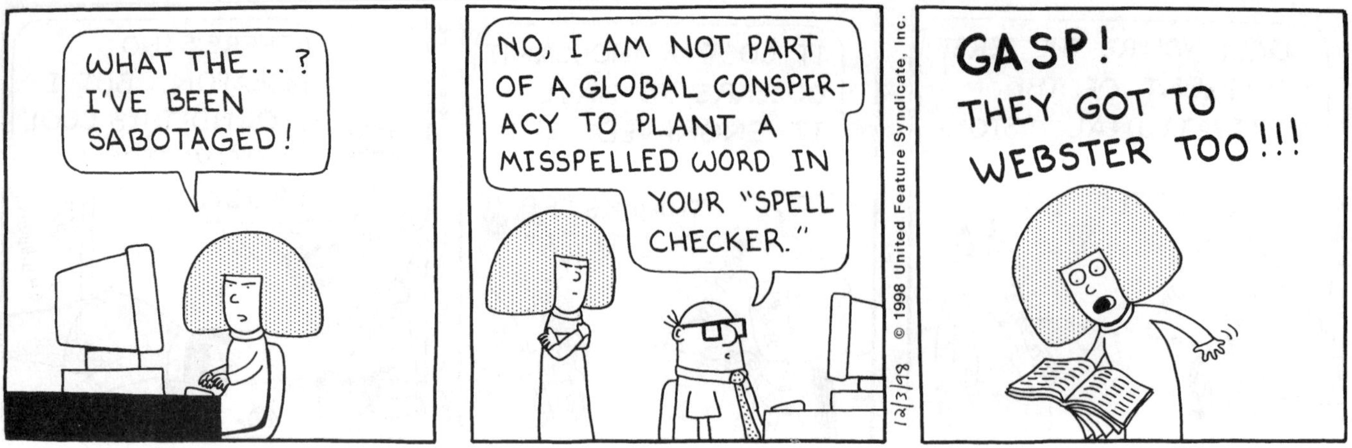
WHAT THE... ? I'VE BEEN SABOTAGED!
NO, I AM NOT PART OF A GLOBAL CONSPIRACY TO PLANT A MISSPELLED WORD IN YOUR "SPELL CHECKER."
12/3/98 © 1998 United Feature Syndicate, Inc.
GASP!
THEY GOT TO WEBSTER TOO!!!

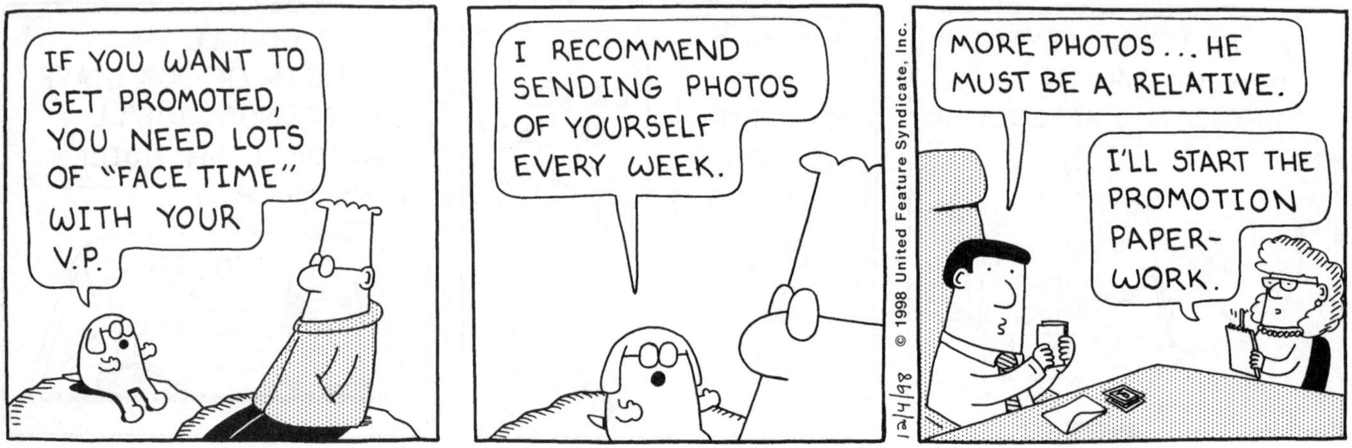
IF YOU WANT TO GET PROMOTED, YOU NEED LOTS OF "FACE TIME" WITH YOUR V.P.
I RECOMMEND SENDING PHOTOS OF YOURSELF EVERY WEEK.
12/4/98 © 1998 United Feature Syndicate, Inc.
MORE PHOTOS... HE MUST BE A RELATIVE.
I'LL START THE PROMOTION PAPERWORK.

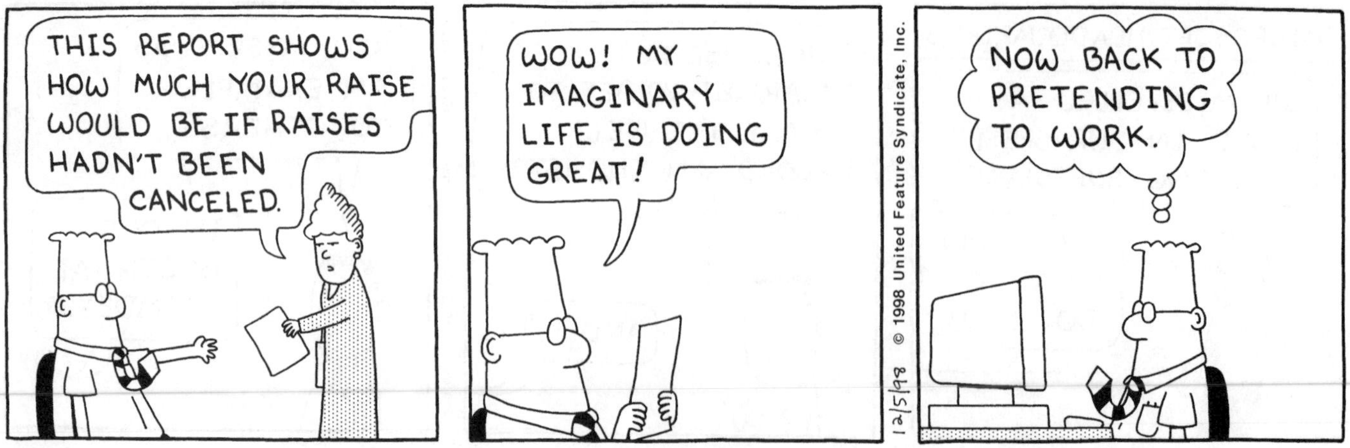
THIS REPORT SHOWS HOW MUCH YOUR RAISE WOULD BE IF RAISES HADN'T BEEN CANCELED.
WOW! MY IMAGINARY LIFE IS DOING GREAT!
12/5/98 © 1998 United Feature Syndicate, Inc.
NOW BACK TO PRETENDING TO WORK.

WALLY, MAY I TAP IN TO YOUR VAST WISDOM?
OKAY, BUT MAKE SURE YOU PULL OUT BEFORE YOUR HEAD EXPLODES.
I'VE NOTICED THAT MANY EMPLOYEES ARE EVIL, SADISTIC OBSTRUCTIONISTS.
DO ALL THE NUTS WORK HERE BY SOME STRANGE COINCIDENCE?
OR ARE MOST EMPLOYEES EVIL?
DON'T FOCUS ON THE EVIL, ASOK.
FOCUS ON THE FEW EMPLOYEES WHO SEEM GOOD.
THEY'RE THE ONES WHO WILL STAB YOU WHEN YOU'RE SLEEPING!
TRUST NO ONE BUT THE LAZY!
OW! OW! OW!
I WARNED YOU TO PULL OUT!
12/6/98

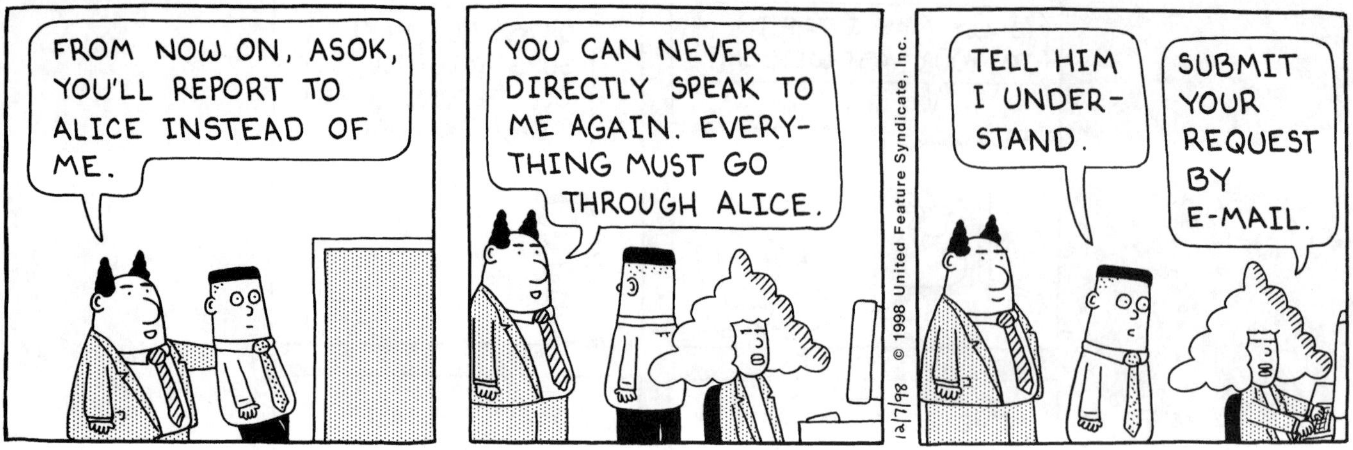
FROM NOW ON, ASOK, YOU'LL REPORT TO ALICE INSTEAD OF ME.
YOU CAN NEVER DIRECTLY SPEAK TO ME AGAIN. EVERYTHING MUST GO THROUGH ALICE.
12/7/98 © 1998 United Feature Syndicate, Inc.
TELL HIM I UNDERSTAND.
SUBMIT YOUR REQUEST BY E-MAIL.

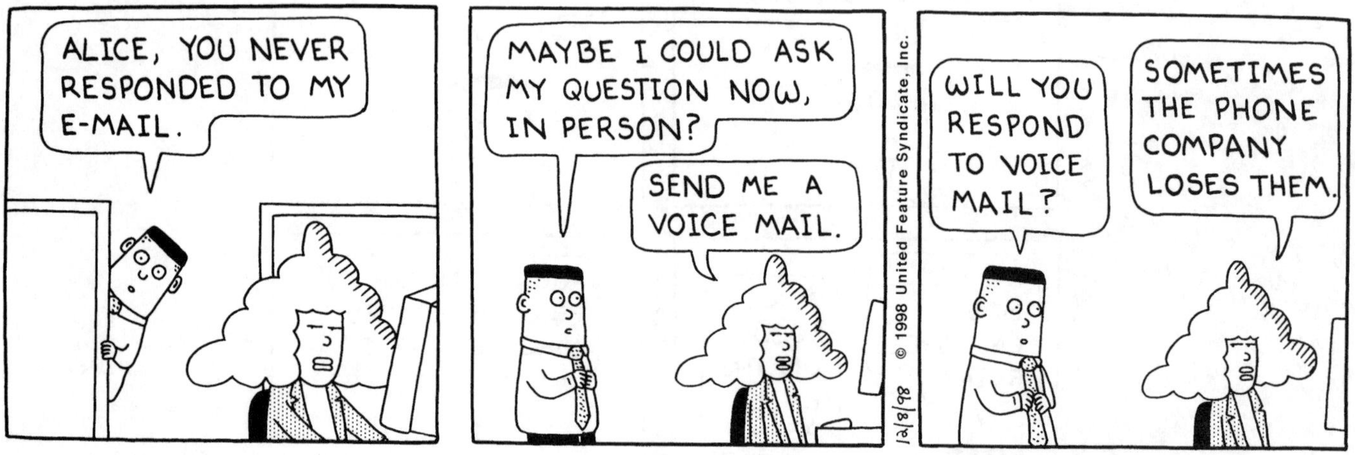
ALICE, YOU NEVER RESPONDED TO MY E-MAIL.
MAYBE I COULD ASK MY QUESTION NOW, IN PERSON?
SEND ME A VOICE MAIL.
12/8/98 © 1998 United Feature Syndicate, Inc.
WILL YOU RESPOND TO VOICE MAIL?
SOMETIMES THE PHONE COMPANY LOSES THEM.

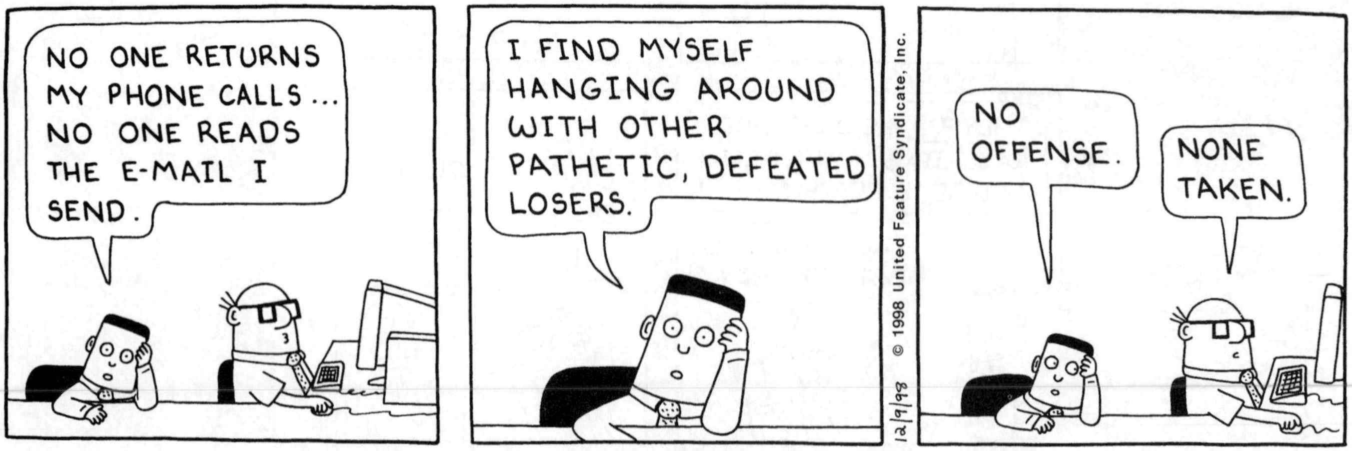
NO ONE RETURNS MY PHONE CALLS... NO ONE READS THE E-MAIL I SEND.
I FIND MYSELF HANGING AROUND WITH OTHER PATHETIC, DEFEATED LOSERS.
12/9/98 © 1998 United Feature Syndicate, Inc.
NO OFFENSE.
NONE TAKEN.

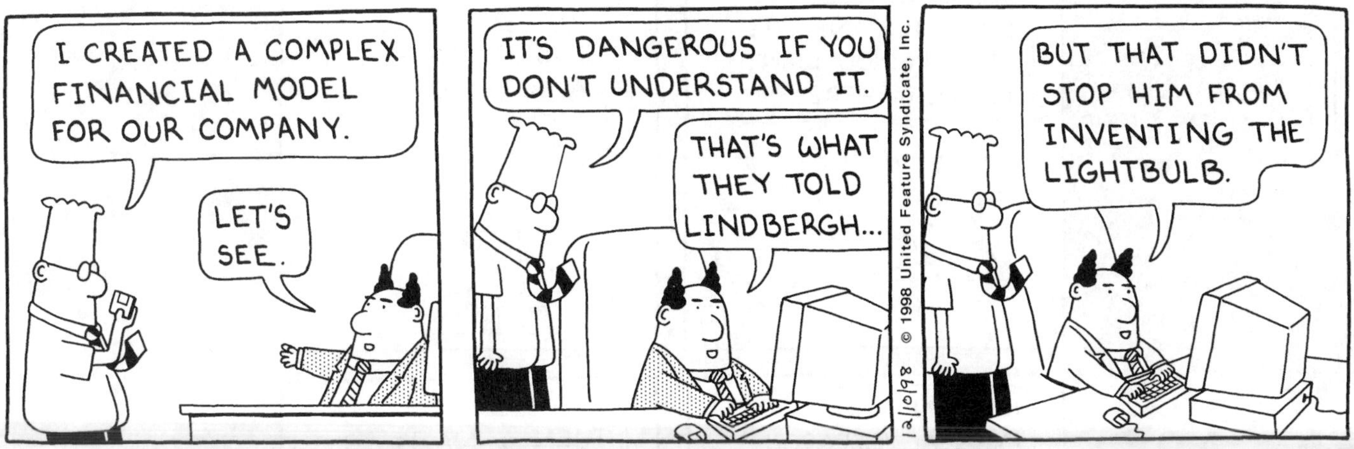
I CREATED A COMPLEX FINANCIAL MODEL FOR OUR COMPANY.
LET'S SEE.
IT'S DANGEROUS IF YOU DON'T UNDERSTAND IT.
THAT'S WHAT THEY TOLD LINDBERGH...
12/10/98 © 1998 United Feature Syndicate, Inc.
BUT THAT DIDN'T STOP HIM FROM INVENTING THE LIGHTBULB.

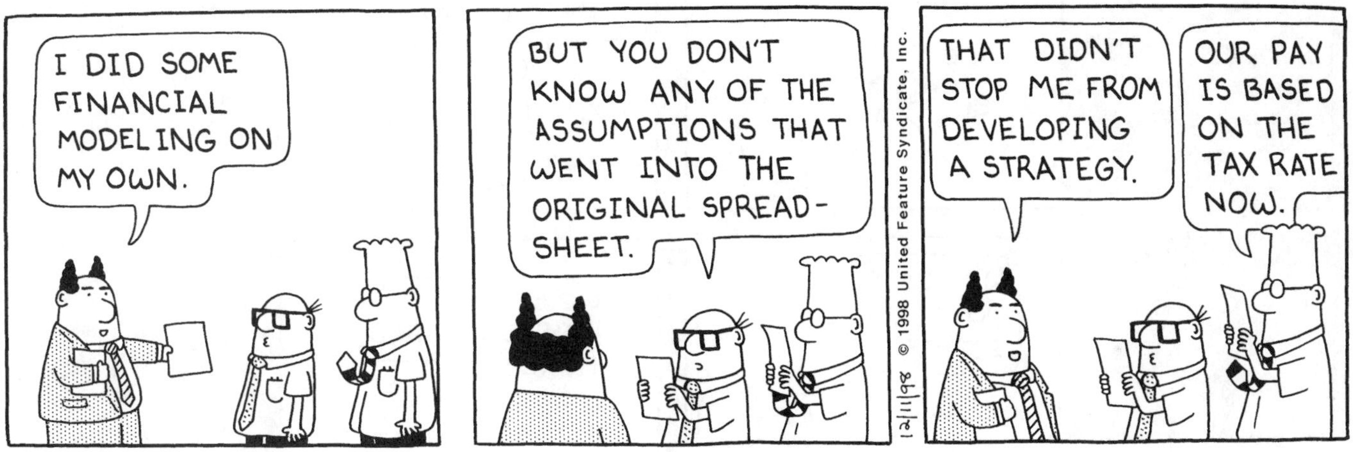
I DID SOME FINANCIAL MODELING ON MY OWN.
BUT YOU DON'T KNOW ANY OF THE ASSUMPTIONS THAT WENT INTO THE ORIGINAL SPREAD-SHEET.
12/11/98 © 1998 United Feature Syndicate, Inc.
THAT DIDN'T STOP ME FROM DEVELOPING A STRATEGY.
OUR PAY IS BASED ON THE TAX RATE NOW.

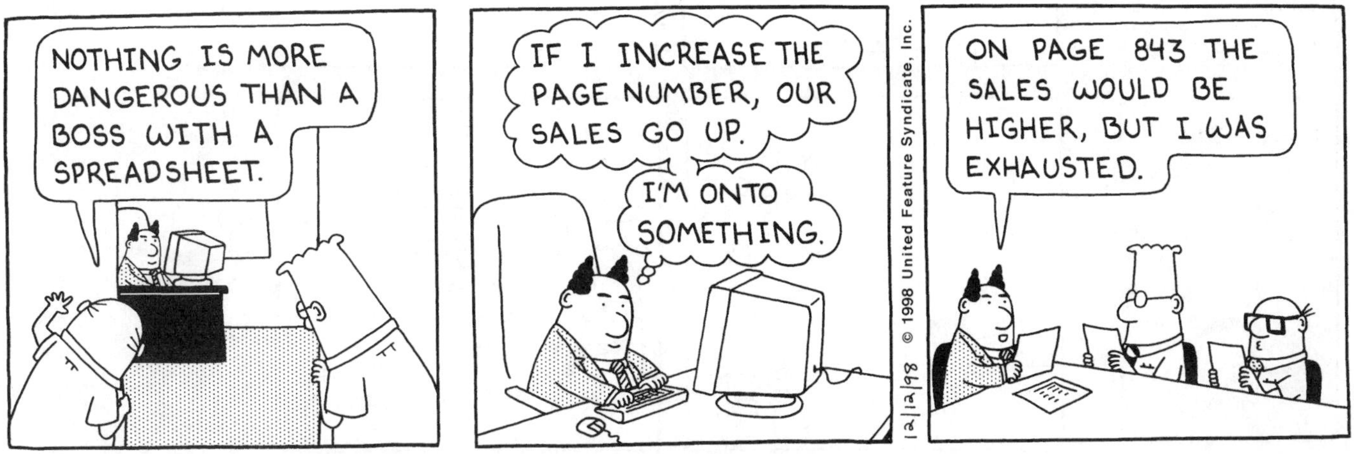
NOTHING IS MORE DANGEROUS THAN A BOSS WITH A SPREADSHEET.
IF I INCREASE THE PAGE NUMBER, OUR SALES GO UP.
I'M ONTO SOMETHING.
12/12/98 © 1998 United Feature Syndicate, Inc.
ON PAGE 843 THE SALES WOULD BE HIGHER, BUT I WAS EXHAUSTED.

SO... JUSTIN, TELL ME WHY YOU WANT TO WORK HERE.
I WANT TO FIND A CURE FOR ASTHMA!
WE DON'T DO MEDICAL RESEARCH HERE.
OH
THEN I WANT TO BUILD THE BIGGEST HYDROELECTRIC DAM IN THE WORLD!
WE DON'T DO THAT EITHER.
WHAT DO YOU DO?
12/13/98 © 1998 United Feature Syndicate, Inc.
WE SIT IN FABRIC-COVERED BOXES.
SHRIVEL CRINKLE ACK!
THAT WAS THE SOUND OF YOUR IDEALISM DYING.
SHOW ME TO MY BOX.

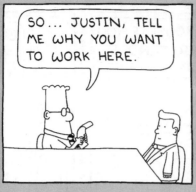

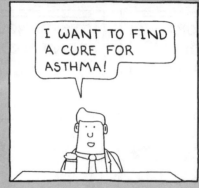

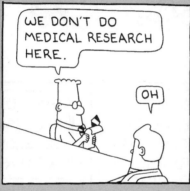

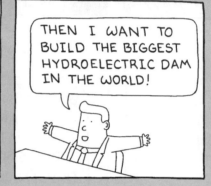

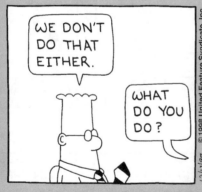

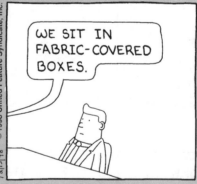

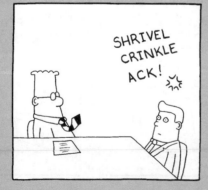

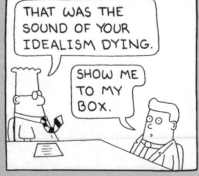

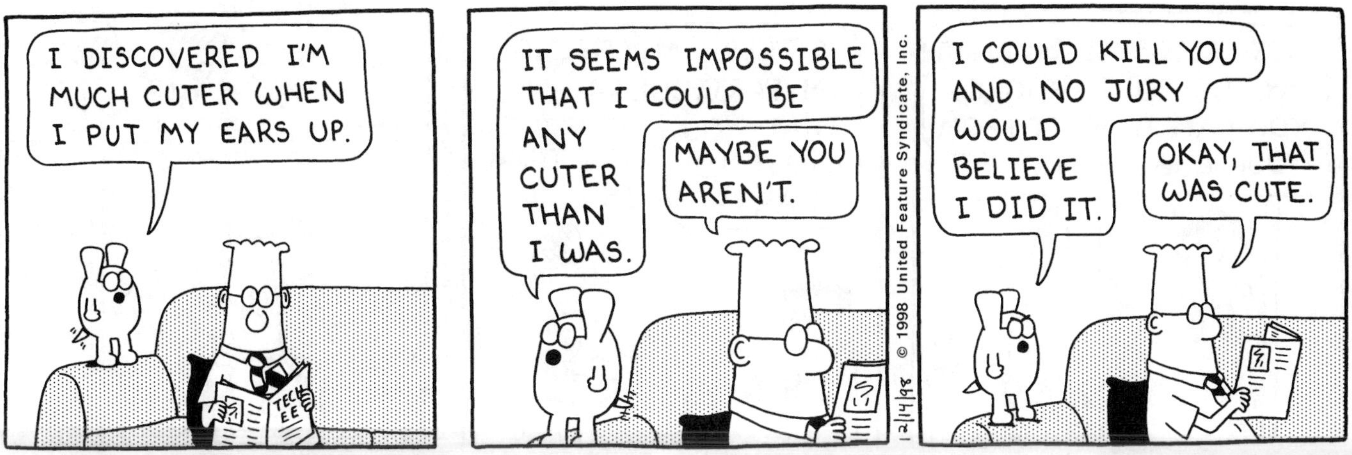
I DISCOVERED I'M MUCH CUTER WHEN I PUT MY EARS UP.
IT SEEMS IMPOSSIBLE THAT I COULD BE ANY CUTER THAN I WAS.
MAYBE YOU AREN'T.
I COULD KILL YOU AND NO JURY WOULD BELIEVE I DID IT.
OKAY, THAT WAS CUTE.
12/14/98 © 1998 United Feature Syndicate, Inc.

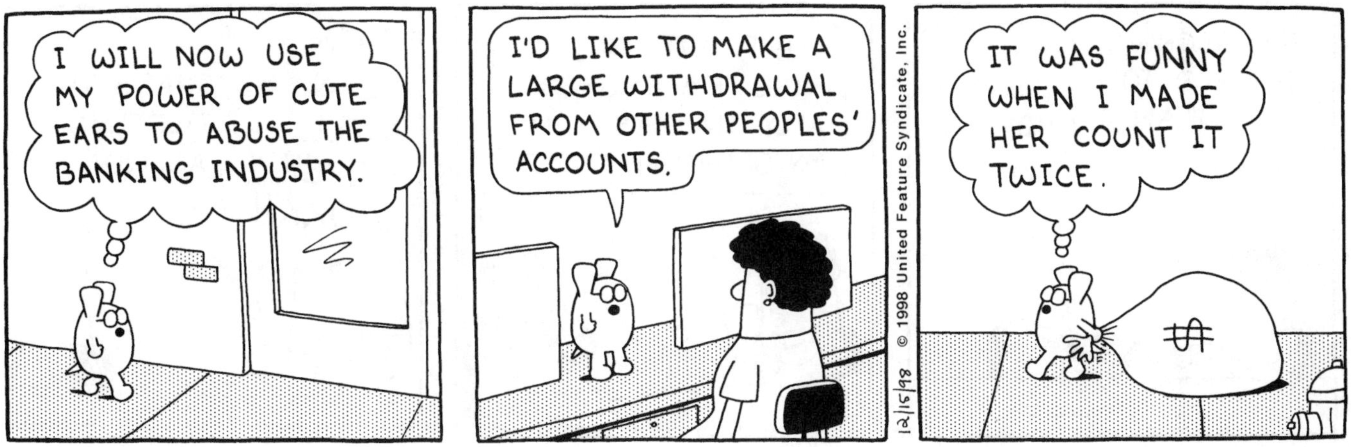
I WILL NOW USE MY POWER OF CUTE EARS TO ABUSE THE BANKING INDUSTRY.
I'D LIKE TO MAKE A LARGE WITHDRAWAL FROM OTHER PEOPLES' ACCOUNTS.
IT WAS FUNNY WHEN I MADE HER COUNT IT TWICE.
12/15/98 © 1998 United Feature Syndicate, Inc.

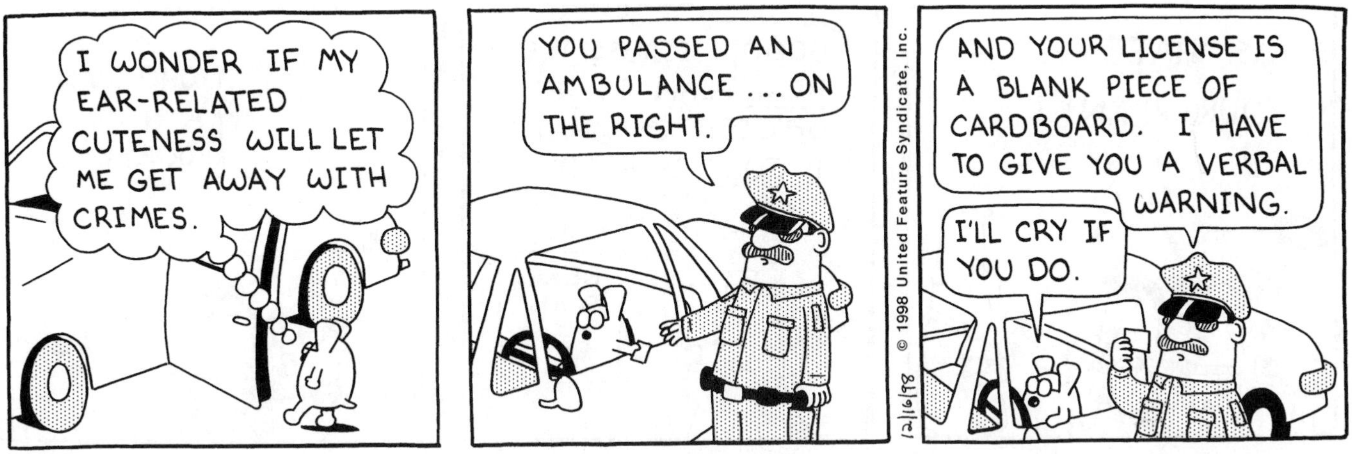
I WONDER IF MY EAR-RELATED CUTENESS WILL LET ME GET AWAY WITH CRIMES.
YOU PASSED AN AMBULANCE ... ON THE RIGHT.
AND YOUR LICENSE IS A BLANK PIECE OF CARDBOARD. I HAVE TO GIVE YOU A VERBAL WARNING.
I'LL CRY IF YOU DO.
12/16/98 © 1998 United Feature Syndicate, Inc.

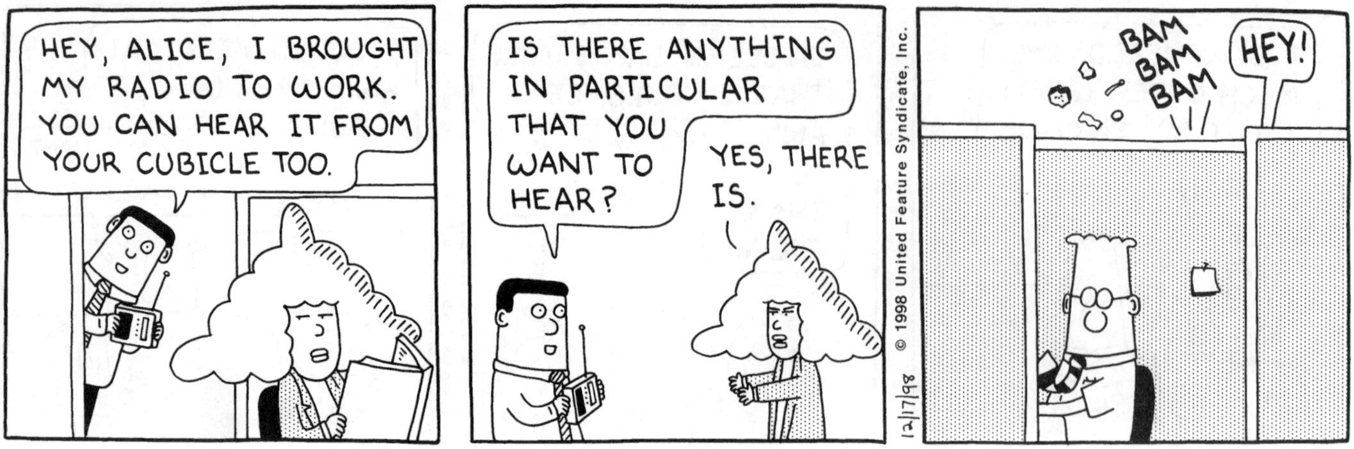
HEY, ALICE, I BROUGHT MY RADIO TO WORK. YOU CAN HEAR IT FROM YOUR CUBICLE TOO.
IS THERE ANYTHING IN PARTICULAR THAT YOU WANT TO HEAR?
YES, THERE IS.
12/17/98 © 1998 United Feature Syndicate, Inc.
BAM BAM BAM
HEY!

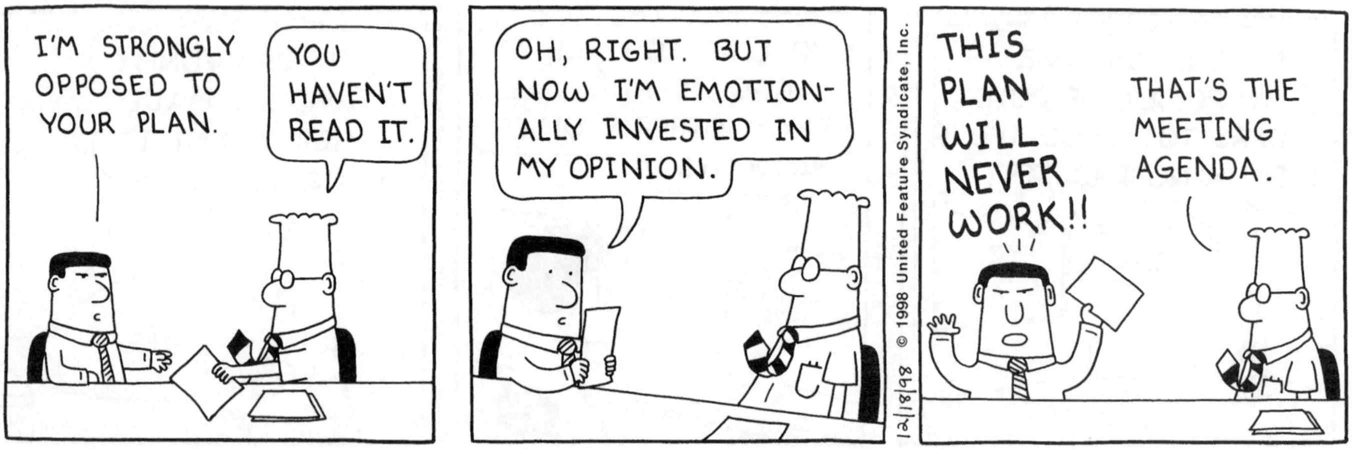
I'M STRONGLY OPPOSED TO YOUR PLAN.
YOU HAVEN'T READ IT.
OH, RIGHT. BUT NOW I'M EMOTIONALLY INVESTED IN MY OPINION.
12/18/98 © 1998 United Feature Syndicate, Inc.
THIS PLAN WILL NEVER WORK!!
THAT'S THE MEETING AGENDA.

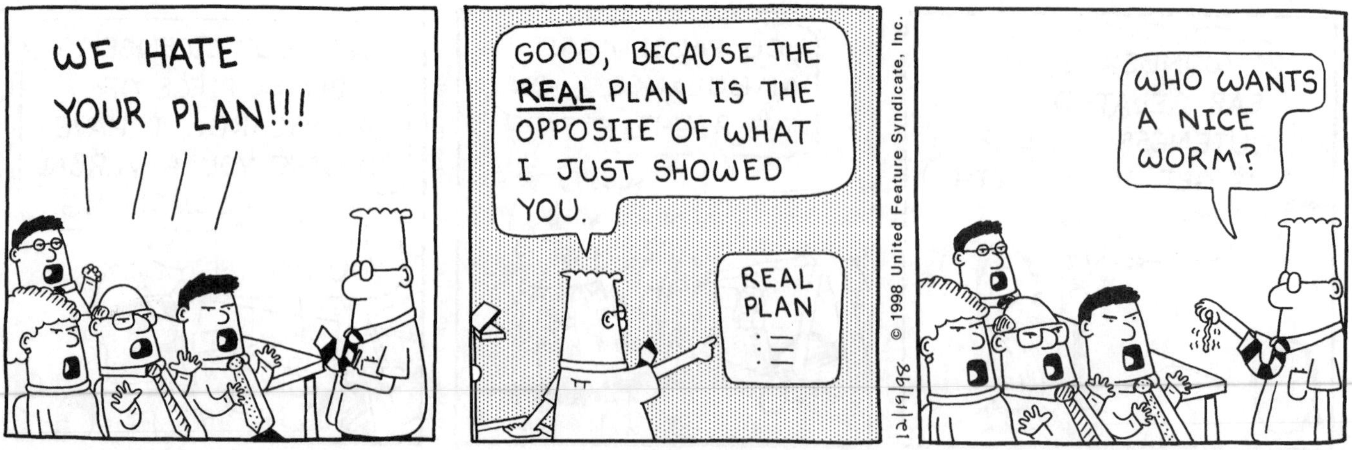
WE HATE YOUR PLAN!!!
GOOD, BECAUSE THE REAL PLAN IS THE OPPOSITE OF WHAT I JUST SHOWED YOU.
REAL PLAN
12/19/98 © 1998 United Feature Syndicate, Inc.
WHO WANTS A NICE WORM?

WE HAVE A PROBLEM.
I ORDERED THESE DIRECTION SIGNS FOR OUR CONFERENCE TOMORROW.
BUT THEY ALL POINT TO THE RIGHT. I NEED LEFT ARROWS.
IS IT TOO LATE TO CHANGE THE SITE OF THE CONFERENCE TO MATCH THE ARROWS?
WELL, THAT WOULD PUT US IN THE MIDDLE OF THE LAKE.
I SUPPOSE WE COULD USE HELICOPTERS TO BUILD A DEEP-WATER PLATFORM HOTEL . . .
BY TOMORROW.
OKAY, BUT GET TWO BIDS . . .
WHAT?
SPOOKY.

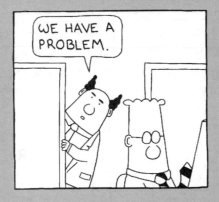

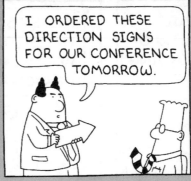

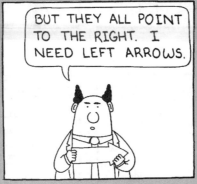

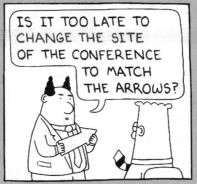

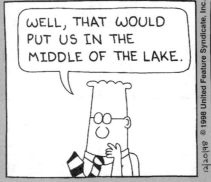

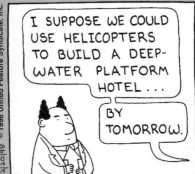

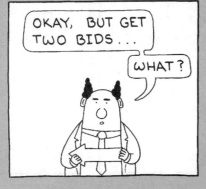

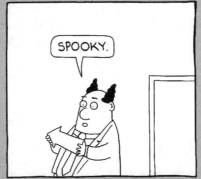

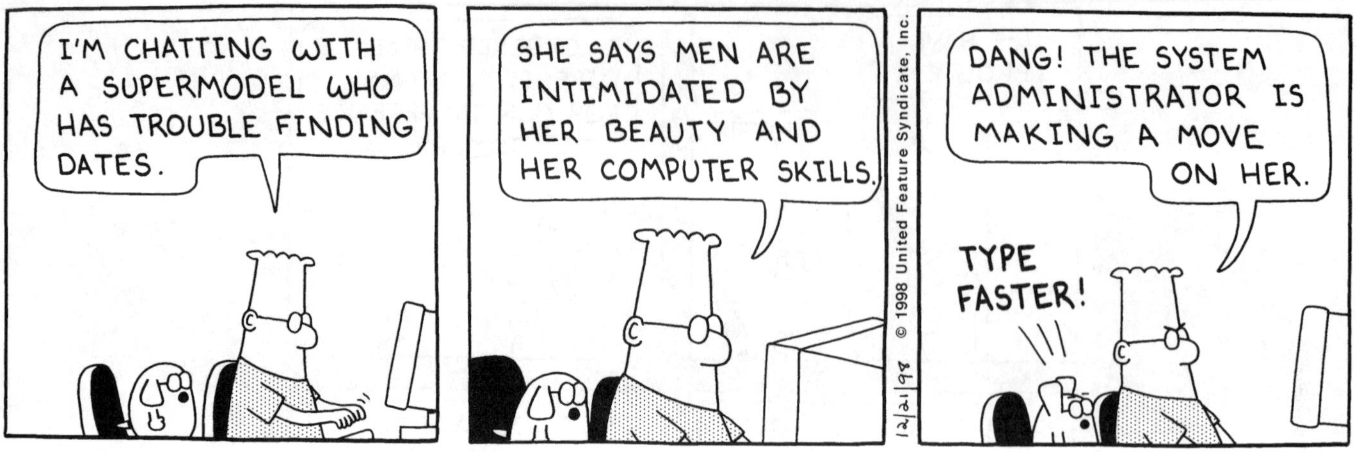
I'M CHATTING WITH A SUPERMODEL WHO HAS TROUBLE FINDING DATES.
SHE SAYS MEN ARE INTIMIDATED BY HER BEAUTY AND HER COMPUTER SKILLS.
12/21/98 © 1998 United Feature Syndicate, Inc.
DANG! THE SYSTEM ADMINISTRATOR IS MAKING A MOVE ON HER.
TYPE FASTER!

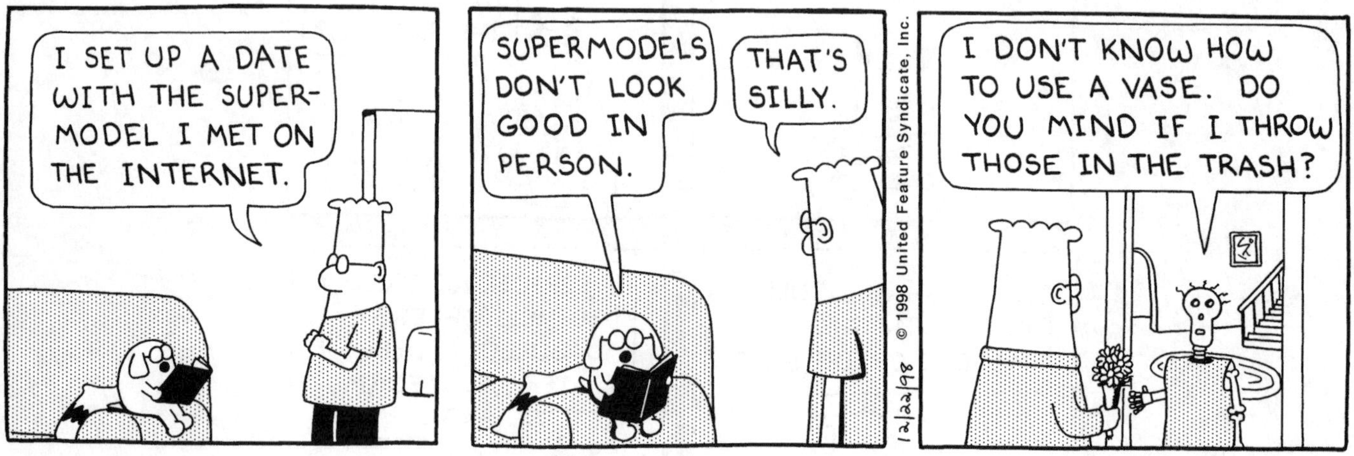
I SET UP A DATE WITH THE SUPER-MODEL I MET ON THE INTERNET.
SUPERMODELS DON'T LOOK GOOD IN PERSON.
THAT'S SILLY.
12/22/98 © 1998 United Feature Syndicate, Inc.
I DON'T KNOW HOW TO USE A VASE. DO YOU MIND IF I THROW THOSE IN THE TRASH?

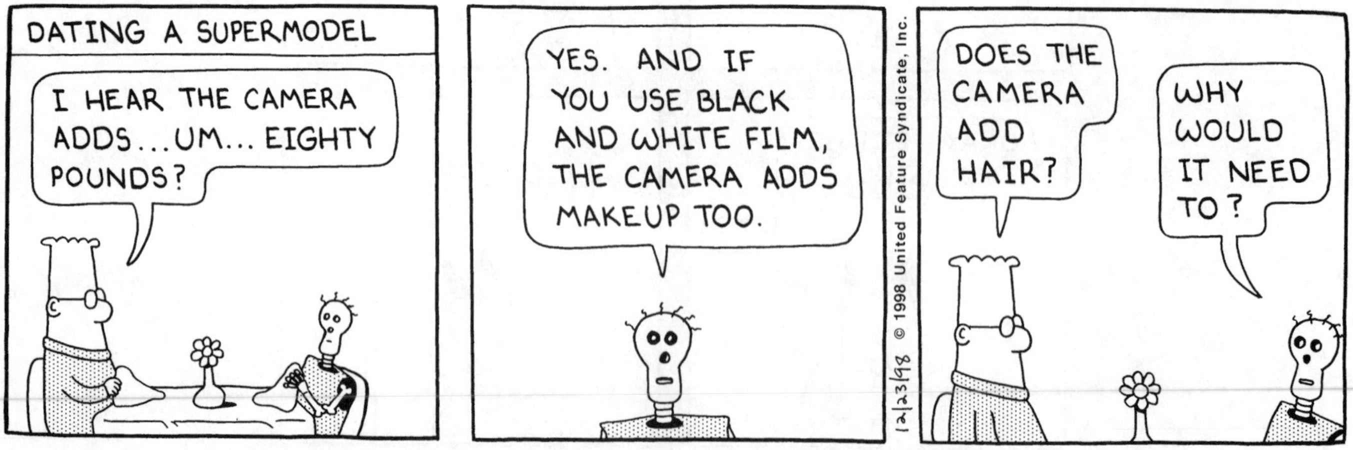
DATING A SUPERMODEL
I HEAR THE CAMERA ADDS...UM... EIGHTY POUNDS?
YES. AND IF YOU USE BLACK AND WHITE FILM, THE CAMERA ADDS MAKEUP TOO.
12/23/98 © 1998 United Feature Syndicate, Inc.
DOES THE CAMERA ADD HAIR?
WHY WOULD IT NEED TO?

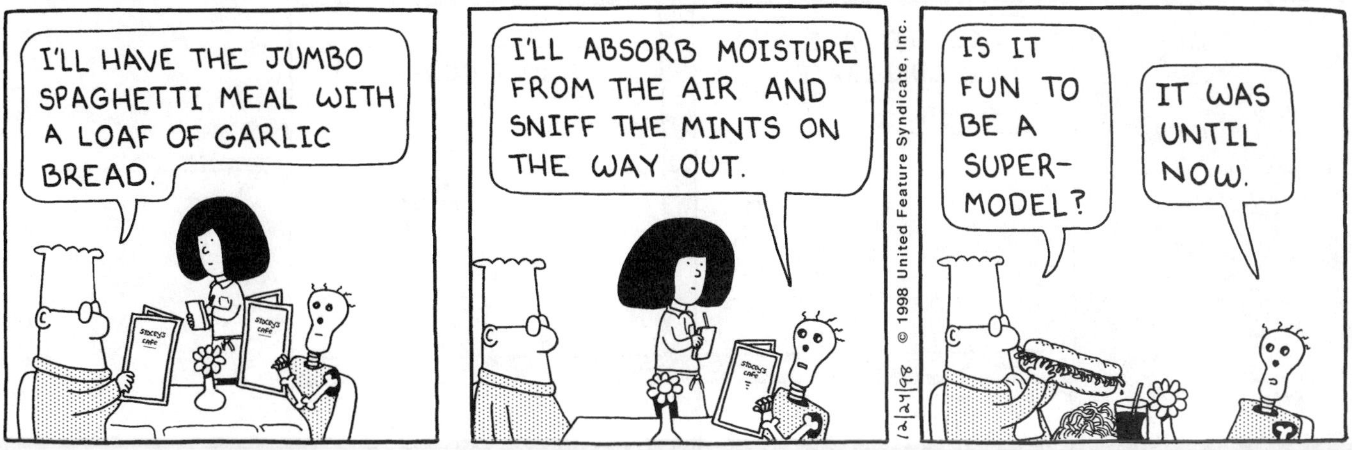
I'LL HAVE THE JUMBO SPAGHETTI MEAL WITH A LOAF OF GARLIC BREAD.
I'LL ABSORB MOISTURE FROM THE AIR AND SNIFF THE MINTS ON THE WAY OUT.
12/24/98 © 1998 United Feature Syndicate, Inc.
IS IT FUN TO BE A SUPER-MODEL?
IT WAS UNTIL NOW.

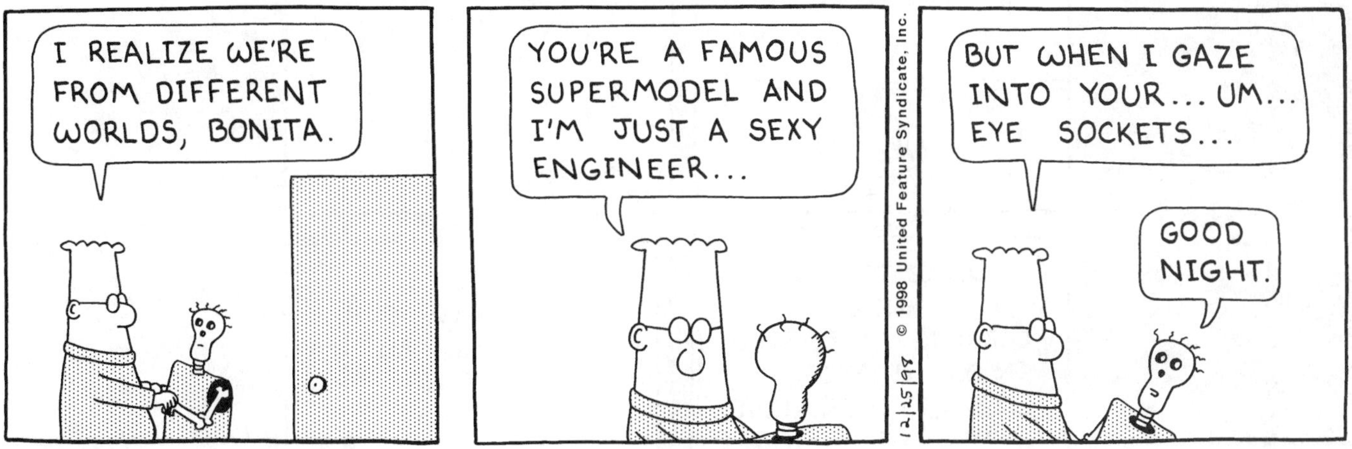
I REALIZE WE'RE FROM DIFFERENT WORLDS, BONITA.
YOU'RE A FAMOUS SUPERMODEL AND I'M JUST A SEXY ENGINEER...
12/25/98 © 1998 United Feature Syndicate, Inc.
BUT WHEN I GAZE INTO YOUR... UM... EYE SOCKETS...
GOOD NIGHT.

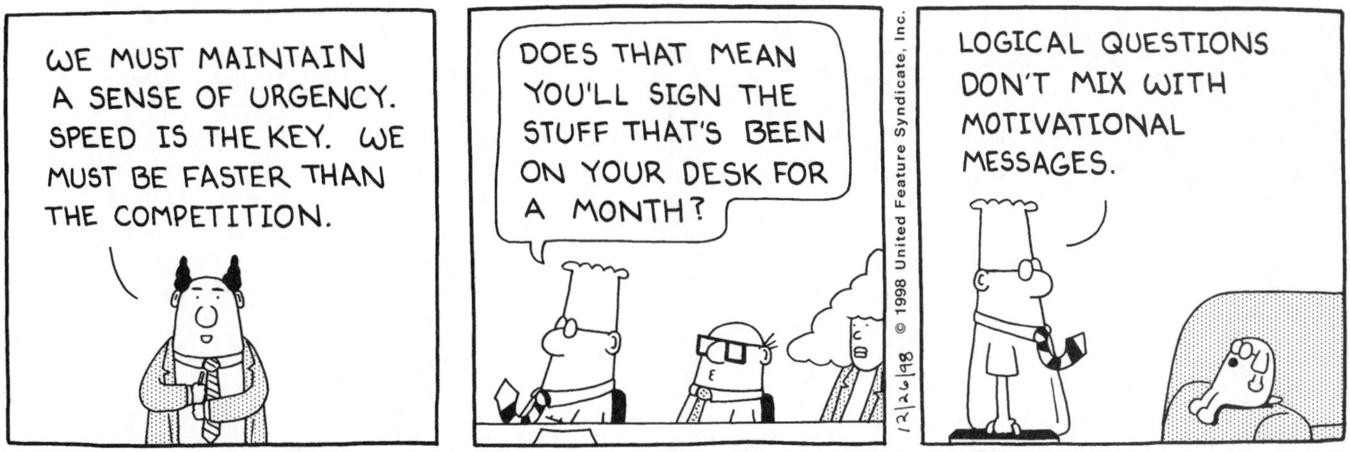
WE MUST MAINTAIN A SENSE OF URGENCY. SPEED IS THE KEY. WE MUST BE FASTER THAN THE COMPETITION.
DOES THAT MEAN YOU'LL SIGN THE STUFF THAT'S BEEN ON YOUR DESK FOR A MONTH?
12/26/98 © 1998 United Feature Syndicate, Inc.
LOGICAL QUESTIONS DON'T MIX WITH MOTIVATIONAL MESSAGES.

ALICE, WE HAVE A NEW CORPORATE POLICY.
AND I QUOTE...
"... INITIATE THE DESCRIPTION OF THE CRITERIA FOR REQUIREMENTS...
"... BY DEVELOPING A FRAMEWORK FOR THE APPLICATION ARCHITECTURE...
"... CONSISTENT WITH THE PLANNING CORRIDOR SPECIFIED IN OUR STRATEGIC INITIATIVE."
SO TIRED
12/27/98 © 1998 United Feature Syndicate, Inc.
DID YOU GET ALL THAT?
ZZZZ
WALLY, COME HERE FOR A MINUTE.
READ THIS AND TELL ME IF SHE'S DOING ANY OF IT RIGHT NOW.
ZZZZZ

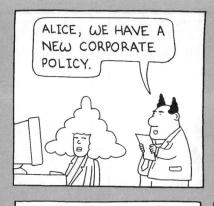

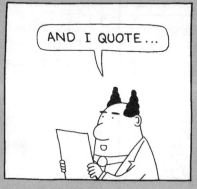

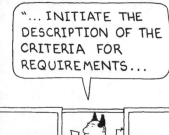

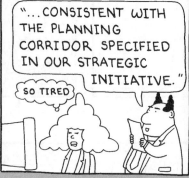

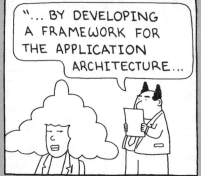

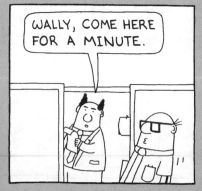

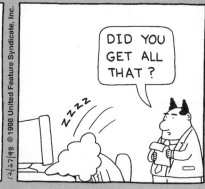

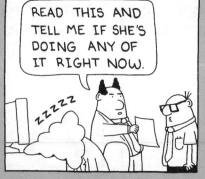

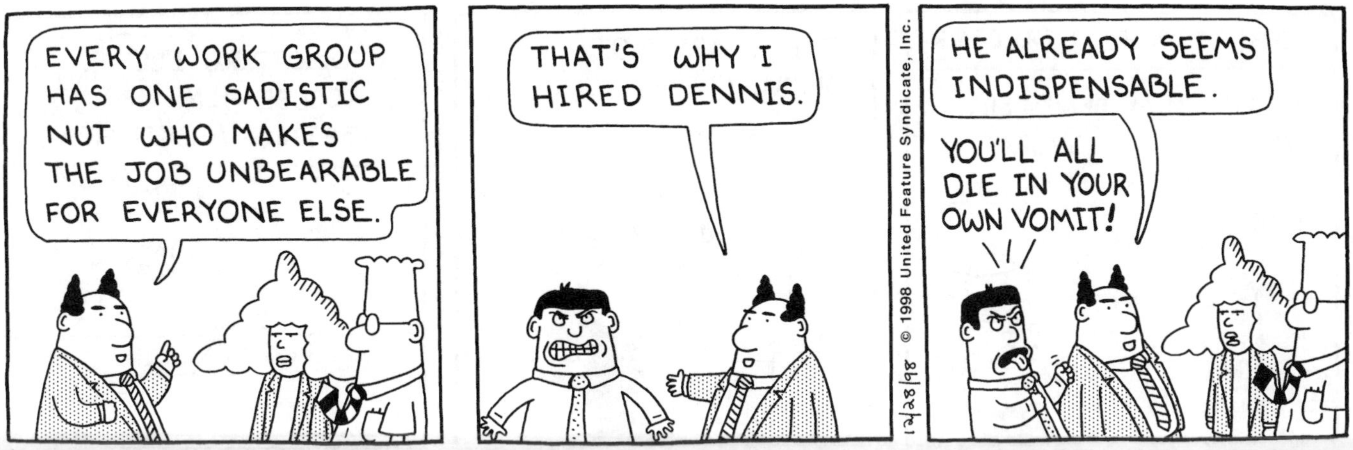
EVERY WORK GROUP HAS ONE SADISTIC NUT WHO MAKES THE JOB UNBEARABLE FOR EVERYONE ELSE.
THAT'S WHY I HIRED DENNIS.
12/28/98 © 1998 United Feature Syndicate, Inc.
HE ALREADY SEEMS INDISPENSABLE.
YOU'LL ALL DIE IN YOUR OWN VOMIT!

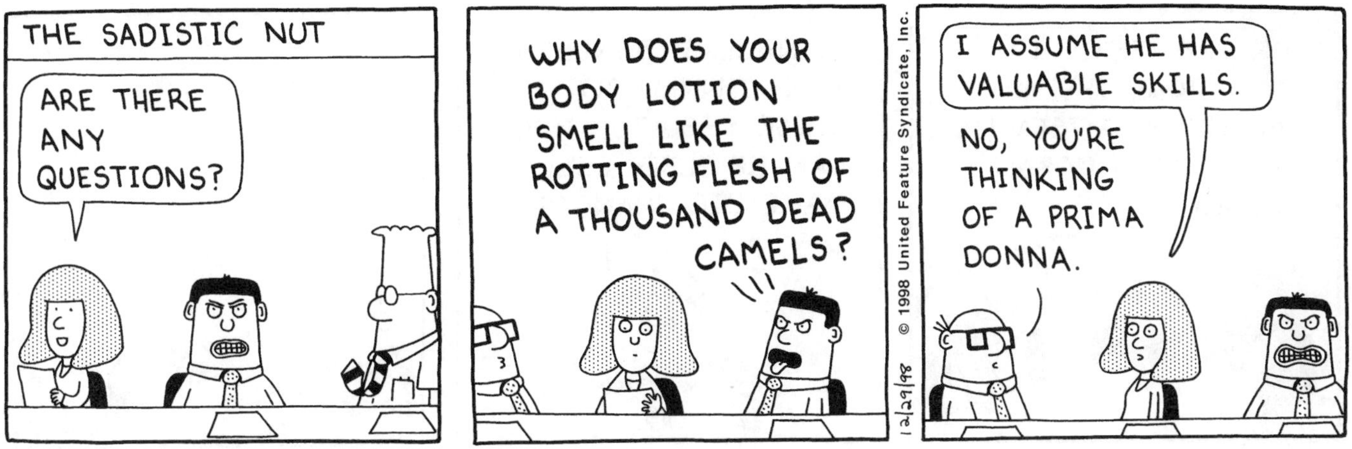
THE SADISTIC NUT
ARE THERE ANY QUESTIONS?
WHY DOES YOUR BODY LOTION SMELL LIKE THE ROTTING FLESH OF A THOUSAND DEAD CAMELS?
12/29/98 © 1998 United Feature Syndicate, Inc.
I ASSUME HE HAS VALUABLE SKILLS.
NO, YOU'RE THINKING OF A PRIMA DONNA.

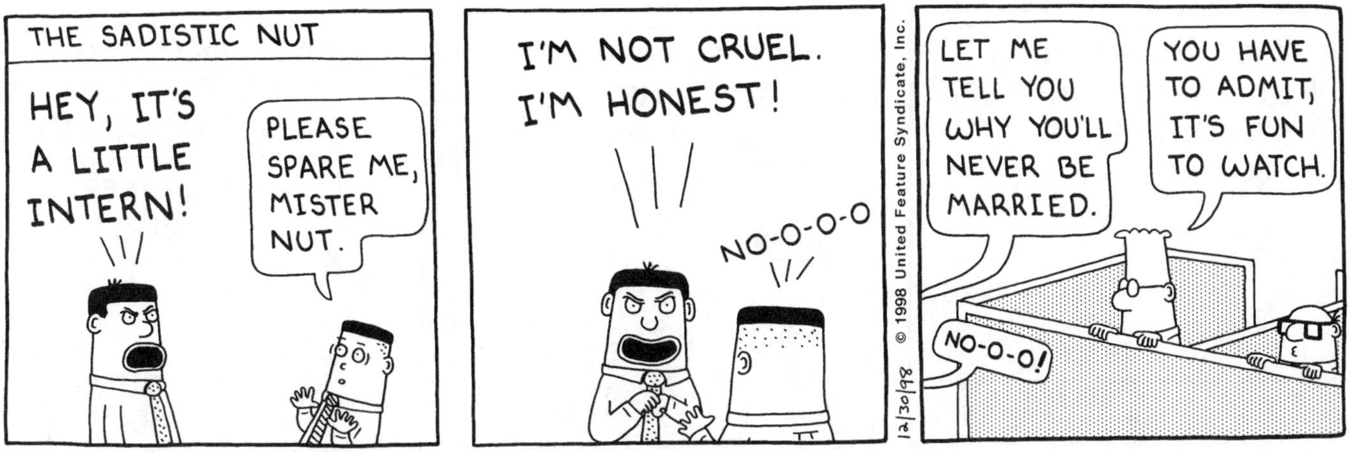
THE SADISTIC NUT
HEY, IT'S A LITTLE INTERN!
PLEASE SPARE ME, MISTER NUT.
I'M NOT CRUEL. I'M HONEST!
NO-O-O-O
12/30/98 © 1998 United Feature Syndicate, Inc.
LET ME TELL YOU WHY YOU'LL NEVER BE MARRIED.
YOU HAVE TO ADMIT, IT'S FUN TO WATCH.
NO-O-O!

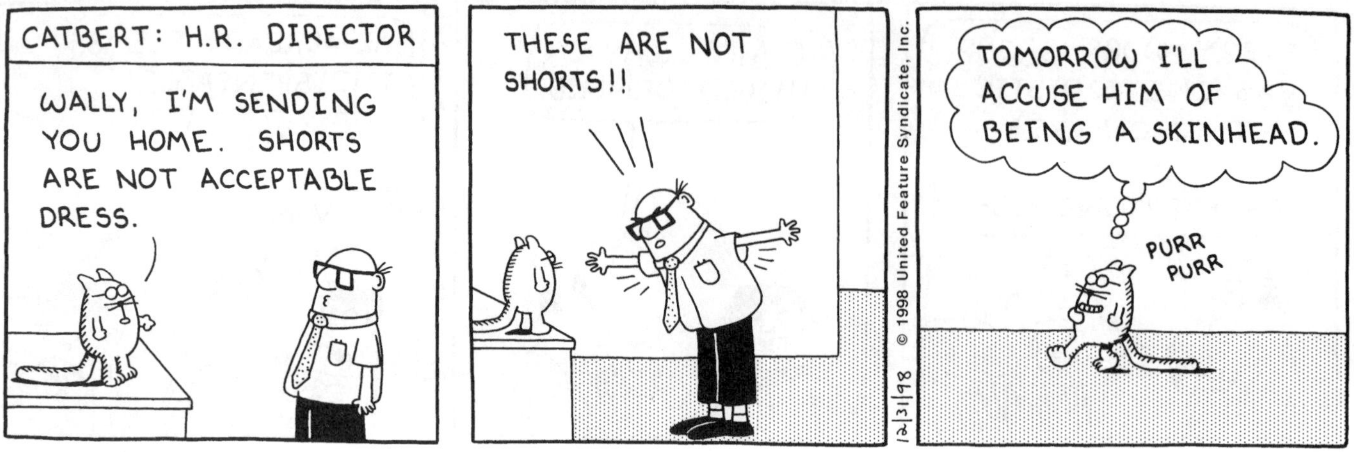
CATBERT: H.R. DIRECTOR
WALLY, I'M SENDING YOU HOME. SHORTS ARE NOT ACCEPTABLE DRESS.
THESE ARE NOT SHORTS!!
12/31/98 © 1998 United Feature Syndicate, Inc.
TOMORROW I'LL ACCUSE HIM OF BEING A SKINHEAD.
PURR PURR

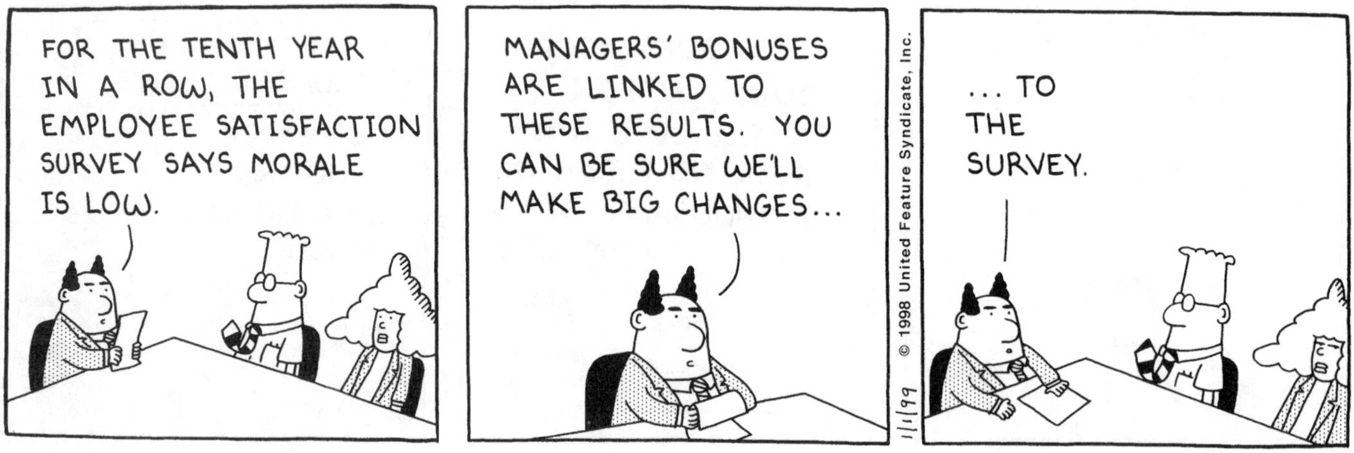
FOR THE TENTH YEAR IN A ROW, THE EMPLOYEE SATISFACTION SURVEY SAYS MORALE IS LOW.
MANAGERS' BONUSES ARE LINKED TO THESE RESULTS. YOU CAN BE SURE WE'LL MAKE BIG CHANGES...
1/1/99 © 1998 United Feature Syndicate, Inc.
... TO THE SURVEY.

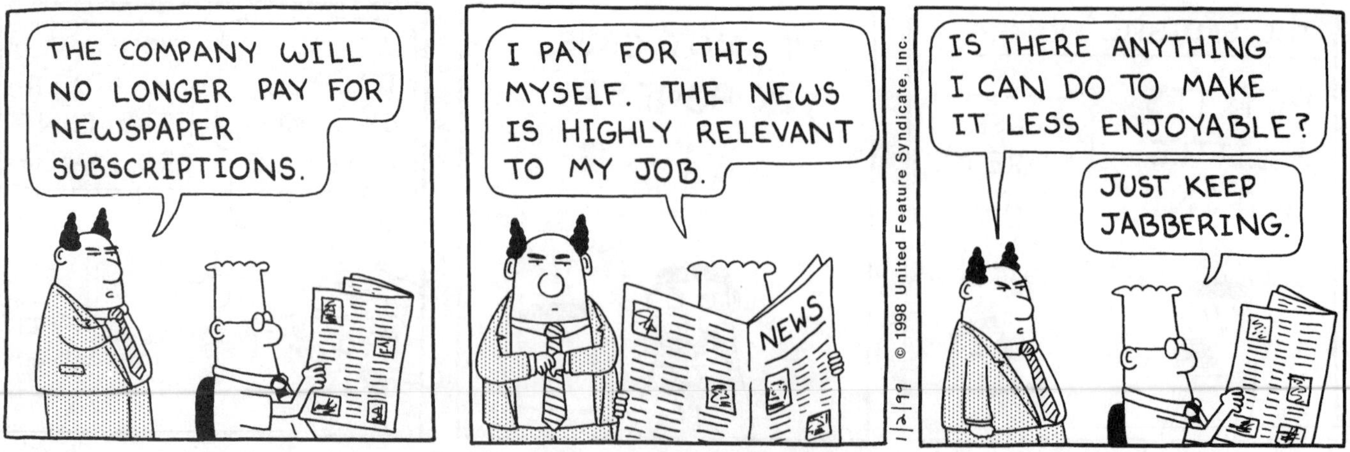
THE COMPANY WILL NO LONGER PAY FOR NEWSPAPER SUBSCRIPTIONS.
I PAY FOR THIS MYSELF. THE NEWS IS HIGHLY RELEVANT TO MY JOB.
NEWS
1/2/99 © 1998 United Feature Syndicate, Inc.
IS THERE ANYTHING I CAN DO TO MAKE IT LESS ENJOYABLE?
JUST KEEP JABBERING.

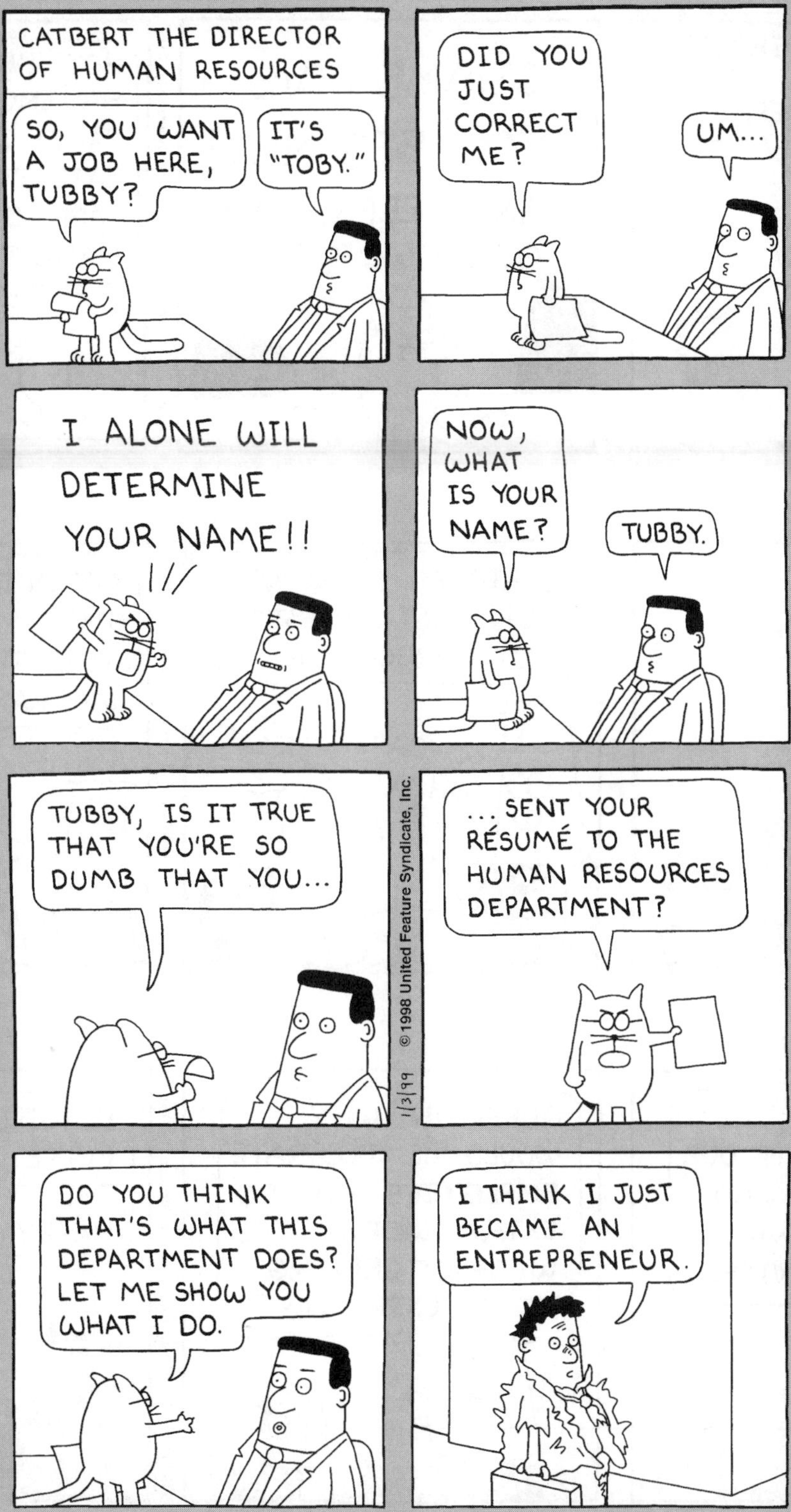
CATBERT THE DIRECTOR OF HUMAN RESOURCES
SO, YOU WANT A JOB HERE, TUBBY?
IT'S "TOBY."
DID YOU JUST CORRECT ME?
UM...
I ALONE WILL DETERMINE YOUR NAME!!
NOW, WHAT IS YOUR NAME?
TUBBY.
TUBBY, IS IT TRUE THAT YOU'RE SO DUMB THAT YOU...
© 1998 United Feature Syndicate, Inc.
1/3/99
...SENT YOUR RÉSUMÉ TO THE HUMAN RESOURCES DEPARTMENT?
DO YOU THINK THAT'S WHAT THIS DEPARTMENT DOES? LET ME SHOW YOU WHAT I DO.
I THINK I JUST BECAME AN ENTREPRENEUR.

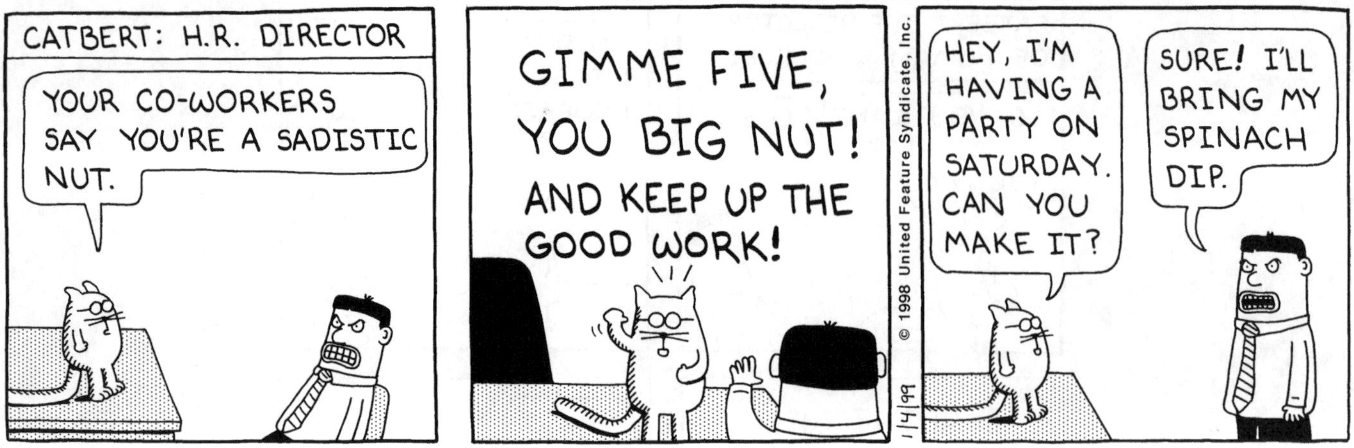
CATBERT: H.R. DIRECTOR
YOUR CO-WORKERS SAY YOU'RE A SADISTIC NUT.
GIMME FIVE, YOU BIG NUT!
AND KEEP UP THE GOOD WORK!
HEY, I'M HAVING A PARTY ON SATURDAY. CAN YOU MAKE IT?
SURE! I'LL BRING MY SPINACH DIP.
1/4/99 © 1998 United Feature Syndicate, Inc.

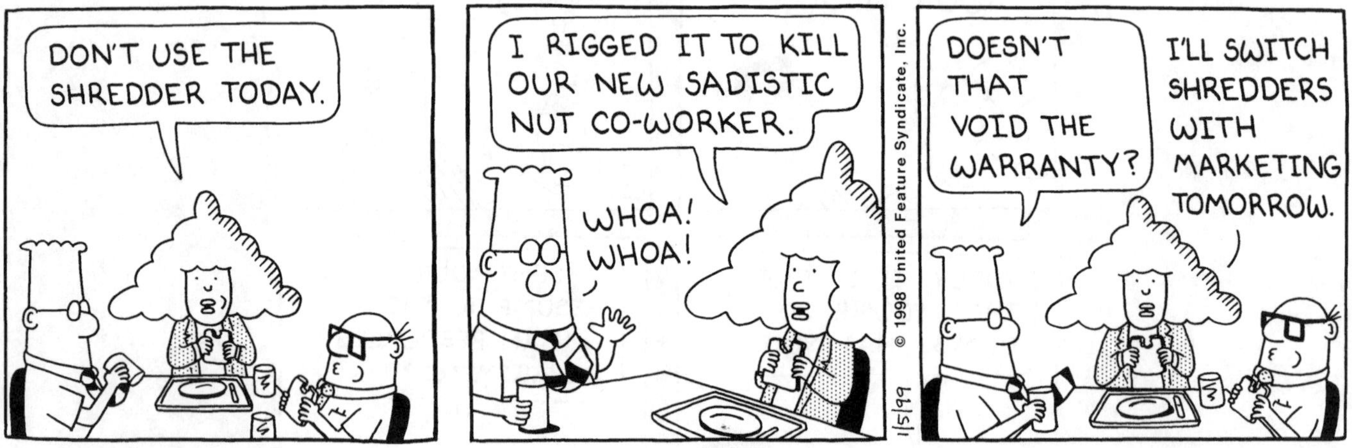
DON'T USE THE SHREDDER TODAY.
I RIGGED IT TO KILL OUR NEW SADISTIC NUT CO-WORKER.
WHOA! WHOA!
DOESN'T THAT VOID THE WARRANTY?
I'LL SWITCH SHREDDERS WITH MARKETING TOMORROW.
1/5/99 © 1998 United Feature Syndicate, Inc.

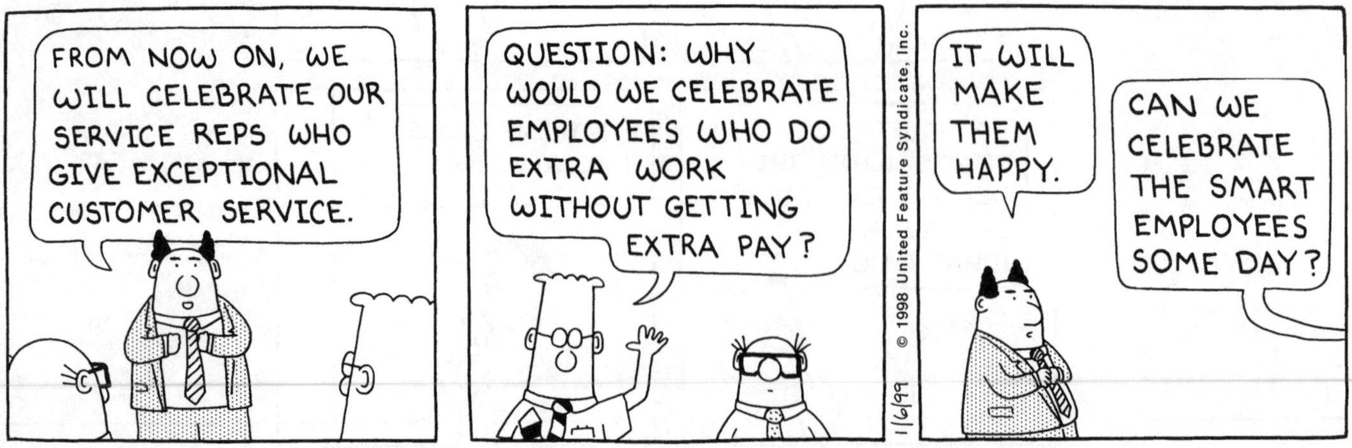
FROM NOW ON, WE WILL CELEBRATE OUR SERVICE REPS WHO GIVE EXCEPTIONAL CUSTOMER SERVICE.
QUESTION: WHY WOULD WE CELEBRATE EMPLOYEES WHO DO EXTRA WORK WITHOUT GETTING EXTRA PAY?
IT WILL MAKE THEM HAPPY.
CAN WE CELEBRATE THE SMART EMPLOYEES SOME DAY?
1/6/99 © 1998 United Feature Syndicate, Inc.

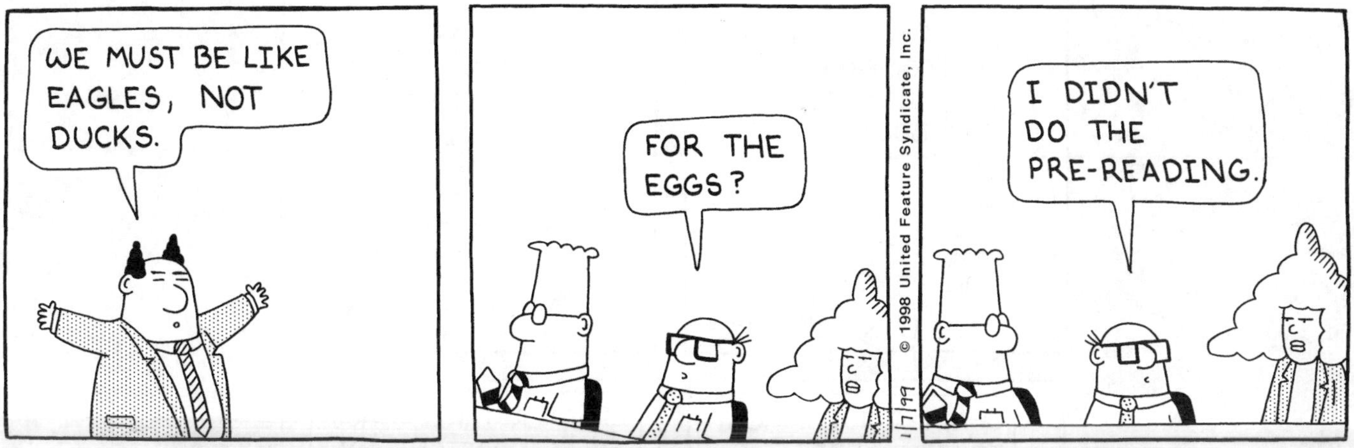
WE MUST BE LIKE EAGLES, NOT DUCKS.
FOR THE EGGS?
I DIDN'T DO THE PRE-READING.
© 1998 United Feature Syndicate, Inc.
1/7/99

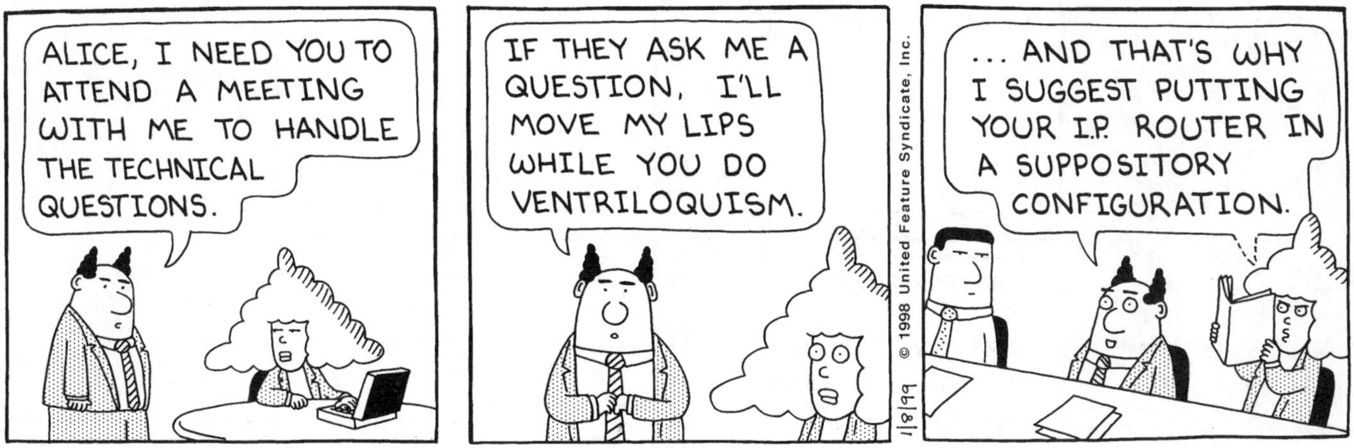
ALICE, I NEED YOU TO ATTEND A MEETING WITH ME TO HANDLE THE TECHNICAL QUESTIONS.
IF THEY ASK ME A QUESTION, I'LL MOVE MY LIPS WHILE YOU DO VENTRILOQUISM.
... AND THAT'S WHY I SUGGEST PUTTING YOUR I.P. ROUTER IN A SUPPOSITORY CONFIGURATION.
© 1998 United Feature Syndicate, Inc.
1/8/99

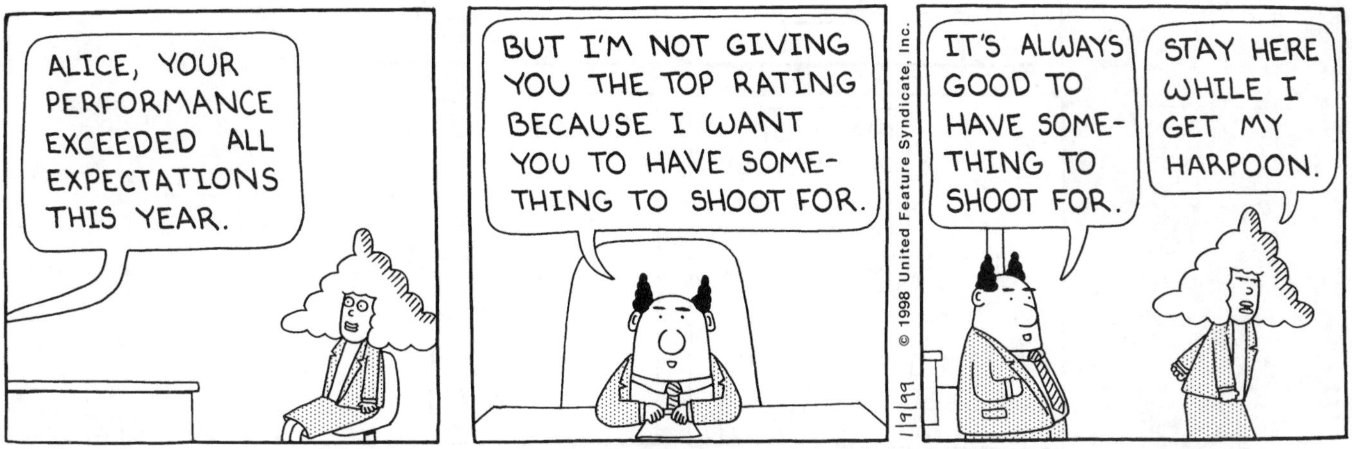
ALICE, YOUR PERFORMANCE EXCEEDED ALL EXPECTATIONS THIS YEAR.
BUT I'M NOT GIVING YOU THE TOP RATING BECAUSE I WANT YOU TO HAVE SOME-THING TO SHOOT FOR.
IT'S ALWAYS GOOD TO HAVE SOME-THING TO SHOOT FOR.
STAY HERE WHILE I GET MY HARPOON.
© 1998 United Feature Syndicate, Inc.
1/9/99

I'M WRITING A COMPREHENSIVE "HOW TO" BOOK.
IN CHAPTER ONE, I TEACH PEOPLE HOW TO PICK WINNING LOTTERY NUMBERS.
CHAPTER TWO: HOW TO FIND FREE REAL ESTATE IN VERY NICE NEIGHBOR-HOODS.
CHAPTER THREE: HOW TO LOSE WEIGHT BY EATING HUGE TUBS OF ICE CREAM.
CHAPTER FOUR: HOW TO BUILD STRONG ABS BY JOINING A GYM AND NEVER GOING.
FINALLY, HOW TO SEE ANGELS BY GIVING YOURSELF A NEAR DEATH EXPERIENCE.
THAT LAST ONE IS JUST TO GET RID OF ALL THE WITNESSES.
ON THE PLUS SIDE, I DON'T FEEL SO BAD ABOUT NOT RECYCLING.
1/10/99 © 1999 United Feature Syndicate, Inc.

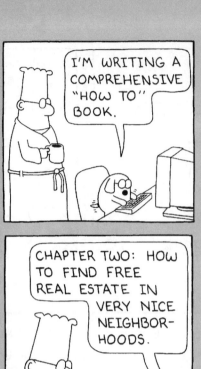

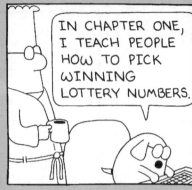

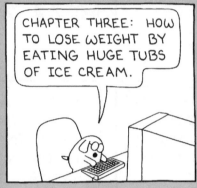

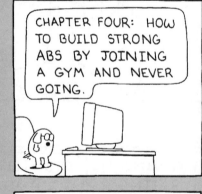

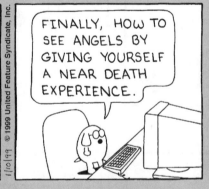

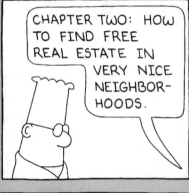

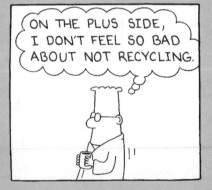

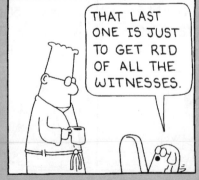

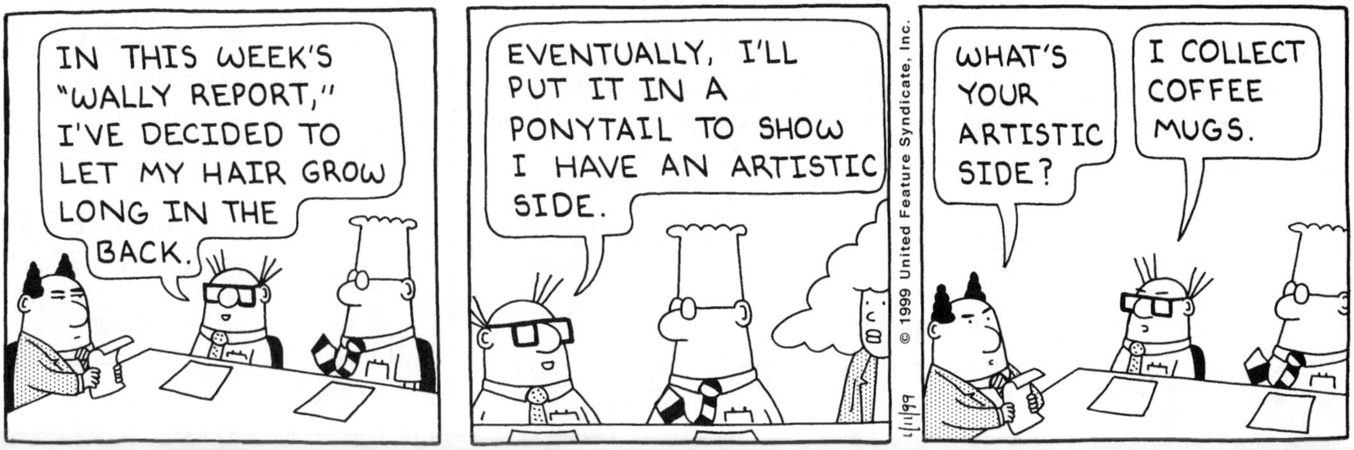
IN THIS WEEK'S "WALLY REPORT," I'VE DECIDED TO LET MY HAIR GROW LONG IN THE BACK.
EVENTUALLY, I'LL PUT IT IN A PONYTAIL TO SHOW I HAVE AN ARTISTIC SIDE.
© 1999 United Feature Syndicate, Inc.
1/11/99
WHAT'S YOUR ARTISTIC SIDE?
I COLLECT COFFEE MUGS.

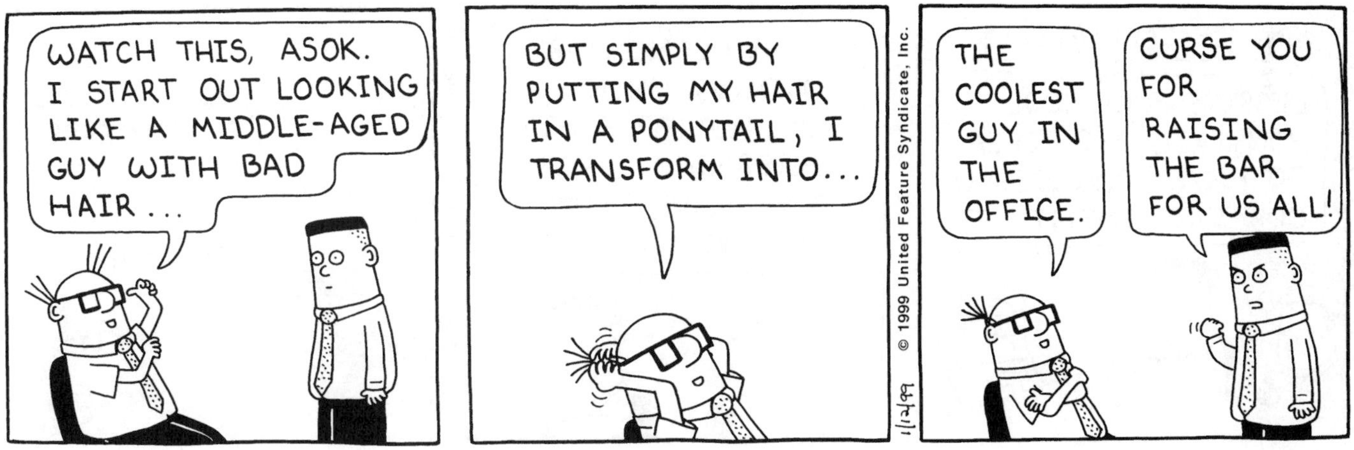
WATCH THIS, ASOK. I START OUT LOOKING LIKE A MIDDLE-AGED GUY WITH BAD HAIR...
BUT SIMPLY BY PUTTING MY HAIR IN A PONYTAIL, I TRANSFORM INTO...
© 1999 United Feature Syndicate, Inc.
1/12/99
THE COOLEST GUY IN THE OFFICE.
CURSE YOU FOR RAISING THE BAR FOR US ALL!

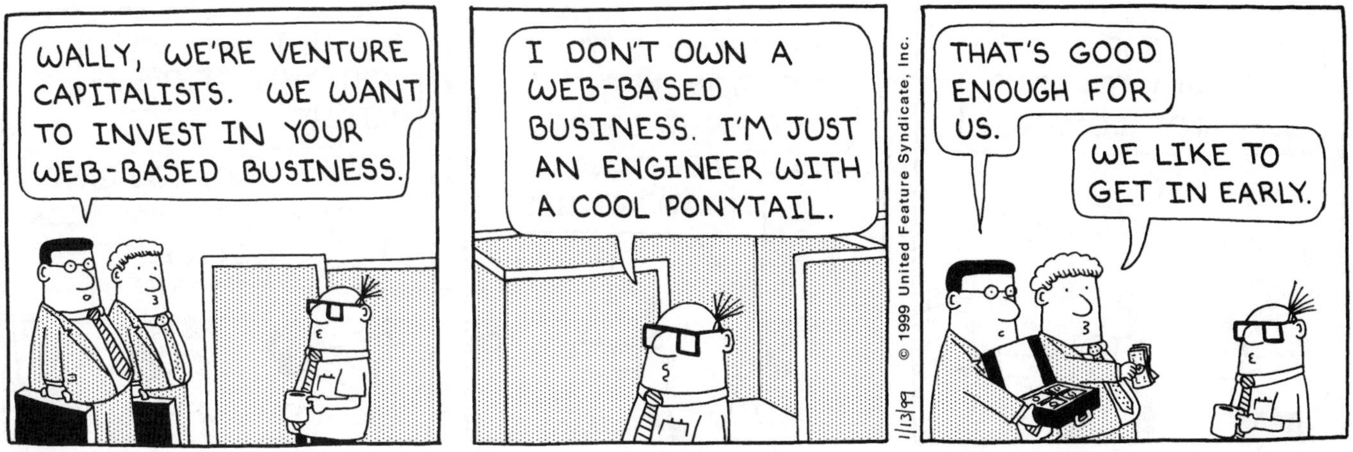
WALLY, WE'RE VENTURE CAPITALISTS. WE WANT TO INVEST IN YOUR WEB-BASED BUSINESS.
I DON'T OWN A WEB-BASED BUSINESS. I'M JUST AN ENGINEER WITH A COOL PONYTAIL.
© 1999 United Feature Syndicate, Inc.
1/13/99
THAT'S GOOD ENOUGH FOR US.
WE LIKE TO GET IN EARLY.

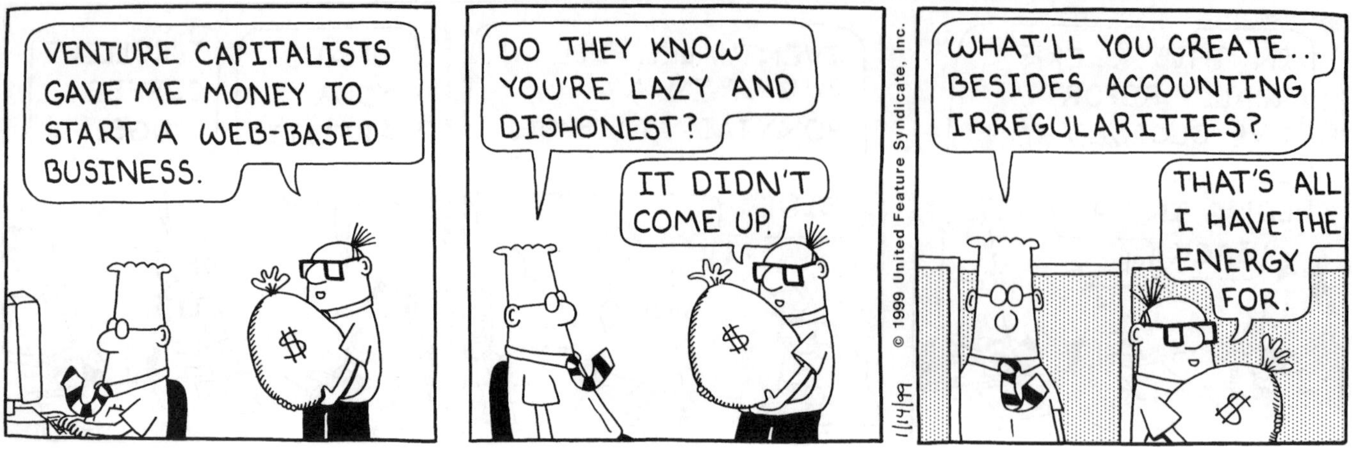
VENTURE CAPITALISTS GAVE ME MONEY TO START A WEB-BASED BUSINESS.
DO THEY KNOW YOU'RE LAZY AND DISHONEST?
IT DIDN'T COME UP.
1/14/99 © 1999 United Feature Syndicate, Inc.
WHAT'LL YOU CREATE... BESIDES ACCOUNTING IRREGULARITIES?
THAT'S ALL I HAVE THE ENERGY FOR.

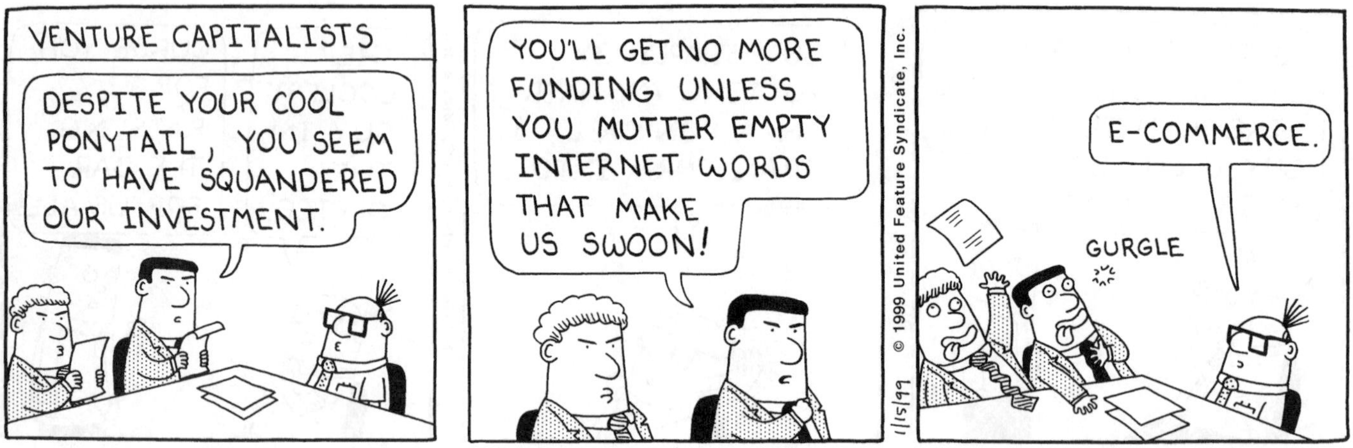
VENTURE CAPITALISTS
DESPITE YOUR COOL PONYTAIL, YOU SEEM TO HAVE SQUANDERED OUR INVESTMENT.
YOU'LL GET NO MORE FUNDING UNLESS YOU MUTTER EMPTY INTERNET WORDS THAT MAKE US SWOON!
1/15/99 © 1999 United Feature Syndicate, Inc.
E-COMMERCE.
GURGLE

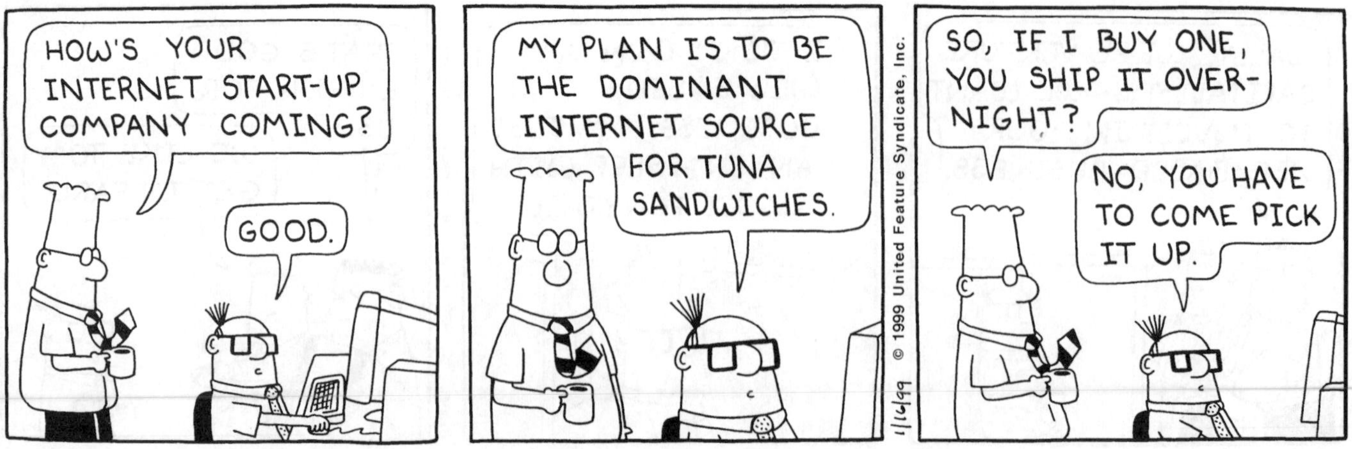
HOW'S YOUR INTERNET START-UP COMPANY COMING?
GOOD.
MY PLAN IS TO BE THE DOMINANT INTERNET SOURCE FOR TUNA SANDWICHES.
1/16/99 © 1999 United Feature Syndicate, Inc.
SO, IF I BUY ONE, YOU SHIP IT OVER-NIGHT?
NO, YOU HAVE TO COME PICK IT UP.

STOP.
SECURITY
SHOW ME YOUR "EQUIPMENT REMOVAL AUTHORIZATION FORM."
THIS REQUIRES THE SIGNATURE OF TWO EMPLOYEES.
GOOD CATCH. YOU'D BETTER SIGN IT SO IT'S LEGAL.
THIS SEEMS WRONG ... BUT I DON'T KNOW WHY.
AND I'LL NEED TO SEE YOUR BIRTH CERTIFICATE.
I DON'T HAVE ONE.
THEN HOW DO YOU KNOW YOU WERE BORN?
I HAVE BABY PICTURES, BUT THEY COULD HAVE BEEN DOCTORED BY MY ALLEGED MOM.
1/17/99 © 1999 United Feature Syndicate, Inc.

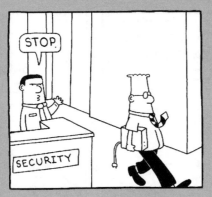

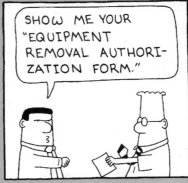

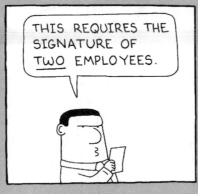

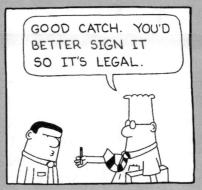

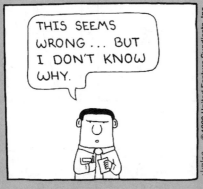

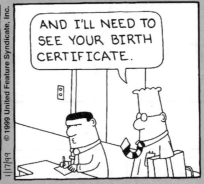

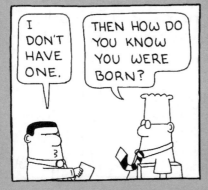

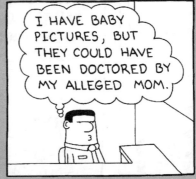

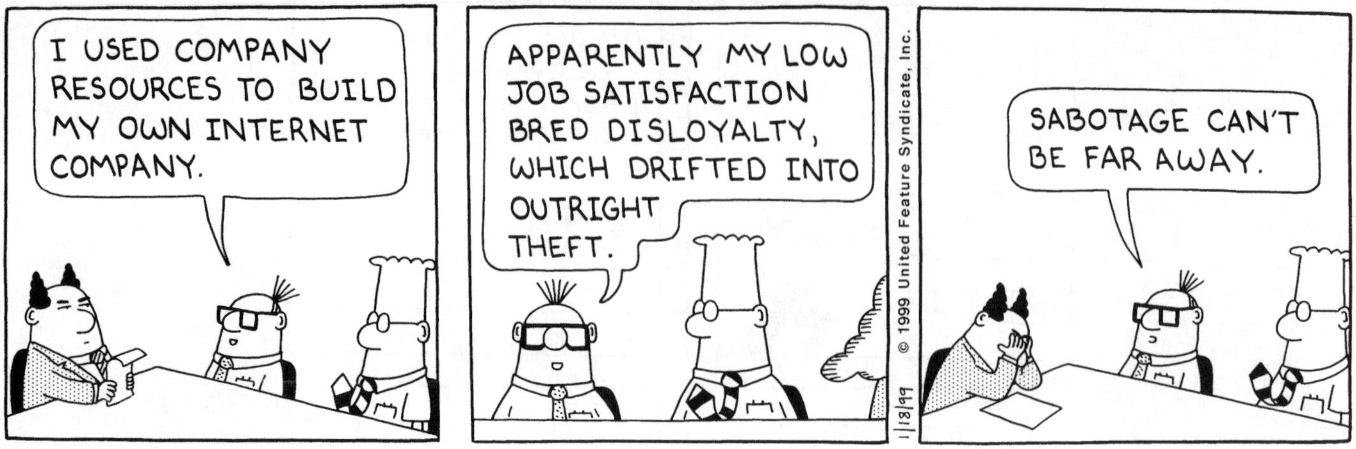
I USED COMPANY RESOURCES TO BUILD MY OWN INTERNET COMPANY.
APPARENTLY MY LOW JOB SATISFACTION BRED DISLOYALTY, WHICH DRIFTED INTO OUTRIGHT THEFT.
SABOTAGE CAN'T BE FAR AWAY.
1/18/99 © 1999 United Feature Syndicate, Inc.

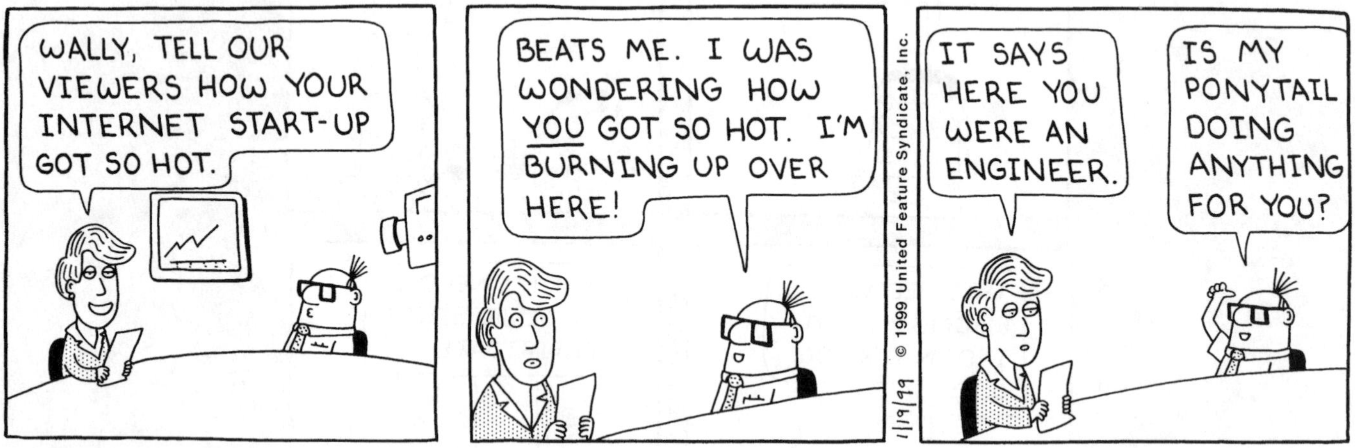
WALLY, TELL OUR VIEWERS HOW YOUR INTERNET START-UP GOT SO HOT.
BEATS ME. I WAS WONDERING HOW YOU GOT SO HOT. I'M BURNING UP OVER HERE!
IT SAYS HERE YOU WERE AN ENGINEER.
IS MY PONYTAIL DOING ANYTHING FOR YOU?
1/19/99 © 1999 United Feature Syndicate, Inc.

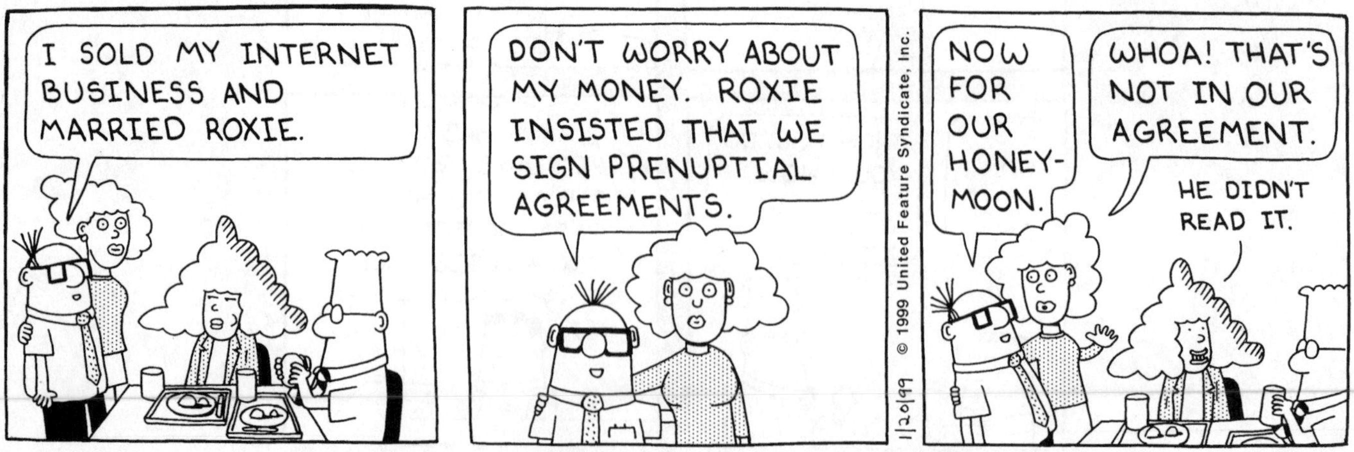
I SOLD MY INTERNET BUSINESS AND MARRIED ROXIE.
DON'T WORRY ABOUT MY MONEY. ROXIE INSISTED THAT WE SIGN PRENUPTIAL AGREEMENTS.
NOW FOR OUR HONEY-MOON.
WHOA! THAT'S NOT IN OUR AGREEMENT.
HE DIDN'T READ IT.
1/20/99 © 1999 United Feature Syndicate, Inc.

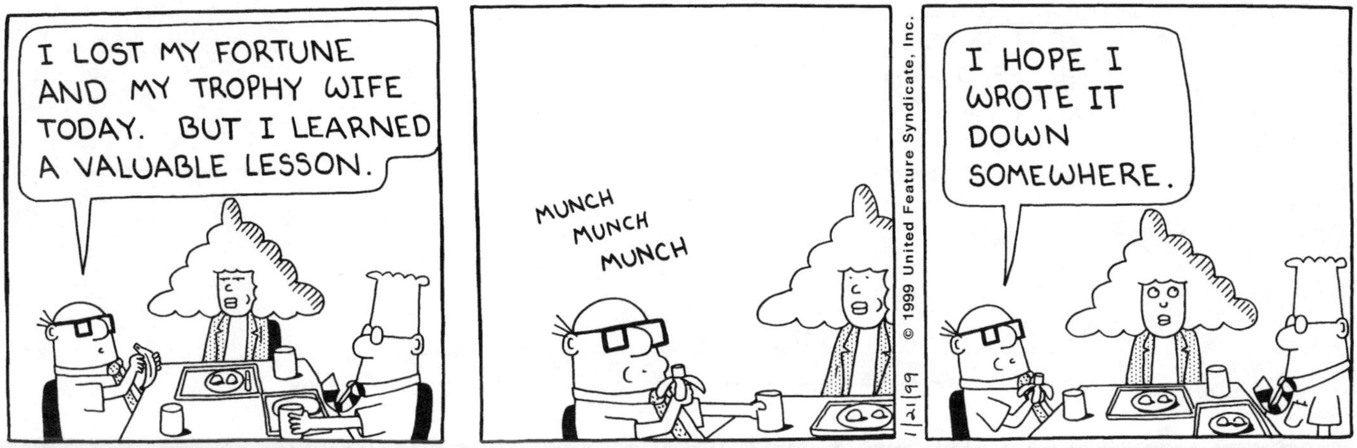
I LOST MY FORTUNE AND MY TROPHY WIFE TODAY. BUT I LEARNED A VALUABLE LESSON.
MUNCH MUNCH MUNCH
I HOPE I WROTE IT DOWN SOMEWHERE.
1/21/99 © 1999 United Feature Syndicate, Inc.

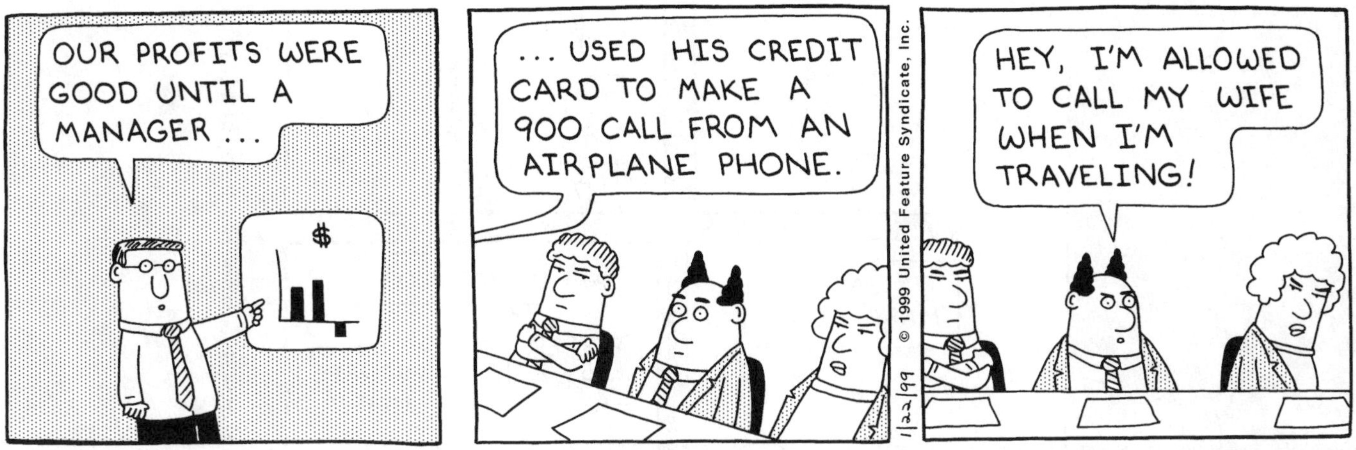
OUR PROFITS WERE GOOD UNTIL A MANAGER ...
$
... USED HIS CREDIT CARD TO MAKE A 900 CALL FROM AN AIRPLANE PHONE.
HEY, I'M ALLOWED TO CALL MY WIFE WHEN I'M TRAVELING!
1/22/99 © 1999 United Feature Syndicate, Inc.

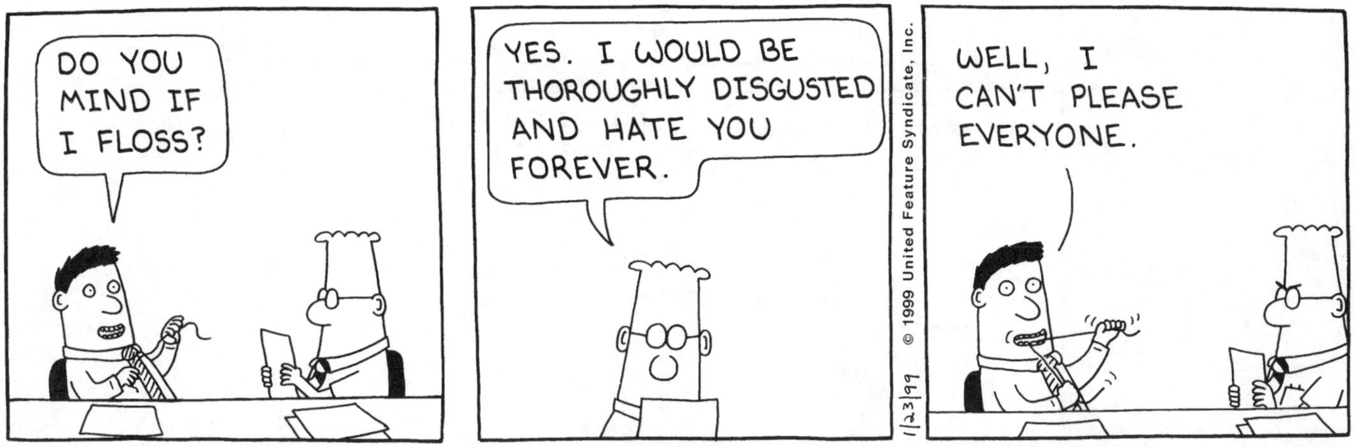
DO YOU MIND IF I FLOSS?
YES. I WOULD BE THOROUGHLY DISGUSTED AND HATE YOU FOREVER.
WELL, I CAN'T PLEASE EVERYONE.
1/23/99 © 1999 United Feature Syndicate, Inc.

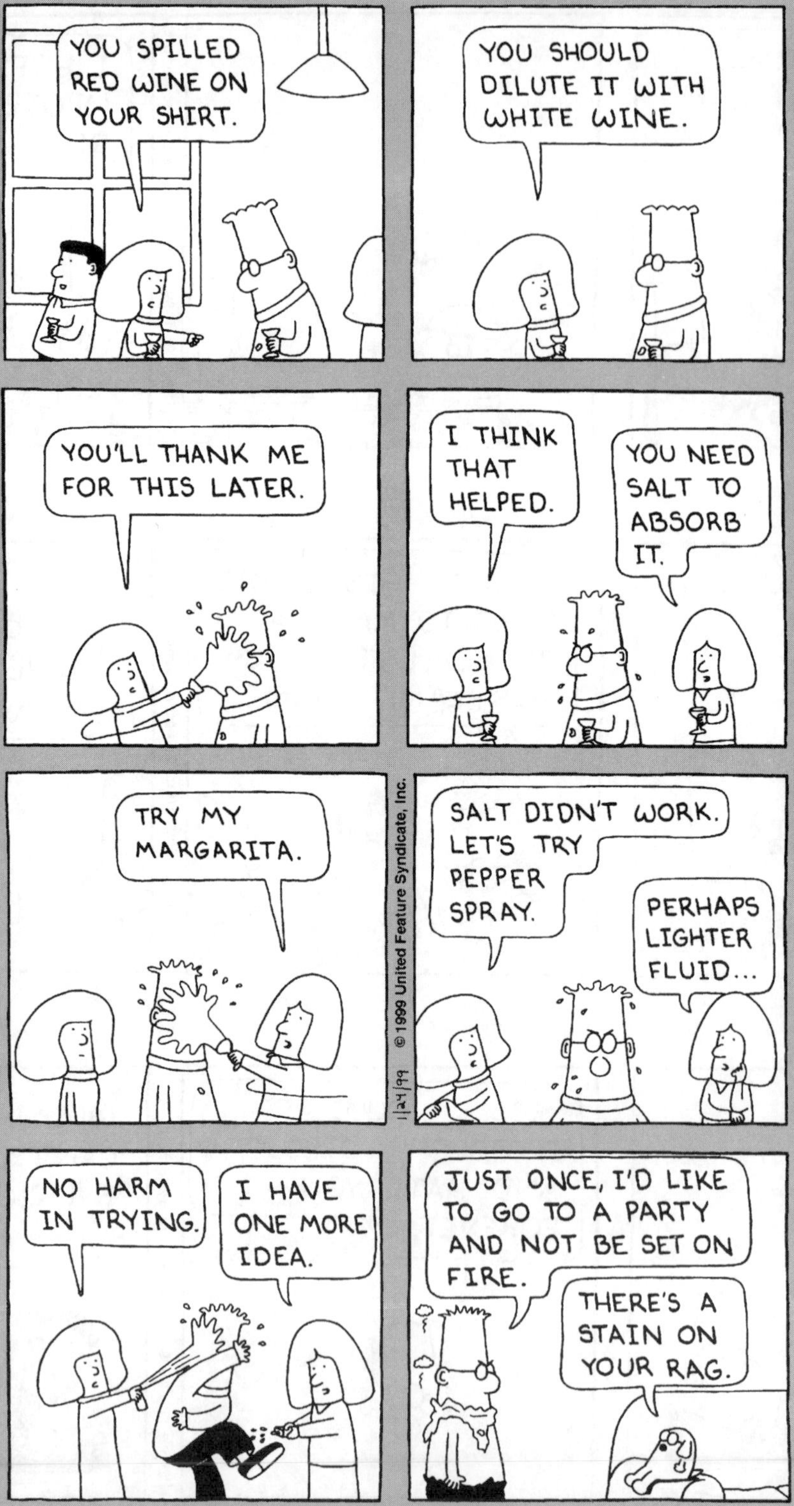
YOU SPILLED RED WINE ON YOUR SHIRT.
YOU SHOULD DILUTE IT WITH WHITE WINE.
YOU'LL THANK ME FOR THIS LATER.
I THINK THAT HELPED.
YOU NEED SALT TO ABSORB IT.
TRY MY MARGARITA.
SALT DIDN'T WORK. LET'S TRY PEPPER SPRAY.
PERHAPS LIGHTER FLUID...
NO HARM IN TRYING.
I HAVE ONE MORE IDEA.
JUST ONCE, I'D LIKE TO GO TO A PARTY AND NOT BE SET ON FIRE.
THERE'S A STAIN ON YOUR RAG.
© 1999 United Feature Syndicate, Inc.
1/24/99

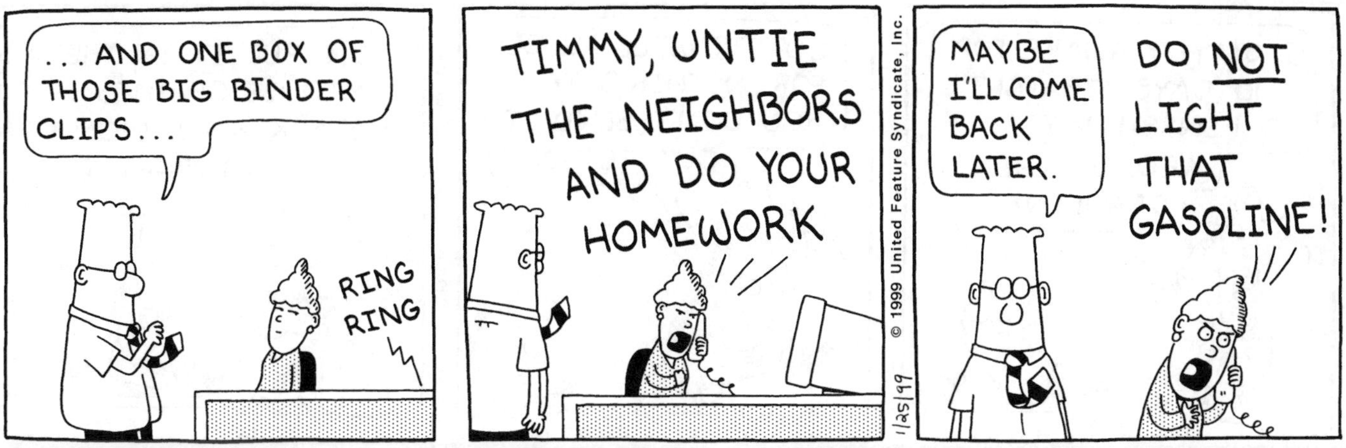
...AND ONE BOX OF THOSE BIG BINDER CLIPS...
RING RING
TIMMY, UNTIE THE NEIGHBORS AND DO YOUR HOMEWORK
MAYBE I'LL COME BACK LATER.
DO NOT LIGHT THAT GASOLINE!

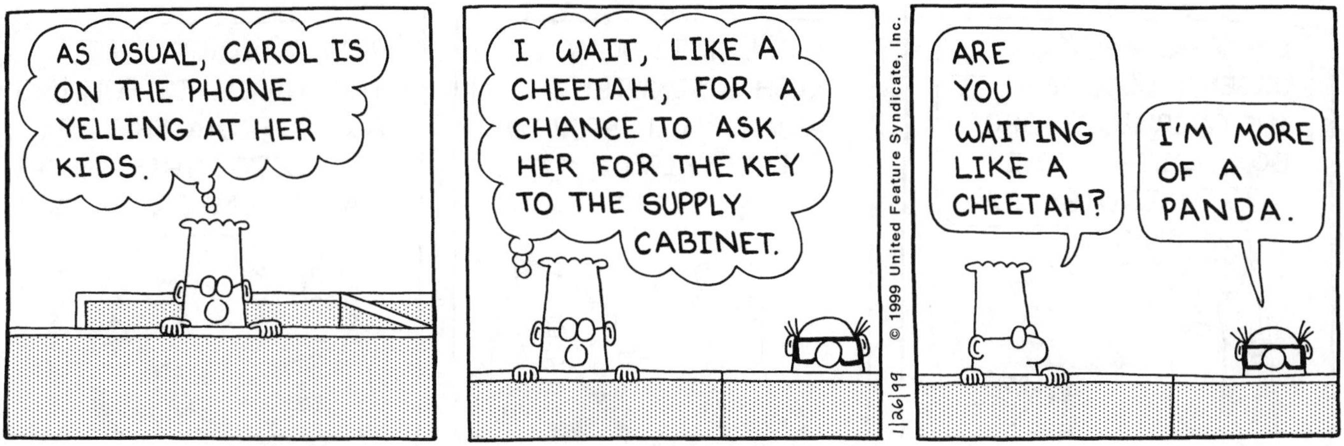
AS USUAL, CAROL IS ON THE PHONE YELLING AT HER KIDS.
I WAIT, LIKE A CHEETAH, FOR A CHANCE TO ASK HER FOR THE KEY TO THE SUPPLY CABINET.
ARE YOU WAITING LIKE A CHEETAH?
I'M MORE OF A PANDA.

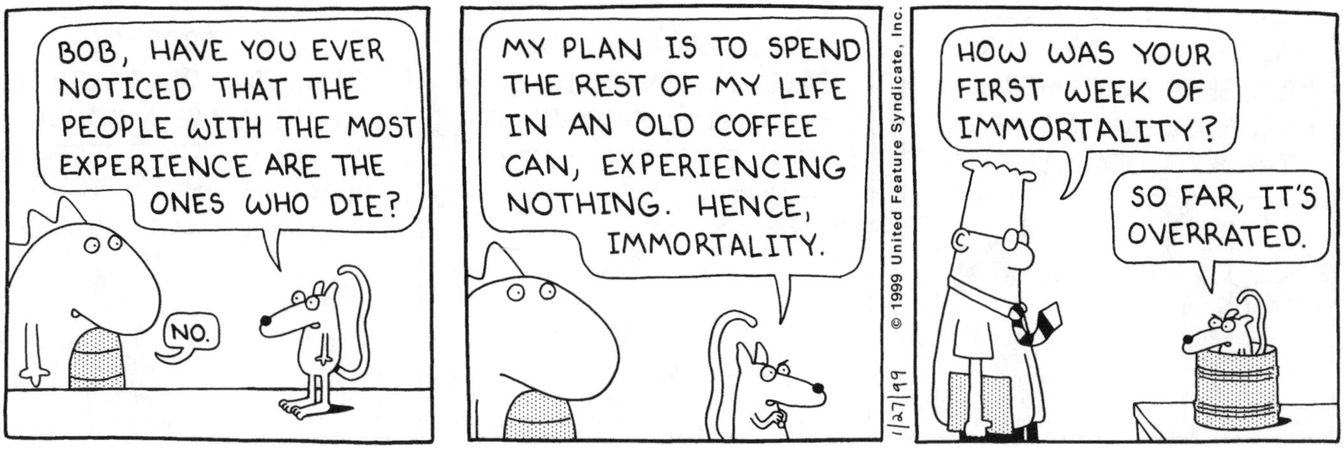
BOB, HAVE YOU EVER NOTICED THAT THE PEOPLE WITH THE MOST EXPERIENCE ARE THE ONES WHO DIE?
NO.
MY PLAN IS TO SPEND THE REST OF MY LIFE IN AN OLD COFFEE CAN, EXPERIENCING NOTHING. HENCE, IMMORTALITY.
HOW WAS YOUR FIRST WEEK OF IMMORTALITY?
SO FAR, IT'S OVERRATED.

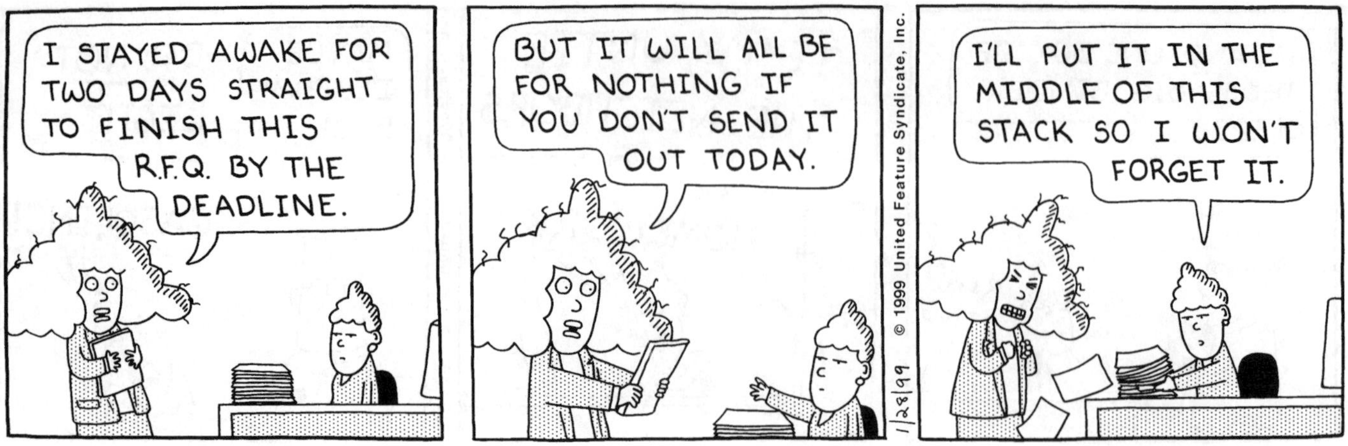
I STAYED AWAKE FOR TWO DAYS STRAIGHT TO FINISH THIS R.F.Q. BY THE DEADLINE.
BUT IT WILL ALL BE FOR NOTHING IF YOU DON'T SEND IT OUT TODAY.
1/28/99 © 1999 United Feature Syndicate, Inc.
I'LL PUT IT IN THE MIDDLE OF THIS STACK SO I WON'T FORGET IT.

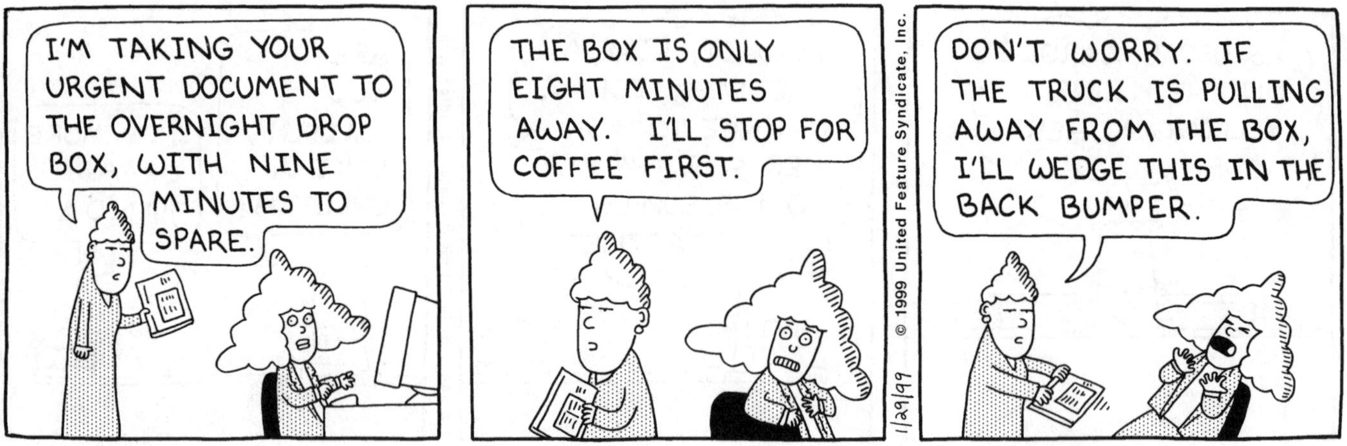
I'M TAKING YOUR URGENT DOCUMENT TO THE OVERNIGHT DROP BOX, WITH NINE MINUTES TO SPARE.
THE BOX IS ONLY EIGHT MINUTES AWAY. I'LL STOP FOR COFFEE FIRST.
1/29/99 © 1999 United Feature Syndicate, Inc.
DON'T WORRY. IF THE TRUCK IS PULLING AWAY FROM THE BOX, I'LL WEDGE THIS IN THE BACK BUMPER.

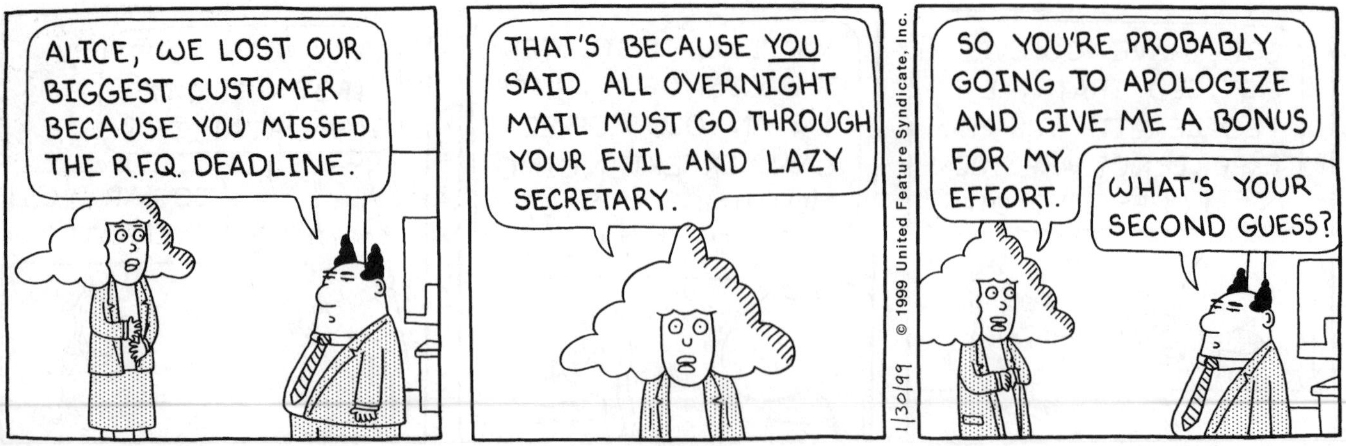
ALICE, WE LOST OUR BIGGEST CUSTOMER BECAUSE YOU MISSED THE R.F.Q. DEADLINE.
THAT'S BECAUSE YOU SAID ALL OVERNIGHT MAIL MUST GO THROUGH YOUR EVIL AND LAZY SECRETARY.
1/30/99 © 1999 United Feature Syndicate, Inc.
SO YOU'RE PROBABLY GOING TO APOLOGIZE AND GIVE ME A BONUS FOR MY EFFORT.
WHAT'S YOUR SECOND GUESS?

MAKE YOUR REPORT CONSISTENT WITH OUR STRATEGIC PLAN.
WHAT'S OUR STRATEGIC PLAN?
IT'S A SECRET.
ARE YOU SAYING YOU DON'T TRUST ME?
I DON'T THINK IT'S A COINCIDENCE THAT MOST EMPLOYEE SABOTAGE IS DONE BY EMPLOYEES.
HOW CAN I DO MY REPORT IF I DON'T KNOW THE STRATEGY?!
OKAY, OKAY.
I'LL LET YOU GLANCE AT IT.
TIME'S UP! THAT'S LONG ENOUGH!
THAT'S THE WARRANTY FOR YOUR CHAIR.
REALLY? I'VE BEEN MANAGING TO THIS FOR YEARS.
1/31/99 © 1999 United Feature Syndicate, Inc.

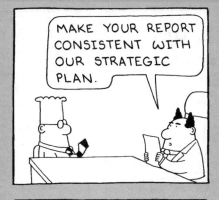

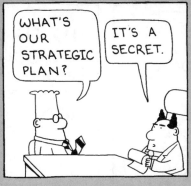

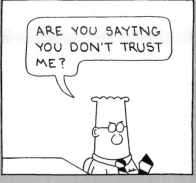

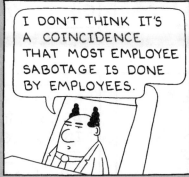

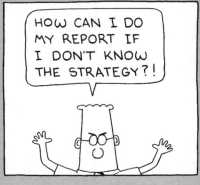

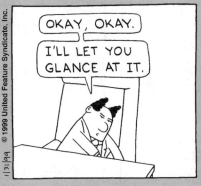

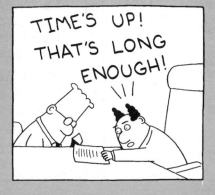

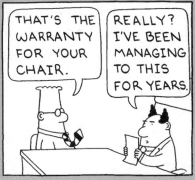

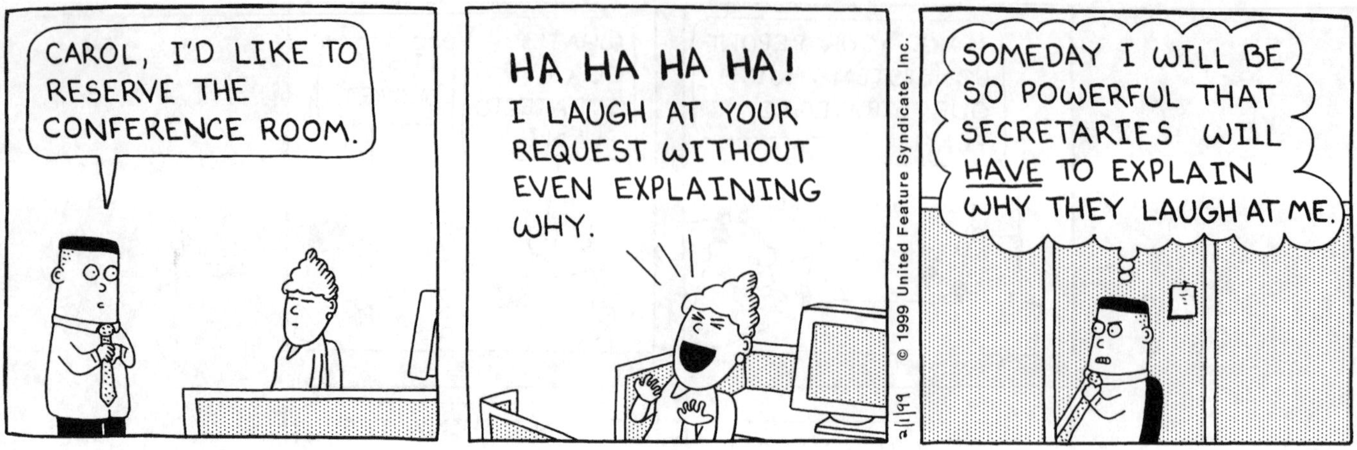
CAROL, I'D LIKE TO RESERVE THE CONFERENCE ROOM.
HA HA HA HA! I LAUGH AT YOUR REQUEST WITHOUT EVEN EXPLAINING WHY.
2/1/99 © 1999 United Feature Syndicate, Inc.
SOMEDAY I WILL BE SO POWERFUL THAT SECRETARIES WILL HAVE TO EXPLAIN WHY THEY LAUGH AT ME.

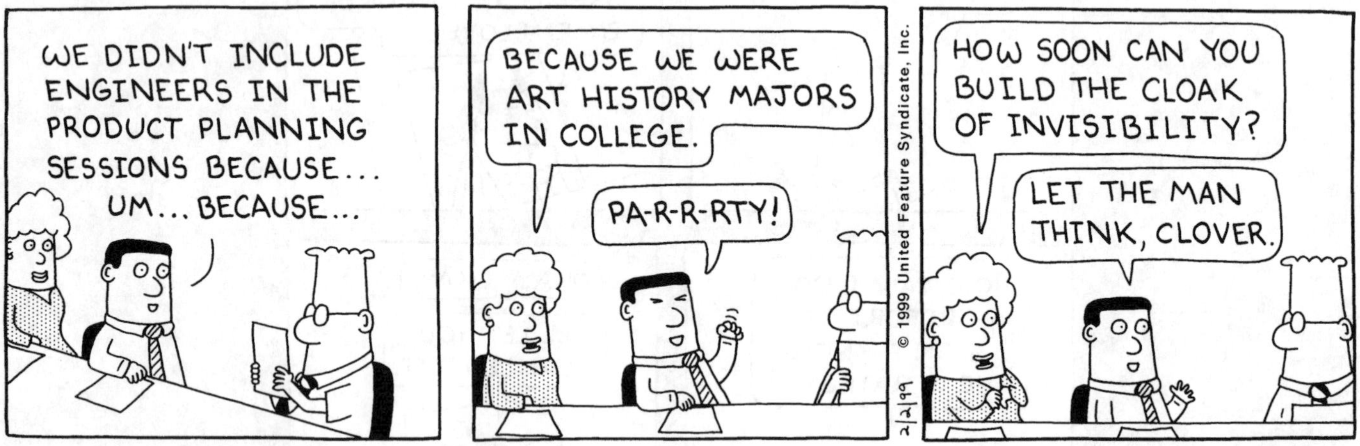
WE DIDN'T INCLUDE ENGINEERS IN THE PRODUCT PLANNING SESSIONS BECAUSE... UM... BECAUSE...
BECAUSE WE WERE ART HISTORY MAJORS IN COLLEGE.
PA-R-R-RTY!
2/2/99 © 1999 United Feature Syndicate, Inc.
HOW SOON CAN YOU BUILD THE CLOAK OF INVISIBILITY?
LET THE MAN THINK, CLOVER.

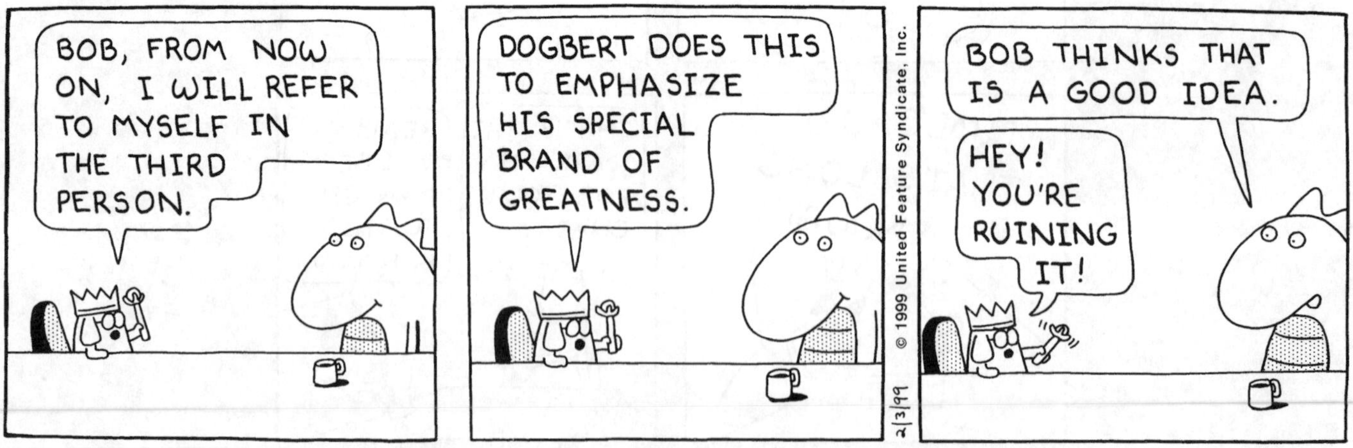
BOB, FROM NOW ON, I WILL REFER TO MYSELF IN THE THIRD PERSON.
DOGBERT DOES THIS TO EMPHASIZE HIS SPECIAL BRAND OF GREATNESS.
2/3/99 © 1999 United Feature Syndicate, Inc.
BOB THINKS THAT IS A GOOD IDEA.
HEY! YOU'RE RUINING IT!

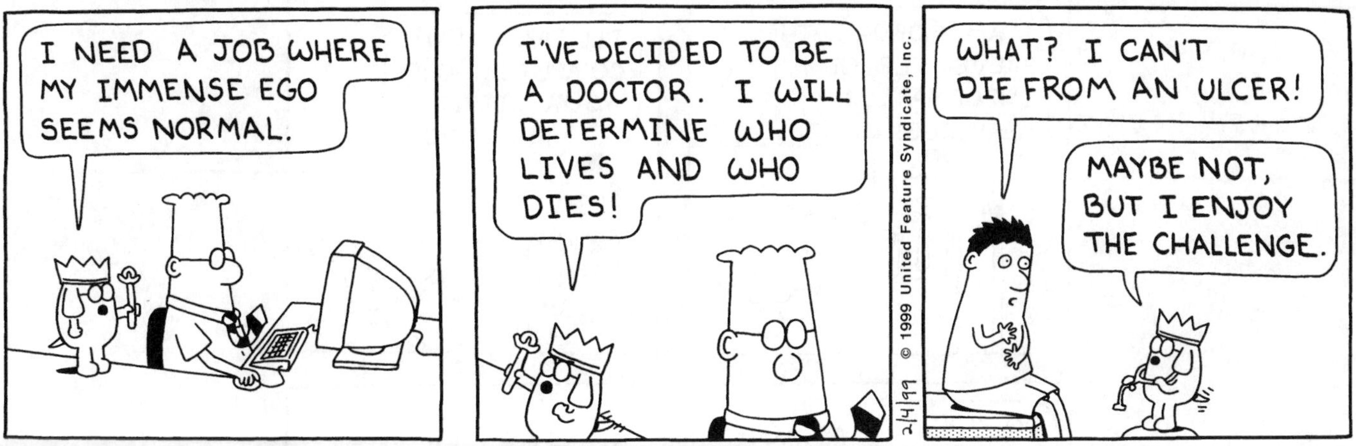
I NEED A JOB WHERE MY IMMENSE EGO SEEMS NORMAL.
I'VE DECIDED TO BE A DOCTOR. I WILL DETERMINE WHO LIVES AND WHO DIES!
2/4/99 © 1999 United Feature Syndicate, Inc.
WHAT? I CAN'T DIE FROM AN ULCER!
MAYBE NOT, BUT I ENJOY THE CHALLENGE.

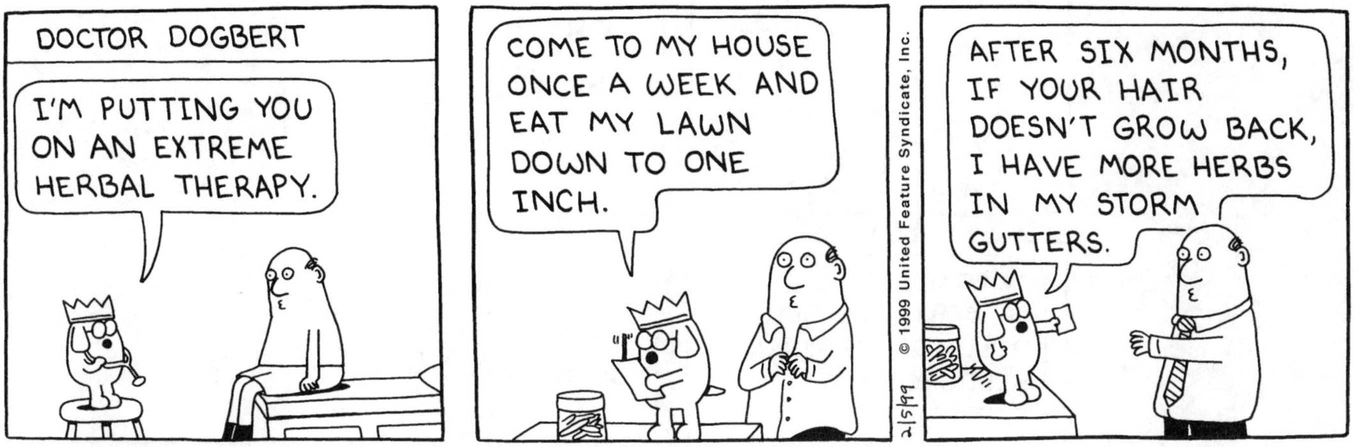
DOCTOR DOGBERT
I'M PUTTING YOU ON AN EXTREME HERBAL THERAPY.
COME TO MY HOUSE ONCE A WEEK AND EAT MY LAWN DOWN TO ONE INCH.
2/5/99 © 1999 United Feature Syndicate, Inc.
AFTER SIX MONTHS, IF YOUR HAIR DOESN'T GROW BACK, I HAVE MORE HERBS IN MY STORM GUTTERS.

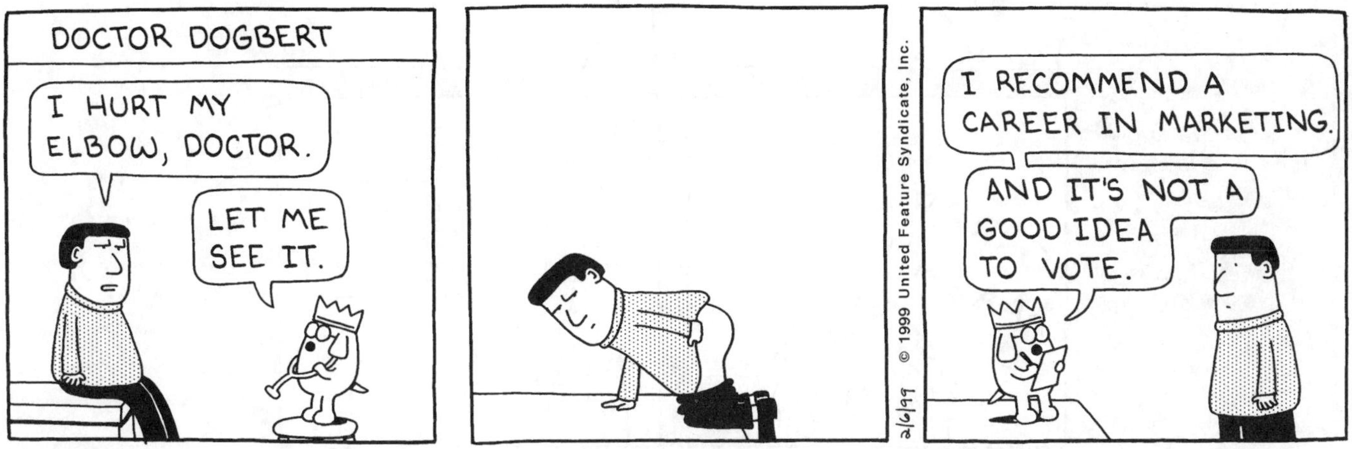
DOCTOR DOGBERT
I HURT MY ELBOW, DOCTOR.
LET ME SEE IT.
2/6/99 © 1999 United Feature Syndicate, Inc.
I RECOMMEND A CAREER IN MARKETING.
AND IT'S NOT A GOOD IDEA TO VOTE.

I AM MORDAC, THE PREVENTER OF INFORMATION SERVICES!
I'LL TAKE YOUR COMPUTER AND YOUR LITTLE P.D.A. TOO!
DO YOU RECOGNIZE THIS?
AAAGH! THAT'S MY NETWORK CABLE!
WHAT DO YOU WANT FROM ME?!
© 1999 United Feature Syndicate, Inc.
2/7/99
MORDAC, IT IS I, CATBERT, THE EVIL DIRECTOR OF HUMAN RESOURCES!
YOU MADE MY PERSONAL PRINTER A SHARED DEVICE!
GRRRR!! AAAGH!!
TWO WRONGS MADE A RIGHT.
WELCOME TO MY REALITY.

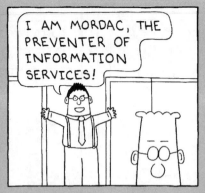

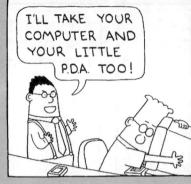

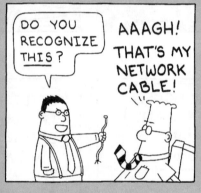

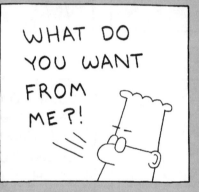

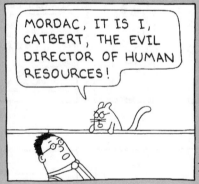

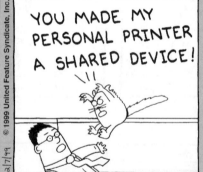

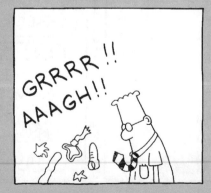

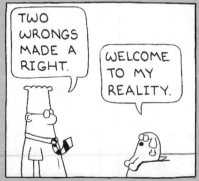

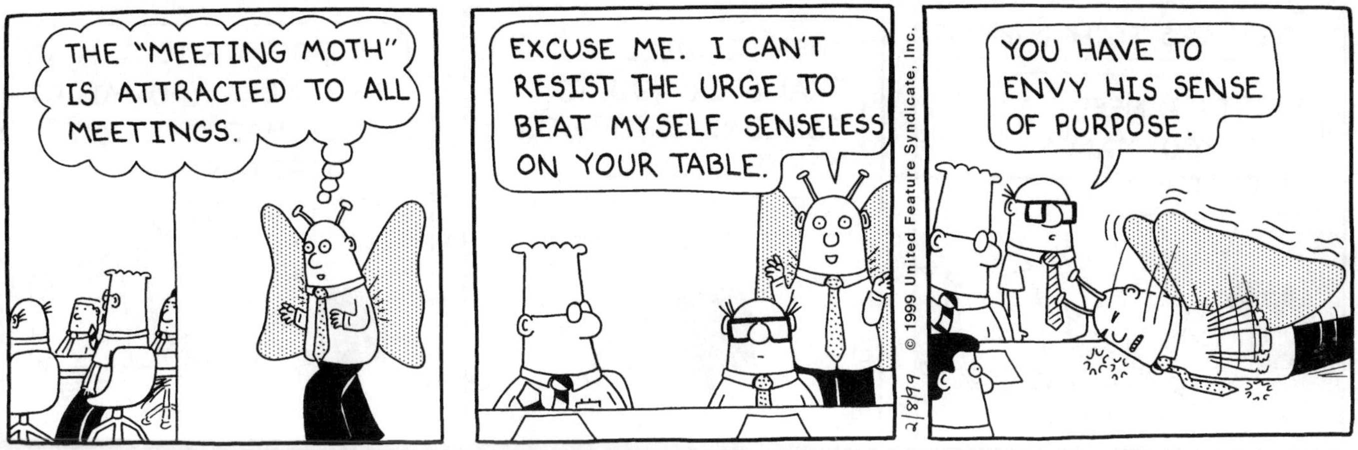
THE "MEETING MOTH" IS ATTRACTED TO ALL MEETINGS.
EXCUSE ME. I CAN'T RESIST THE URGE TO BEAT MYSELF SENSELESS ON YOUR TABLE.
2/8/99 © 1999 United Feature Syndicate, Inc.
YOU HAVE TO ENVY HIS SENSE OF PURPOSE.

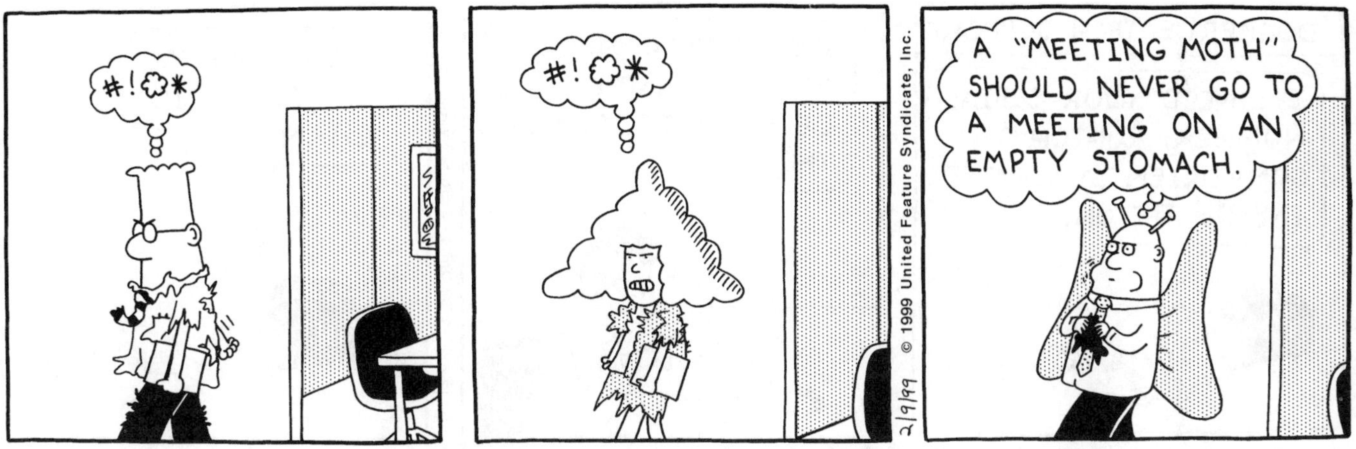
2/9/99 © 1999 United Feature Syndicate, Inc.
A "MEETING MOTH" SHOULD NEVER GO TO A MEETING ON AN EMPTY STOMACH.

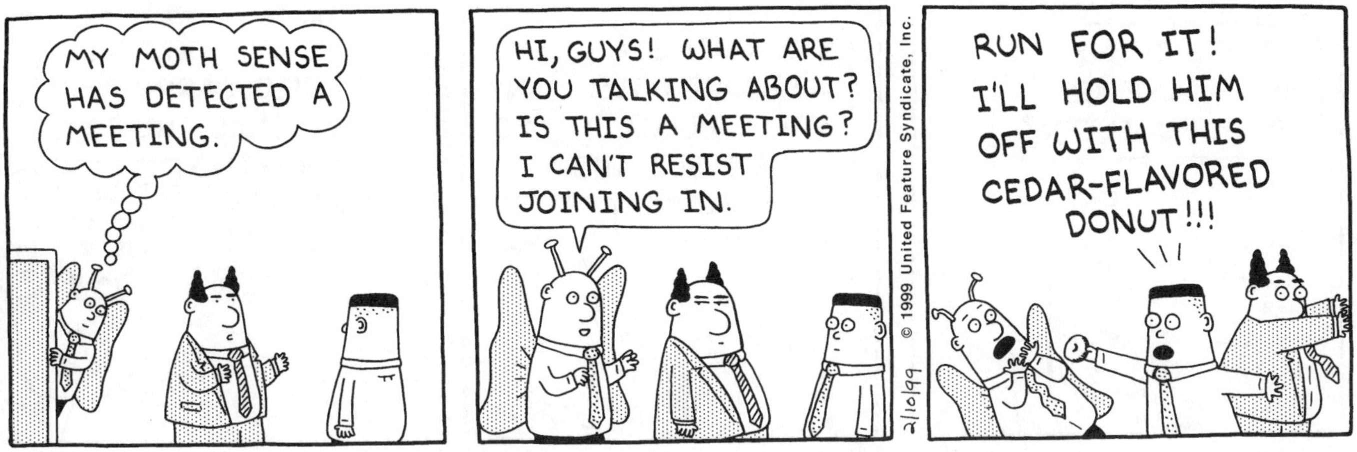
MY MOTH SENSE HAS DETECTED A MEETING.
HI, GUYS! WHAT ARE YOU TALKING ABOUT? IS THIS A MEETING? I CAN'T RESIST JOINING IN.
2/10/99 © 1999 United Feature Syndicate, Inc.
RUN FOR IT! I'LL HOLD HIM OFF WITH THIS CEDAR-FLAVORED DONUT!!!

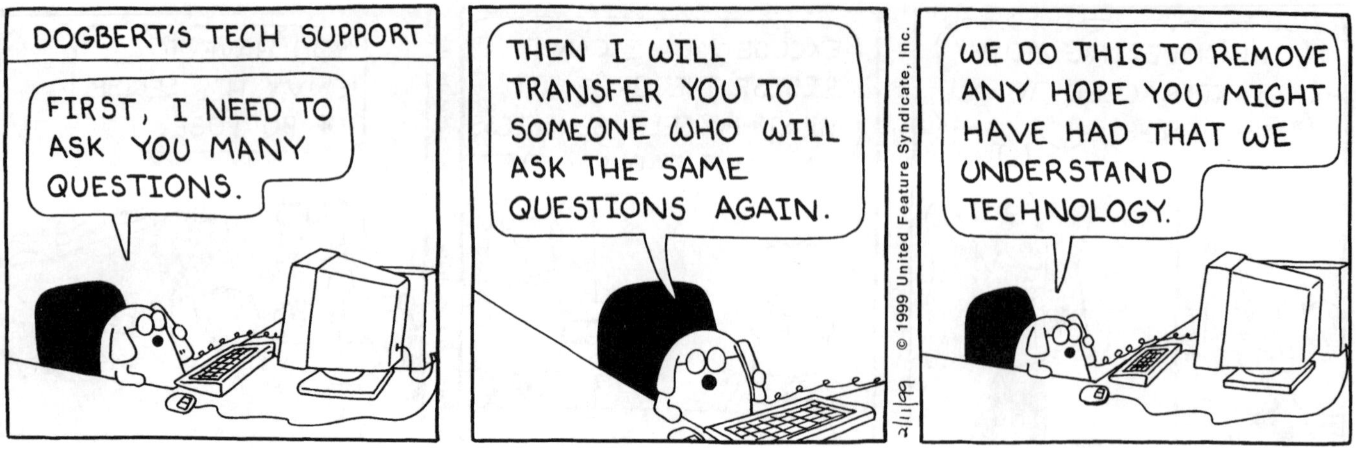
DOGBERT'S TECH SUPPORT
FIRST, I NEED TO ASK YOU MANY QUESTIONS.
THEN I WILL TRANSFER YOU TO SOMEONE WHO WILL ASK THE SAME QUESTIONS AGAIN.
© 1999 United Feature Syndicate, Inc.
2/11/99
WE DO THIS TO REMOVE ANY HOPE YOU MIGHT HAVE HAD THAT WE UNDERSTAND TECHNOLOGY.

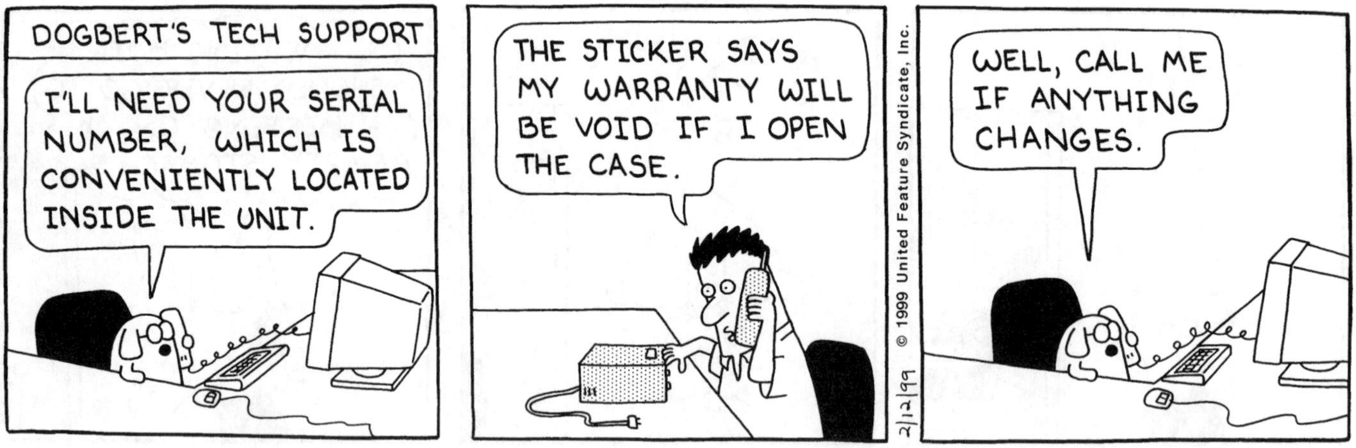
DOGBERT'S TECH SUPPORT
I'LL NEED YOUR SERIAL NUMBER, WHICH IS CONVENIENTLY LOCATED INSIDE THE UNIT.
THE STICKER SAYS MY WARRANTY WILL BE VOID IF I OPEN THE CASE.
© 1999 United Feature Syndicate, Inc.
2/12/99
WELL, CALL ME IF ANYTHING CHANGES.

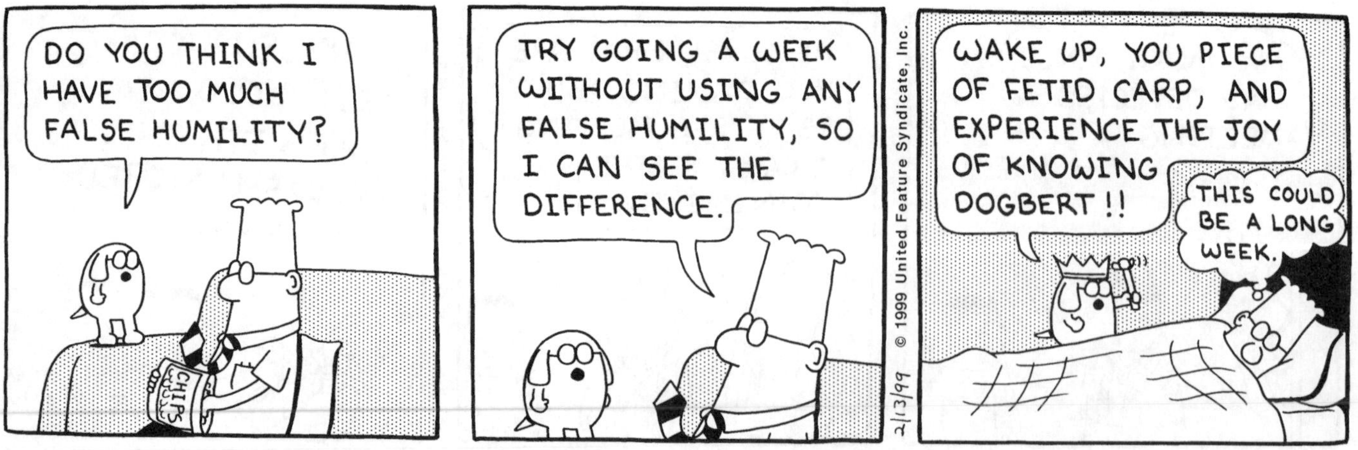
DO YOU THINK I HAVE TOO MUCH FALSE HUMILITY?
CHIPS
TRY GOING A WEEK WITHOUT USING ANY FALSE HUMILITY, SO I CAN SEE THE DIFFERENCE.
© 1999 United Feature Syndicate, Inc.
2/13/99
WAKE UP, YOU PIECE OF FETID CARP, AND EXPERIENCE THE JOY OF KNOWING DOGBERT!!
THIS COULD BE A LONG WEEK.

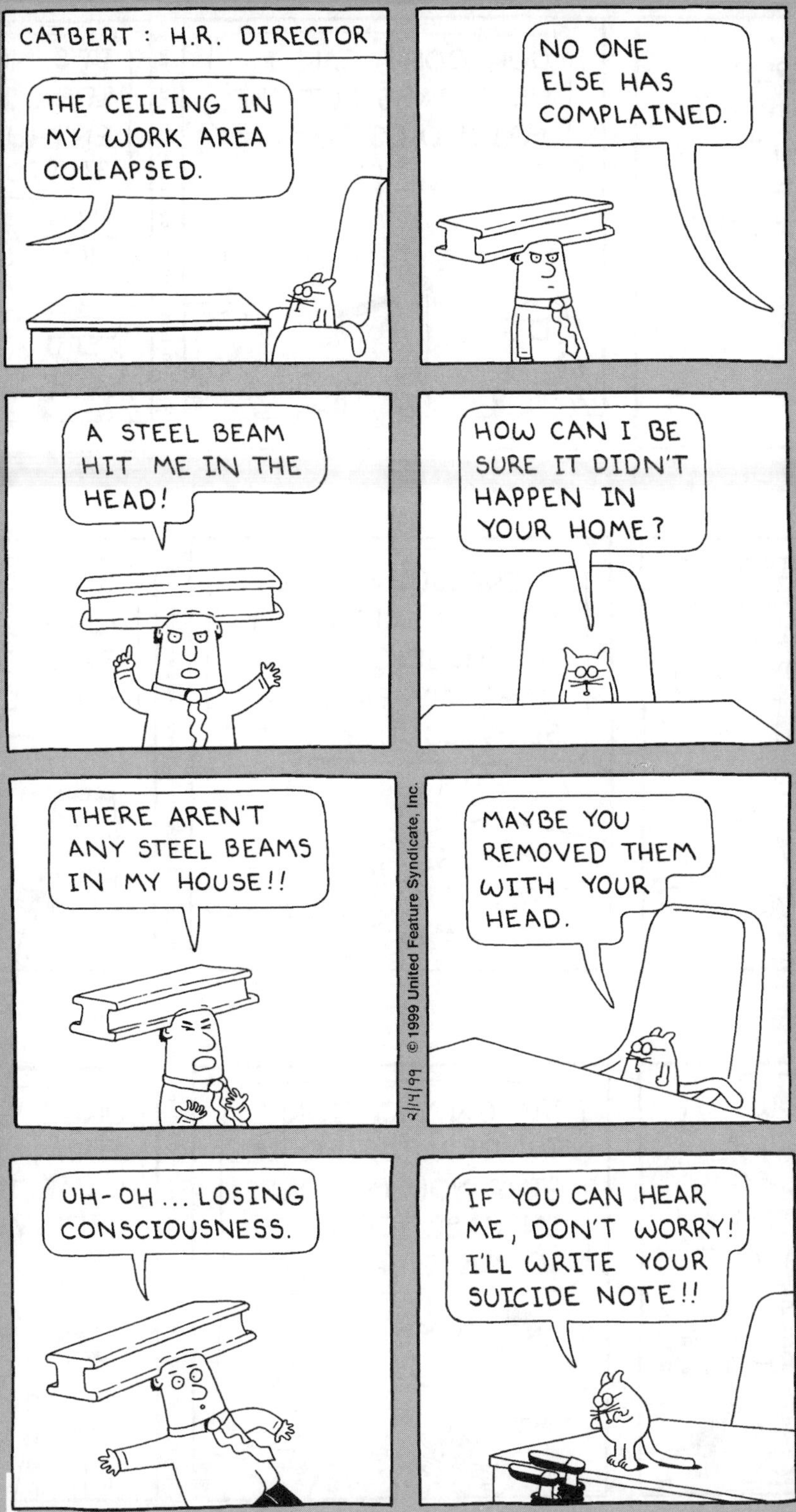
CATBERT : H.R. DIRECTOR
THE CEILING IN MY WORK AREA COLLAPSED.
NO ONE ELSE HAS COMPLAINED.
A STEEL BEAM HIT ME IN THE HEAD!
HOW CAN I BE SURE IT DIDN'T HAPPEN IN YOUR HOME?
THERE AREN'T ANY STEEL BEAMS IN MY HOUSE!!
MAYBE YOU REMOVED THEM WITH YOUR HEAD.
2/4/99 © 1999 United Feature Syndicate, Inc.
UH-OH ... LOSING CONSCIOUSNESS.
IF YOU CAN HEAR ME, DON'T WORRY! I'LL WRITE YOUR SUICIDE NOTE!!

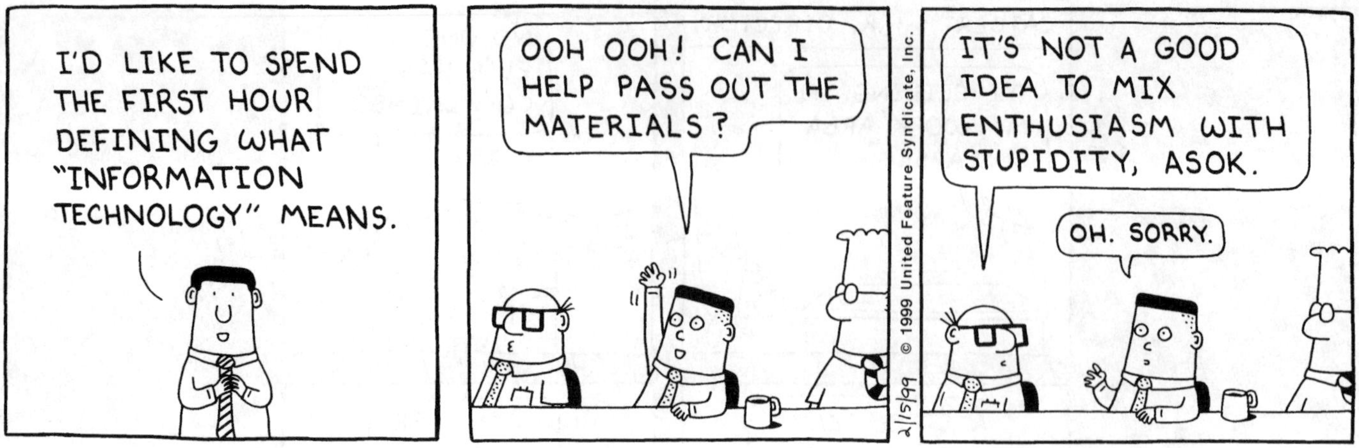
I'D LIKE TO SPEND THE FIRST HOUR DEFINING WHAT "INFORMATION TECHNOLOGY" MEANS.
OOH OOH! CAN I HELP PASS OUT THE MATERIALS?
2/5/99 © 1999 United Feature Syndicate, Inc.
IT'S NOT A GOOD IDEA TO MIX ENTHUSIASM WITH STUPIDITY, ASOK.
OH. SORRY.

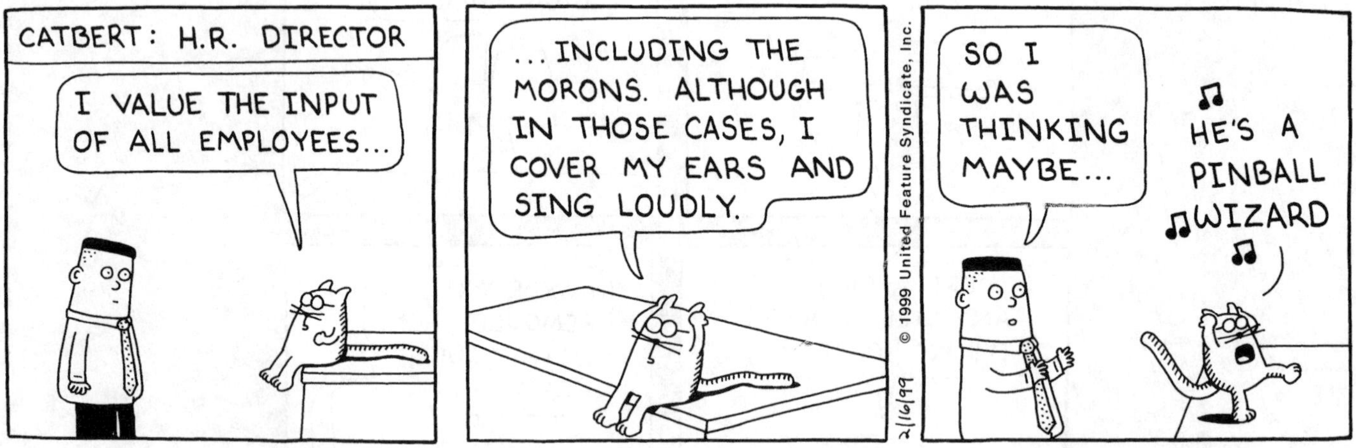
CATBERT: H.R. DIRECTOR
I VALUE THE INPUT OF ALL EMPLOYEES...
...INCLUDING THE MORONS. ALTHOUGH IN THOSE CASES, I COVER MY EARS AND SING LOUDLY.
2/16/99 © 1999 United Feature Syndicate, Inc.
SO I WAS THINKING MAYBE...
♫ HE'S A PINBALL ♫ WIZARD ♫

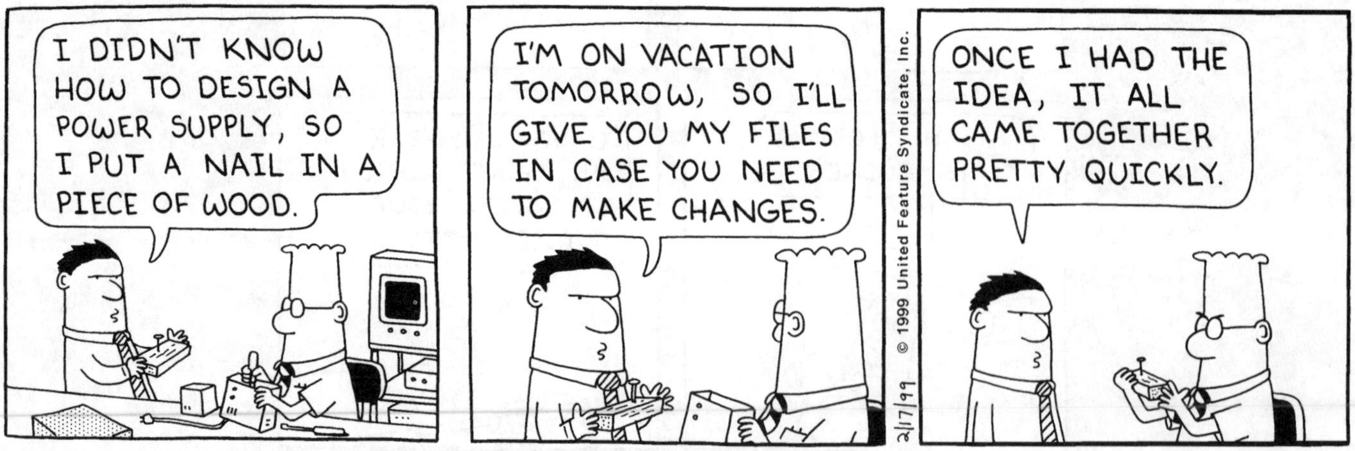
I DIDN'T KNOW HOW TO DESIGN A POWER SUPPLY, SO I PUT A NAIL IN A PIECE OF WOOD.
I'M ON VACATION TOMORROW, SO I'LL GIVE YOU MY FILES IN CASE YOU NEED TO MAKE CHANGES.
2/17/99 © 1999 United Feature Syndicate, Inc.
ONCE I HAD THE IDEA, IT ALL CAME TOGETHER PRETTY QUICKLY.

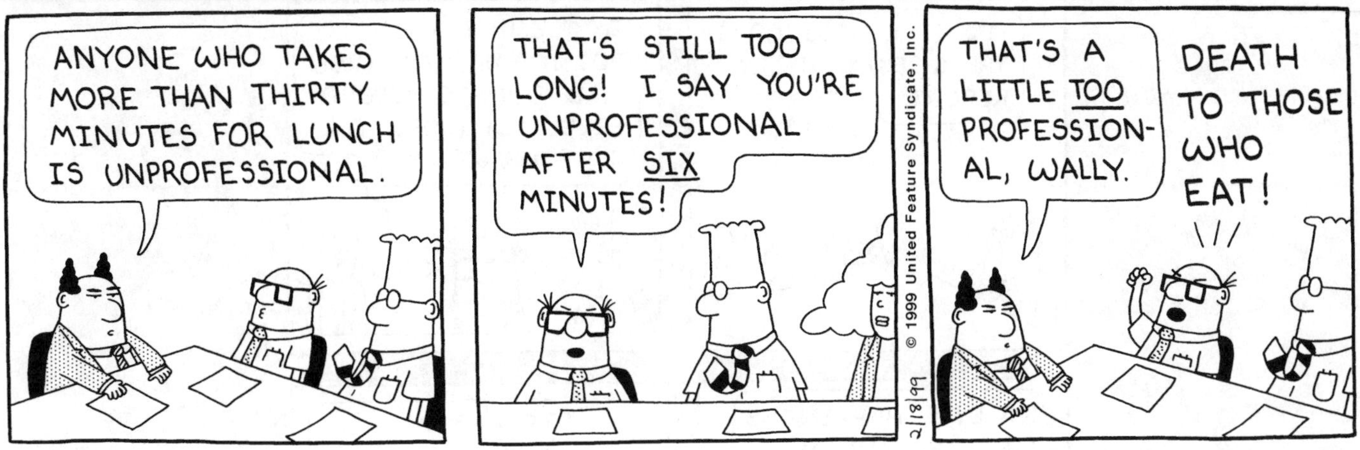
ANYONE WHO TAKES MORE THAN THIRTY MINUTES FOR LUNCH IS UNPROFESSIONAL.
THAT'S STILL TOO LONG! I SAY YOU'RE UNPROFESSIONAL AFTER SIX MINUTES!
2/18/99 © 1999 United Feature Syndicate, Inc.
THAT'S A LITTLE TOO PROFESSION-AL, WALLY.
DEATH TO THOSE WHO EAT!

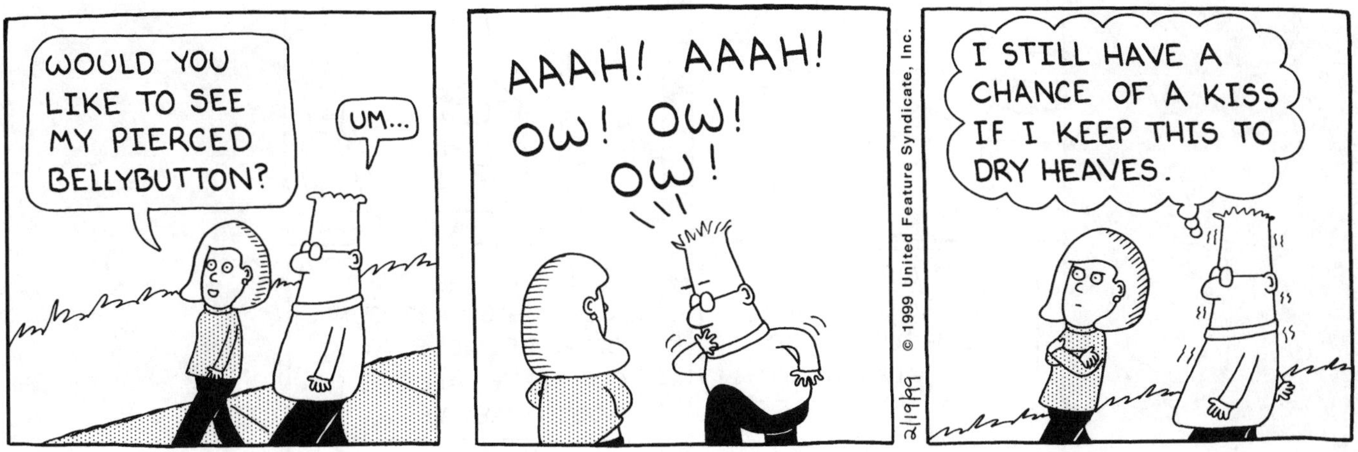
WOULD YOU LIKE TO SEE MY PIERCED BELLYBUTTON?
UM...
AAAH! AAAH! OW! OW! OW!
2/19/99 © 1999 United Feature Syndicate, Inc.
I STILL HAVE A CHANCE OF A KISS IF I KEEP THIS TO DRY HEAVES.

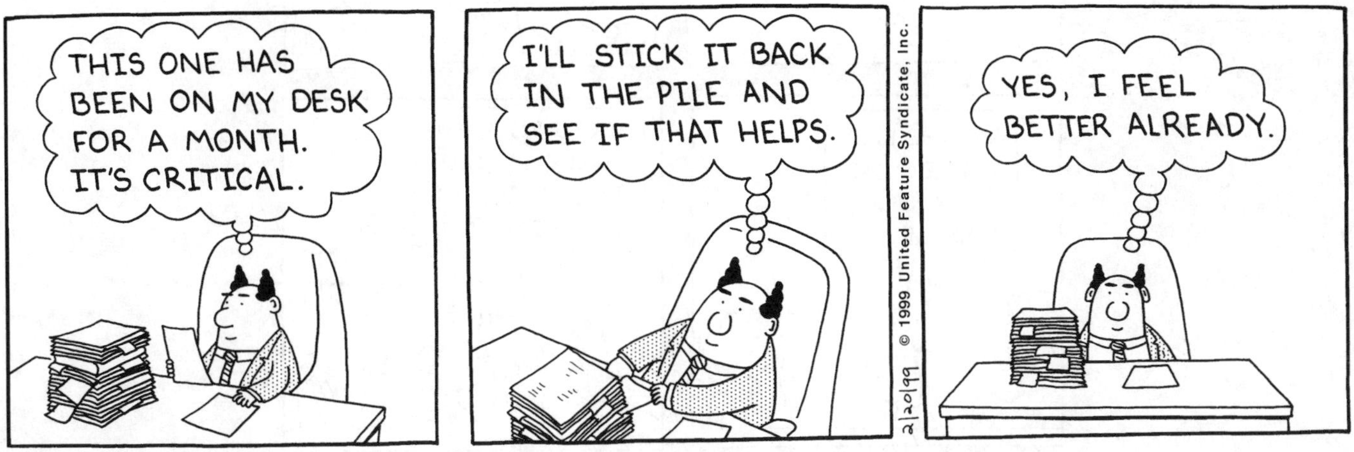
THIS ONE HAS BEEN ON MY DESK FOR A MONTH. IT'S CRITICAL.
I'LL STICK IT BACK IN THE PILE AND SEE IF THAT HELPS.
2/20/99 © 1999 United Feature Syndicate, Inc.
YES, I FEEL BETTER ALREADY.

IT'S TIME NOW FOR THE WEEKLY WALLY REPORT.
BY TUESDAY THE POINTY-HAIRED TROLL HAD DUMPED RECORD LEVELS OF WORK ON POOR WALLY.
WALLY'S HAPPINESS WAS IN EXTREME JEOPARDY.
IT WAS A MORAL DILEMMA TOO.
WOULD WALLY DISAPPOINT THE STOCKHOLDERS TO SAVE HIS OWN SKIN?
OR WOULD HE FIGHT WITH HIS LAST OUNCE OF HAPPINESS TO COMPLETE ALL THE ASSIGNMENTS?
IN THE END THERE WAS ONLY ONE CHOICE.
YOU WROTE THE WALLY REPORT INSTEAD OF WORKING?
STOP READING AHEAD!

2/21/99

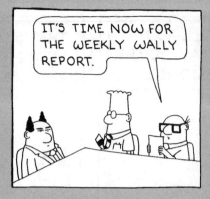

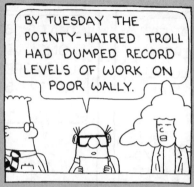

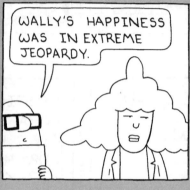

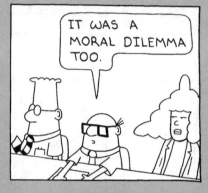

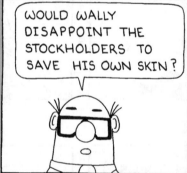

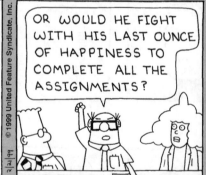

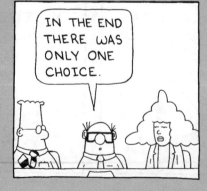

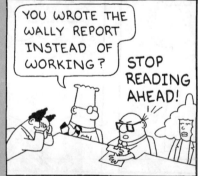

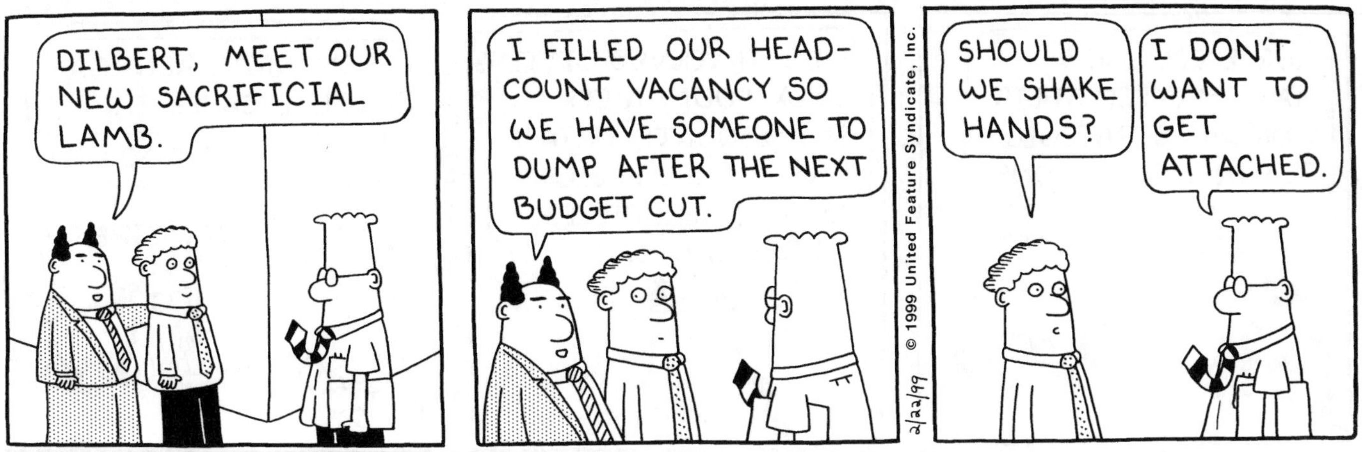
DILBERT, MEET OUR NEW SACRIFICIAL LAMB.
I FILLED OUR HEAD-COUNT VACANCY SO WE HAVE SOMEONE TO DUMP AFTER THE NEXT BUDGET CUT.
SHOULD WE SHAKE HANDS?
I DON'T WANT TO GET ATTACHED.
2/22/99 © 1999 United Feature Syndicate, Inc.

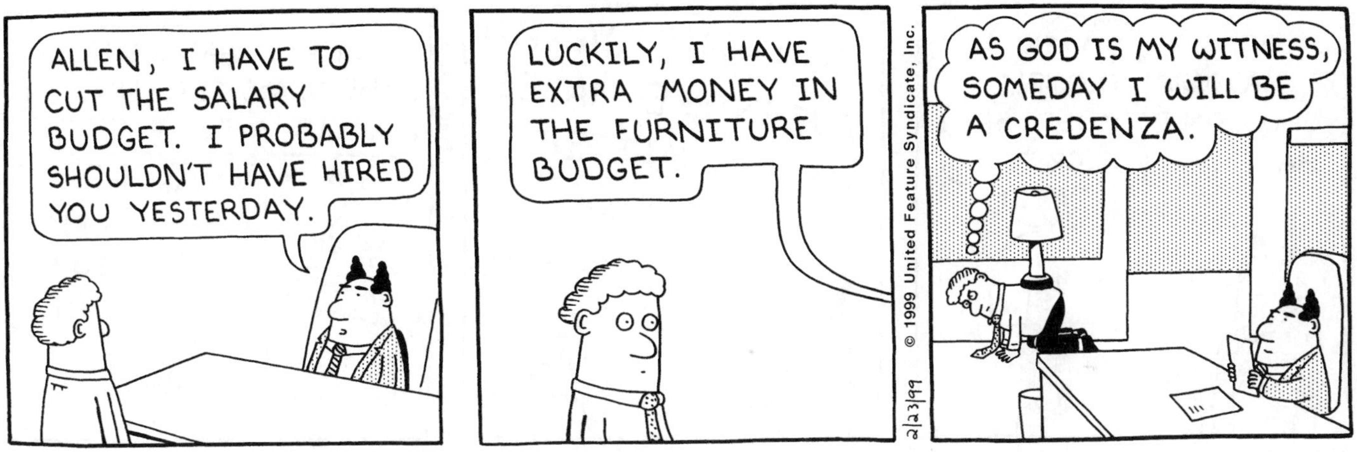
ALLEN, I HAVE TO CUT THE SALARY BUDGET. I PROBABLY SHOULDN'T HAVE HIRED YOU YESTERDAY.
LUCKILY, I HAVE EXTRA MONEY IN THE FURNITURE BUDGET.
AS GOD IS MY WITNESS, SOMEDAY I WILL BE A CREDENZA.
2/23/99 © 1999 United Feature Syndicate, Inc.

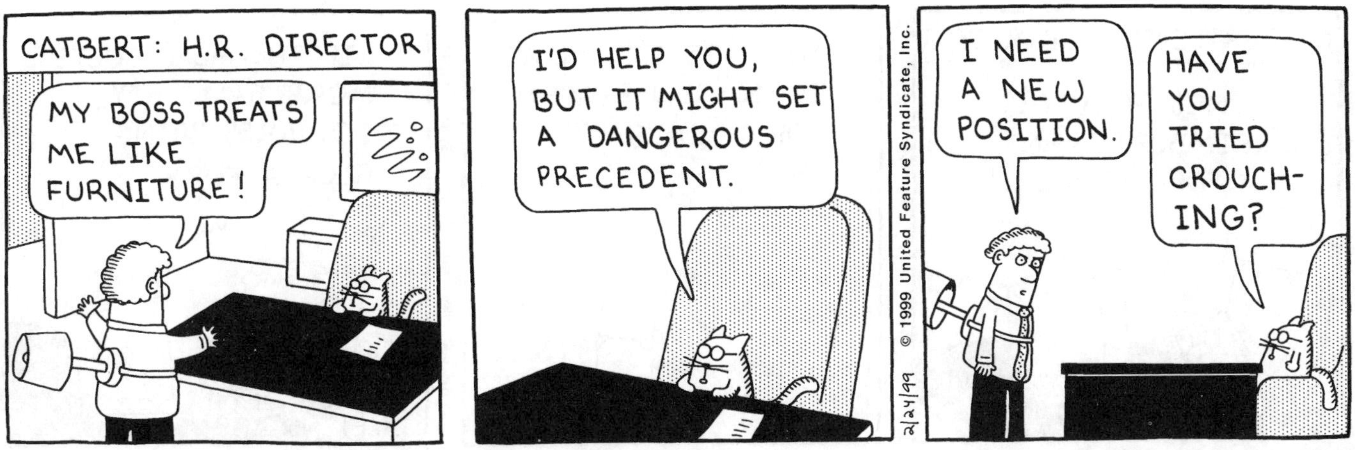
CATBERT: H.R. DIRECTOR
MY BOSS TREATS ME LIKE FURNITURE!
I'D HELP YOU, BUT IT MIGHT SET A DANGEROUS PRECEDENT.
I NEED A NEW POSITION.
HAVE YOU TRIED CROUCH-ING?
2/24/99 © 1999 United Feature Syndicate, Inc.

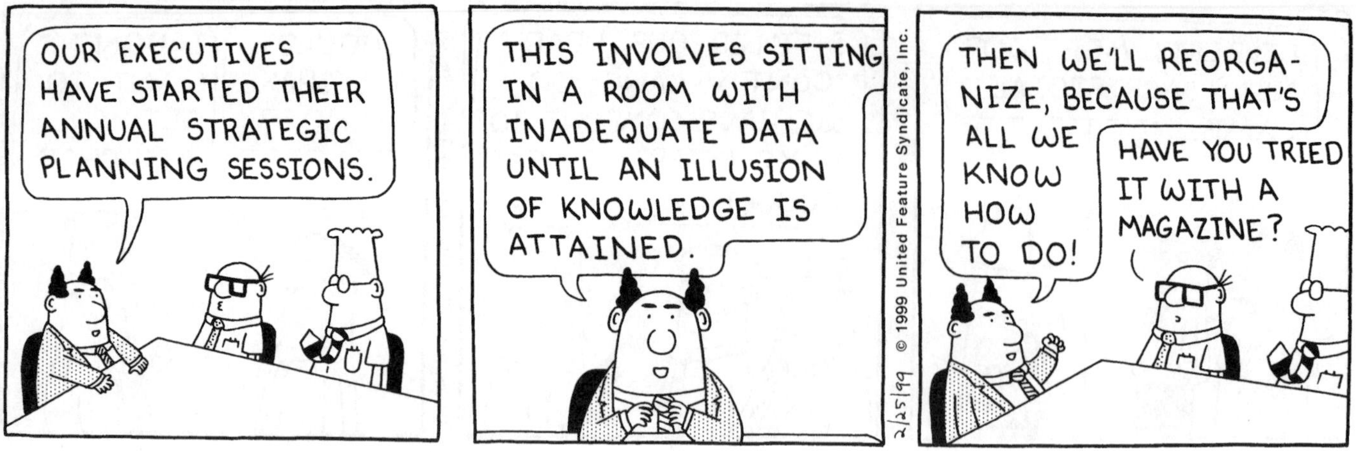
OUR EXECUTIVES HAVE STARTED THEIR ANNUAL STRATEGIC PLANNING SESSIONS.
THIS INVOLVES SITTING IN A ROOM WITH INADEQUATE DATA UNTIL AN ILLUSION OF KNOWLEDGE IS ATTAINED.
2/25/99 © 1999 United Feature Syndicate, Inc.
THEN WE'LL REORGANIZE, BECAUSE THAT'S ALL WE KNOW HOW TO DO!
HAVE YOU TRIED IT WITH A MAGAZINE?

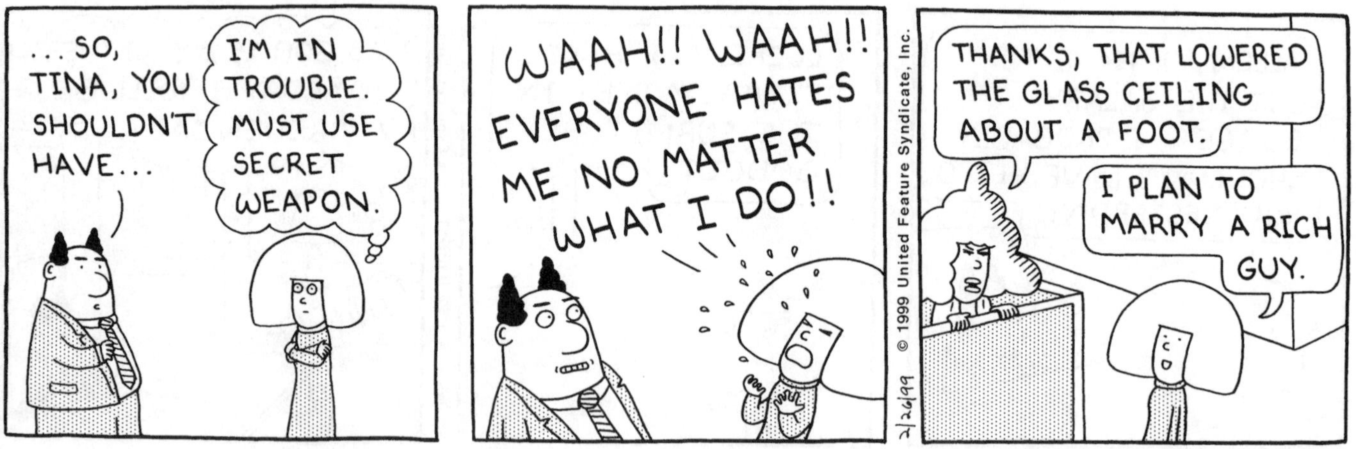
... SO, TINA, YOU SHOULDN'T HAVE...
I'M IN TROUBLE. MUST USE SECRET WEAPON.
WAAH!! WAAH!! EVERYONE HATES ME NO MATTER WHAT I DO!!
2/26/99 © 1999 United Feature Syndicate, Inc.
THANKS, THAT LOWERED THE GLASS CEILING ABOUT A FOOT.
I PLAN TO MARRY A RICH GUY.

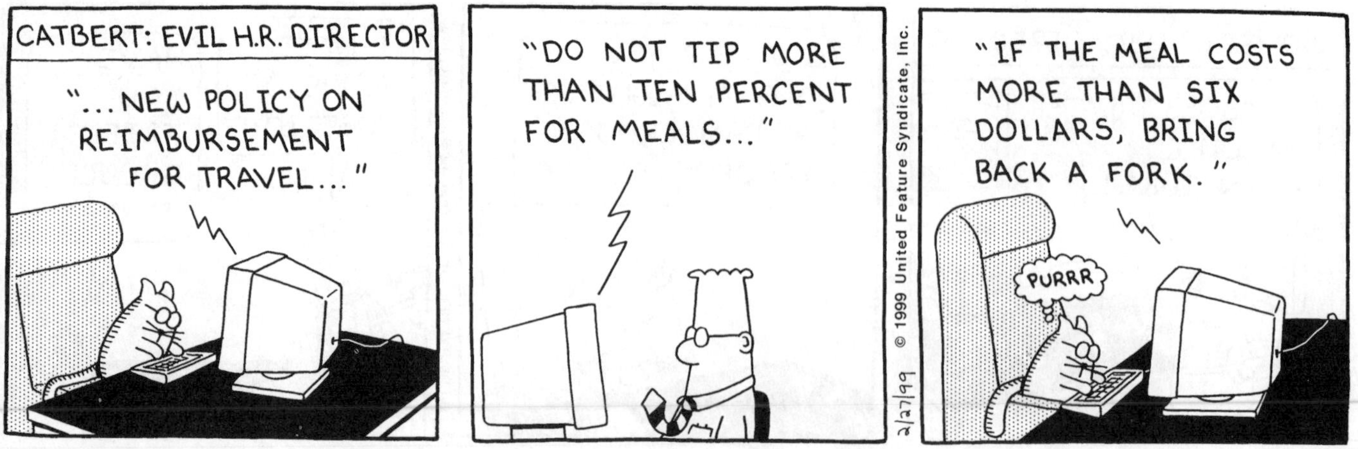
CATBERT: EVIL H.R. DIRECTOR
"...NEW POLICY ON REIMBURSEMENT FOR TRAVEL..."
"DO NOT TIP MORE THAN TEN PERCENT FOR MEALS..."
2/27/99 © 1999 United Feature Syndicate, Inc.
"IF THE MEAL COSTS MORE THAN SIX DOLLARS, BRING BACK A FORK."
PURRR

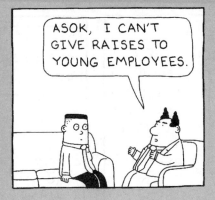

ASOK, I CAN'T GIVE RAISES TO YOUNG EMPLOYEES.
BECAUSE AS SOON AS YOU GET A FEW DOLLARS IN YOUR POCKET...
YOU BUY SMALL MOTORCYCLES AND DISAPPEAR IN THE NIGHT.
I KNOW THAT'S A GENERALIZATION.
SOME OF YOU PREFER THE CRACK COCAINE.
THE GOOD NEWS IS THAT I'M WILLING TO BE YOUR MENTOR.
AAAGH! I GOT DOUBLE EIGHT HUNDREDS ON MY SAT!!! FOR WHAT?!!
SOMETIMES WHEN I'M IN A BAD MOOD I TICKLE MY OWN FEET.
2/28/99 © 1999 United Feature Syndicate, Inc.

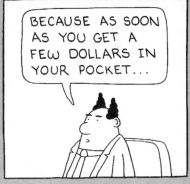

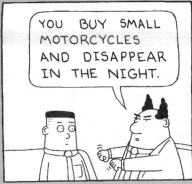

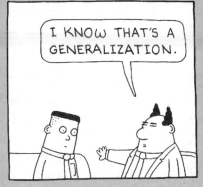

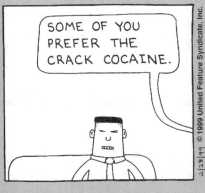

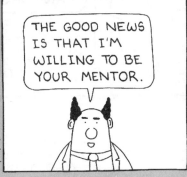

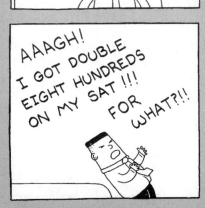

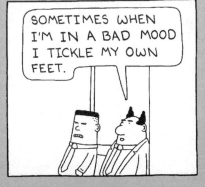

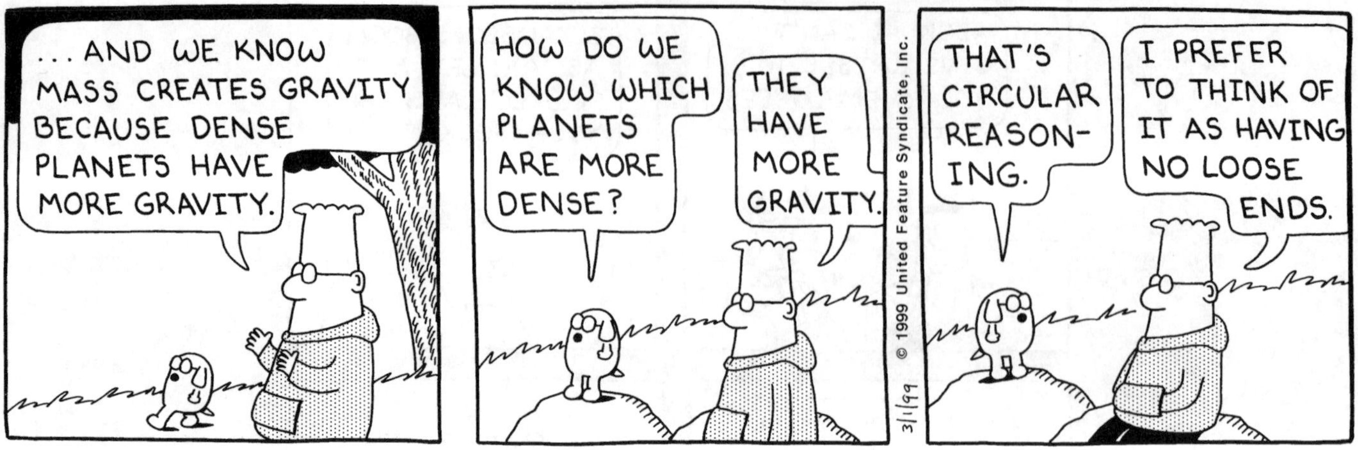
... AND WE KNOW MASS CREATES GRAVITY BECAUSE DENSE PLANETS HAVE MORE GRAVITY.
HOW DO WE KNOW WHICH PLANETS ARE MORE DENSE?
THEY HAVE MORE GRAVITY.
THAT'S CIRCULAR REASON-ING.
I PREFER TO THINK OF IT AS HAVING NO LOOSE ENDS.
© 1999 United Feature Syndicate, Inc.
3/1/99

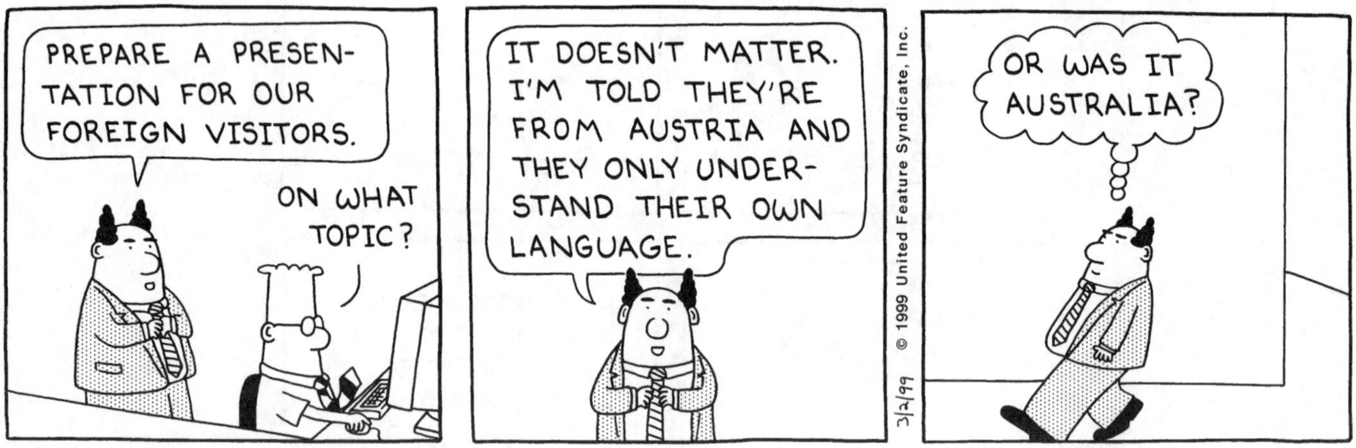
PREPARE A PRESEN-TATION FOR OUR FOREIGN VISITORS.
ON WHAT TOPIC?
IT DOESN'T MATTER. I'M TOLD THEY'RE FROM AUSTRIA AND THEY ONLY UNDER-STAND THEIR OWN LANGUAGE.
OR WAS IT AUSTRALIA?
© 1999 United Feature Syndicate, Inc.
3/2/99

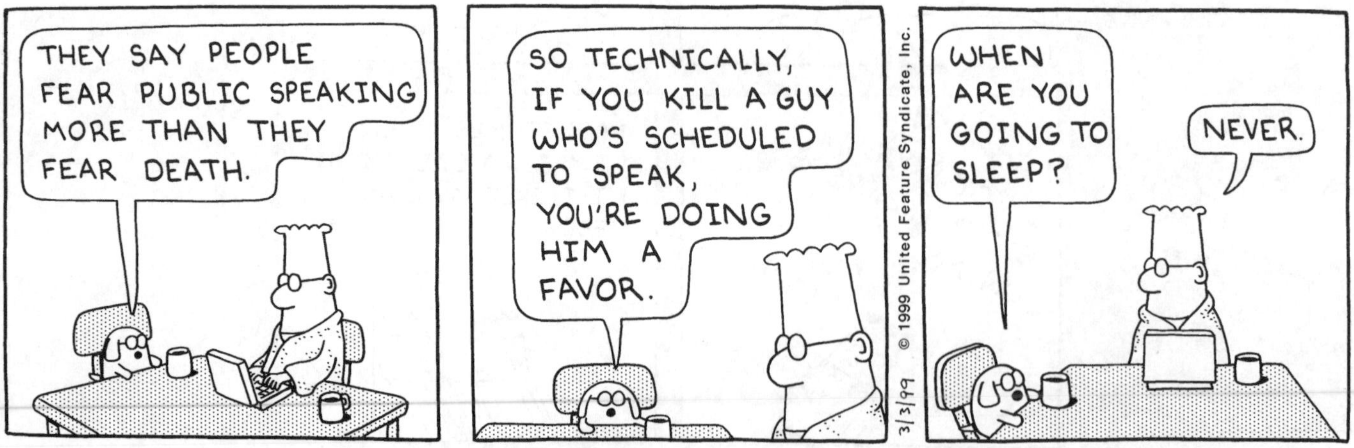
THEY SAY PEOPLE FEAR PUBLIC SPEAKING MORE THAN THEY FEAR DEATH.
SO TECHNICALLY, IF YOU KILL A GUY WHO'S SCHEDULED TO SPEAK, YOU'RE DOING HIM A FAVOR.
WHEN ARE YOU GOING TO SLEEP?
NEVER.
© 1999 United Feature Syndicate, Inc.
3/3/99

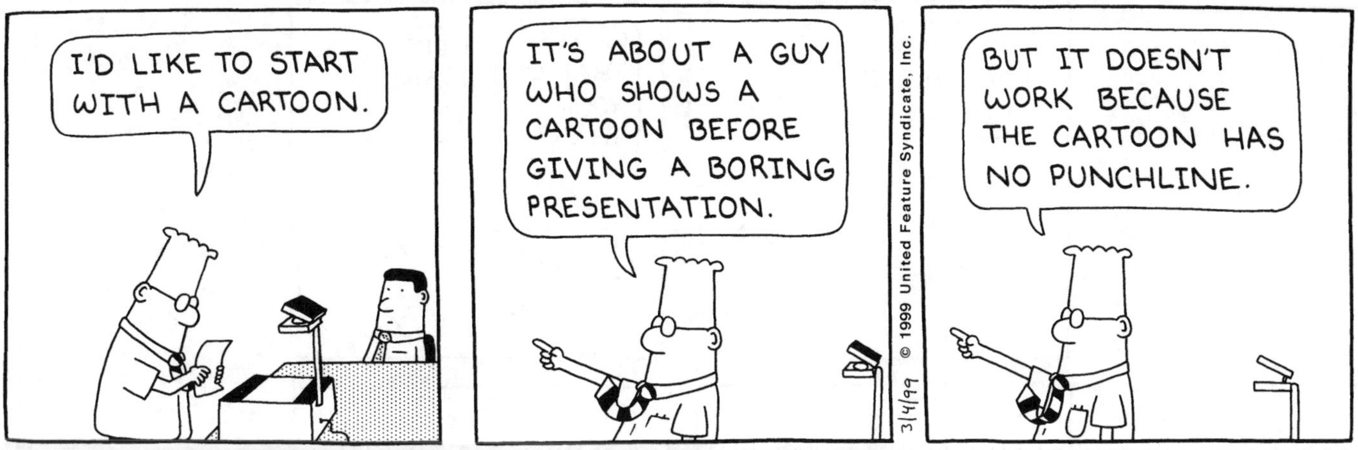
I'D LIKE TO START WITH A CARTOON.
IT'S ABOUT A GUY WHO SHOWS A CARTOON BEFORE GIVING A BORING PRESENTATION.
3/4/99 © 1999 United Feature Syndicate, Inc.
BUT IT DOESN'T WORK BECAUSE THE CARTOON HAS NO PUNCHLINE.

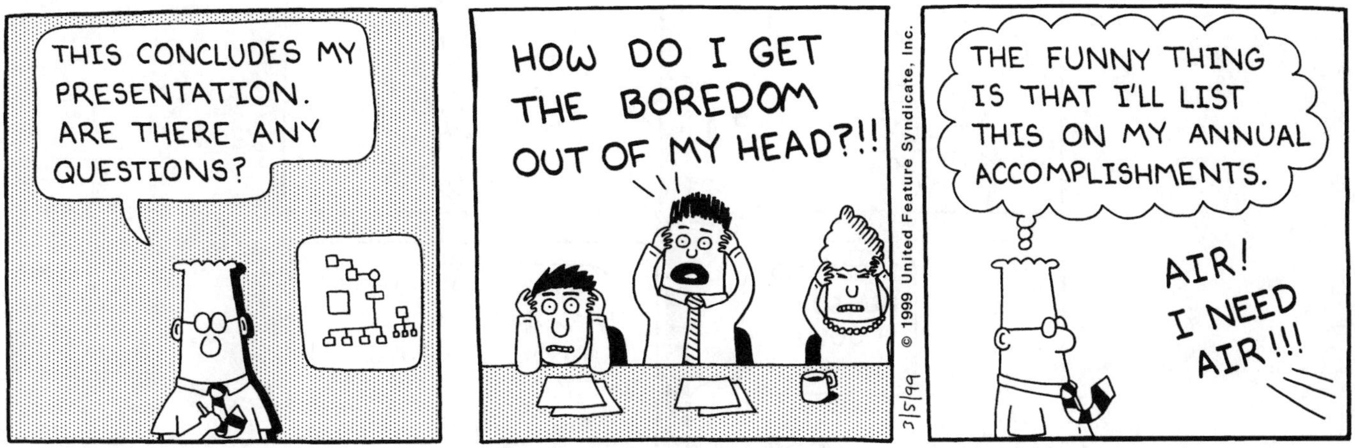
THIS CONCLUDES MY PRESENTATION. ARE THERE ANY QUESTIONS?
HOW DO I GET THE BOREDOM OUT OF MY HEAD?!!
3/5/99 © 1999 United Feature Syndicate, Inc.
THE FUNNY THING IS THAT I'LL LIST THIS ON MY ANNUAL ACCOMPLISHMENTS.
AIR! I NEED AIR!!!

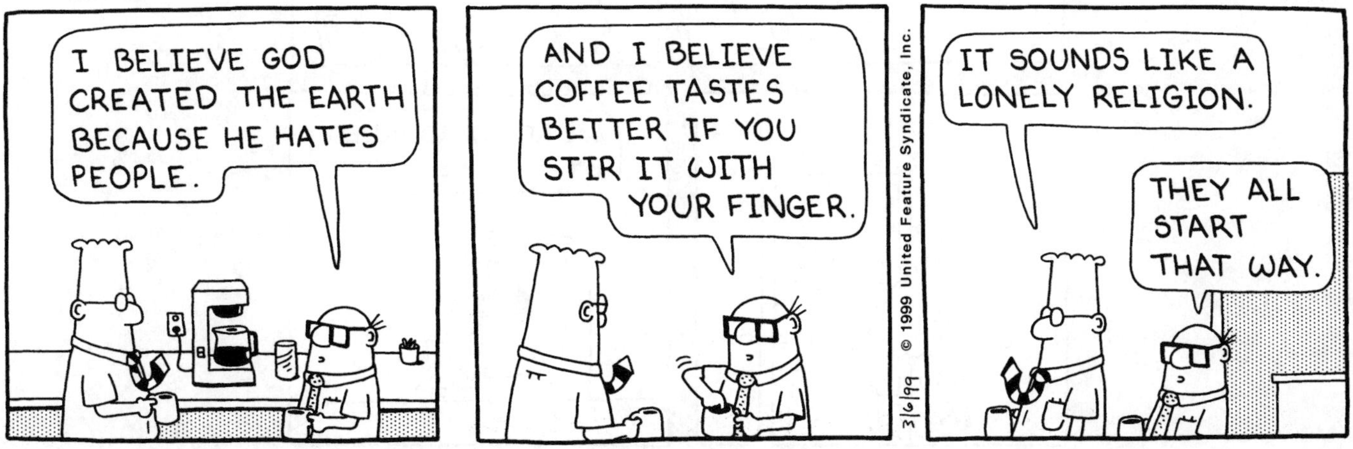
I BELIEVE GOD CREATED THE EARTH BECAUSE HE HATES PEOPLE.
AND I BELIEVE COFFEE TASTES BETTER IF YOU STIR IT WITH YOUR FINGER.
3/6/99 © 1999 United Feature Syndicate, Inc.
IT SOUNDS LIKE A LONELY RELIGION.
THEY ALL START THAT WAY.

... SO OUR MORALE IS... UMM...
WHAT'S THAT ON YOUR DESK?
IT'S A FAMILY PICTURE.
I MIGHT BE WRONG, BUT I THINK IT'S ONLY A PICTURE OF YOU.
THE REST OF THE FAMILY IS HARD TO LOOK AT.
I SEE NO REASON I SHOULD SUFFER.
NOW WHAT WAS YOUR QUESTION ABOUT MORALE?
ALICE?
WE'RE SURROUNDED BY FREAKS.
3/7/99 © 1999 United Feature Syndicate, Inc.

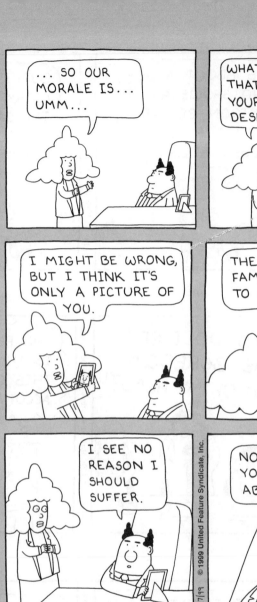

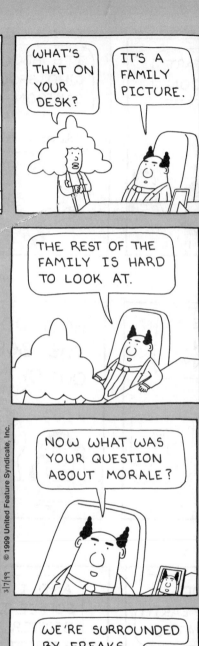

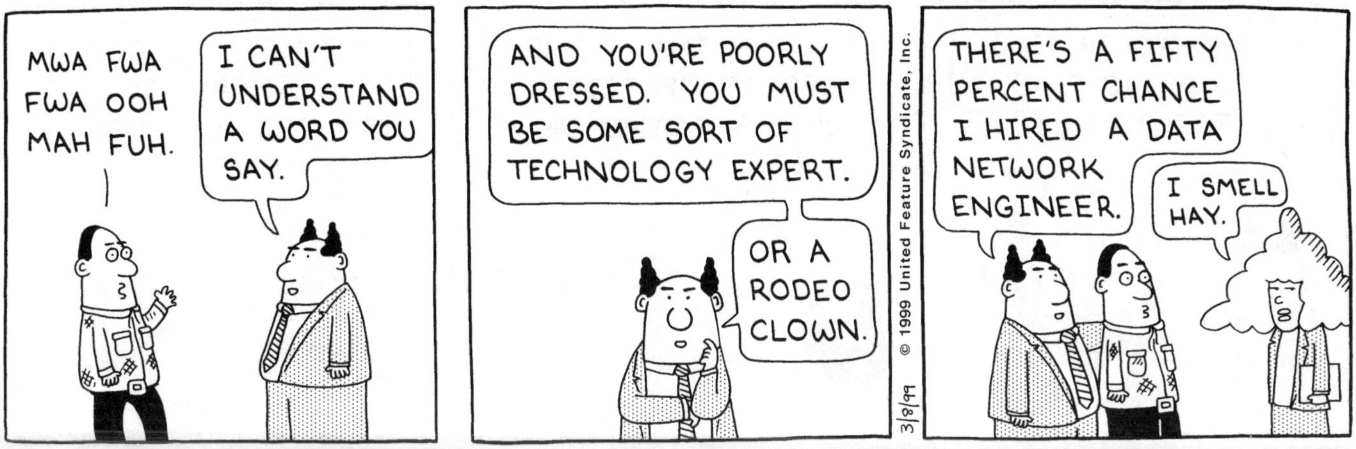
MWA FWA FWA OOH MAH FUH.
I CAN'T UNDERSTAND A WORD YOU SAY.
AND YOU'RE POORLY DRESSED. YOU MUST BE SOME SORT OF TECHNOLOGY EXPERT.
OR A RODEO CLOWN.
THERE'S A FIFTY PERCENT CHANCE I HIRED A DATA NETWORK ENGINEER.
I SMELL HAY.
3/8/99 © 1999 United Feature Syndicate, Inc.

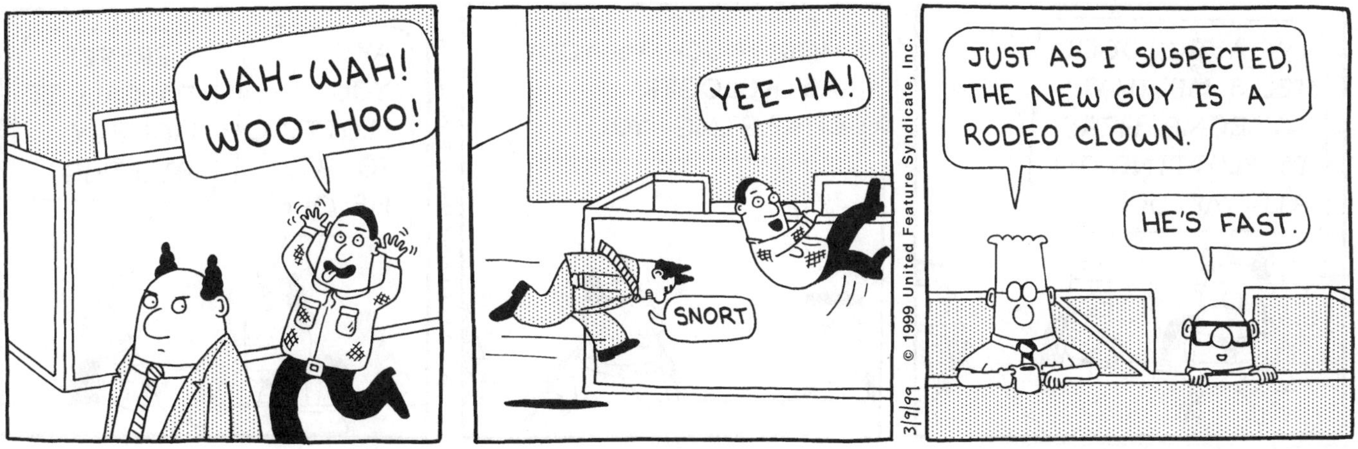
WAH-WAH! WOO-HOO!
YEE-HA!
SNORT
JUST AS I SUSPECTED, THE NEW GUY IS A RODEO CLOWN.
HE'S FAST.
3/9/99 © 1999 United Feature Syndicate, Inc.

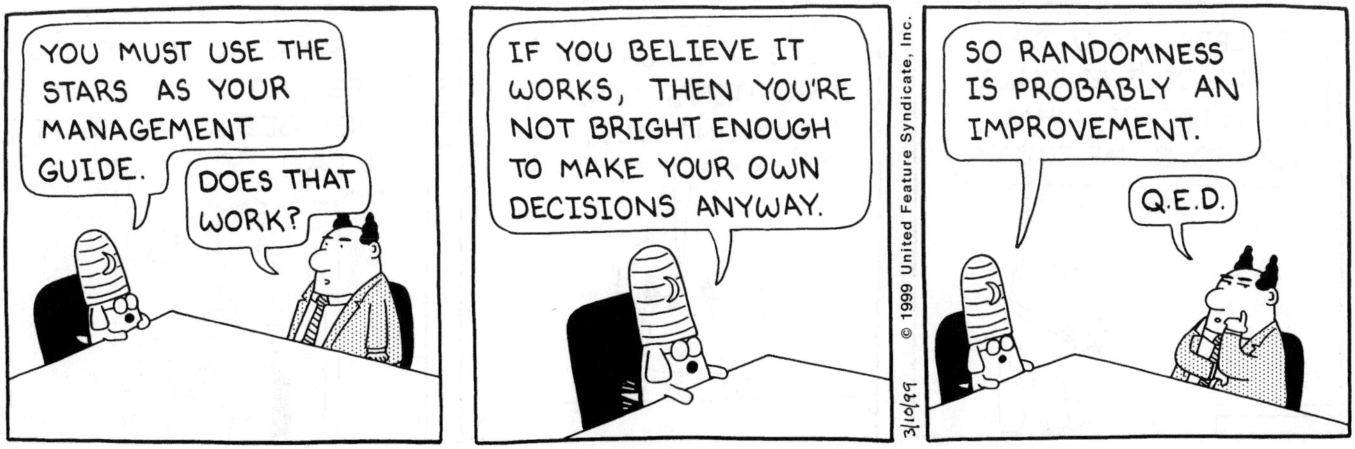
YOU MUST USE THE STARS AS YOUR MANAGEMENT GUIDE.
DOES THAT WORK?
IF YOU BELIEVE IT WORKS, THEN YOU'RE NOT BRIGHT ENOUGH TO MAKE YOUR OWN DECISIONS ANYWAY.
SO RANDOMNESS IS PROBABLY AN IMPROVEMENT.
Q.E.D.
3/10/99 © 1999 United Feature Syndicate, Inc.

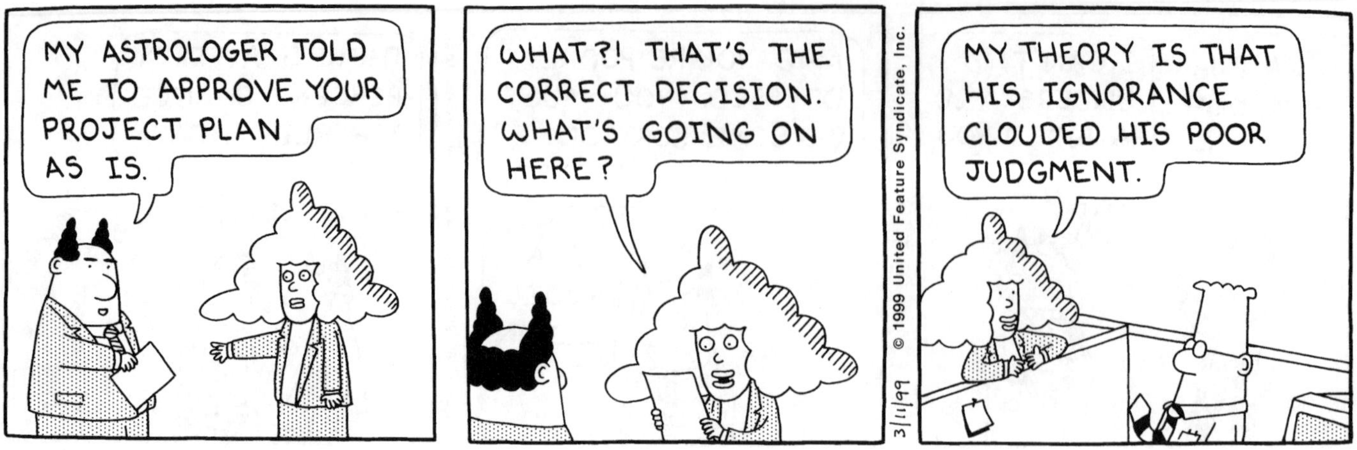
MY ASTROLOGER TOLD ME TO APPROVE YOUR PROJECT PLAN AS IS.
WHAT?! THAT'S THE CORRECT DECISION. WHAT'S GOING ON HERE?
3/11/99 © 1999 United Feature Syndicate, Inc.
MY THEORY IS THAT HIS IGNORANCE CLOUDED HIS POOR JUDGMENT.

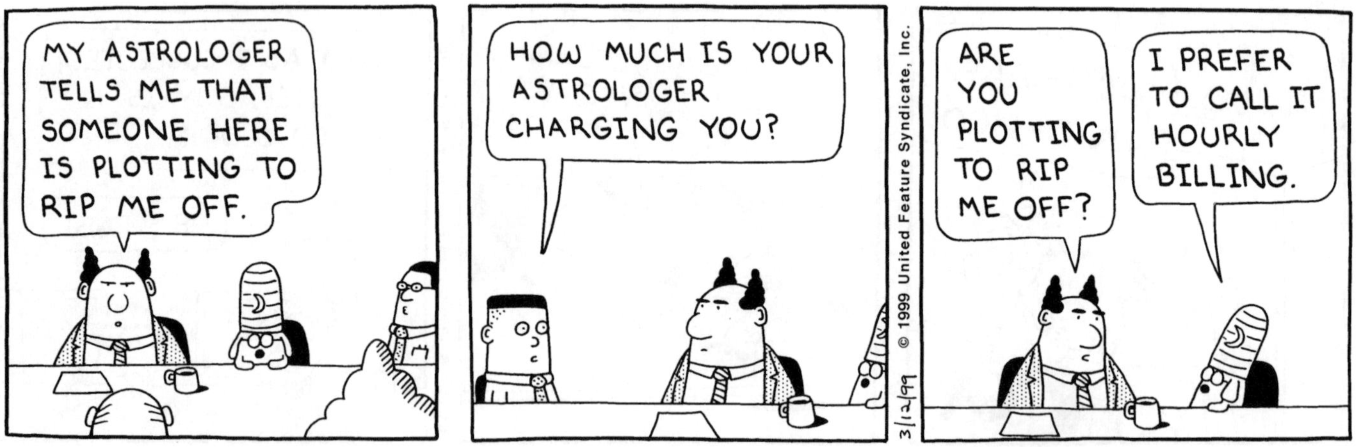
MY ASTROLOGER TELLS ME THAT SOMEONE HERE IS PLOTTING TO RIP ME OFF.
HOW MUCH IS YOUR ASTROLOGER CHARGING YOU?
3/12/99 © 1999 United Feature Syndicate, Inc.
ARE YOU PLOTTING TO RIP ME OFF?
I PREFER TO CALL IT HOURLY BILLING.

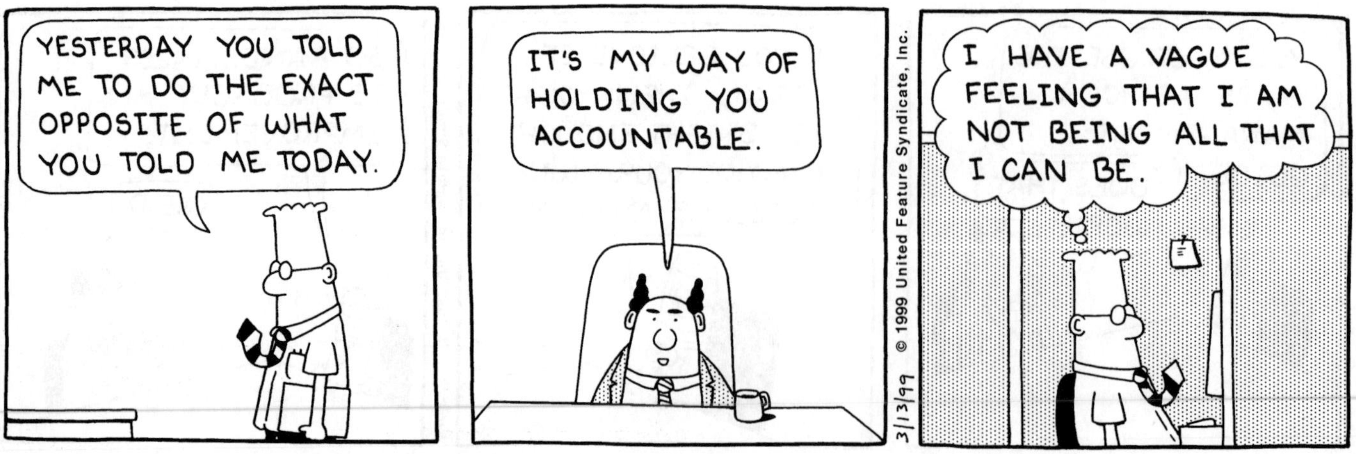
YESTERDAY YOU TOLD ME TO DO THE EXACT OPPOSITE OF WHAT YOU TOLD ME TODAY.
IT'S MY WAY OF HOLDING YOU ACCOUNTABLE.
3/13/99 © 1999 United Feature Syndicate, Inc.
I HAVE A VAGUE FEELING THAT I AM NOT BEING ALL THAT I CAN BE.

I'M FROM THE DOGBERT WRECKING COMPANY.
I'M RUNNING A SPECIAL ON CRUSHING YOUR BOSS'S NEW CAR IN THE PARKING LOT.
WHAT DOES IT COST?
THE FIRST ONE IS FREE.
IF YOU'RE SATISFIED, I HOPE YOU'LL CONSIDER MY MONTHLY PLAN.
IT'S THE RED ONE. HE BRAGS ABOUT IT EVERY DAY.
© 1999 United Feature Syndicate, Inc.
3/14/99
AND WHEN YOU SPEND THAT MUCH, THE DEALER GIVES YOU A FREE MODEL OF YOUR CAR!
BEEP BEEP BEEP
AND NEXT MONTH CAN YOU CRUSH THE LITTLE ONE ON HIS DESK TOO?

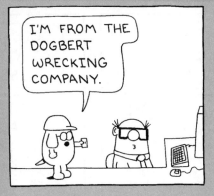

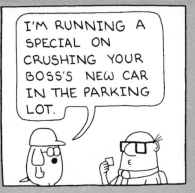

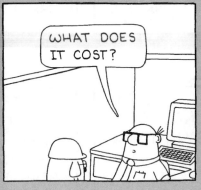

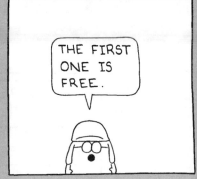

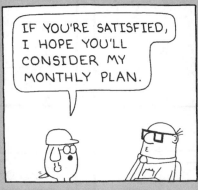

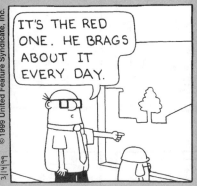

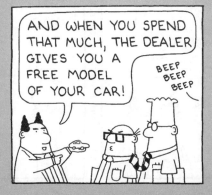

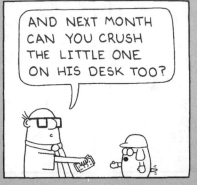

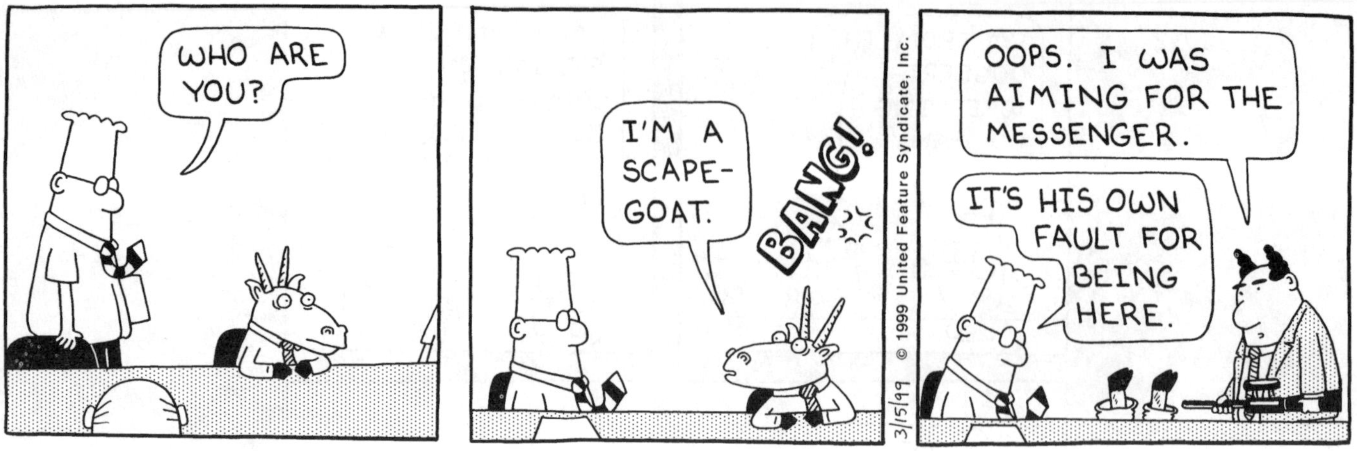
WHO ARE YOU?
I'M A SCAPE-GOAT.
BANG!
OOPS. I WAS AIMING FOR THE MESSENGER.
IT'S HIS OWN FAULT FOR BEING HERE.
3/5/99 © 1999 United Feature Syndicate, Inc.

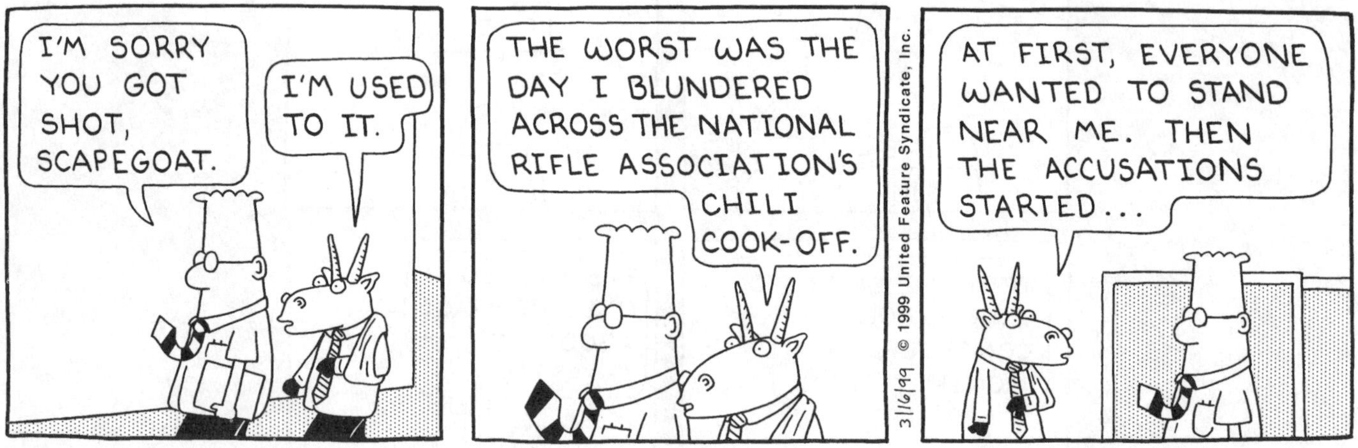
I'M SORRY YOU GOT SHOT, SCAPEGOAT.
I'M USED TO IT.
THE WORST WAS THE DAY I BLUNDERED ACROSS THE NATIONAL RIFLE ASSOCIATION'S CHILI COOK-OFF.
AT FIRST, EVERYONE WANTED TO STAND NEAR ME. THEN THE ACCUSATIONS STARTED...
3/6/99 © 1999 United Feature Syndicate, Inc.

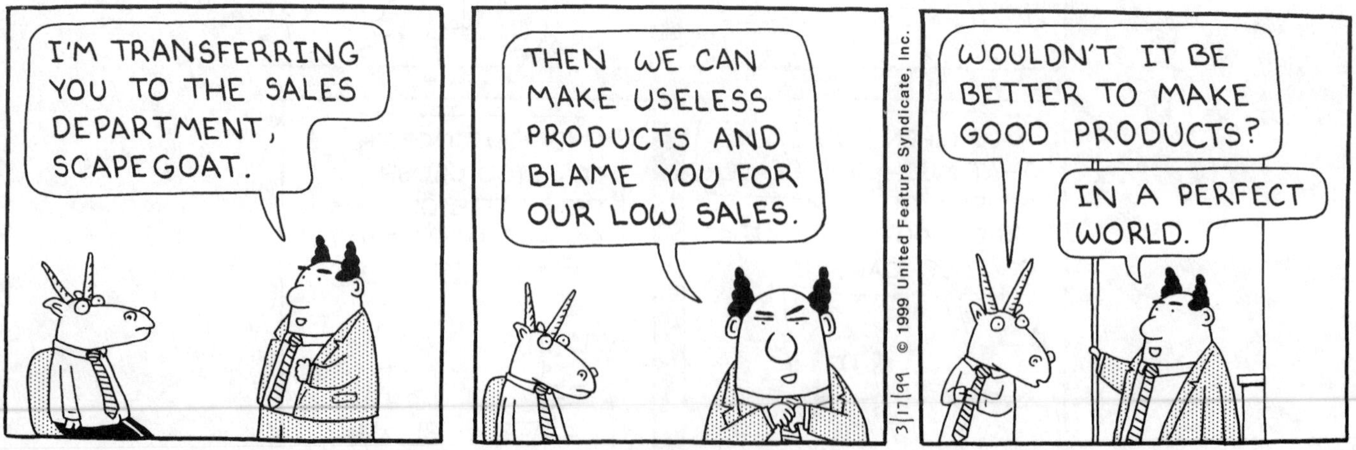
I'M TRANSFERRING YOU TO THE SALES DEPARTMENT, SCAPEGOAT.
THEN WE CAN MAKE USELESS PRODUCTS AND BLAME YOU FOR OUR LOW SALES.
WOULDN'T IT BE BETTER TO MAKE GOOD PRODUCTS?
IN A PERFECT WORLD.
3/17/99 © 1999 United Feature Syndicate, Inc.

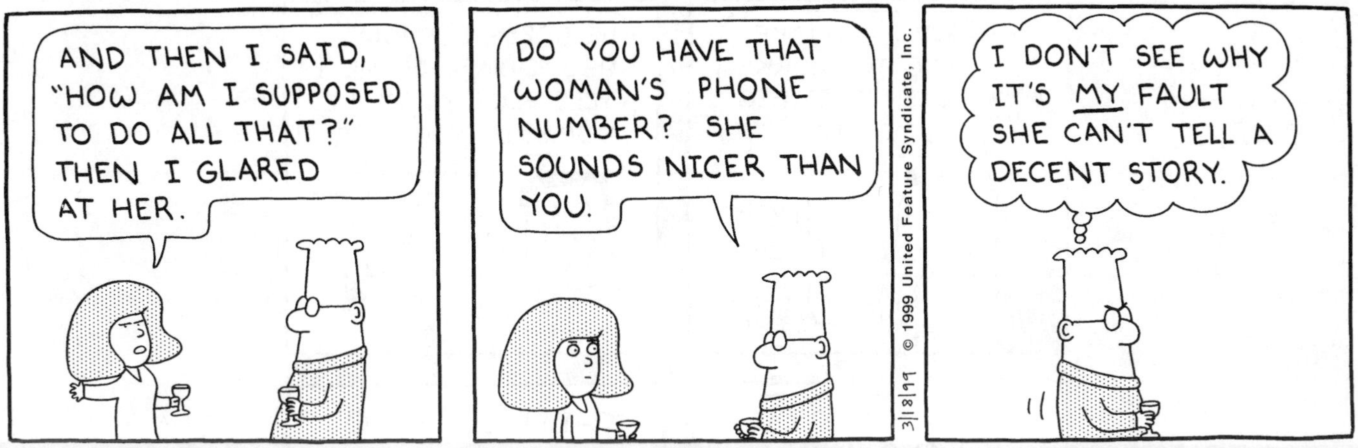
AND THEN I SAID, "HOW AM I SUPPOSED TO DO ALL THAT?" THEN I GLARED AT HER.
DO YOU HAVE THAT WOMAN'S PHONE NUMBER? SHE SOUNDS NICER THAN YOU.
3/8/99 © 1999 United Feature Syndicate, Inc.
I DON'T SEE WHY IT'S MY FAULT SHE CAN'T TELL A DECENT STORY.

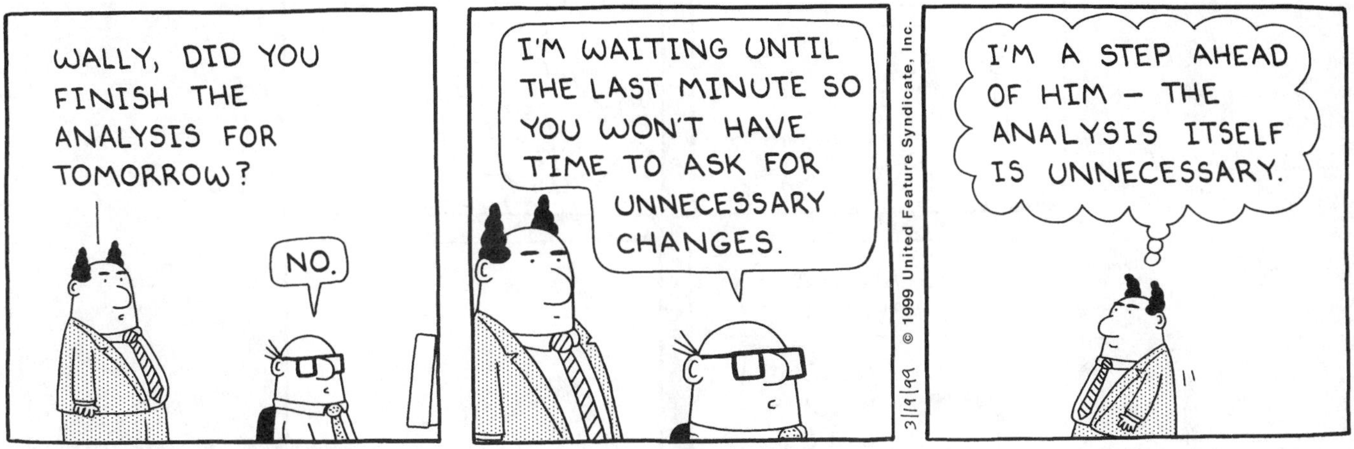
WALLY, DID YOU FINISH THE ANALYSIS FOR TOMORROW?
NO.
I'M WAITING UNTIL THE LAST MINUTE SO YOU WON'T HAVE TIME TO ASK FOR UNNECESSARY CHANGES.
3/9/99 © 1999 United Feature Syndicate, Inc.
I'M A STEP AHEAD OF HIM – THE ANALYSIS ITSELF IS UNNECESSARY.

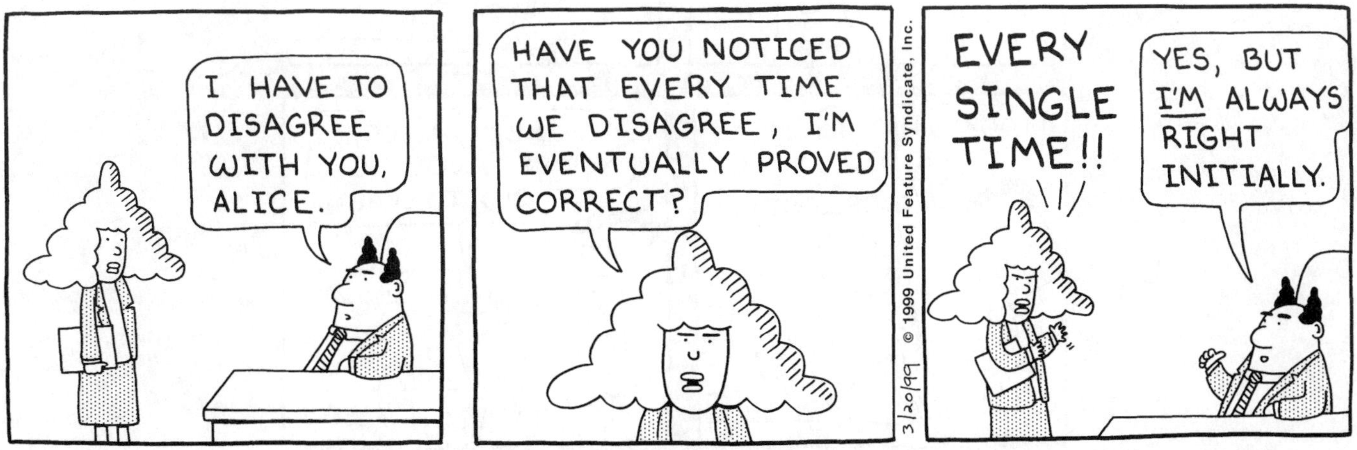
I HAVE TO DISAGREE WITH YOU, ALICE.
HAVE YOU NOTICED THAT EVERY TIME WE DISAGREE, I'M EVENTUALLY PROVED CORRECT?
3/20/99 © 1999 United Feature Syndicate, Inc.
EVERY SINGLE TIME!!
YES, BUT I'M ALWAYS RIGHT INITIALLY.

ALICE, I'D LIKE YOU TO WORK WITH THIS BIG DUMB GUY.
HE DOESN'T KNOW HE'S DUMB, SO HE'LL TELL PEOPLE YOU'RE DUMB IF YOU EVER DISAGREE.
HE'S ALSO LAZY AND A HABITUAL LIAR.
THEN WHY DO YOU LET HIM WORK HERE?!
HE HAS AN EXCELLENT TRACK RECORD.
NO ONE KNOWS WHY.
© 1999 United Feature Syndicate, Inc.
3/21/99
LOOK WHAT I JUST DID.
EXCELLENT WORK.
REMEMBER, ALICE, YOU'RE NEVER TOO OLD TO LEARN.

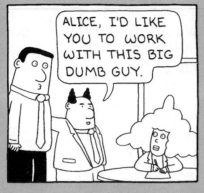

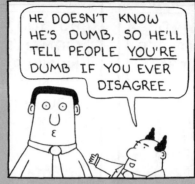

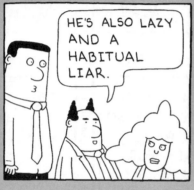

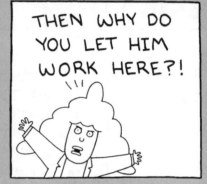

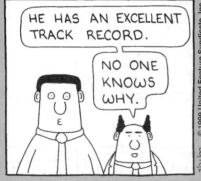

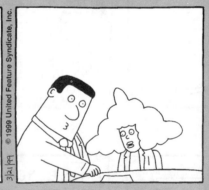

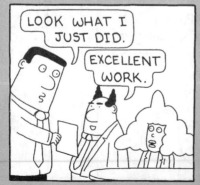

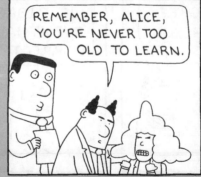

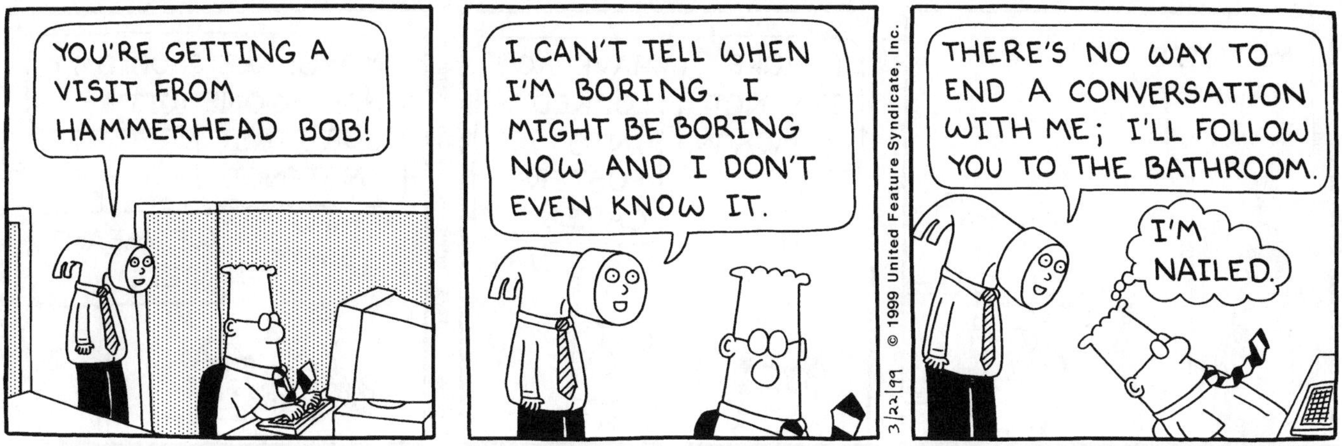
YOU'RE GETTING A VISIT FROM HAMMERHEAD BOB!
I CAN'T TELL WHEN I'M BORING. I MIGHT BE BORING NOW AND I DON'T EVEN KNOW IT.
3/22/99 © 1999 United Feature Syndicate, Inc.
THERE'S NO WAY TO END A CONVERSATION WITH ME; I'LL FOLLOW YOU TO THE BATHROOM.
I'M NAILED.

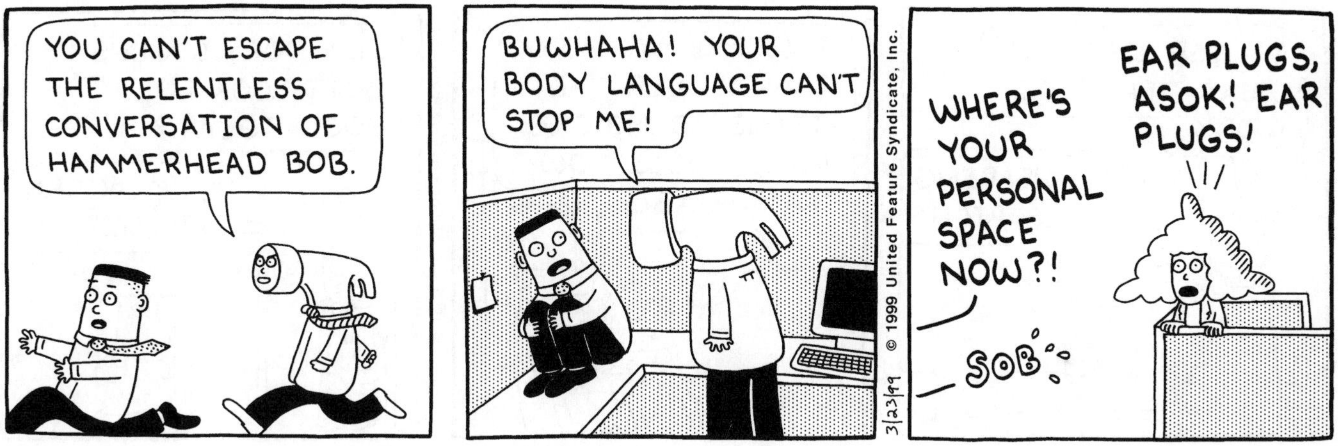
YOU CAN'T ESCAPE THE RELENTLESS CONVERSATION OF HAMMERHEAD BOB.
BUWHAHA! YOUR BODY LANGUAGE CAN'T STOP ME!
3/23/99 © 1999 United Feature Syndicate, Inc.
WHERE'S YOUR PERSONAL SPACE NOW?!
SOB
EAR PLUGS, ASOK! EAR PLUGS!

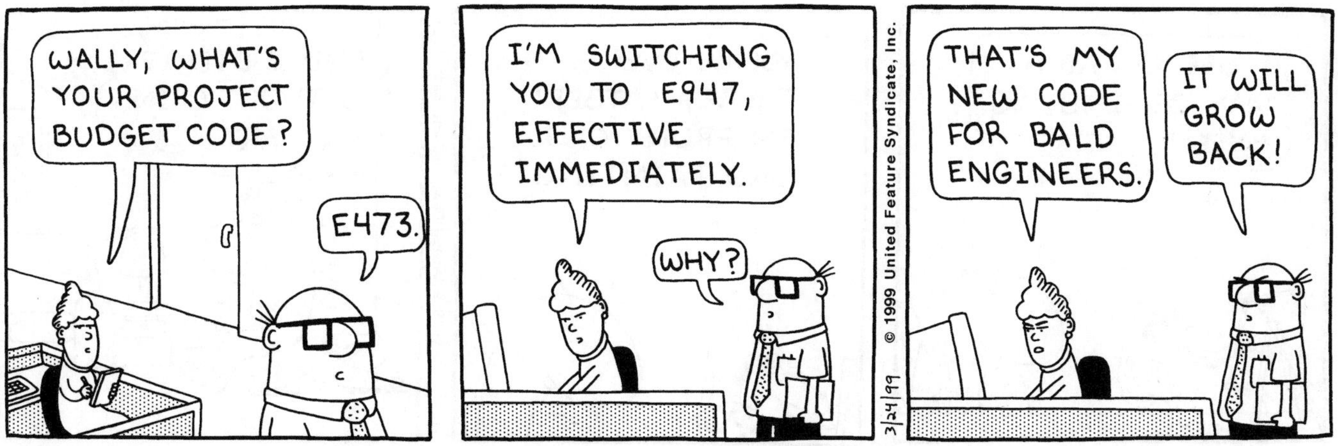
WALLY, WHAT'S YOUR PROJECT BUDGET CODE?
E473.
I'M SWITCHING YOU TO E947, EFFECTIVE IMMEDIATELY.
WHY?
3/24/99 © 1999 United Feature Syndicate, Inc.
THAT'S MY NEW CODE FOR BALD ENGINEERS.
IT WILL GROW BACK!

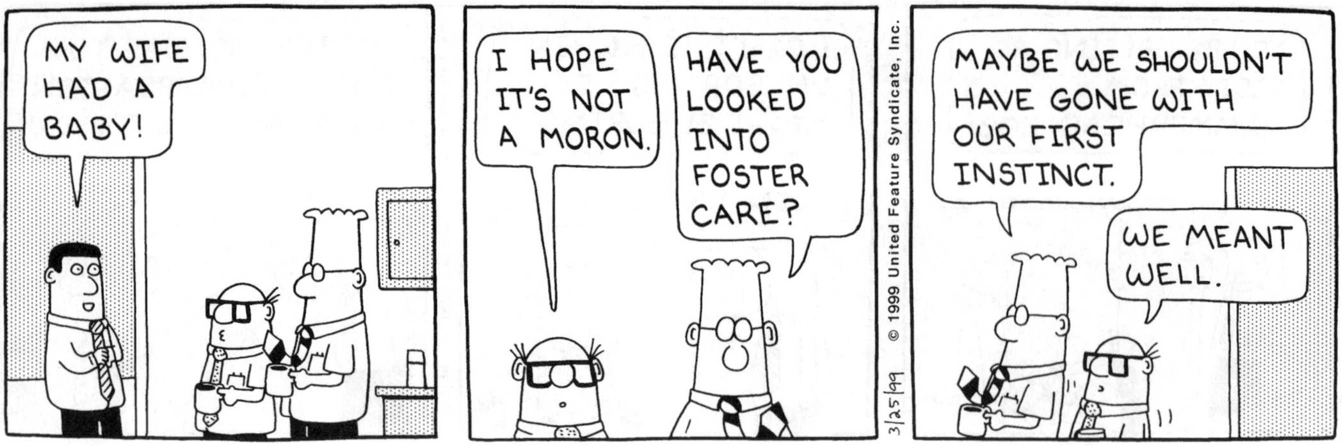
MY WIFE HAD A BABY!
I HOPE IT'S NOT A MORON.
HAVE YOU LOOKED INTO FOSTER CARE?
MAYBE WE SHOULDN'T HAVE GONE WITH OUR FIRST INSTINCT.
WE MEANT WELL.
3/25/99

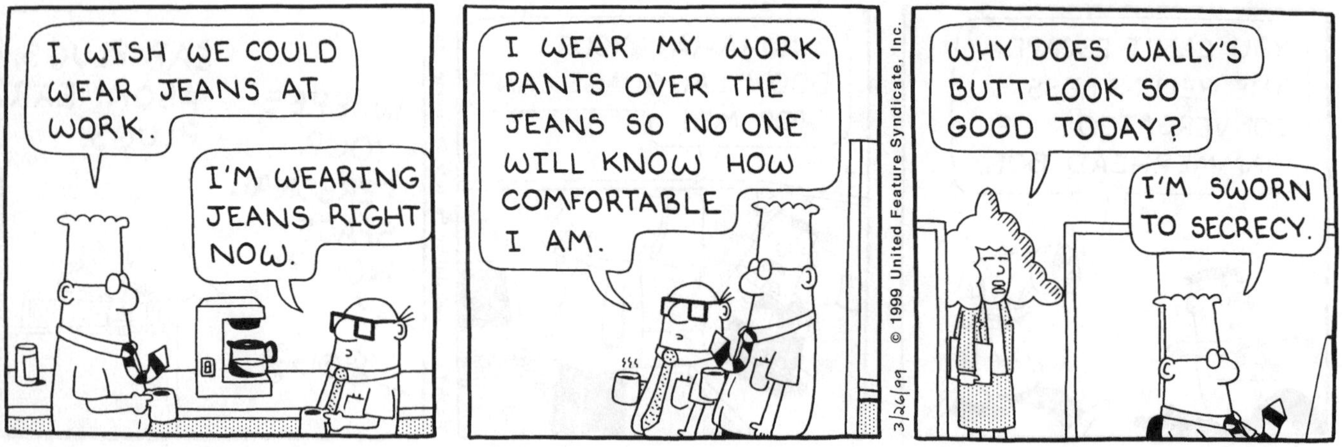
I WISH WE COULD WEAR JEANS AT WORK.
I'M WEARING JEANS RIGHT NOW.
I WEAR MY WORK PANTS OVER THE JEANS SO NO ONE WILL KNOW HOW COMFORTABLE I AM.
WHY DOES WALLY'S BUTT LOOK SO GOOD TODAY?
I'M SWORN TO SECRECY.
3/26/99

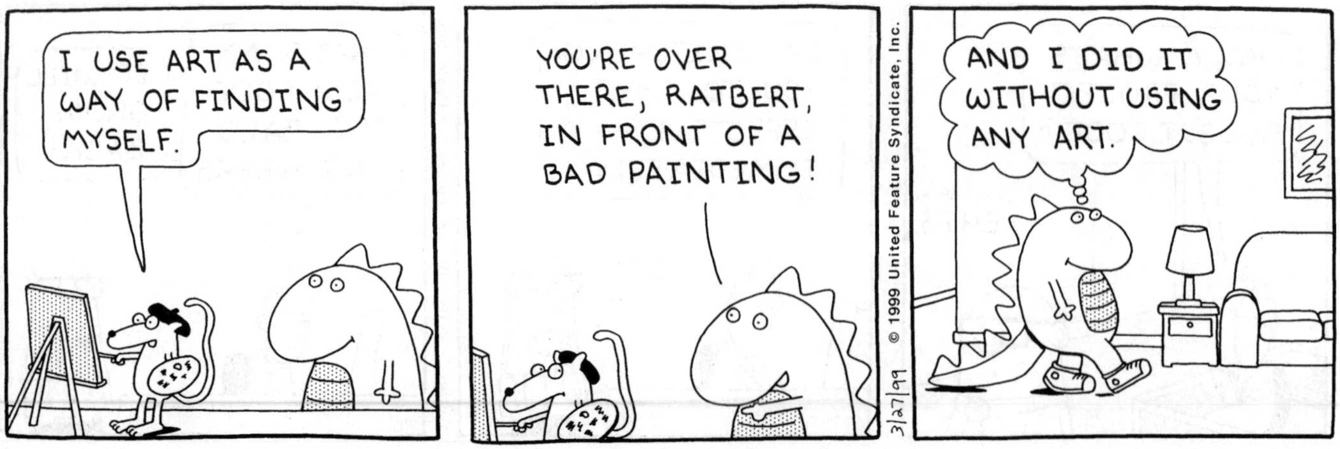
I USE ART AS A WAY OF FINDING MYSELF.
YOU'RE OVER THERE, RATBERT, IN FRONT OF A BAD PAINTING!
AND I DID IT WITHOUT USING ANY ART.
3/27/99

I'M TRYING A LITTLE EXPERIMENT TONIGHT.
I'LL ATTRIBUTE A STUPID OPINION TO YOU...
THEN I'LL AGGRESSIVELY MOCK YOU WHILE YOU SIT THERE SAYING NOTHING.
SO, ACCORDING TO YOU, THE INTERNET IS A PASSING FAD.
YOU MORON! LOOK AROUND YOU! THE INTERNET IS EVERYWHERE!
AND THERE'S NOTHING YOU CAN DO ABOUT IT! NOTHING!!
HOW DID THAT FEEL?
QUITE SATISFYING.
I NEEDED A BACK-UP PLAN IN CASE YOU EVER GET LARYNGITIS.

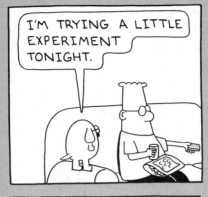

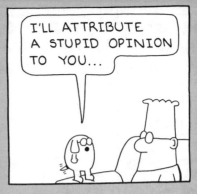

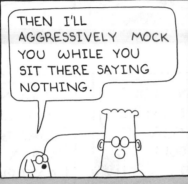

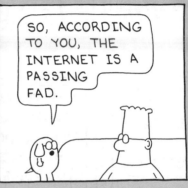

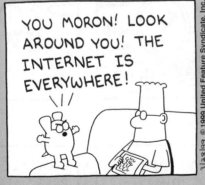

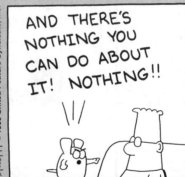

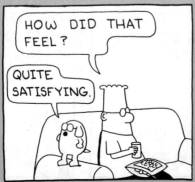

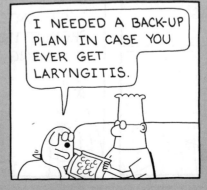

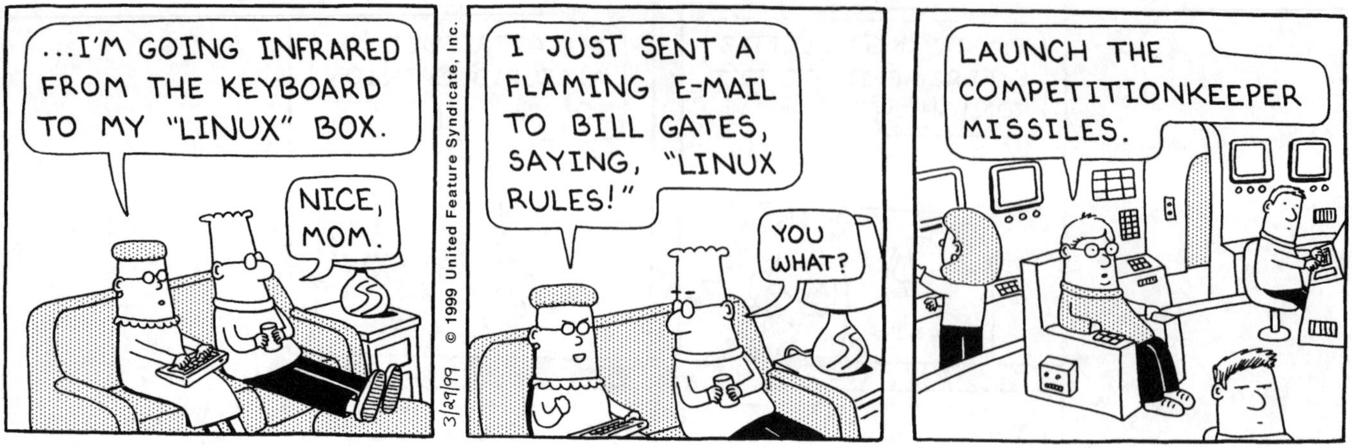
...I'M GOING INFRARED FROM THE KEYBOARD TO MY "LINUX" BOX.
NICE, MOM.
I JUST SENT A FLAMING E-MAIL TO BILL GATES, SAYING, "LINUX RULES!"
YOU WHAT?
LAUNCH THE COMPETITIONKEEPER MISSILES.

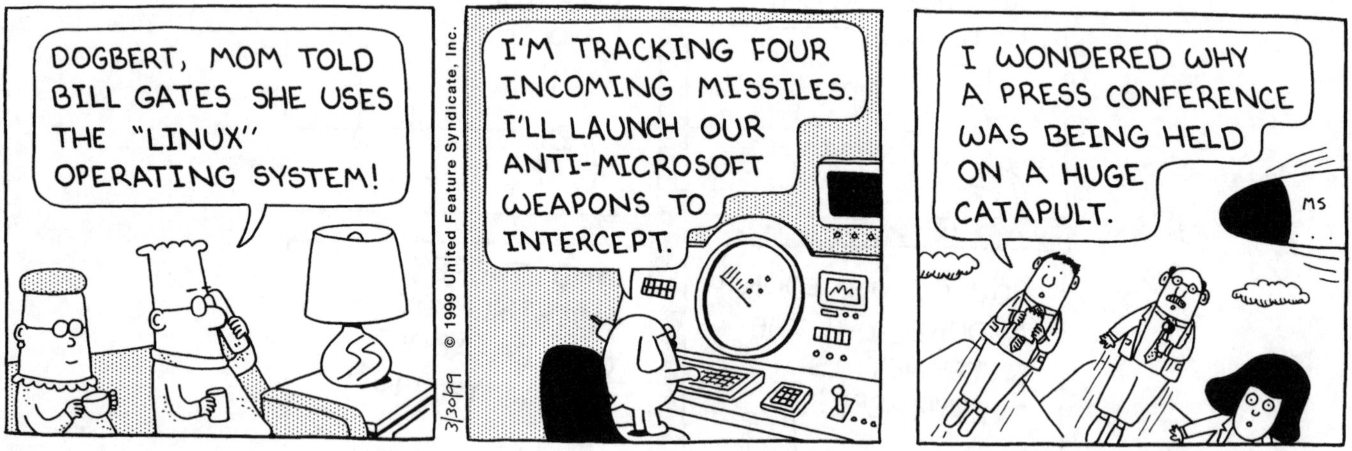
DOGBERT, MOM TOLD BILL GATES SHE USES THE "LINUX" OPERATING SYSTEM!
I'M TRACKING FOUR INCOMING MISSILES. I'LL LAUNCH OUR ANTI-MICROSOFT WEAPONS TO INTERCEPT.
I WONDERED WHY A PRESS CONFERENCE WAS BEING HELD ON A HUGE CATAPULT.
MS

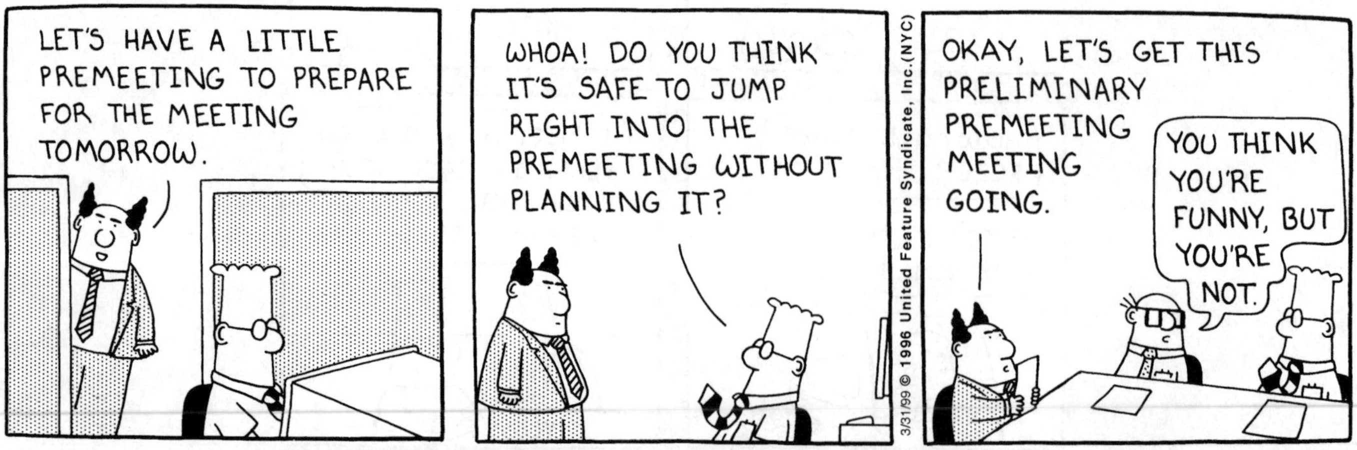
LET'S HAVE A LITTLE PREMEETING TO PREPARE FOR THE MEETING TOMORROW.
WHOA! DO YOU THINK IT'S SAFE TO JUMP RIGHT INTO THE PREMEETING WITHOUT PLANNING IT?
OKAY, LET'S GET THIS PRELIMINARY PREMEETING MEETING GOING.
YOU THINK YOU'RE FUNNY, BUT YOU'RE NOT.

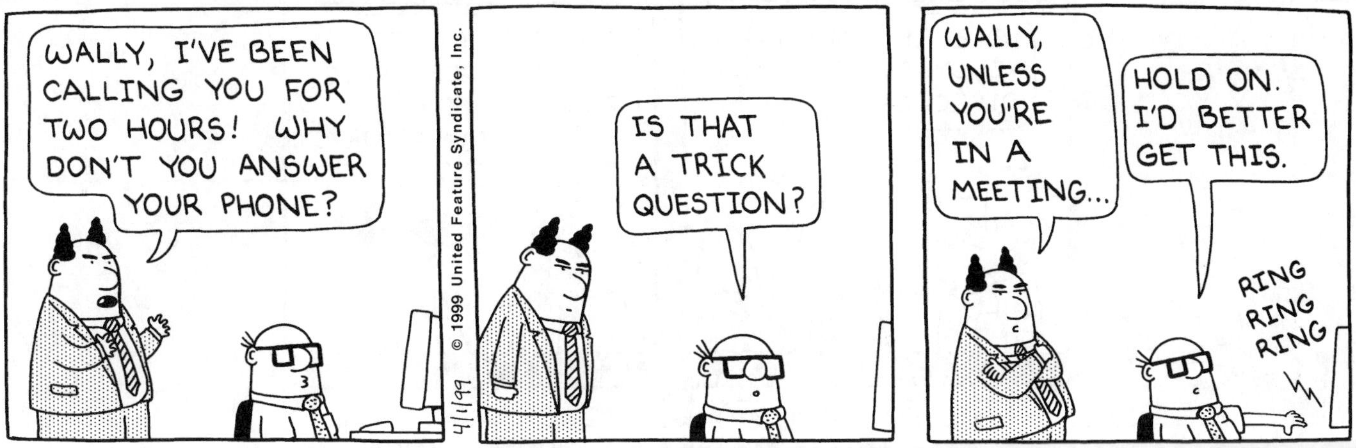
WALLY, I'VE BEEN CALLING YOU FOR TWO HOURS! WHY DON'T YOU ANSWER YOUR PHONE?
4/1/99 © 1999 United Feature Syndicate, Inc.
IS THAT A TRICK QUESTION?
WALLY, UNLESS YOU'RE IN A MEETING...
HOLD ON. I'D BETTER GET THIS.
RING RING RING

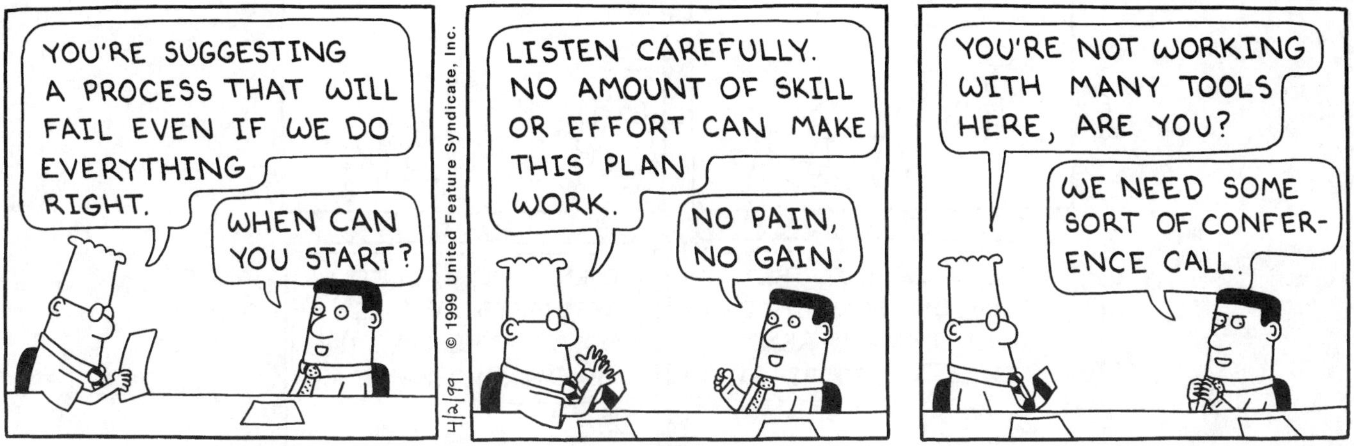
YOU'RE SUGGESTING A PROCESS THAT WILL FAIL EVEN IF WE DO EVERYTHING RIGHT.
WHEN CAN YOU START?
4/2/99 © 1999 United Feature Syndicate, Inc.
LISTEN CAREFULLY. NO AMOUNT OF SKILL OR EFFORT CAN MAKE THIS PLAN WORK.
NO PAIN, NO GAIN.
YOU'RE NOT WORKING WITH MANY TOOLS HERE, ARE YOU?
WE NEED SOME SORT OF CONFER-ENCE CALL.

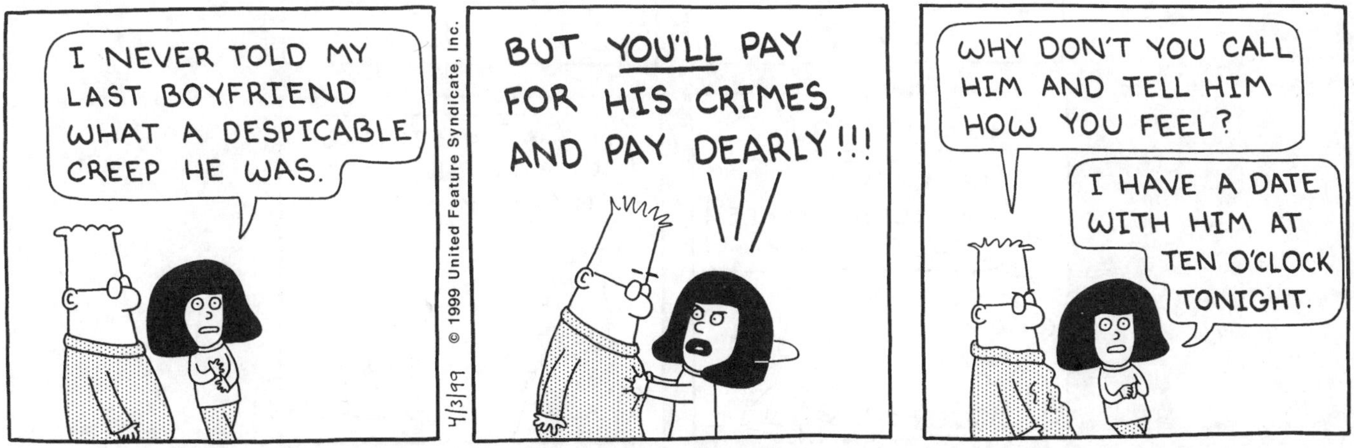
I NEVER TOLD MY LAST BOYFRIEND WHAT A DESPICABLE CREEP HE WAS.
4/3/99 © 1999 United Feature Syndicate, Inc.
BUT YOU'LL PAY FOR HIS CRIMES, AND PAY DEARLY!!!
WHY DON'T YOU CALL HIM AND TELL HIM HOW YOU FEEL?
I HAVE A DATE WITH HIM AT TEN O'CLOCK TONIGHT.

DILBERT, THIS IS PEGGY THE P.R. DIRECTOR.
I WANT YOU TO REVIEW HER PRESS RELEASE FOR TECHNICAL ACCURACY.
WHO WROTE THIS?
A TRAINED SQUIRREL?
I DON'T KNOW WHERE TO BEGIN.
I'LL CROSS OUT THE RUN-ON SENTENCES AND TRANSPARENT LIES FIRST.
THEN THE FAILED ATTEMPTS AT CUTE-NESS ... THE SPELLING ERRORS ... GRAMMAR.
THERE YOU GO.
REMEMBER, CRITICISM MAKES YOU STRONGER.
IT WAS A MISTAKE TO MAKE HER STRONGER.
© 1999 United Feature Syndicate, Inc.
4/4/99

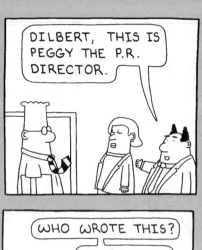

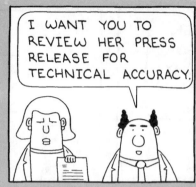

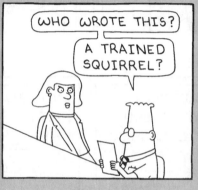

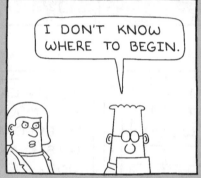

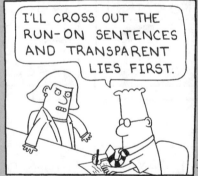

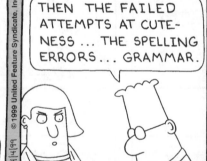

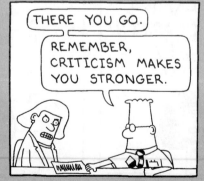

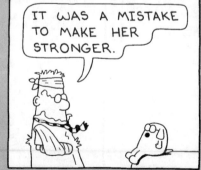

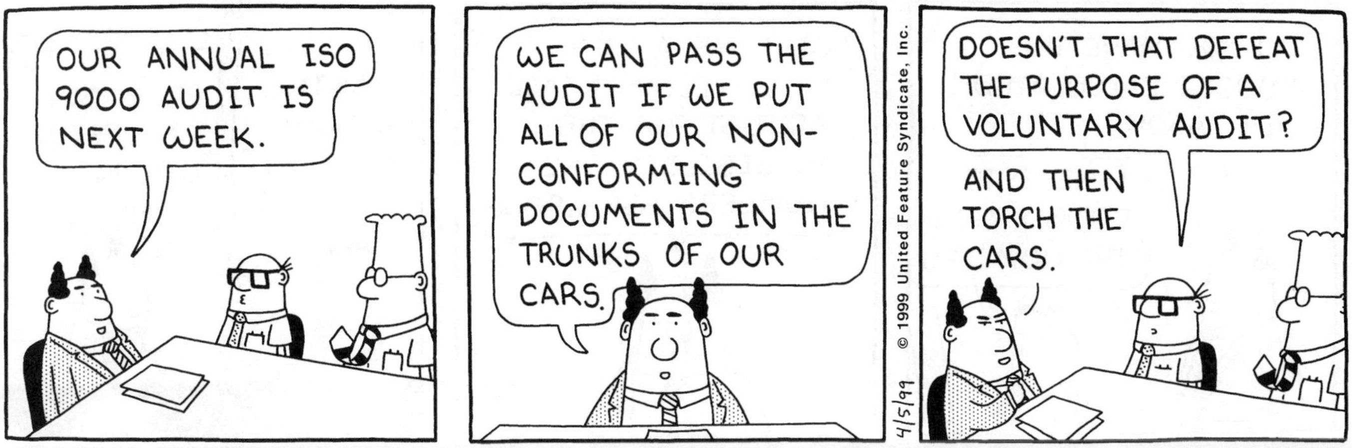
OUR ANNUAL ISO 9000 AUDIT IS NEXT WEEK.
WE CAN PASS THE AUDIT IF WE PUT ALL OF OUR NON-CONFORMING DOCUMENTS IN THE TRUNKS OF OUR CARS.
4/5/99 © 1999 United Feature Syndicate, Inc.
DOESN'T THAT DEFEAT THE PURPOSE OF A VOLUNTARY AUDIT?
AND THEN TORCH THE CARS.

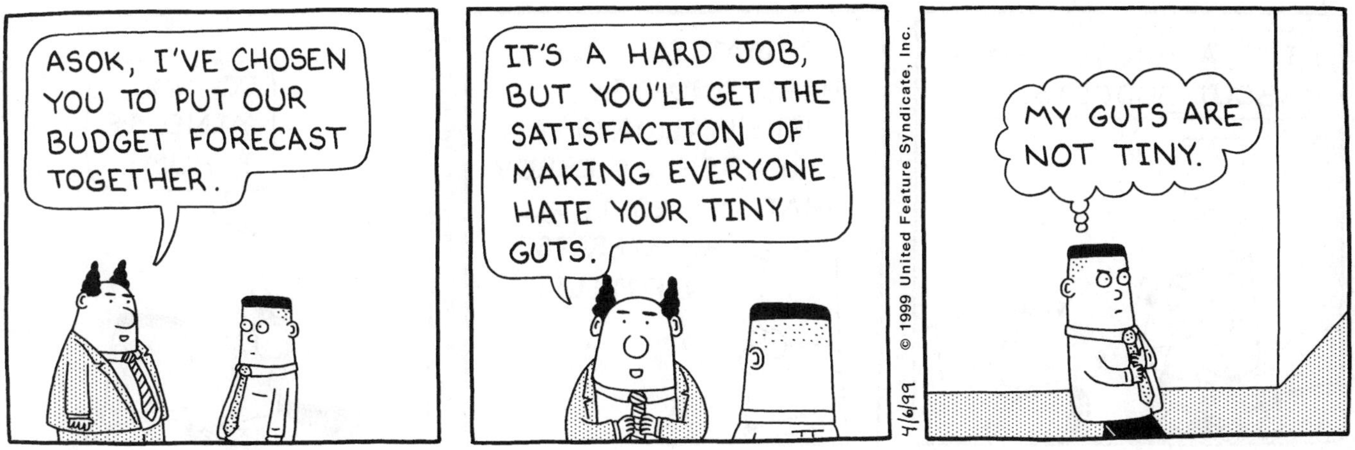
ASOK, I'VE CHOSEN YOU TO PUT OUR BUDGET FORECAST TOGETHER.
IT'S A HARD JOB, BUT YOU'LL GET THE SATISFACTION OF MAKING EVERYONE HATE YOUR TINY GUTS.
4/6/99 © 1999 United Feature Syndicate, Inc.
MY GUTS ARE NOT TINY.

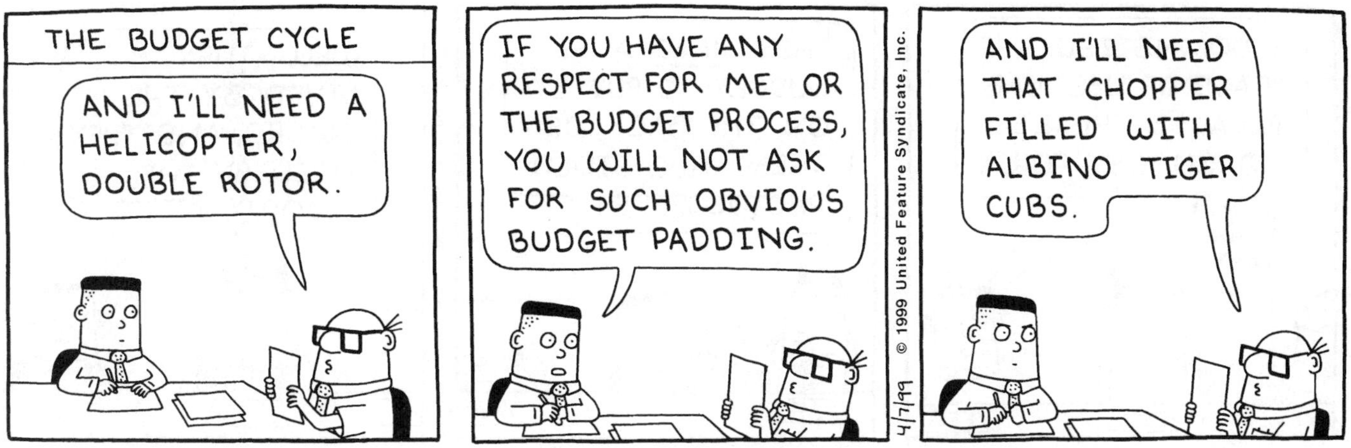
THE BUDGET CYCLE
AND I'LL NEED A HELICOPTER, DOUBLE ROTOR.
IF YOU HAVE ANY RESPECT FOR ME OR THE BUDGET PROCESS, YOU WILL NOT ASK FOR SUCH OBVIOUS BUDGET PADDING.
4/7/99 © 1999 United Feature Syndicate, Inc.
AND I'LL NEED THAT CHOPPER FILLED WITH ALBINO TIGER CUBS.

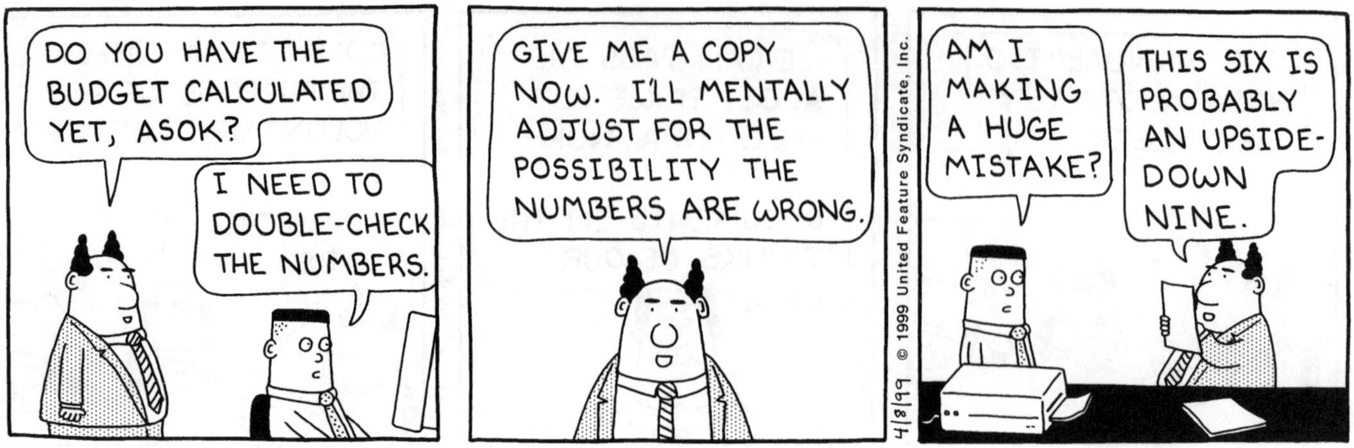
DO YOU HAVE THE BUDGET CALCULATED YET, ASOK?
I NEED TO DOUBLE-CHECK THE NUMBERS.
GIVE ME A COPY NOW. I'LL MENTALLY ADJUST FOR THE POSSIBILITY THE NUMBERS ARE WRONG.
4/8/99 © 1999 United Feature Syndicate, Inc.
AM I MAKING A HUGE MISTAKE?
THIS SIX IS PROBABLY AN UPSIDE-DOWN NINE.

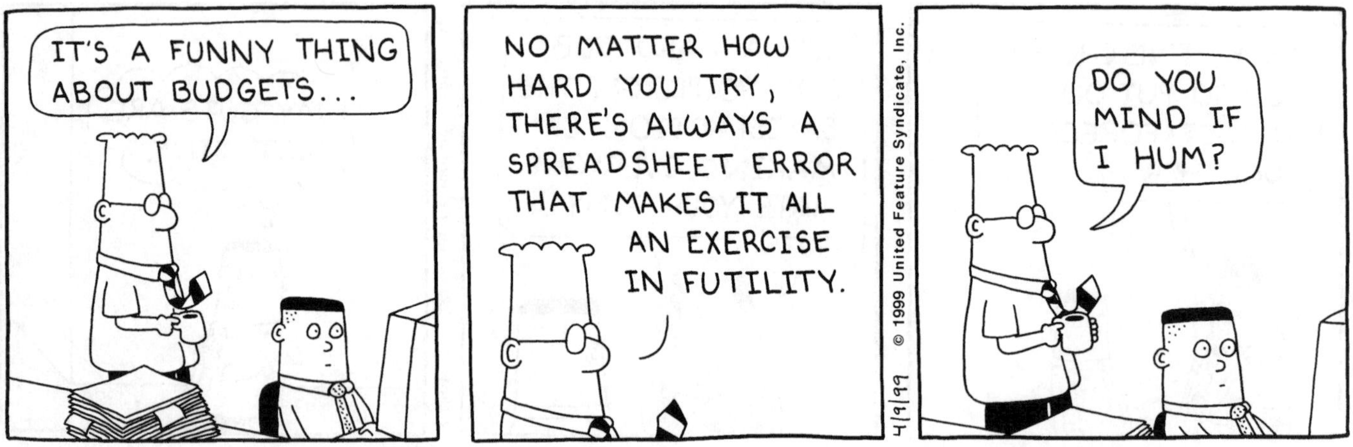
IT'S A FUNNY THING ABOUT BUDGETS...
NO MATTER HOW HARD YOU TRY, THERE'S ALWAYS A SPREADSHEET ERROR THAT MAKES IT ALL AN EXERCISE IN FUTILITY.
4/9/99 © 1999 United Feature Syndicate, Inc.
DO YOU MIND IF I HUM?

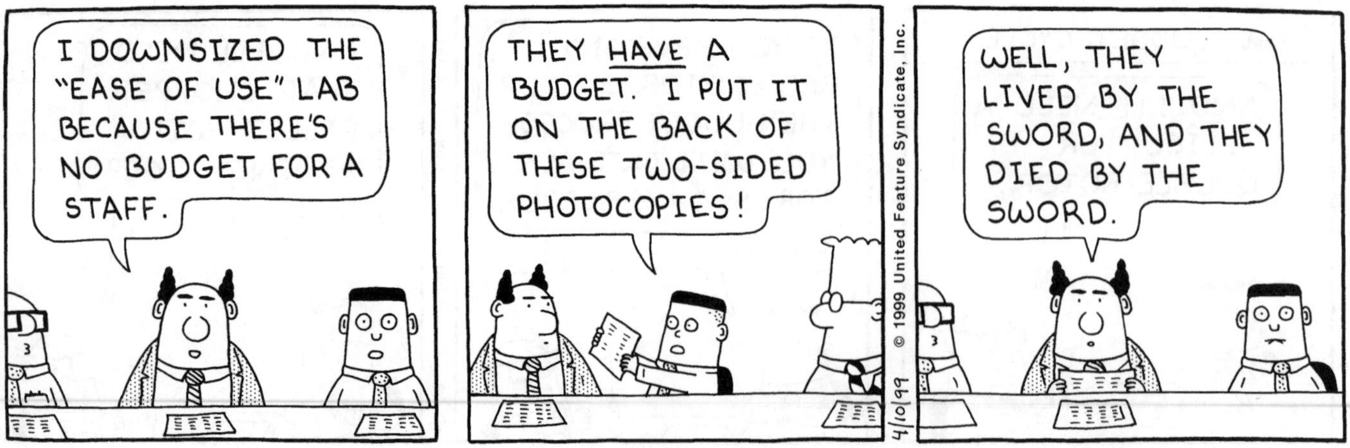
I DOWNSIZED THE "EASE OF USE" LAB BECAUSE THERE'S NO BUDGET FOR A STAFF.
THEY HAVE A BUDGET. I PUT IT ON THE BACK OF THESE TWO-SIDED PHOTOCOPIES!
4/10/99 © 1999 United Feature Syndicate, Inc.
WELL, THEY LIVED BY THE SWORD, AND THEY DIED BY THE SWORD.

THERE'S TED. HE NEVER SENT ME THE INFORMATION HE PROMISED.
WHY HAVE YOU IGNORED MY REQUEST, TED?
I WAS KILLED BY A SQUADRON OF GIANT MILITARY SQUIRRELS.
HE DOESN'T RESPECT YOU ENOUGH TO TELL A PLAUSIBLE LIE.
I DEMAND A PLAUSIBLE LIE!
OKAY, MAYBE I WASN'T KILLED BY GIANT MILITARY SQUIRRELS.
BUT I WAS IMPRISONED IN THEIR SECRET LAIR AT THE CENTER OF THE EARTH.
YOU CAN'T PROVE THAT ONE EITHER WAY.
HE DID SAY IT WAS A "SECRET" LAIR.
4/11/99

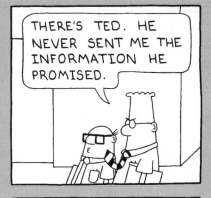

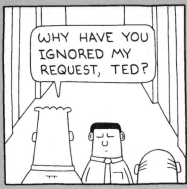

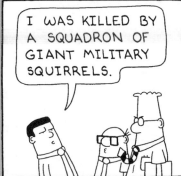

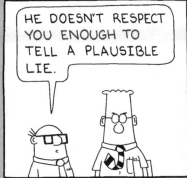

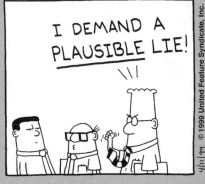

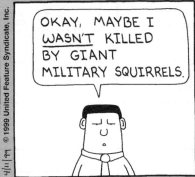

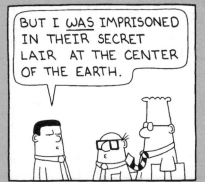

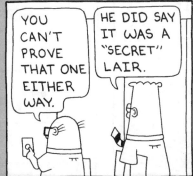

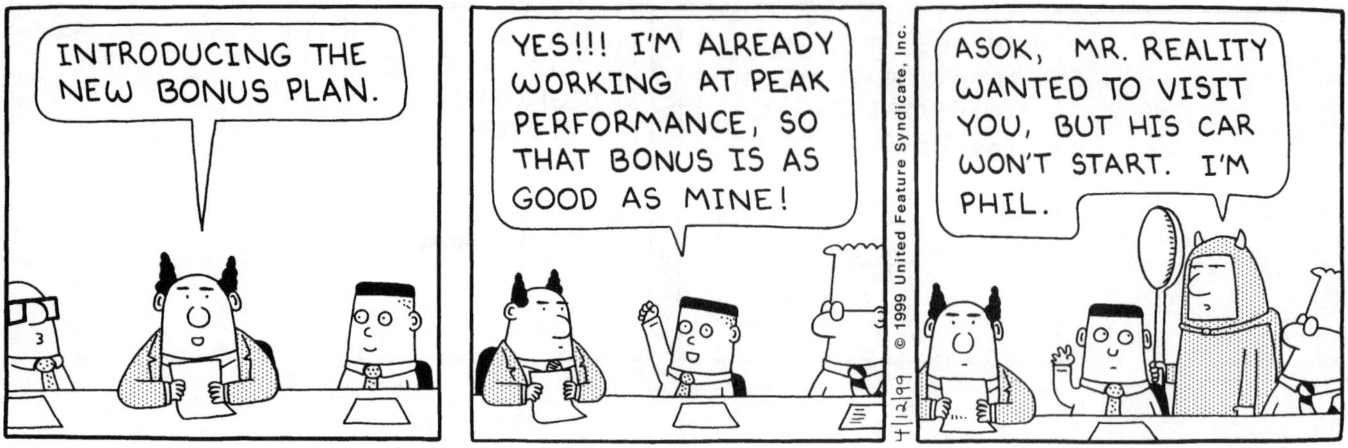
INTRODUCING THE NEW BONUS PLAN.
YES!!! I'M ALREADY WORKING AT PEAK PERFORMANCE, SO THAT BONUS IS AS GOOD AS MINE!
4/12/99 © 1999 United Feature Syndicate, Inc.
ASOK, MR. REALITY WANTED TO VISIT YOU, BUT HIS CAR WON'T START. I'M PHIL.

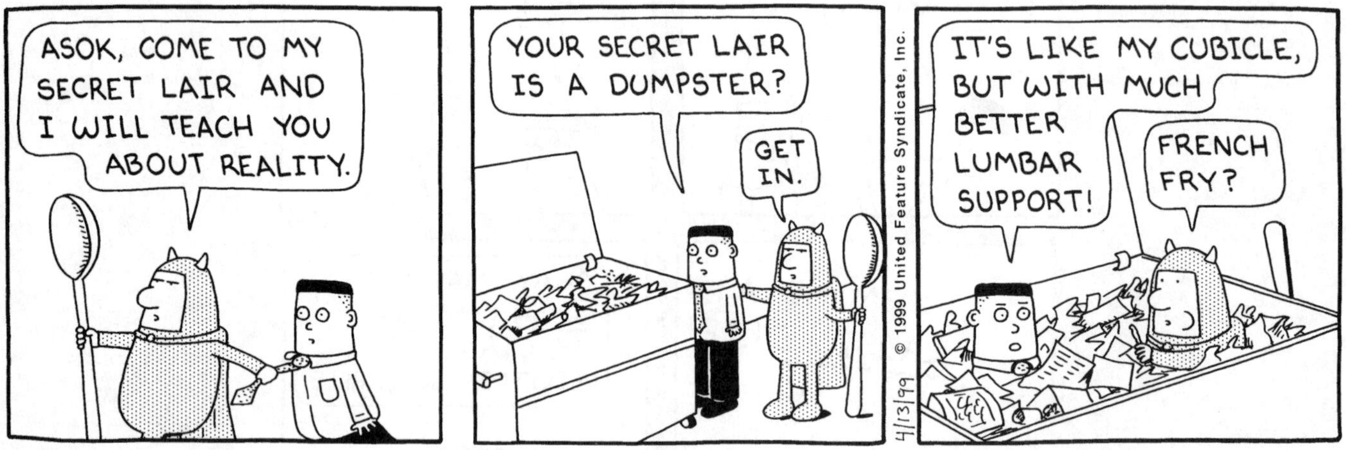
ASOK, COME TO MY SECRET LAIR AND I WILL TEACH YOU ABOUT REALITY.
YOUR SECRET LAIR IS A DUMPSTER?
GET IN.
4/13/99 © 1999 United Feature Syndicate, Inc.
IT'S LIKE MY CUBICLE, BUT WITH MUCH BETTER LUMBAR SUPPORT!
FRENCH FRY?

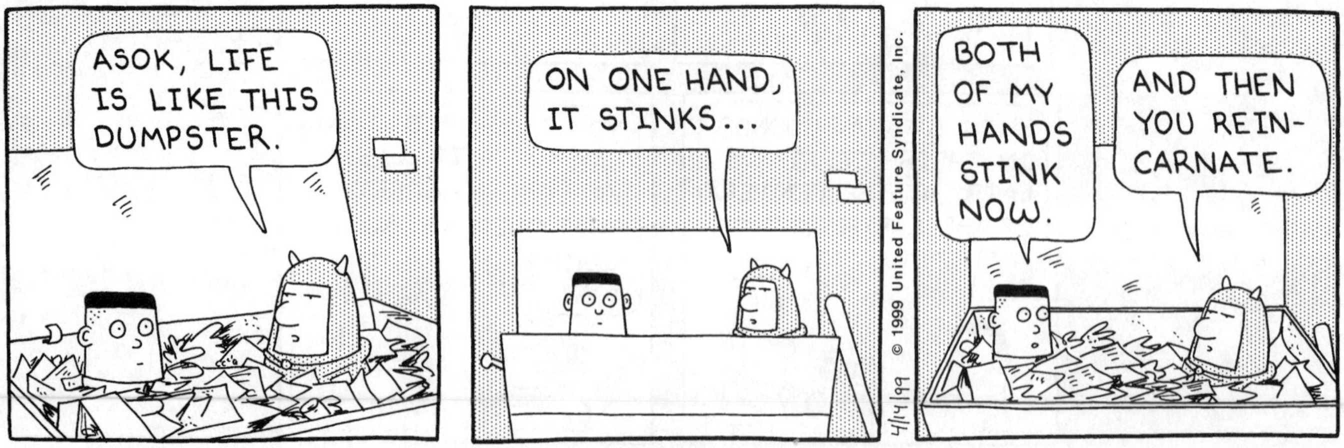
ASOK, LIFE IS LIKE THIS DUMPSTER.
ON ONE HAND, IT STINKS...
4/14/99 © 1999 United Feature Syndicate, Inc.
BOTH OF MY HANDS STINK NOW.
AND THEN YOU REIN-CARNATE.

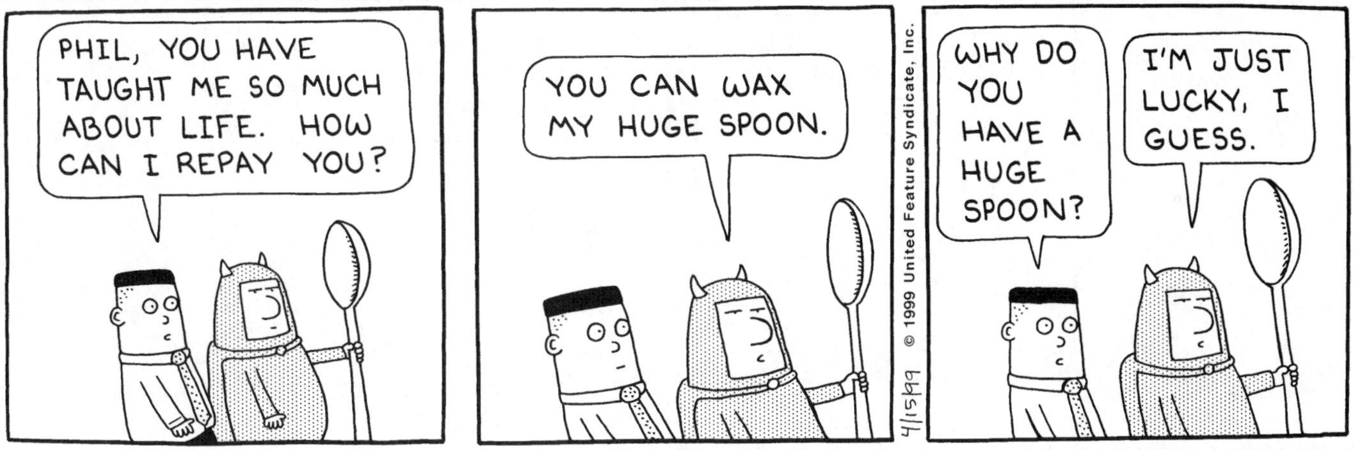
PHIL, YOU HAVE TAUGHT ME SO MUCH ABOUT LIFE. HOW CAN I REPAY YOU?
YOU CAN WAX MY HUGE SPOON.
4/15/99 © 1999 United Feature Syndicate, Inc.
WHY DO YOU HAVE A HUGE SPOON?
I'M JUST LUCKY, I GUESS.

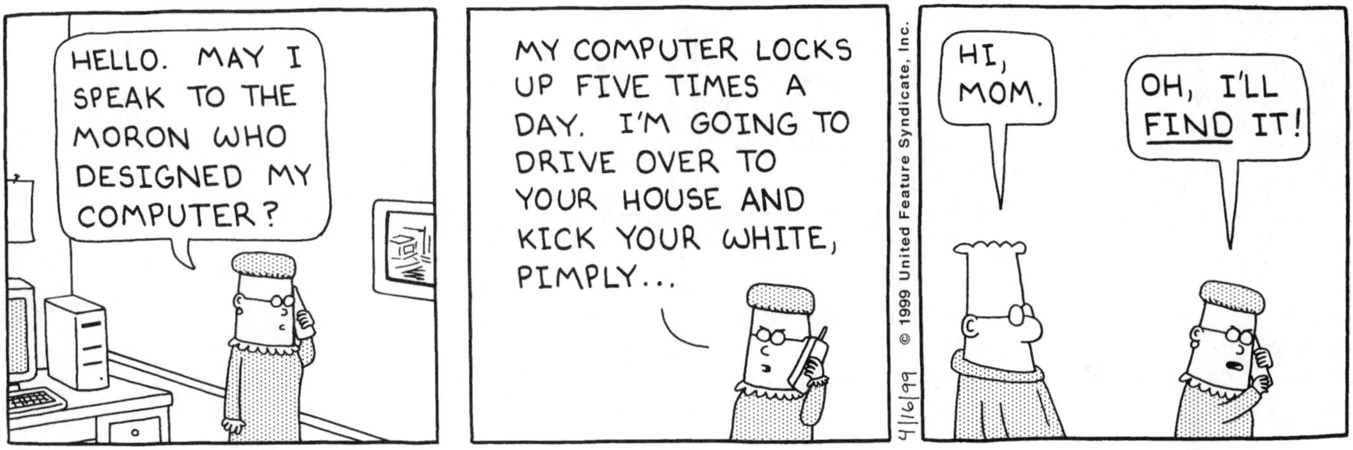
HELLO. MAY I SPEAK TO THE MORON WHO DESIGNED MY COMPUTER?
MY COMPUTER LOCKS UP FIVE TIMES A DAY. I'M GOING TO DRIVE OVER TO YOUR HOUSE AND KICK YOUR WHITE, PIMPLY...
4/16/99 © 1999 United Feature Syndicate, Inc.
HI, MOM.
OH, I'LL FIND IT!

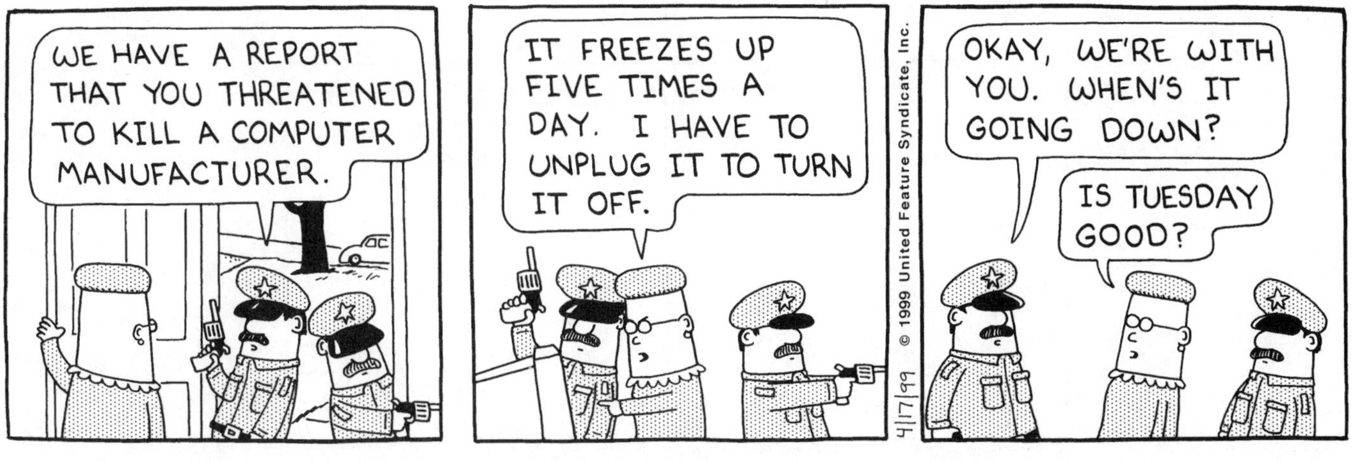
WE HAVE A REPORT THAT YOU THREATENED TO KILL A COMPUTER MANUFACTURER.
IT FREEZES UP FIVE TIMES A DAY. I HAVE TO UNPLUG IT TO TURN IT OFF.
4/17/99 © 1999 United Feature Syndicate, Inc.
OKAY, WE'RE WITH YOU. WHEN'S IT GOING DOWN?
IS TUESDAY GOOD?

PATTY IS OUR NEW "PROCESS MANAGER."
PATTY DOESN'T KNOW HOW TO DO ANYTHING.
SHE ONLY KNOWS HOW TO DO THINGS BETTER!
PROCESS!
FOR EXAMPLE, THIS MEETING IS POORLY MANAGED BECAUSE YOU HAVE NO PROCESS.
AND THIS INTERN OBVIOUSLY HAD NO PROCESS FOR DECIDING WHETHER TO ATTEND.
© 1999 United Feature Syndicate, Inc.
4/18/99
OKAY, PATTY IS ANNOYING.
ALL IN FAVOR OF GETTING RID OF HER.
YOU LASTED LONGER THAN TIMMY THE "FACILITATOR."

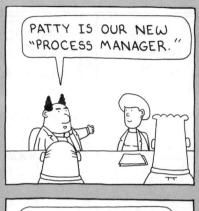

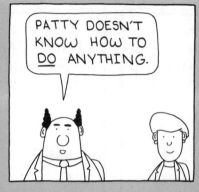

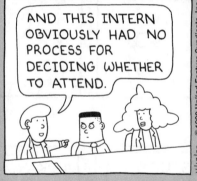

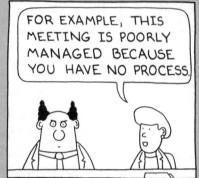

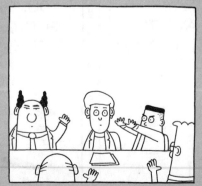

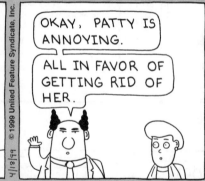

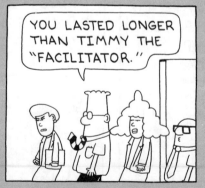

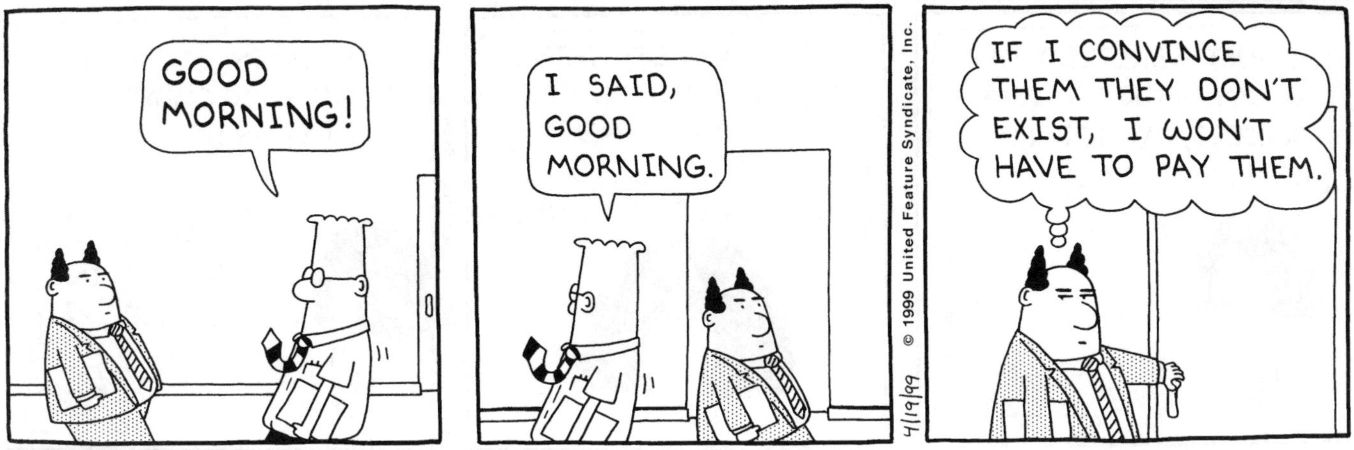
GOOD MORNING!
I SAID, GOOD MORNING.
4/19/99 © 1999 United Feature Syndicate, Inc.
IF I CONVINCE THEM THEY DON'T EXIST, I WON'T HAVE TO PAY THEM.

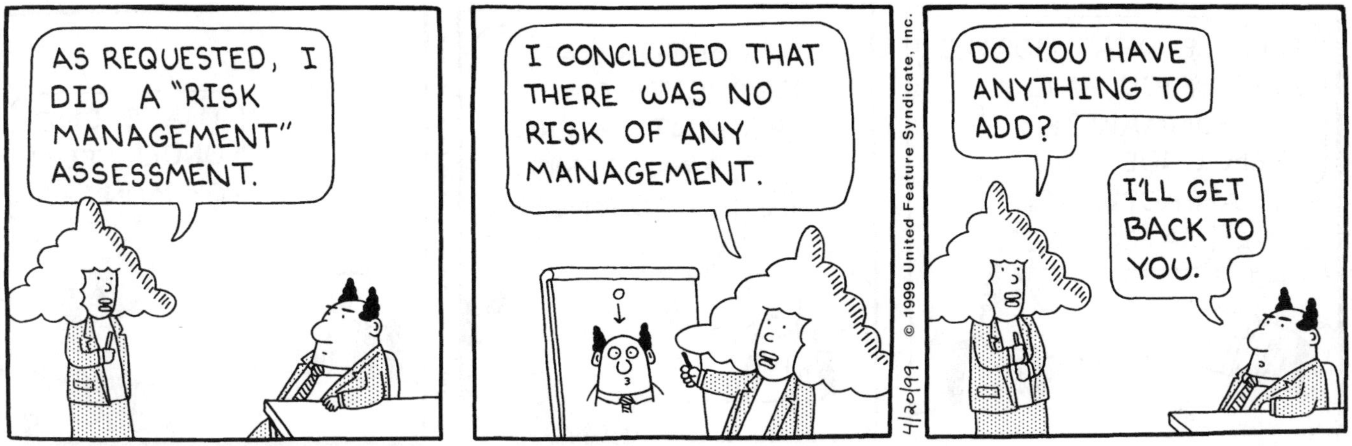
AS REQUESTED, I DID A "RISK MANAGEMENT" ASSESSMENT.
I CONCLUDED THAT THERE WAS NO RISK OF ANY MANAGEMENT.
4/20/99 © 1999 United Feature Syndicate, Inc.
DO YOU HAVE ANYTHING TO ADD?
I'LL GET BACK TO YOU.

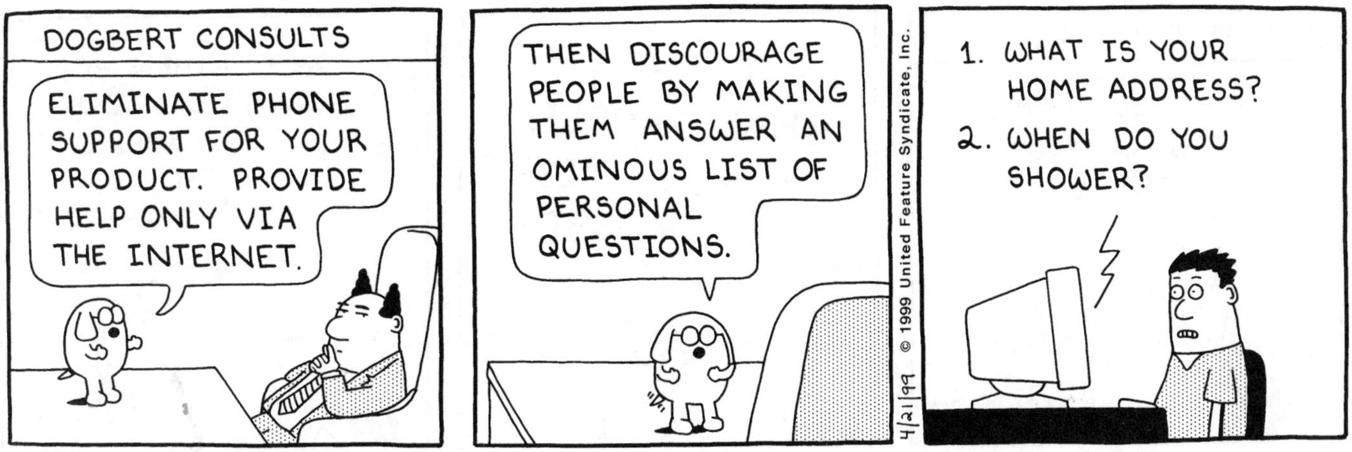
DOGBERT CONSULTS
ELIMINATE PHONE SUPPORT FOR YOUR PRODUCT. PROVIDE HELP ONLY VIA THE INTERNET.
THEN DISCOURAGE PEOPLE BY MAKING THEM ANSWER AN OMINOUS LIST OF PERSONAL QUESTIONS.
4/21/99 © 1999 United Feature Syndicate, Inc.
1. WHAT IS YOUR HOME ADDRESS?
2. WHEN DO YOU SHOWER?

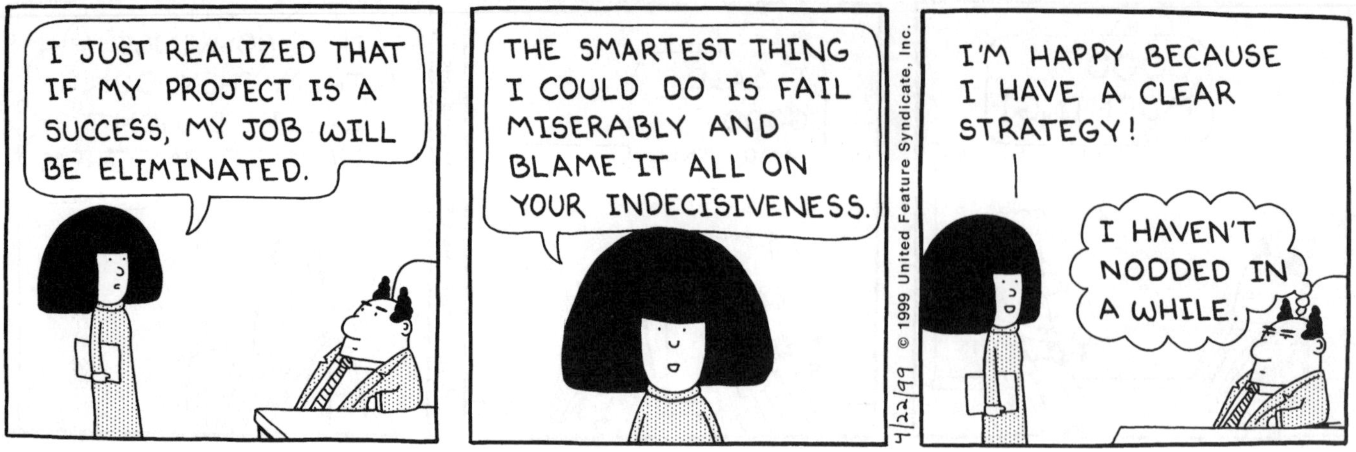
I JUST REALIZED THAT IF MY PROJECT IS A SUCCESS, MY JOB WILL BE ELIMINATED.
THE SMARTEST THING I COULD DO IS FAIL MISERABLY AND BLAME IT ALL ON YOUR INDECISIVENESS.
4/22/99 © 1999 United Feature Syndicate, Inc.
I'M HAPPY BECAUSE I HAVE A CLEAR STRATEGY!
I HAVEN'T NODDED IN A WHILE.

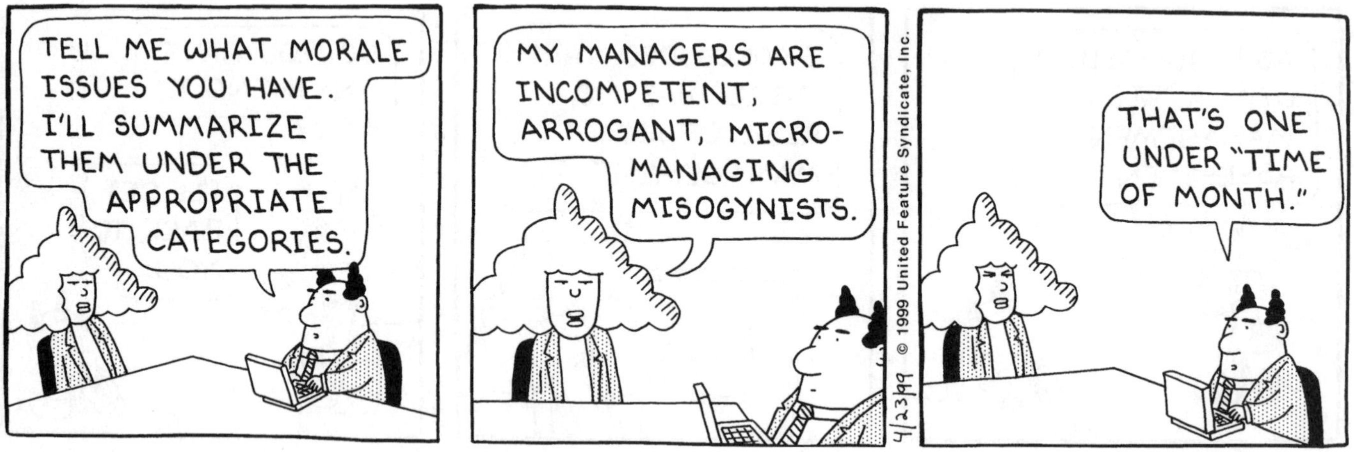
TELL ME WHAT MORALE ISSUES YOU HAVE. I'LL SUMMARIZE THEM UNDER THE APPROPRIATE CATEGORIES.
MY MANAGERS ARE INCOMPETENT, ARROGANT, MICRO-MANAGING MISOGYNISTS.
4/23/99 © 1999 United Feature Syndicate, Inc.
THAT'S ONE UNDER "TIME OF MONTH."

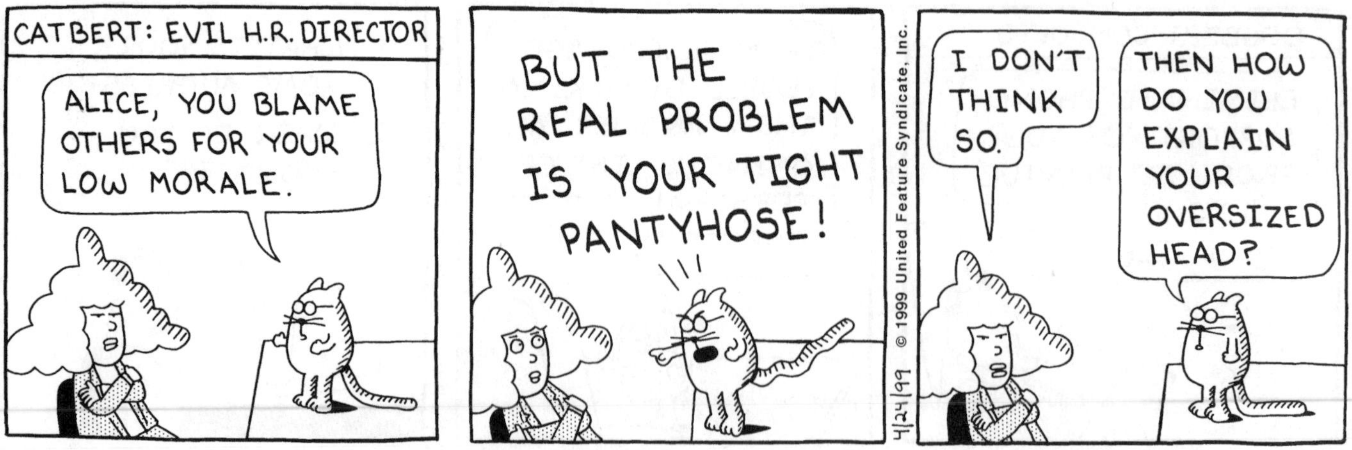
CATBERT: EVIL H.R. DIRECTOR
ALICE, YOU BLAME OTHERS FOR YOUR LOW MORALE.
BUT THE REAL PROBLEM IS YOUR TIGHT PANTYHOSE!
4/24/99 © 1999 United Feature Syndicate, Inc.
I DON'T THINK SO.
THEN HOW DO YOU EXPLAIN YOUR OVERSIZED HEAD?

DOGBERT PRESENTS
MANAGING BY ANALOGIES
IT'S EASY!
WE'LL SOLVE OUR DISTRIBUTION PROBLEM THE ESKIMO WAY.
HUH?
THE ESKIMOS GATHER ICE ALL WINTER LONG.
LATER, DURING THE LEAN SUMMER MONTHS, THE ESKIMOS EAT THE ICE THEY STORED.
WE'LL DO THE SAME THING!
BUT... THE ESKIMOS WOULD STARVE IF THEY ONLY ATE ICE.
MAYBE THEY EAT PENGUINS TOO.
THEY'RE DELICIOUS.
DID YOU KNOW THAT THE ZOO CAN BAN YOU FOR LIFE IF THEY CATCH YOU USING A HIBACHI?
4/25/99 © 1999 United Feature Syndicate, Inc.

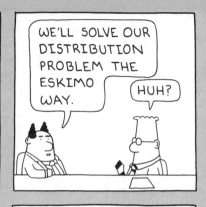

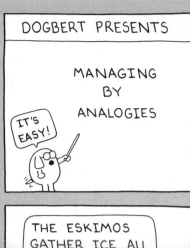

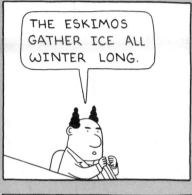

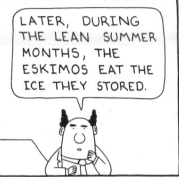

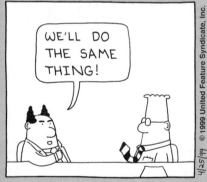

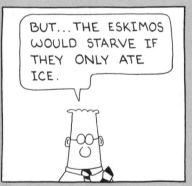

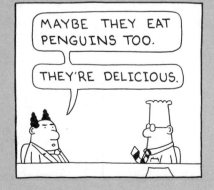

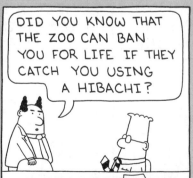

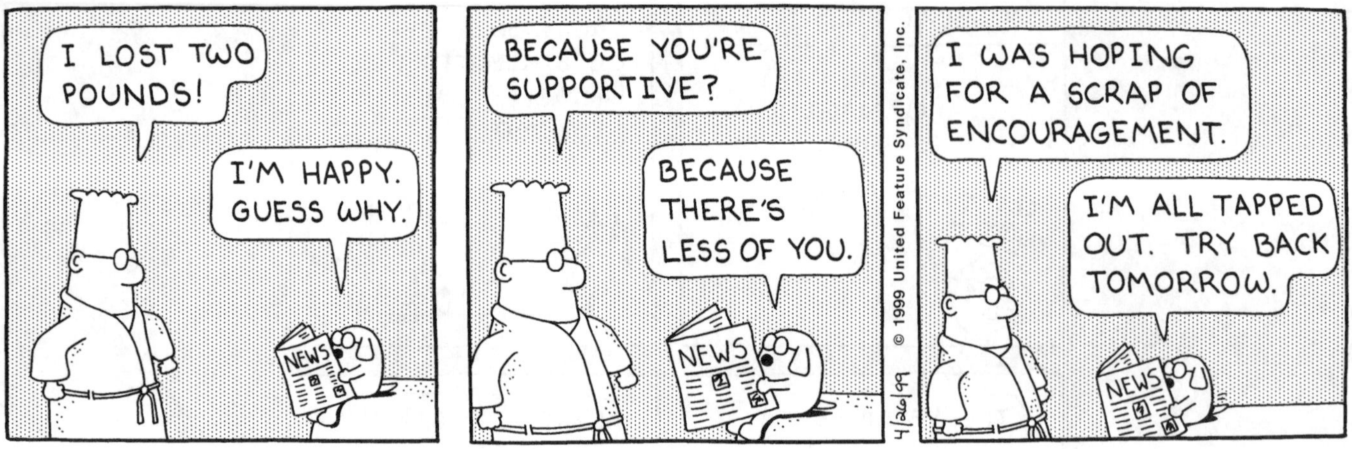
I LOST TWO POUNDS!
I'M HAPPY. GUESS WHY.
BECAUSE YOU'RE SUPPORTIVE?
BECAUSE THERE'S LESS OF YOU.
I WAS HOPING FOR A SCRAP OF ENCOURAGEMENT.
I'M ALL TAPPED OUT. TRY BACK TOMORROW.
NEWS
4/26/99 © 1999 United Feature Syndicate, Inc.

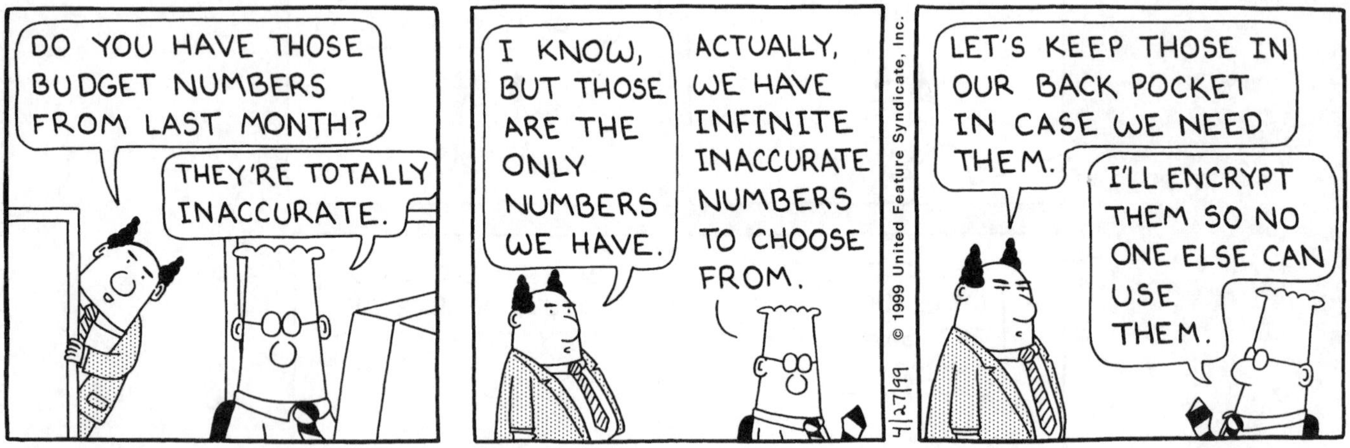
DO YOU HAVE THOSE BUDGET NUMBERS FROM LAST MONTH?
THEY'RE TOTALLY INACCURATE.
I KNOW, BUT THOSE ARE THE ONLY NUMBERS WE HAVE.
ACTUALLY, WE HAVE INFINITE INACCURATE NUMBERS TO CHOOSE FROM.
LET'S KEEP THOSE IN OUR BACK POCKET IN CASE WE NEED THEM.
I'LL ENCRYPT THEM SO NO ONE ELSE CAN USE THEM.
4/27/99 © 1999 United Feature Syndicate, Inc.

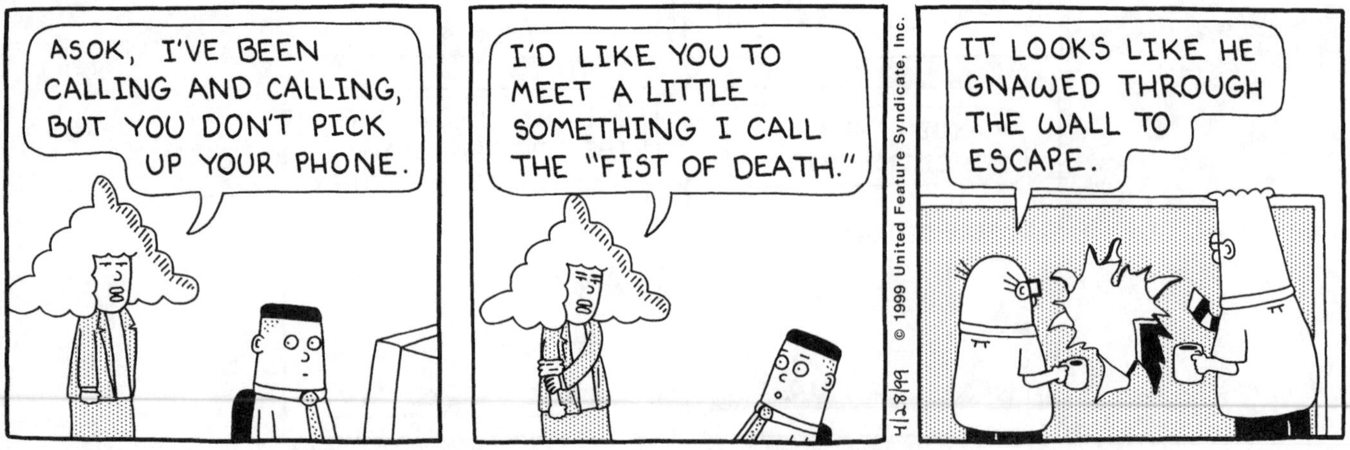
ASOK, I'VE BEEN CALLING AND CALLING, BUT YOU DON'T PICK UP YOUR PHONE.
I'D LIKE YOU TO MEET A LITTLE SOMETHING I CALL THE "FIST OF DEATH."
IT LOOKS LIKE HE GNAWED THROUGH THE WALL TO ESCAPE.
4/28/99 © 1999 United Feature Syndicate, Inc.

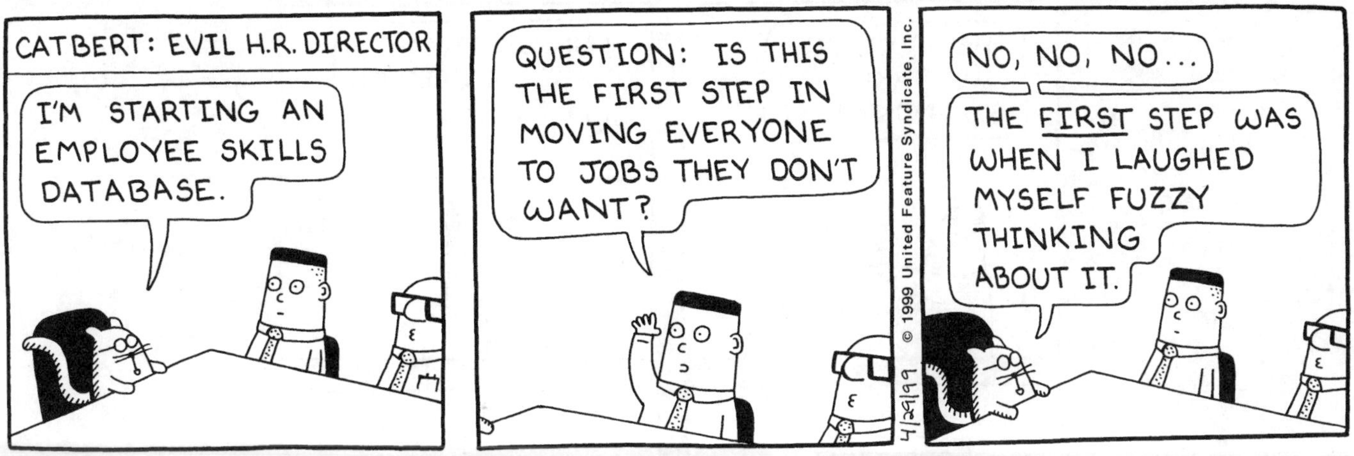
CATBERT: EVIL H.R. DIRECTOR
I'M STARTING AN EMPLOYEE SKILLS DATABASE.
QUESTION: IS THIS THE FIRST STEP IN MOVING EVERYONE TO JOBS THEY DON'T WANT?
NO, NO, NO...
THE FIRST STEP WAS WHEN I LAUGHED MYSELF FUZZY THINKING ABOUT IT.
4/29/99 © 1999 United Feature Syndicate, Inc.

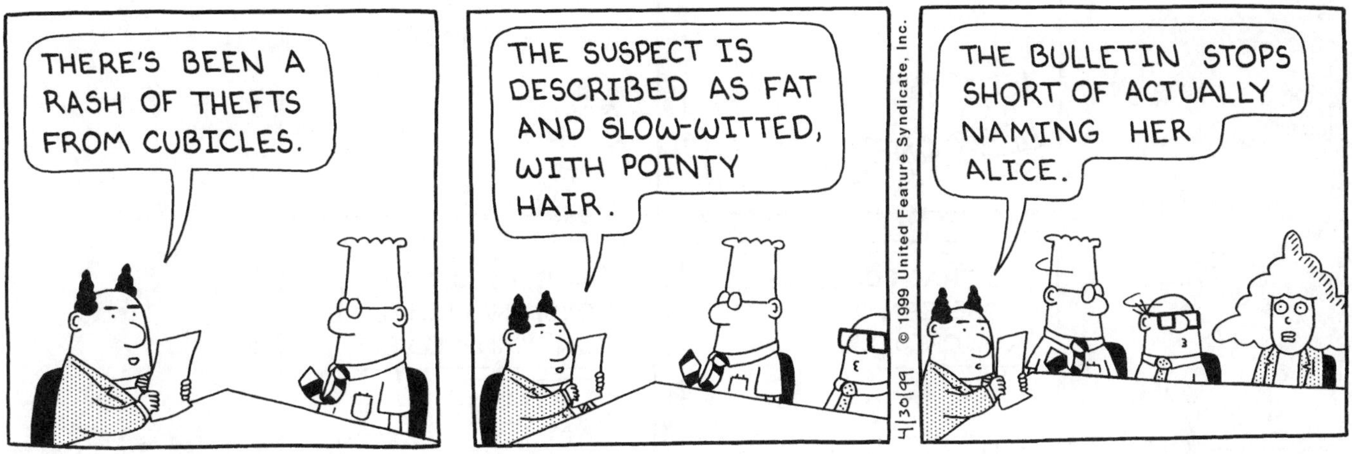
THERE'S BEEN A RASH OF THEFTS FROM CUBICLES.
THE SUSPECT IS DESCRIBED AS FAT AND SLOW-WITTED, WITH POINTY HAIR.
THE BULLETIN STOPS SHORT OF ACTUALLY NAMING HER ALICE.
4/30/99 © 1999 United Feature Syndicate, Inc.

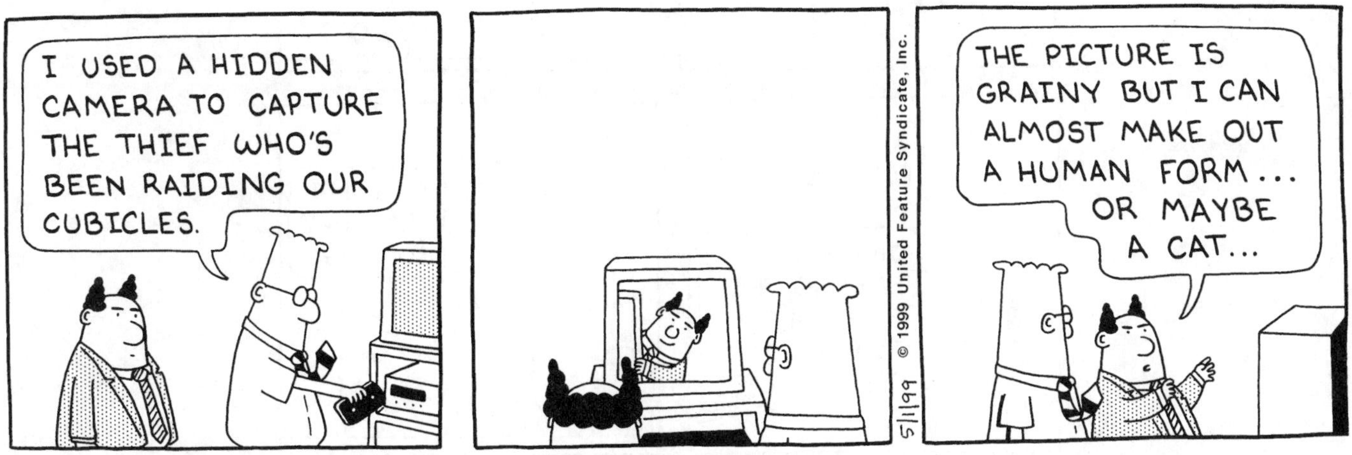
I USED A HIDDEN CAMERA TO CAPTURE THE THIEF WHO'S BEEN RAIDING OUR CUBICLES.
THE PICTURE IS GRAINY BUT I CAN ALMOST MAKE OUT A HUMAN FORM... OR MAYBE A CAT...
5/1/99 © 1999 United Feature Syndicate, Inc.

THE PROJECT WILL TAKE SIX MONTHS...
TIME LINE
UNLESS THERE ARE UNFORESEEN PROBLEMS.
TIM LIN
QUESTION.
YOUR LEADERSHIP HAS MADE ME UNMOTIVATED.
IS THAT CONSIDERED FORESEEN OR UNFORESEEN?
© 1999 United Feature Syndicate, Inc.
5/2/99
AND WALLY IS DYSFUNCTIONAL ON MANY LEVELS.
I REALLY AM.
WAS THAT FORESEEN?
OR ARE YOU SAYING THE SCHEDULE IS RANDOM?
HE LOOKS MAD.
I DIDN'T SEE THAT COMING.

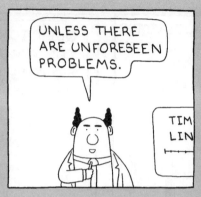

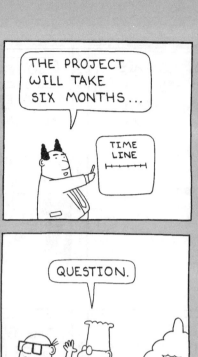

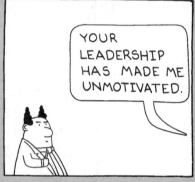

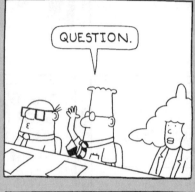

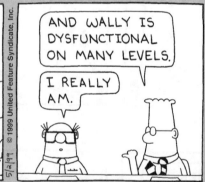

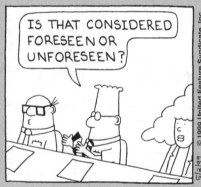

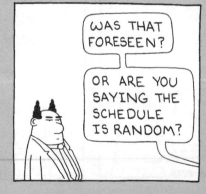

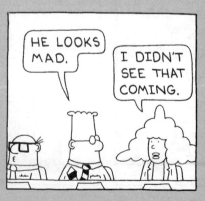

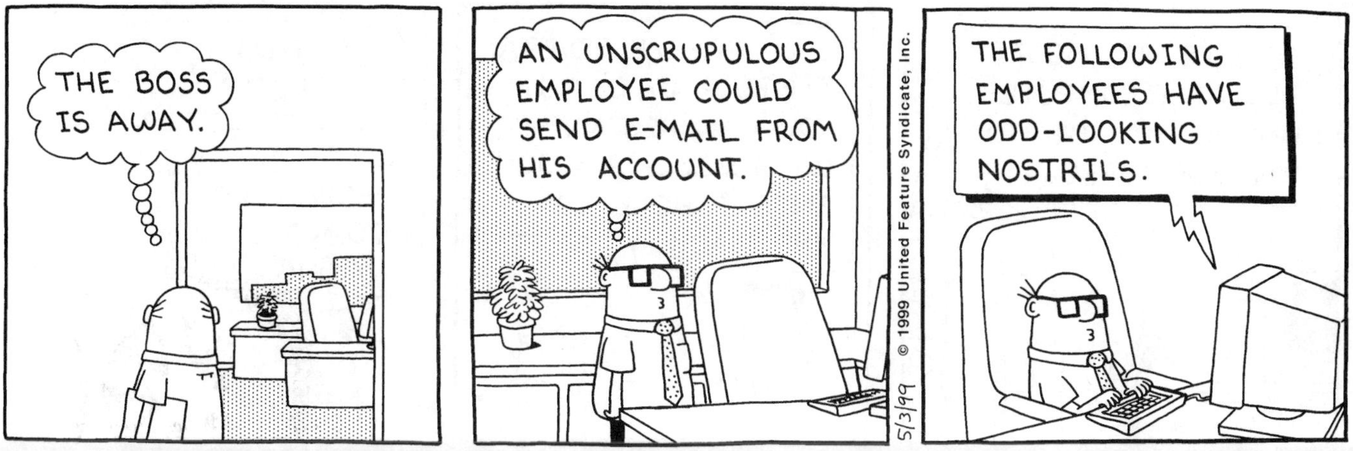
THE BOSS IS AWAY.
AN UNSCRUPULOUS EMPLOYEE COULD SEND E-MAIL FROM HIS ACCOUNT.
THE FOLLOWING EMPLOYEES HAVE ODD-LOOKING NOSTRILS.
5/3/99 © 1999 United Feature Syndicate, Inc.

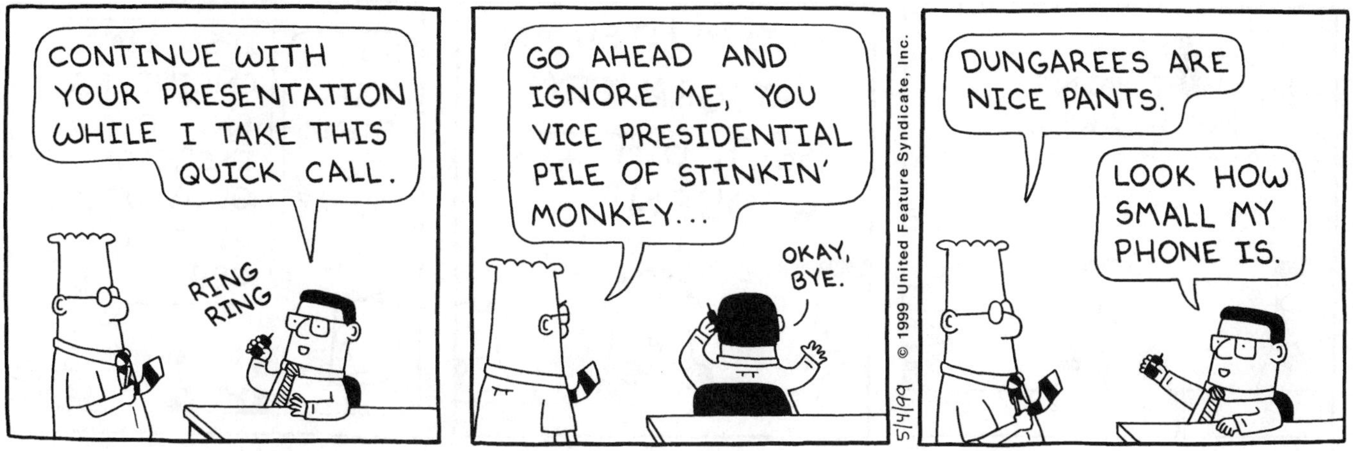
CONTINUE WITH YOUR PRESENTATION WHILE I TAKE THIS QUICK CALL.
RING RING
GO AHEAD AND IGNORE ME, YOU VICE PRESIDENTIAL PILE OF STINKIN' MONKEY...
OKAY, BYE.
DUNGAREES ARE NICE PANTS.
LOOK HOW SMALL MY PHONE IS.
5/4/99 © 1999 United Feature Syndicate, Inc.

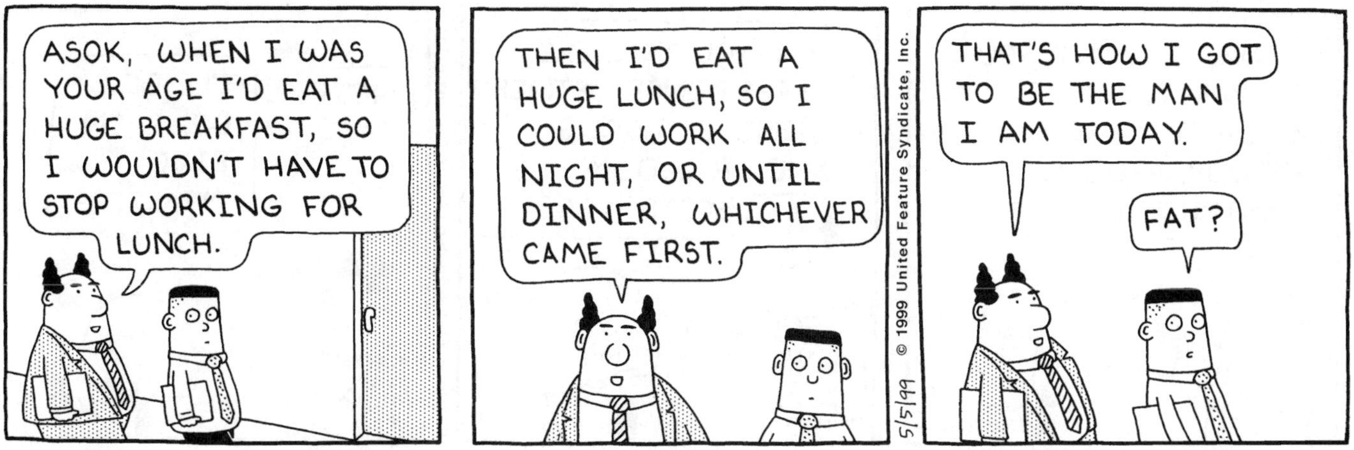
ASOK, WHEN I WAS YOUR AGE I'D EAT A HUGE BREAKFAST, SO I WOULDN'T HAVE TO STOP WORKING FOR LUNCH.
THEN I'D EAT A HUGE LUNCH, SO I COULD WORK ALL NIGHT, OR UNTIL DINNER, WHICHEVER CAME FIRST.
THAT'S HOW I GOT TO BE THE MAN I AM TODAY.
FAT?
5/5/99 © 1999 United Feature Syndicate, Inc.

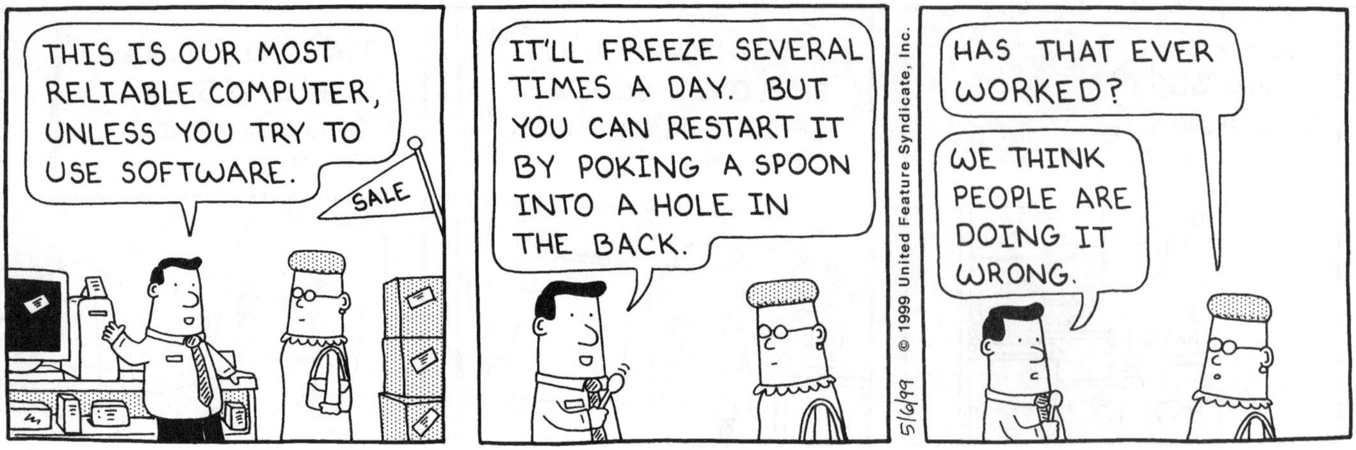
THIS IS OUR MOST RELIABLE COMPUTER, UNLESS YOU TRY TO USE SOFTWARE.
SALE
IT'LL FREEZE SEVERAL TIMES A DAY. BUT YOU CAN RESTART IT BY POKING A SPOON INTO A HOLE IN THE BACK.
5/6/99 © 1999 United Feature Syndicate, Inc.
HAS THAT EVER WORKED?
WE THINK PEOPLE ARE DOING IT WRONG.

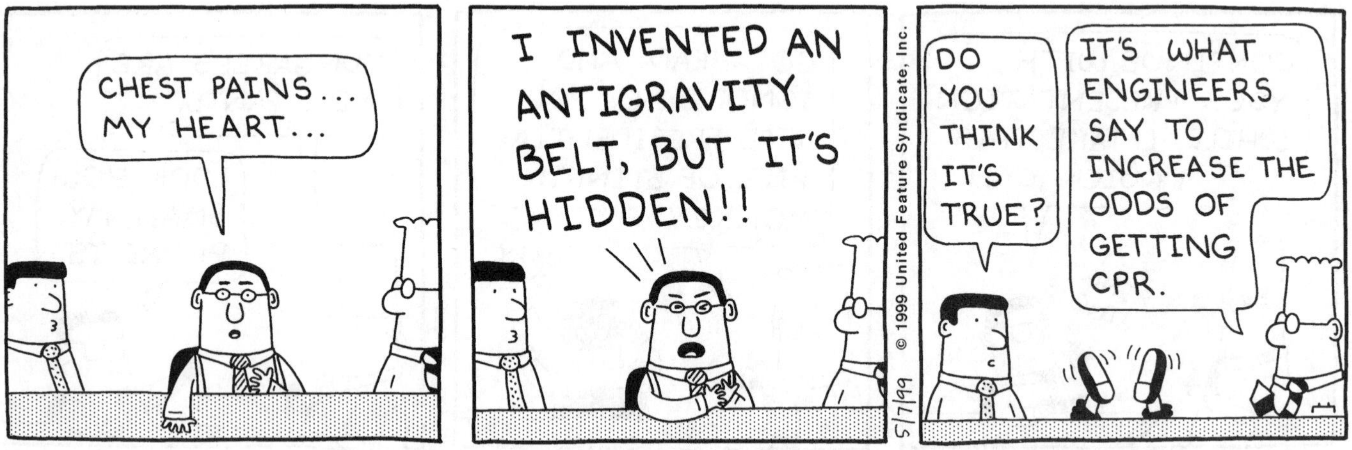
CHEST PAINS... MY HEART...
I INVENTED AN ANTIGRAVITY BELT, BUT IT'S HIDDEN!!
5/7/99 © 1999 United Feature Syndicate, Inc.
DO YOU THINK IT'S TRUE?
IT'S WHAT ENGINEERS SAY TO INCREASE THE ODDS OF GETTING CPR.

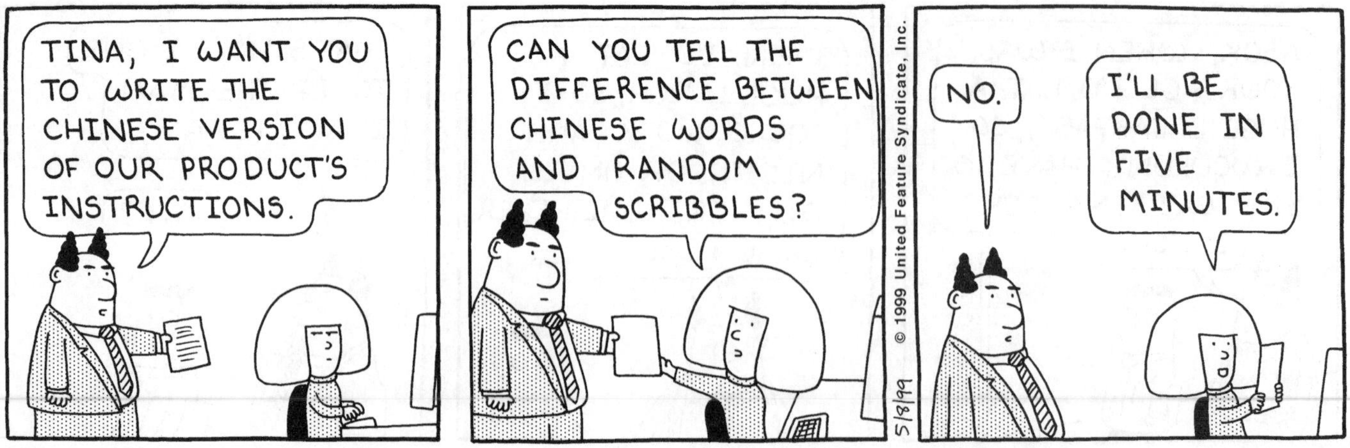
TINA, I WANT YOU TO WRITE THE CHINESE VERSION OF OUR PRODUCT'S INSTRUCTIONS.
CAN YOU TELL THE DIFFERENCE BETWEEN CHINESE WORDS AND RANDOM SCRIBBLES?
5/8/99 © 1999 United Feature Syndicate, Inc.
NO.
I'LL BE DONE IN FIVE MINUTES.

I MADE A FEW UPGRADES TO YOUR DESIGN, ALICE.
DO YOU REALIZE YOU'RE NOT AN ENGINEER?
I'M BETTER! I'M A WELL-ROUNDED GRADUATE OF A LIBERAL ARTS COLLEGE.
THE BROAD EXPOSURE TO DIVERSE TOPICS MADE ME WHAT I AM TODAY.
A MODERN RENAISSANCE MAN.
YOU SCRIBBLED OUT MY TIMING CIRCUIT AND WROTE IN, "MOBY DICK BY CHARLES DICKENS."
EXACTLY. I'LL BET YOU DIDN'T LEARN THAT IN YOUR ENGINEERING CLASSES!
POOR ENGINEERS; THEIR WORLD IS SO SMALL.
5/9/99 © 1999 United Feature Syndicate, Inc.

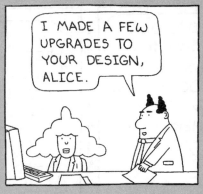

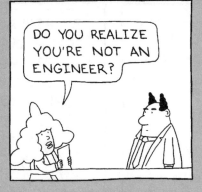

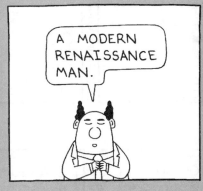

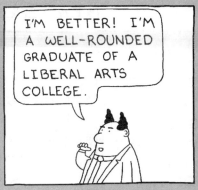

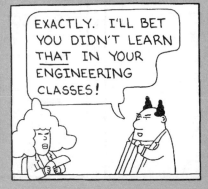

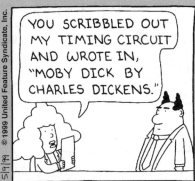

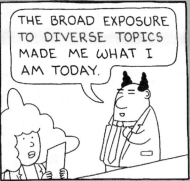

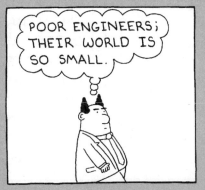

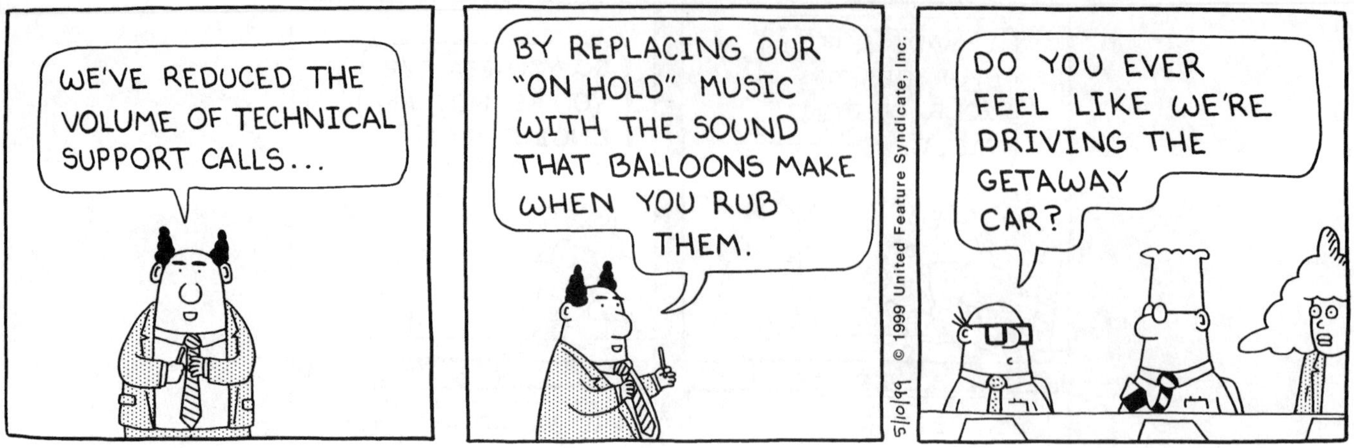
WE'VE REDUCED THE VOLUME OF TECHNICAL SUPPORT CALLS...
BY REPLACING OUR "ON HOLD" MUSIC WITH THE SOUND THAT BALLOONS MAKE WHEN YOU RUB THEM.
5/10/99 © 1999 United Feature Syndicate, Inc.
DO YOU EVER FEEL LIKE WE'RE DRIVING THE GETAWAY CAR?

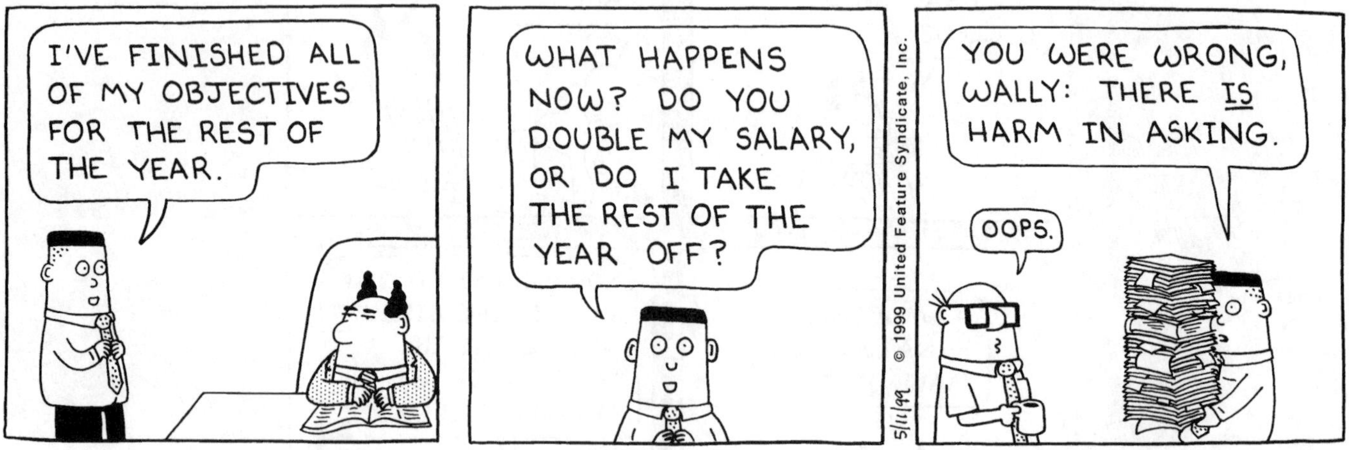
I'VE FINISHED ALL OF MY OBJECTIVES FOR THE REST OF THE YEAR.
WHAT HAPPENS NOW? DO YOU DOUBLE MY SALARY, OR DO I TAKE THE REST OF THE YEAR OFF?
5/11/99 © 1999 United Feature Syndicate, Inc.
YOU WERE WRONG, WALLY: THERE IS HARM IN ASKING.
OOPS.

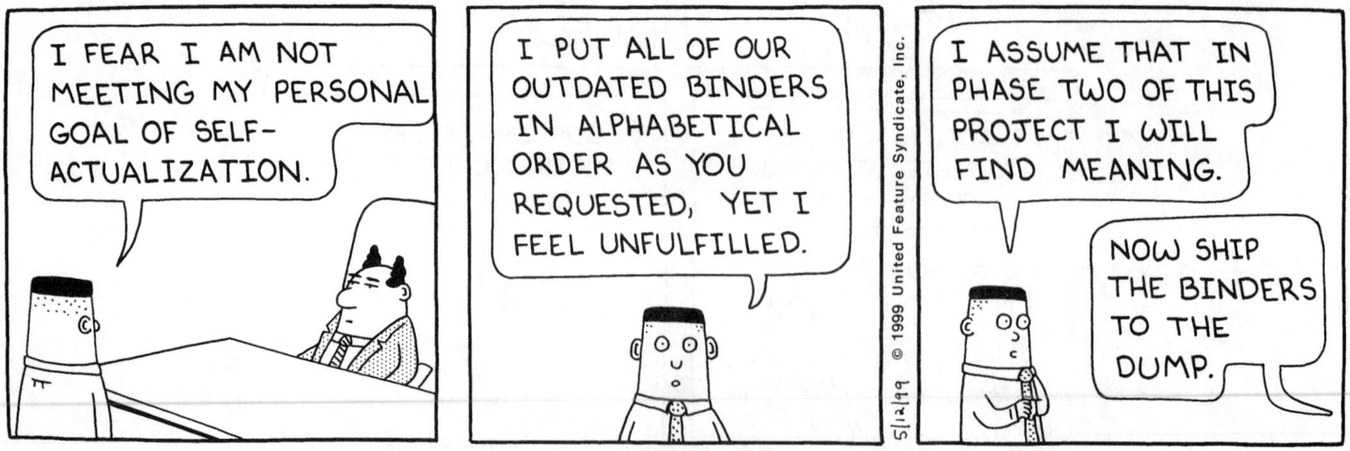
I FEAR I AM NOT MEETING MY PERSONAL GOAL OF SELF-ACTUALIZATION.
I PUT ALL OF OUR OUTDATED BINDERS IN ALPHABETICAL ORDER AS YOU REQUESTED, YET I FEEL UNFULFILLED.
5/12/99 © 1999 United Feature Syndicate, Inc.
I ASSUME THAT IN PHASE TWO OF THIS PROJECT I WILL FIND MEANING.
NOW SHIP THE BINDERS TO THE DUMP.

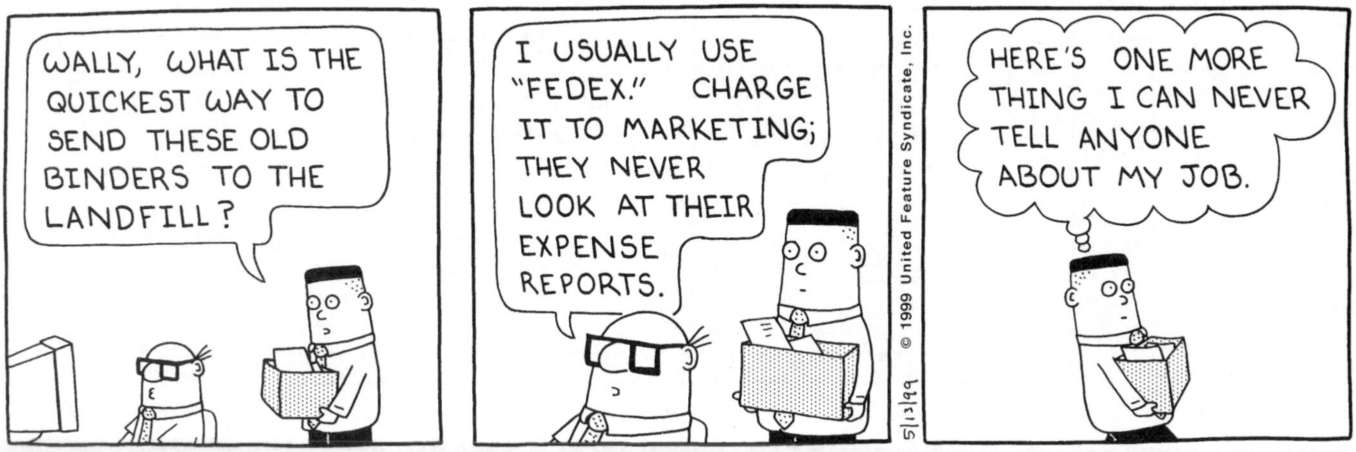
WALLY, WHAT IS THE QUICKEST WAY TO SEND THESE OLD BINDERS TO THE LANDFILL?
I USUALLY USE "FEDEX." CHARGE IT TO MARKETING; THEY NEVER LOOK AT THEIR EXPENSE REPORTS.
5/13/99 © 1999 United Feature Syndicate, Inc.
HERE'S ONE MORE THING I CAN NEVER TELL ANYONE ABOUT MY JOB.

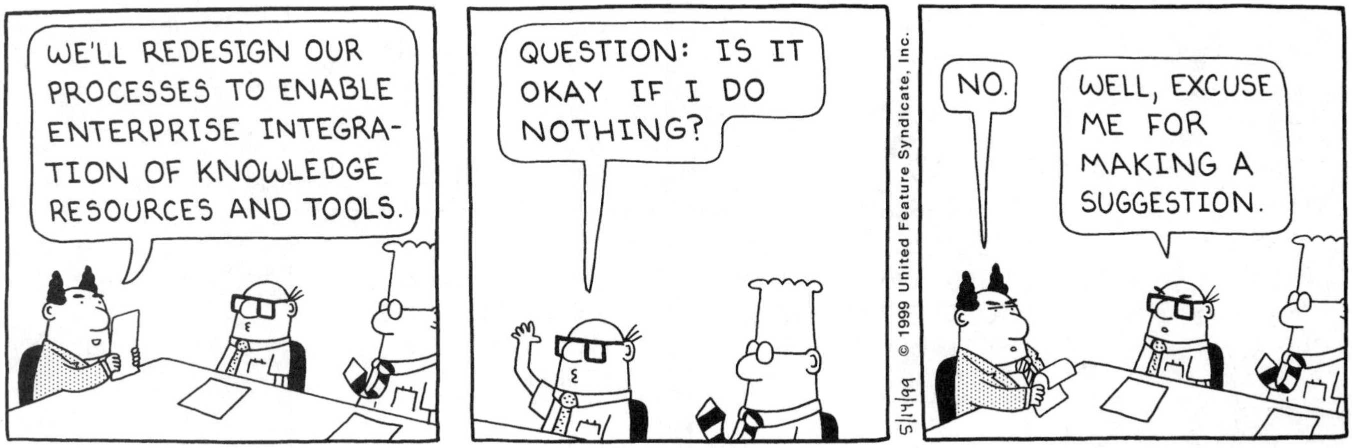
WE'LL REDESIGN OUR PROCESSES TO ENABLE ENTERPRISE INTEGRATION OF KNOWLEDGE RESOURCES AND TOOLS.
QUESTION: IS IT OKAY IF I DO NOTHING?
5/14/99 © 1999 United Feature Syndicate, Inc.
NO.
WELL, EXCUSE ME FOR MAKING A SUGGESTION.

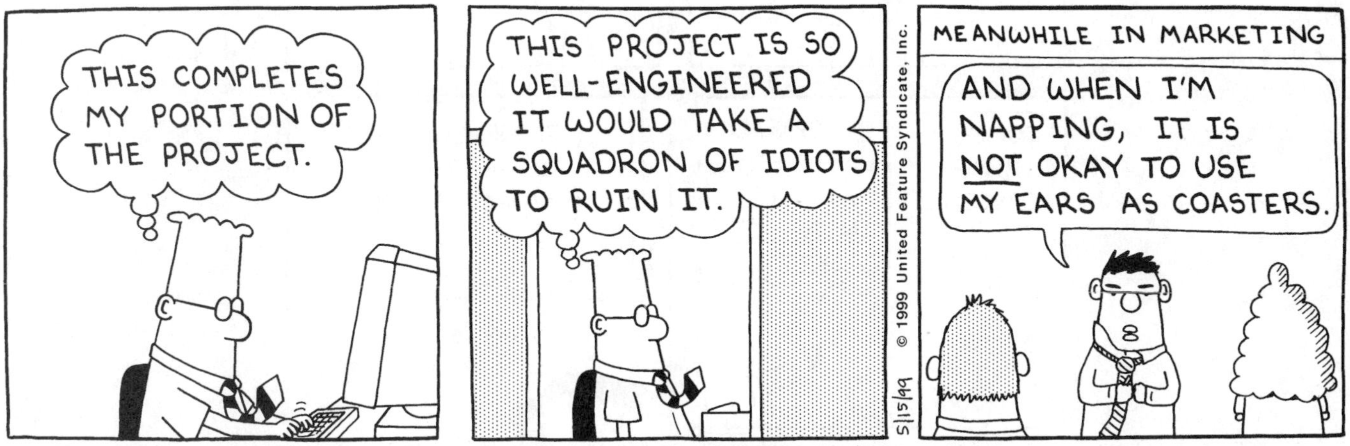
THIS COMPLETES MY PORTION OF THE PROJECT.
THIS PROJECT IS SO WELL-ENGINEERED IT WOULD TAKE A SQUADRON OF IDIOTS TO RUIN IT.
5/15/99 © 1999 United Feature Syndicate, Inc.
MEANWHILE IN MARKETING
AND WHEN I'M NAPPING, IT IS NOT OKAY TO USE MY EARS AS COASTERS.

BLAH BLAH BLAH
I'LL HAVE TO BE PROACTIVE TO ESCAPE THIS BORING MEETING.
I'LL FAKE MY OWN DEATH AND HOPE SOMEONE DRAGS ME INTO THE HALLWAY.
AACK!! MY COFFEE IS POISONED!
MAYBE WE SHOULD DRAG HIM INTO THE HALLWAY.
NO.
LET'S WAIT FOR HIM TO STIFFEN. THEN HE'LL BE EASIER TO DRAG.
© 1999 United Feature Syndicate, Inc.
5/16/99
WE SHOULD POSE HIM BEFORE HE STIFFENS.
SOME-THING OBSCENE?
OR SPREAD EAGLE, SO HE WON'T FIT IN A CASKET.
IT NEVER PAYS TO BE THE PROACTIVE ONE.

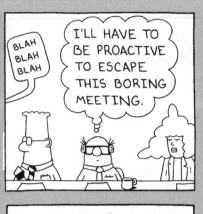

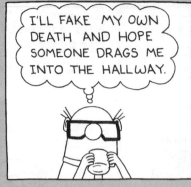

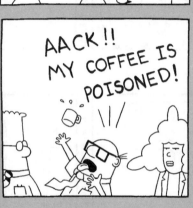

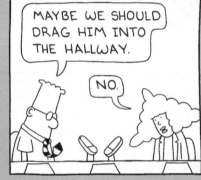

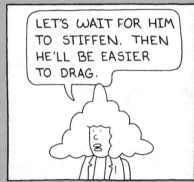

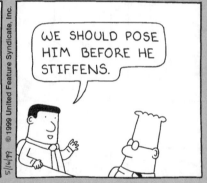

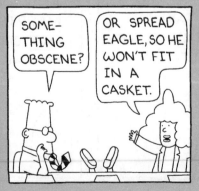

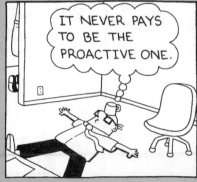

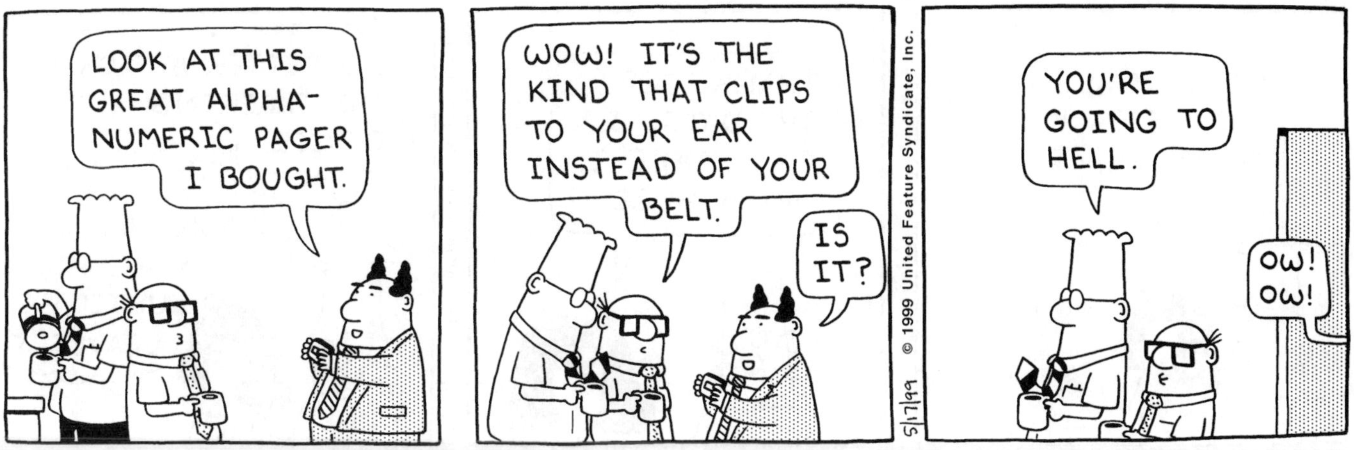
LOOK AT THIS GREAT ALPHA-NUMERIC PAGER I BOUGHT.
WOW! IT'S THE KIND THAT CLIPS TO YOUR EAR INSTEAD OF YOUR BELT.
IS IT?
5/17/99 © 1999 United Feature Syndicate, Inc.
YOU'RE GOING TO HELL.
OW! OW!

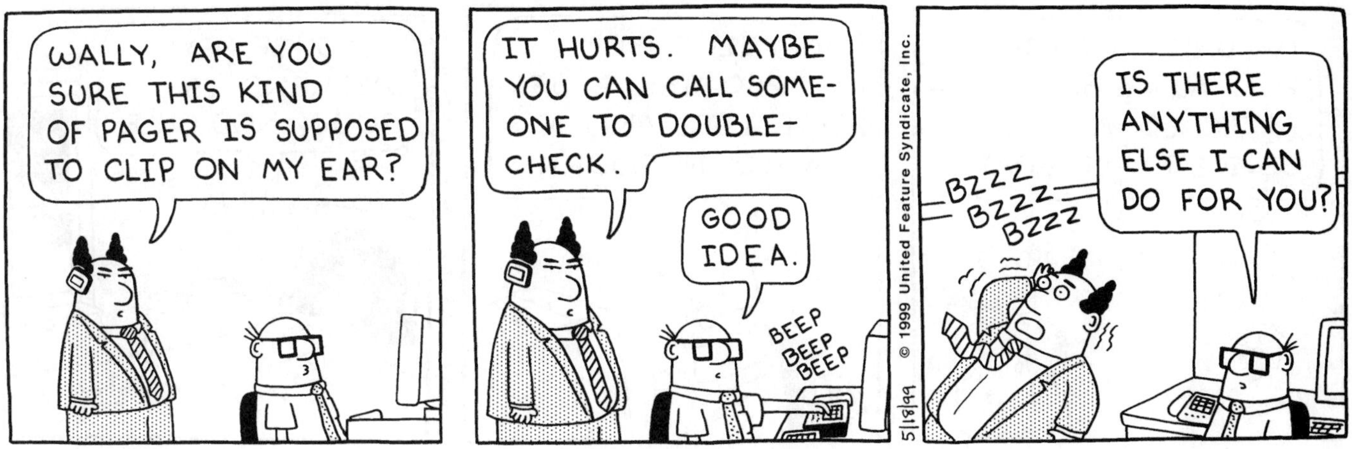
WALLY, ARE YOU SURE THIS KIND OF PAGER IS SUPPOSED TO CLIP ON MY EAR?
IT HURTS. MAYBE YOU CAN CALL SOME-ONE TO DOUBLE-CHECK.
GOOD IDEA.
BEEP BEEP BEEP
5/18/99 © 1999 United Feature Syndicate, Inc.
BZZZ BZZZ BZZZ
IS THERE ANYTHING ELSE I CAN DO FOR YOU?

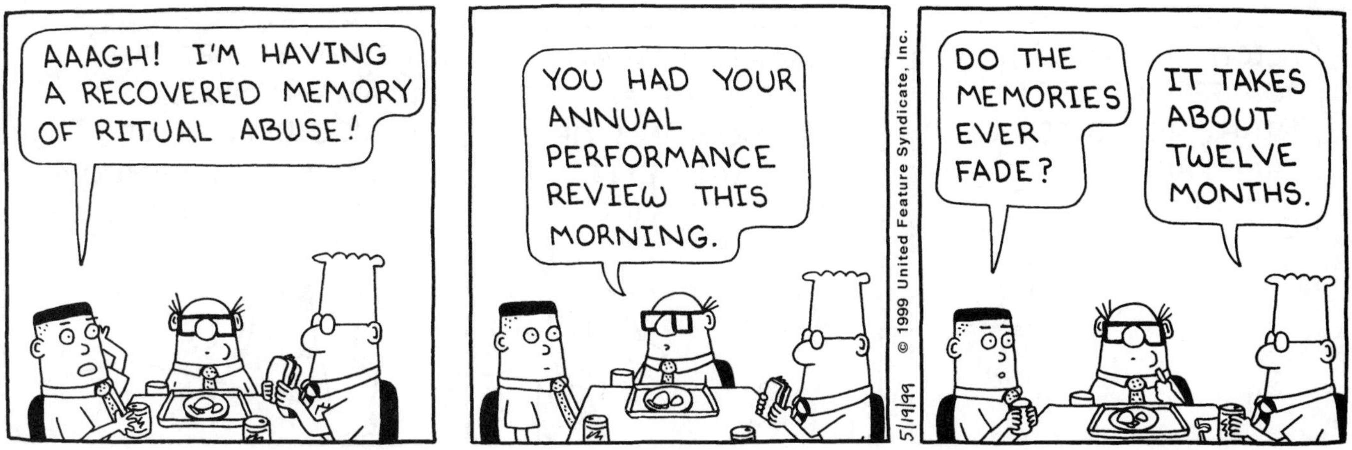
AAAGH! I'M HAVING A RECOVERED MEMORY OF RITUAL ABUSE!
YOU HAD YOUR ANNUAL PERFORMANCE REVIEW THIS MORNING.
5/19/99 © 1999 United Feature Syndicate, Inc.
DO THE MEMORIES EVER FADE?
IT TAKES ABOUT TWELVE MONTHS.

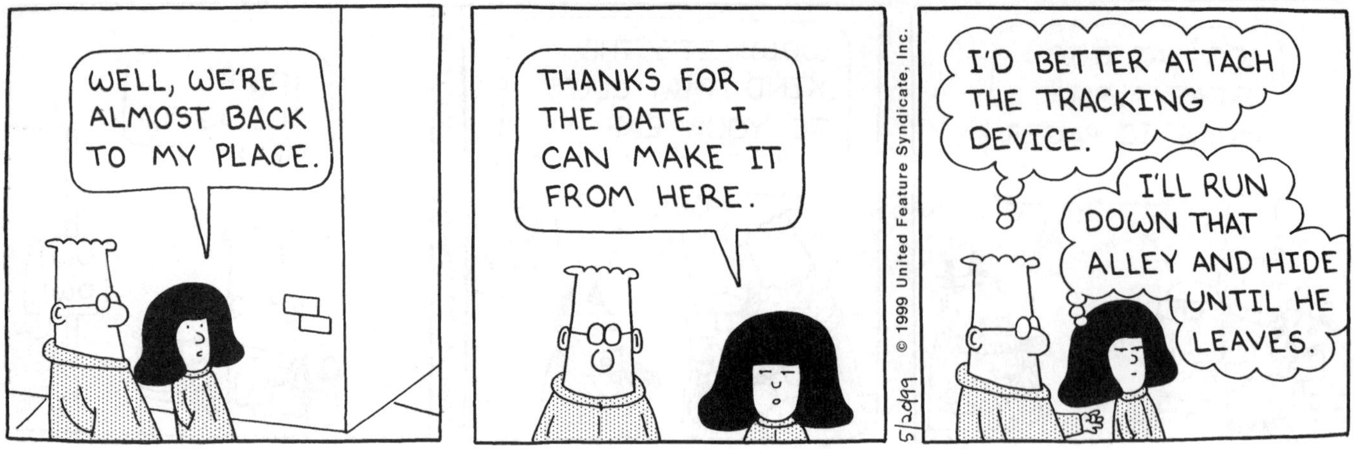
WELL, WE'RE ALMOST BACK TO MY PLACE.
THANKS FOR THE DATE. I CAN MAKE IT FROM HERE.
© 1999 United Feature Syndicate, Inc.
5/20/99
I'D BETTER ATTACH THE TRACKING DEVICE.
I'LL RUN DOWN THAT ALLEY AND HIDE UNTIL HE LEAVES.

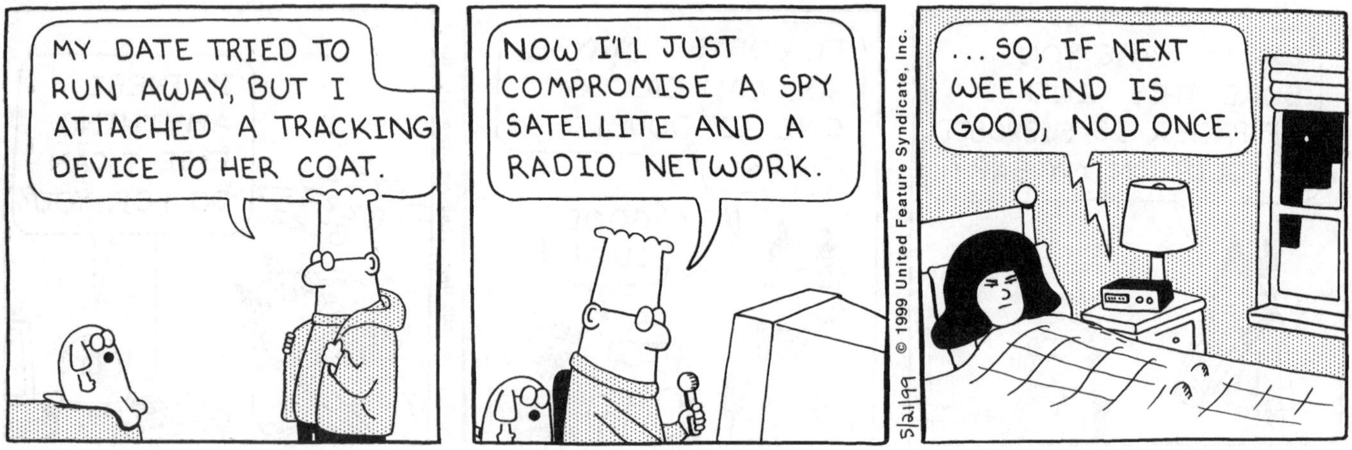
MY DATE TRIED TO RUN AWAY, BUT I ATTACHED A TRACKING DEVICE TO HER COAT.
NOW I'LL JUST COMPROMISE A SPY SATELLITE AND A RADIO NETWORK.
© 1999 United Feature Syndicate, Inc.
5/21/99
... SO, IF NEXT WEEKEND IS GOOD, NOD ONCE.

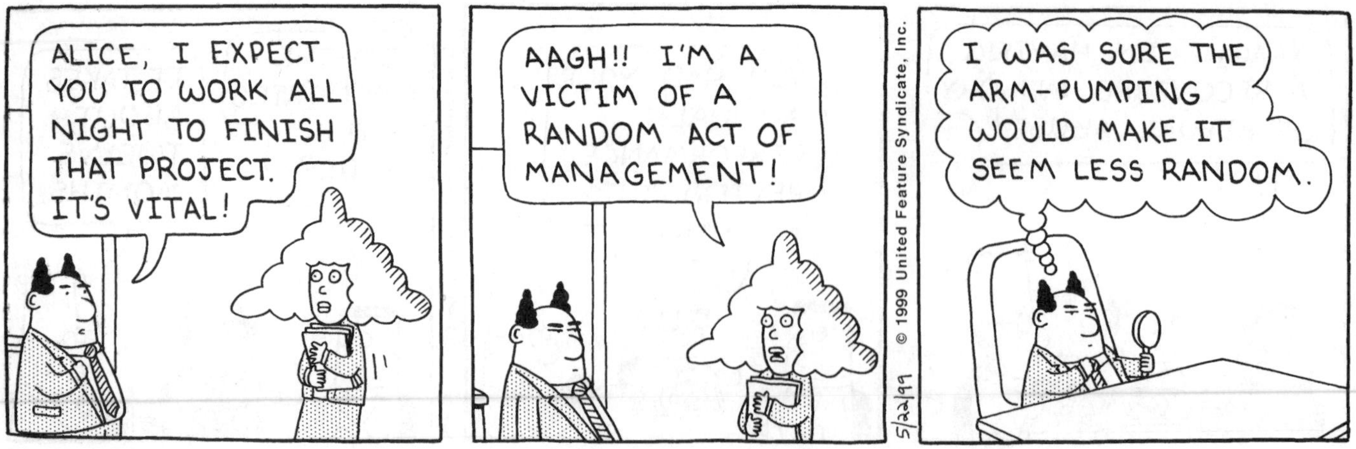
ALICE, I EXPECT YOU TO WORK ALL NIGHT TO FINISH THAT PROJECT. IT'S VITAL!
AAGH!! I'M A VICTIM OF A RANDOM ACT OF MANAGEMENT!
© 1999 United Feature Syndicate, Inc.
5/22/99
I WAS SURE THE ARM-PUMPING WOULD MAKE IT SEEM LESS RANDOM.

CAN I ASK A QUICK QUESTION?
I DOUBT IT.
OH, SURE, IT'LL START AS AN INNOCENT, WORK-RELATED QUESTION.
THEN YOU'LL TRY TO IMPRESS ME WITH YOUR KNOWLEDGE OF ENGINEERING...
...IN THE PATHETIC HOPE THAT I VALUE INTELLIGENCE OVER PHYSICAL APPEARANCE.
5/23/99 © 1999 United Feature Syndicate, Inc.
WELL, I DON'T!! I ONLY CARE ABOUT LOOKS!
DO YOU DRIVE A RED BMW?
THE LIGHTS ARE ON.
AND YOU STILL TRIED TO ASK HER OUT?
SHE'S HARD TO READ.

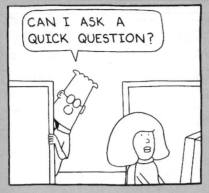

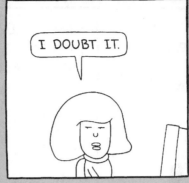

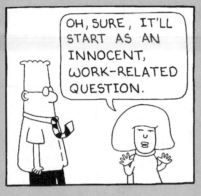

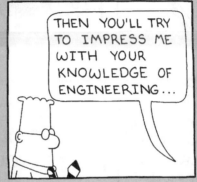

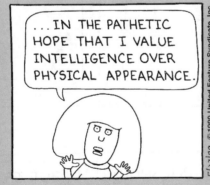

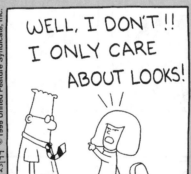

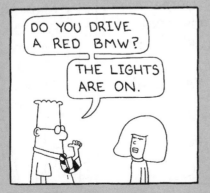

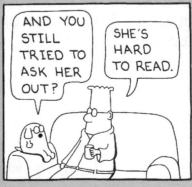

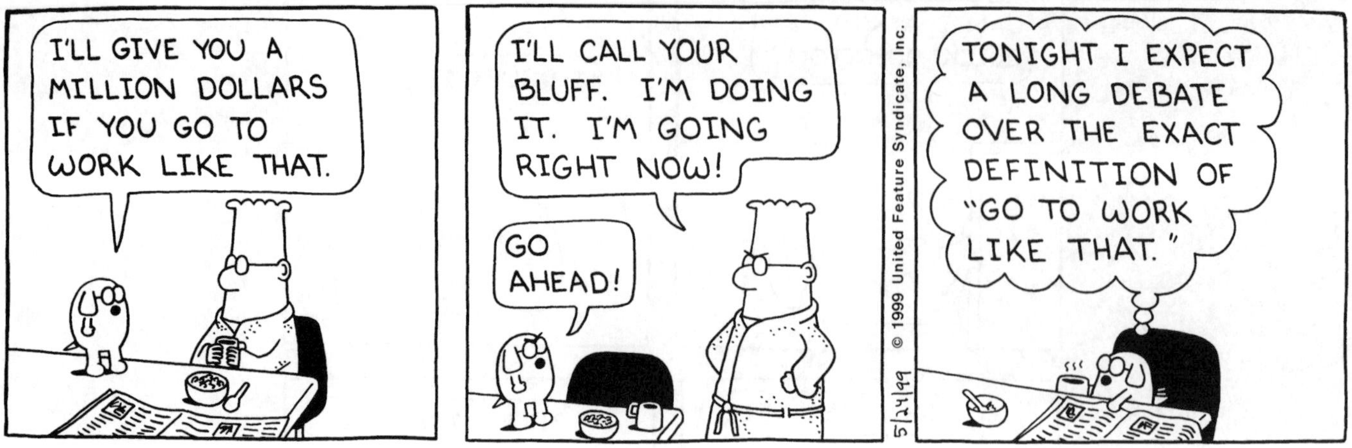
I'LL GIVE YOU A MILLION DOLLARS IF YOU GO TO WORK LIKE THAT.
I'LL CALL YOUR BLUFF. I'M DOING IT. I'M GOING RIGHT NOW!
GO AHEAD!
TONIGHT I EXPECT A LONG DEBATE OVER THE EXACT DEFINITION OF "GO TO WORK LIKE THAT."
5/24/99 © 1999 United Feature Syndicate, Inc.

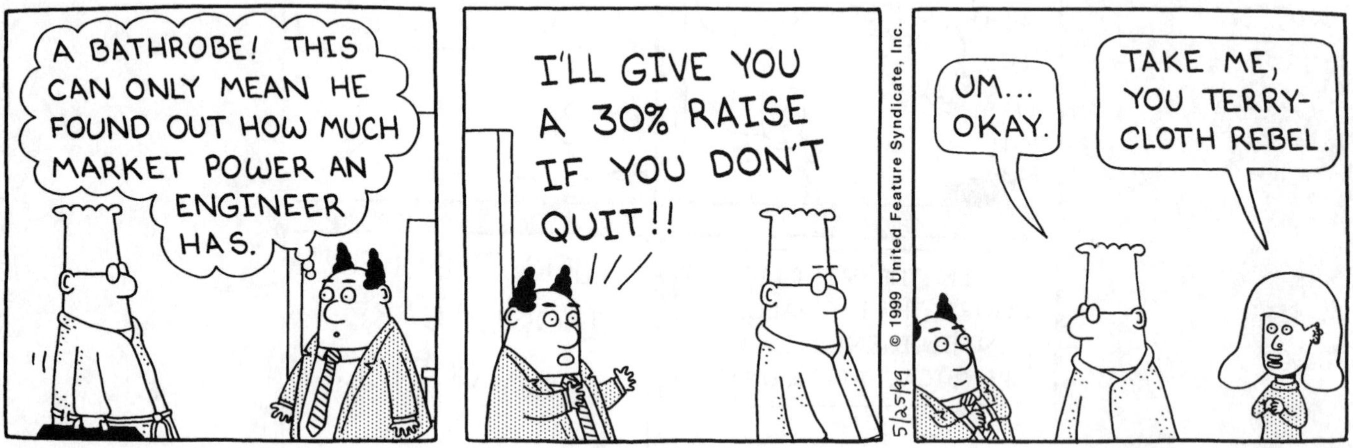
A BATHROBE! THIS CAN ONLY MEAN HE FOUND OUT HOW MUCH MARKET POWER AN ENGINEER HAS.
I'LL GIVE YOU A 30% RAISE IF YOU DON'T QUIT!!
UM... OKAY.
TAKE ME, YOU TERRY-CLOTH REBEL.
5/25/99 © 1999 United Feature Syndicate, Inc.

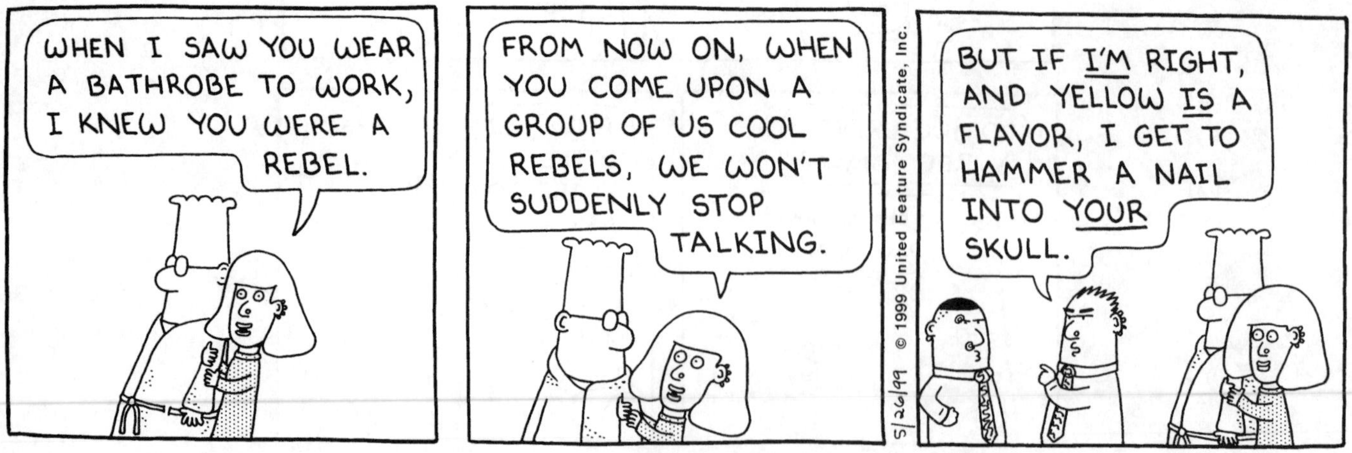
WHEN I SAW YOU WEAR A BATHROBE TO WORK, I KNEW YOU WERE A REBEL.
FROM NOW ON, WHEN YOU COME UPON A GROUP OF US COOL REBELS, WE WON'T SUDDENLY STOP TALKING.
BUT IF I'M RIGHT, AND YELLOW IS A FLAVOR, I GET TO HAMMER A NAIL INTO YOUR SKULL.
5/26/99 © 1999 United Feature Syndicate, Inc.

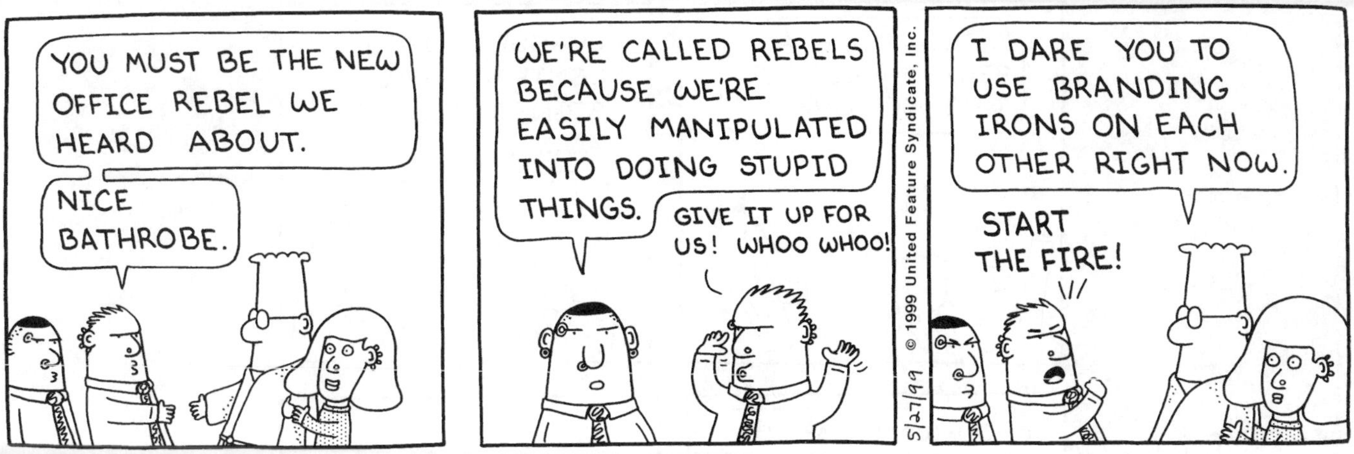
YOU MUST BE THE NEW OFFICE REBEL WE HEARD ABOUT.
NICE BATHROBE.
WE'RE CALLED REBELS BECAUSE WE'RE EASILY MANIPULATED INTO DOING STUPID THINGS.
GIVE IT UP FOR US! WHOO WHOO!
5/27/99 © 1999 United Feature Syndicate, Inc.
I DARE YOU TO USE BRANDING IRONS ON EACH OTHER RIGHT NOW.
START THE FIRE!

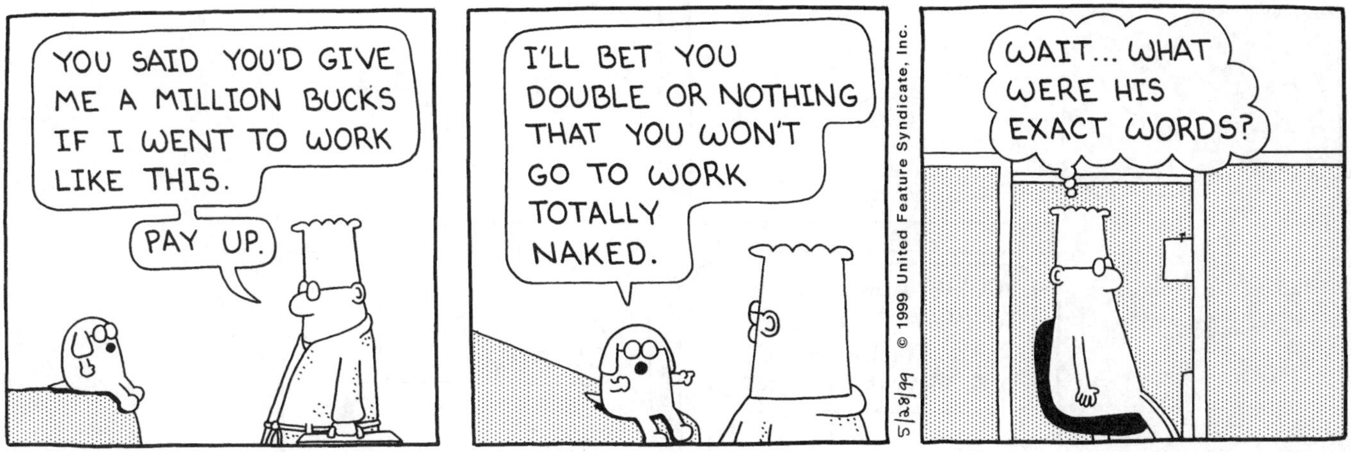
YOU SAID YOU'D GIVE ME A MILLION BUCKS IF I WENT TO WORK LIKE THIS.
PAY UP.
I'LL BET YOU DOUBLE OR NOTHING THAT YOU WON'T GO TO WORK TOTALLY NAKED.
5/28/99 © 1999 United Feature Syndicate, Inc.
WAIT... WHAT WERE HIS EXACT WORDS?

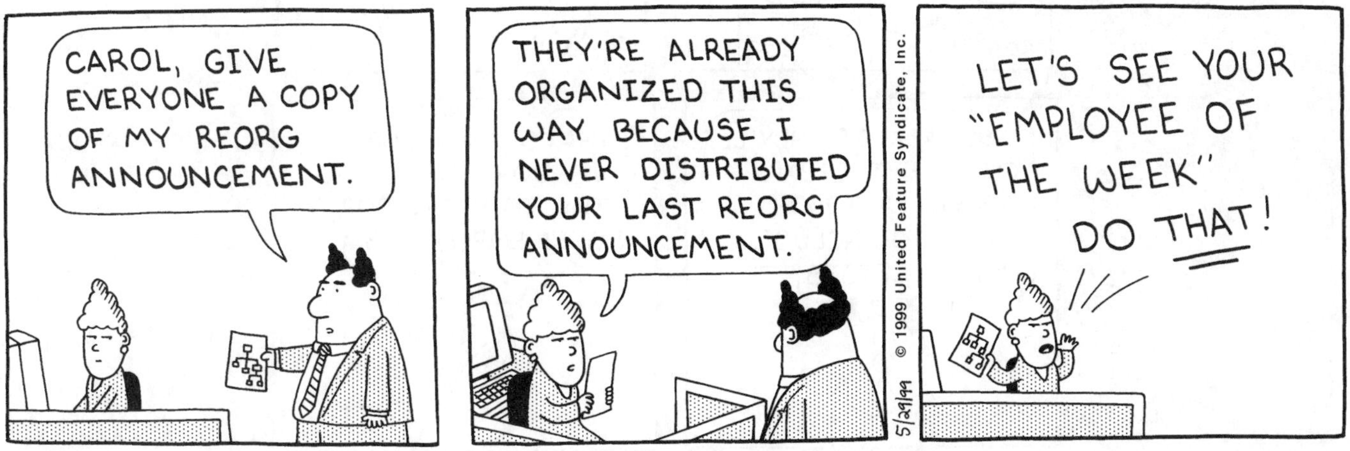
CAROL, GIVE EVERYONE A COPY OF MY REORG ANNOUNCEMENT.
THEY'RE ALREADY ORGANIZED THIS WAY BECAUSE I NEVER DISTRIBUTED YOUR LAST REORG ANNOUNCEMENT.
5/29/99 © 1999 United Feature Syndicate, Inc.
LET'S SEE YOUR "EMPLOYEE OF THE WEEK"
DO THAT!

ALICE, MAKE A FEW CHANGES TO THIS CONTRACT.
CHANGES? THIS CONTRACT WAS SIGNED MONTHS AGO.
IT DOESN'T HURT TO ASK.
YOU WANT ME TO ASK FOR A SIXTY PERCENT DISCOUNT?
NO ONE SAID IT WOULD BE EASY.
YOU'RE ASKING ME TO BE A CLUELESS JERK IN FRONT OF OUR PRIMARY VENDOR.
5/30/99 © 1999 United Feature Syndicate, Inc.
PLEASE DON'T ASK ME TO DO THIS.
AND ASK IF THEY'LL CHANGE THE PART ABOUT "ACTS OF GOD" TO INCLUDE POLTERGEISTS.
THAT'S WHY OUR VENDORS NEVER TRY TO STEAL OUR BEST EMPLOYEES.

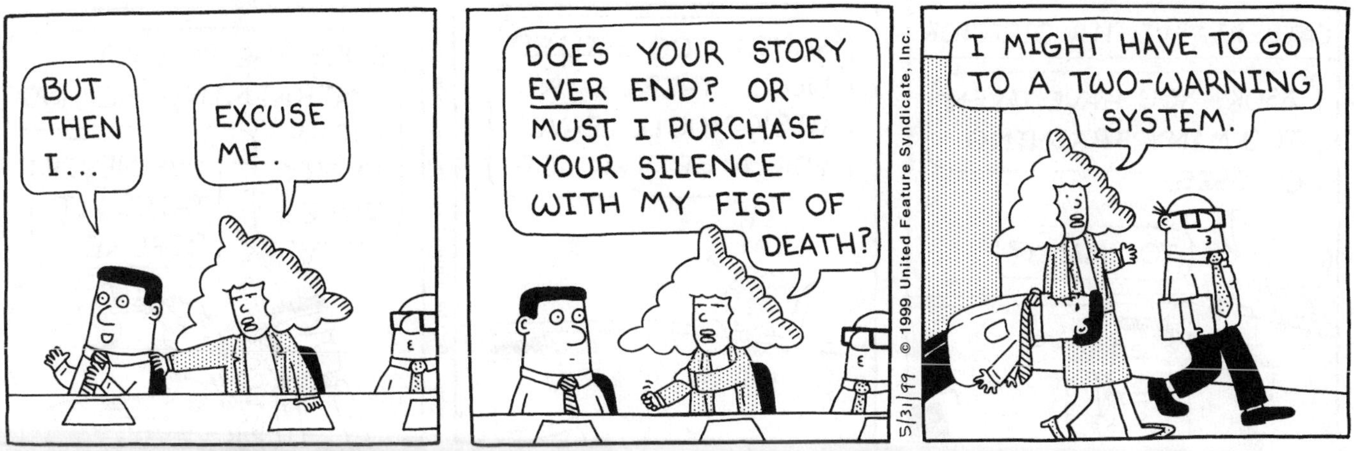
BUT THEN I...
EXCUSE ME.
DOES YOUR STORY EVER END? OR MUST I PURCHASE YOUR SILENCE WITH MY FIST OF DEATH?
5/31/99 © 1999 United Feature Syndicate, Inc.
I MIGHT HAVE TO GO TO A TWO-WARNING SYSTEM.

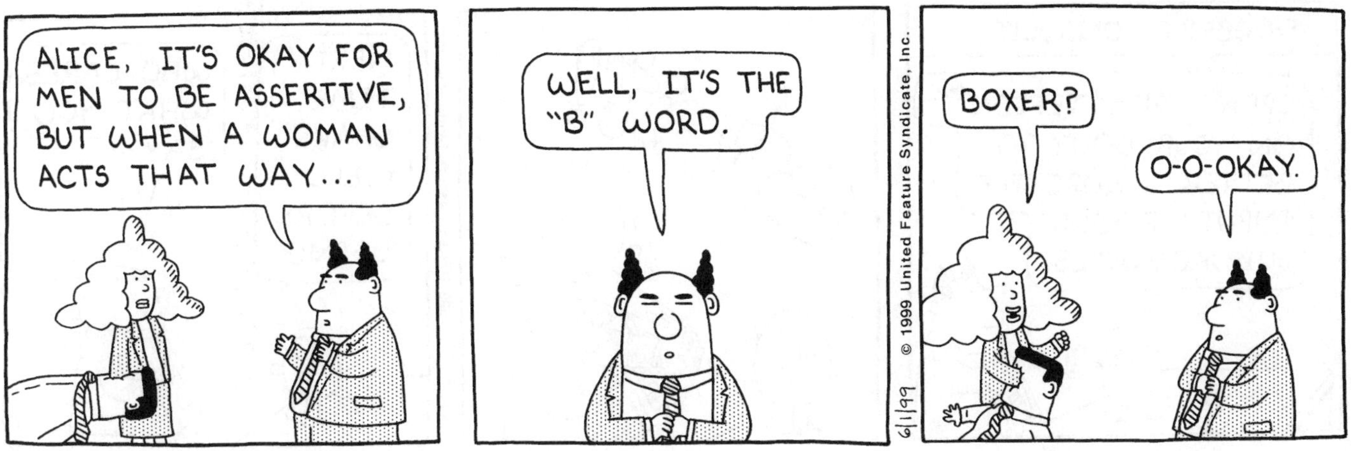
ALICE, IT'S OKAY FOR MEN TO BE ASSERTIVE, BUT WHEN A WOMAN ACTS THAT WAY...
WELL, IT'S THE "B" WORD.
6/1/99 © 1999 United Feature Syndicate, Inc.
BOXER?
O-O-OKAY.

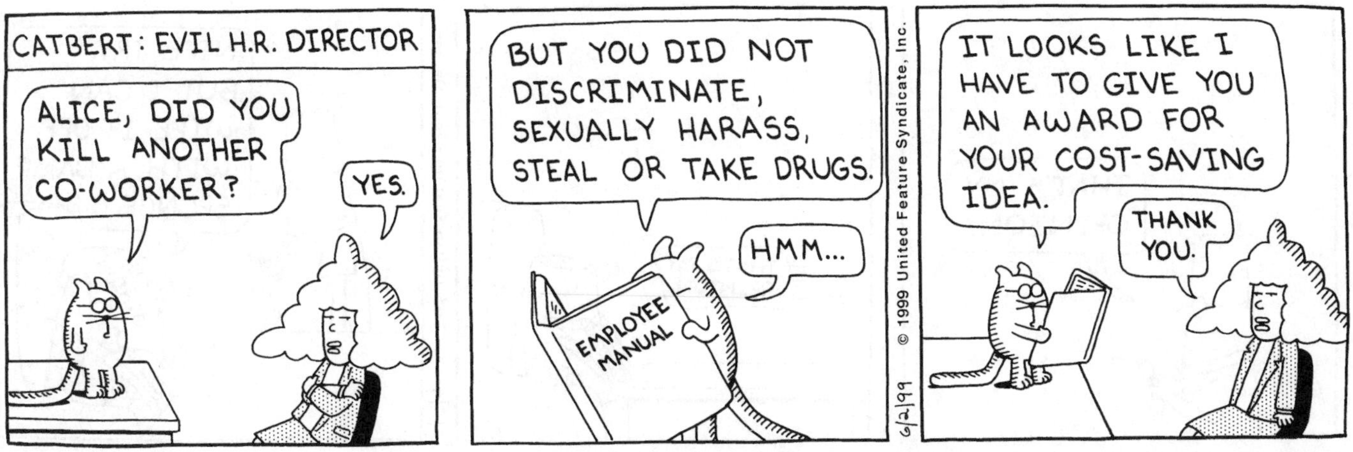
CATBERT: EVIL H.R. DIRECTOR
ALICE, DID YOU KILL ANOTHER CO-WORKER?
YES.
BUT YOU DID NOT DISCRIMINATE, SEXUALLY HARASS, STEAL OR TAKE DRUGS.
HMM...
EMPLOYEE MANUAL
6/2/99 © 1999 United Feature Syndicate, Inc.
IT LOOKS LIKE I HAVE TO GIVE YOU AN AWARD FOR YOUR COST-SAVING IDEA.
THANK YOU.

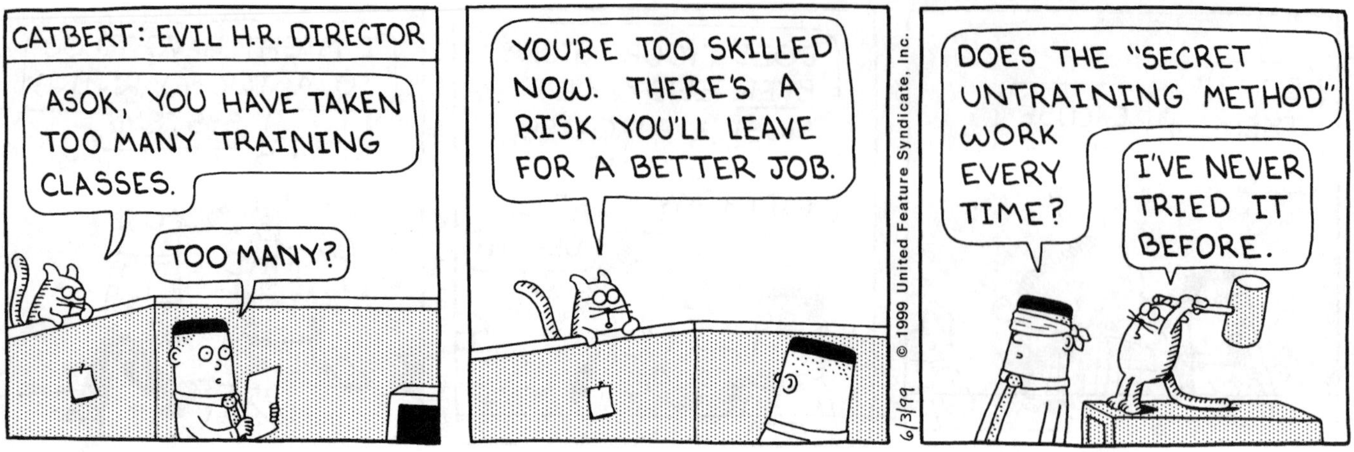
CATBERT: EVIL H.R. DIRECTOR
ASOK, YOU HAVE TAKEN TOO MANY TRAINING CLASSES.
TOO MANY?
YOU'RE TOO SKILLED NOW. THERE'S A RISK YOU'LL LEAVE FOR A BETTER JOB.
6/3/99 © 1999 United Feature Syndicate, Inc.
DOES THE "SECRET UNTRAINING METHOD" WORK EVERY TIME?
I'VE NEVER TRIED IT BEFORE.

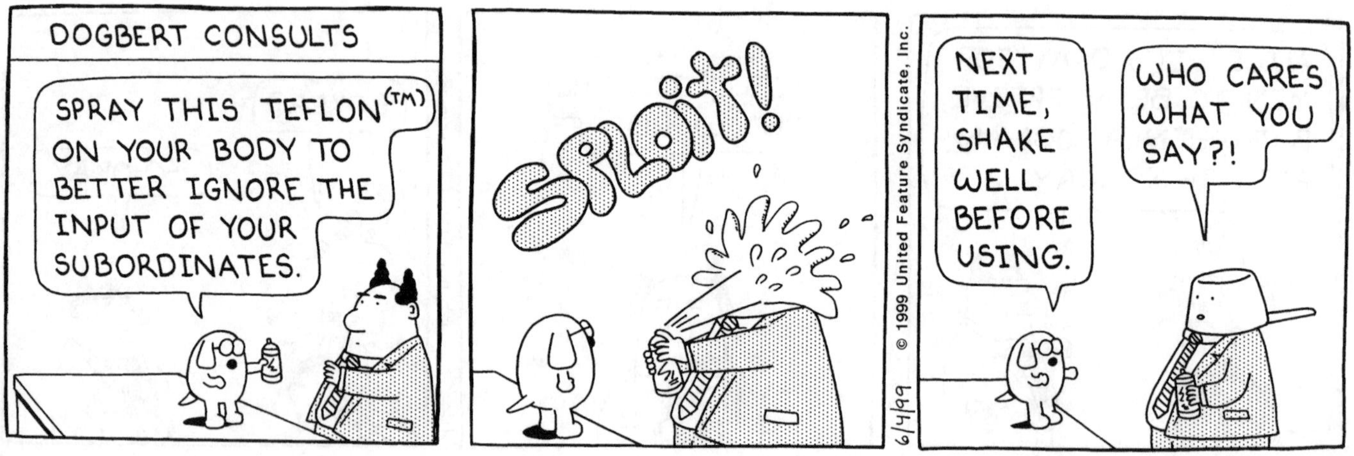
DOGBERT CONSULTS
SPRAY THIS TEFLON(TM) ON YOUR BODY TO BETTER IGNORE THE INPUT OF YOUR SUBORDINATES.
SPLOIT!
6/4/99 © 1999 United Feature Syndicate, Inc.
NEXT TIME, SHAKE WELL BEFORE USING.
WHO CARES WHAT YOU SAY?!

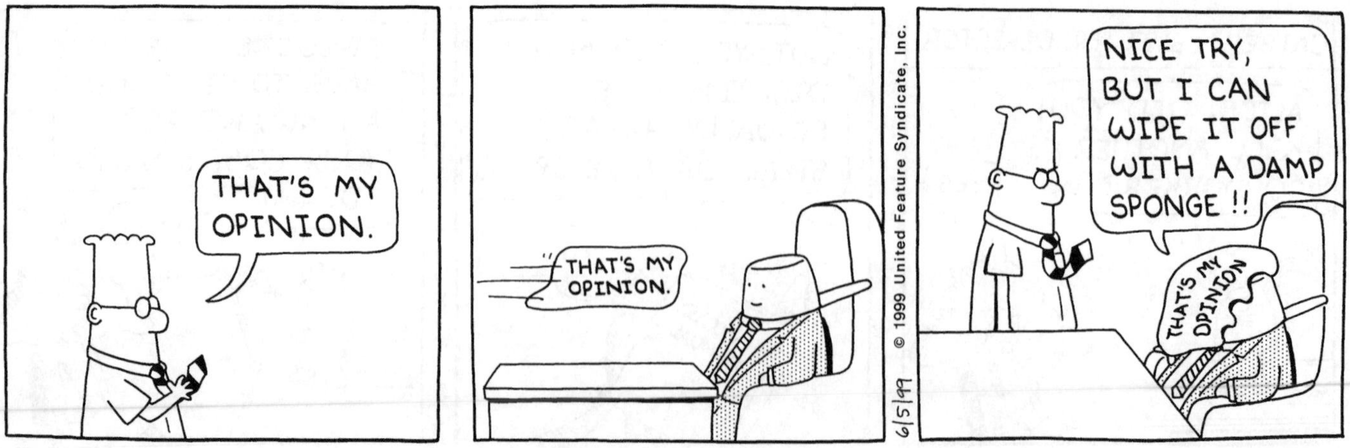
THAT'S MY OPINION.
THAT'S MY OPINION.
6/5/99 © 1999 United Feature Syndicate, Inc.
NICE TRY, BUT I CAN WIPE IT OFF WITH A DAMP SPONGE !!
THAT'S MY OPINION

E-MAIL TWO COPIES TO ME WHEN YOU'RE DONE.
TWO COPIES?
IT'S E-MAIL.
SO?
NEVER MIND.
I'LL E-MAIL TWO COPIES.
AND FAX A COPY ON GREEN PAPER FOR MY FILES.
GREEN? IT'S A FAX!
© 1999 United Feature Syndicate, Inc.
6/6/99
AND BRING ME A HARD COPY OF THE INTERNET SO I CAN DO SOME SERIOUS SURFING.
MOTIVATION ... GONE ... LOSING... CONSCIOUSNESS...
HOW DID I END UP WITH ALL THE LAZY EMPLOYEES?

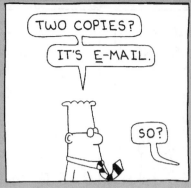

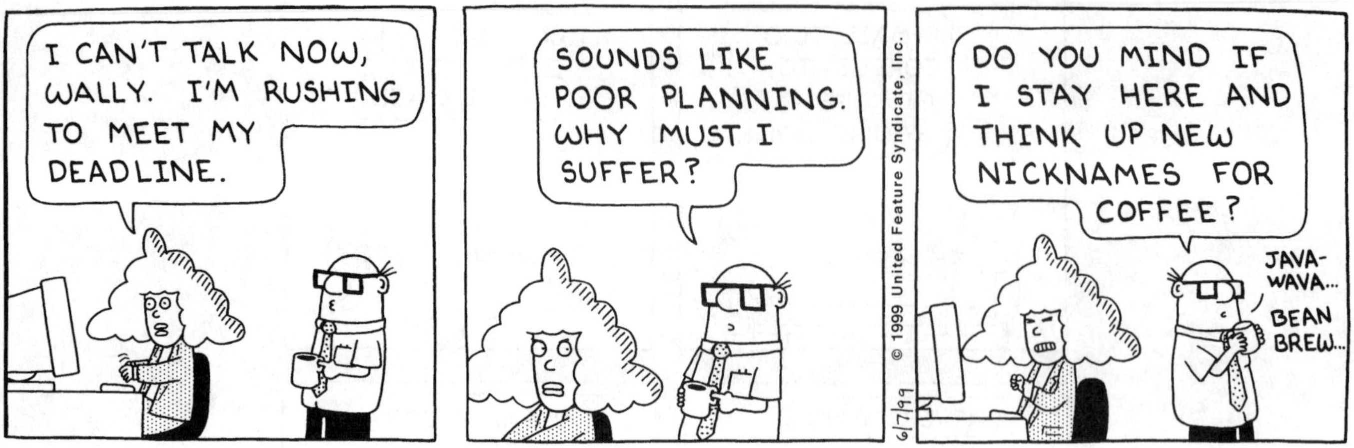
I CAN'T TALK NOW, WALLY. I'M RUSHING TO MEET MY DEADLINE.
SOUNDS LIKE POOR PLANNING. WHY MUST I SUFFER?
DO YOU MIND IF I STAY HERE AND THINK UP NEW NICKNAMES FOR COFFEE?
JAVA-WAVA... BEAN BREW...
© 1999 United Feature Syndicate, Inc.
6/7/99

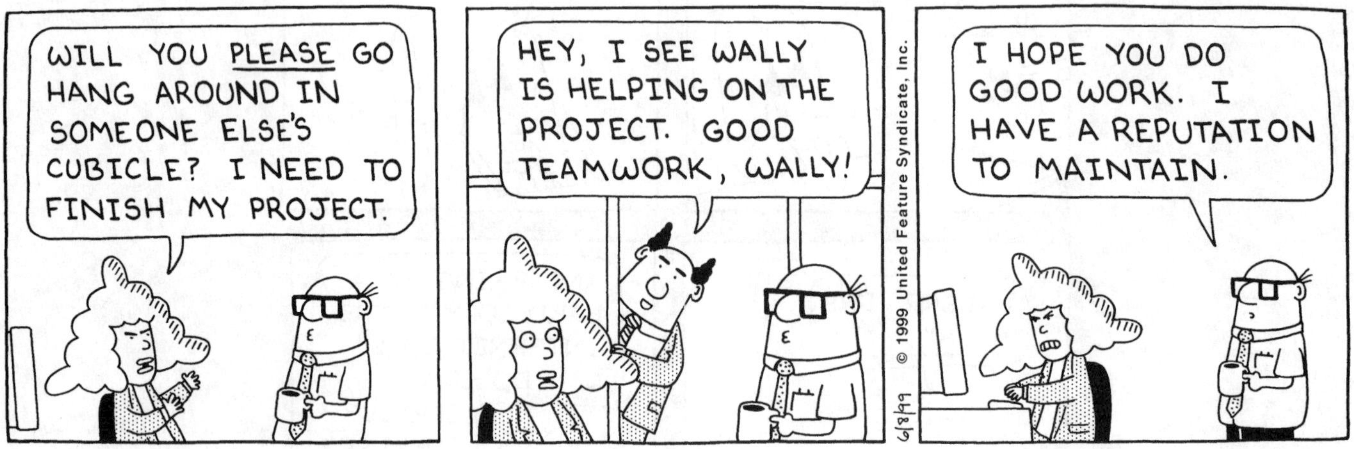
WILL YOU PLEASE GO HANG AROUND IN SOMEONE ELSE'S CUBICLE? I NEED TO FINISH MY PROJECT.
HEY, I SEE WALLY IS HELPING ON THE PROJECT. GOOD TEAMWORK, WALLY!
I HOPE YOU DO GOOD WORK. I HAVE A REPUTATION TO MAINTAIN.
© 1999 United Feature Syndicate, Inc.
6/8/99

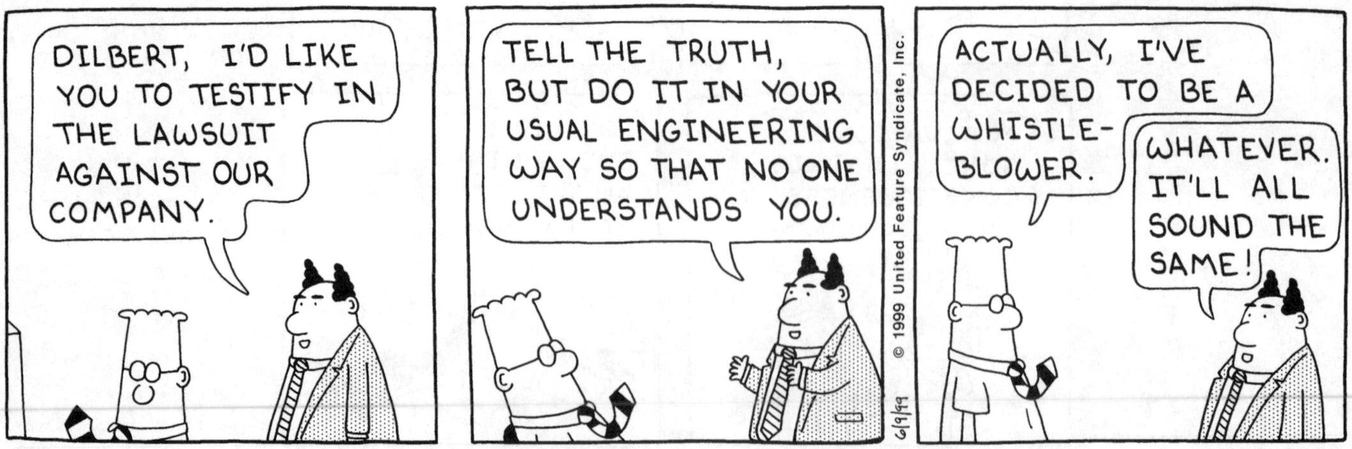
DILBERT, I'D LIKE YOU TO TESTIFY IN THE LAWSUIT AGAINST OUR COMPANY.
TELL THE TRUTH, BUT DO IT IN YOUR USUAL ENGINEERING WAY SO THAT NO ONE UNDERSTANDS YOU.
ACTUALLY, I'VE DECIDED TO BE A WHISTLE-BLOWER.
WHATEVER. IT'LL ALL SOUND THE SAME!
© 1999 United Feature Syndicate, Inc.
6/9/99

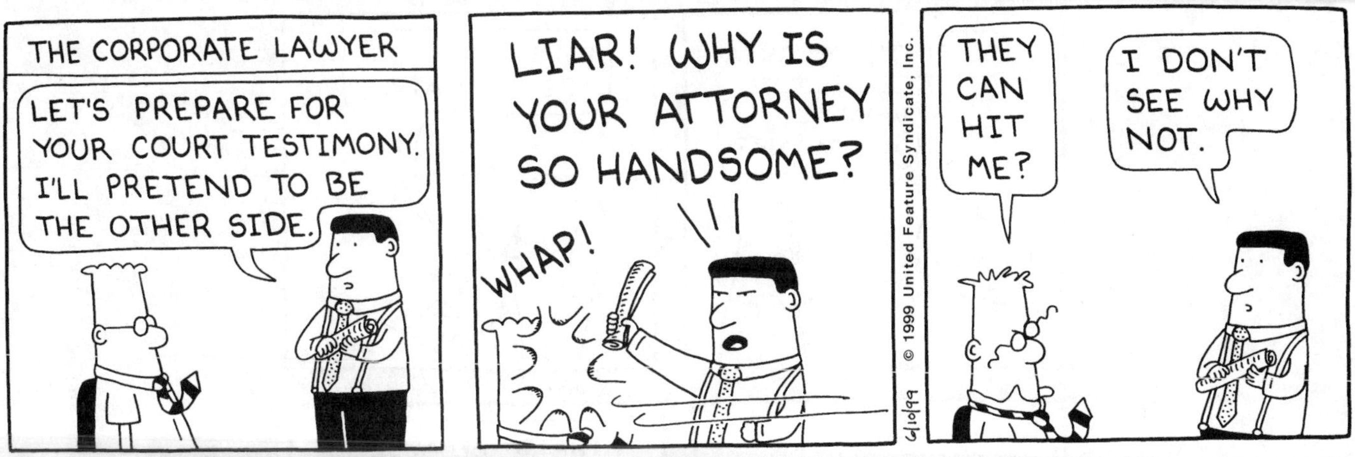
THE CORPORATE LAWYER
LET'S PREPARE FOR YOUR COURT TESTIMONY. I'LL PRETEND TO BE THE OTHER SIDE.
LIAR! WHY IS YOUR ATTORNEY SO HANDSOME?
WHAP!
THEY CAN HIT ME?
I DON'T SEE WHY NOT.
6/10/99 © 1999 United Feature Syndicate, Inc.

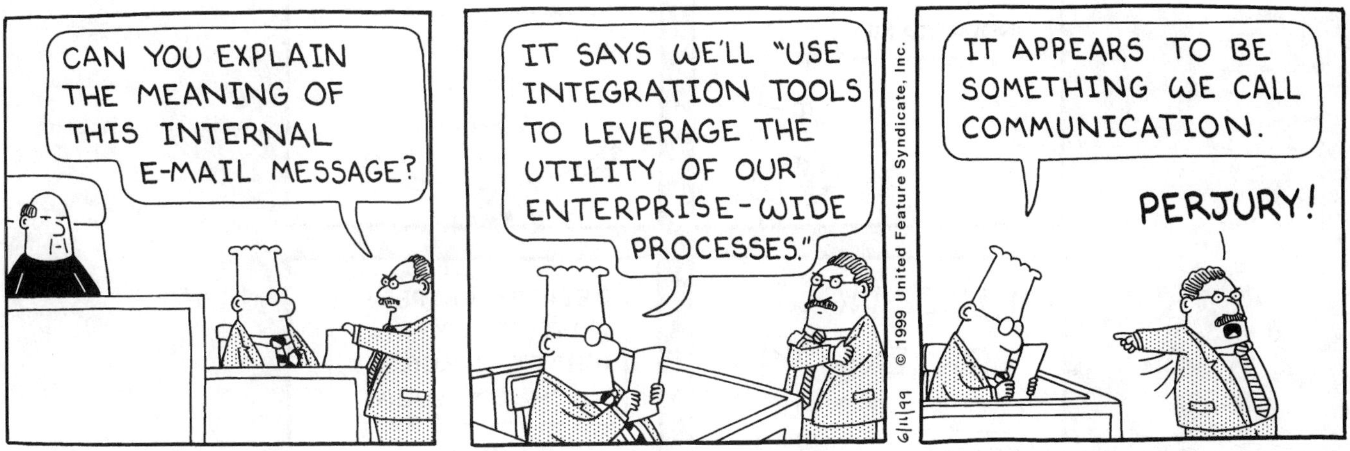
CAN YOU EXPLAIN THE MEANING OF THIS INTERNAL E-MAIL MESSAGE?
IT SAYS WE'LL "USE INTEGRATION TOOLS TO LEVERAGE THE UTILITY OF OUR ENTERPRISE-WIDE PROCESSES."
IT APPEARS TO BE SOMETHING WE CALL COMMUNICATION.
PERJURY!
6/11/99 © 1999 United Feature Syndicate, Inc.

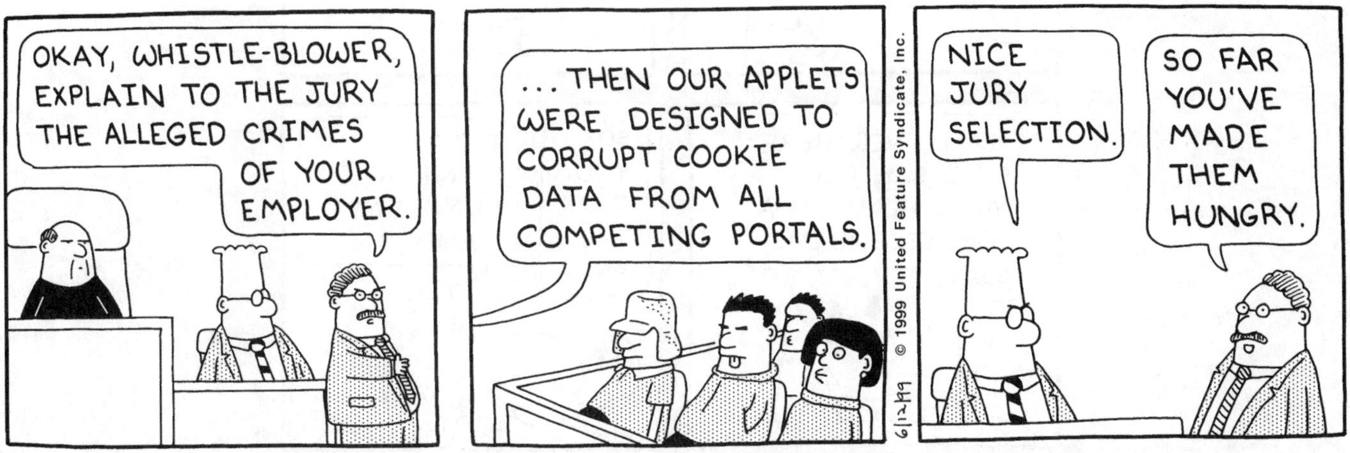
OKAY, WHISTLE-BLOWER, EXPLAIN TO THE JURY THE ALLEGED CRIMES OF YOUR EMPLOYER.
... THEN OUR APPLETS WERE DESIGNED TO CORRUPT COOKIE DATA FROM ALL COMPETING PORTALS.
NICE JURY SELECTION.
SO FAR YOU'VE MADE THEM HUNGRY.
6/12/99 © 1999 United Feature Syndicate, Inc.

SO, THAT'S MY IDEA.
WHAT DO YOU THINK?
DILBERT, YOU ARE SO NAIVE.
THERE ARE MANY THINGS YOU DON'T UNDERSTAND.
THAT'S BECAUSE YOU NEVER TELL ME ANYTHING!
LIKE NOW, FOR EXAMPLE!
DILBERT, DILBERT, DILBERT...
JEEPERS CRIPES! JUST TELL ME WHAT'S WRONG WITH MY IDEA!
LEAN OVER HERE SO I CAN PAT YOUR HEAD IN A CONDESCENDING WAY.
SO YOU TOOK THE PAT?
I DIDN'T WANT TO LEAVE EMPTY-HANDED.
6/13/99 © 1999 United Feature Syndicate, Inc.

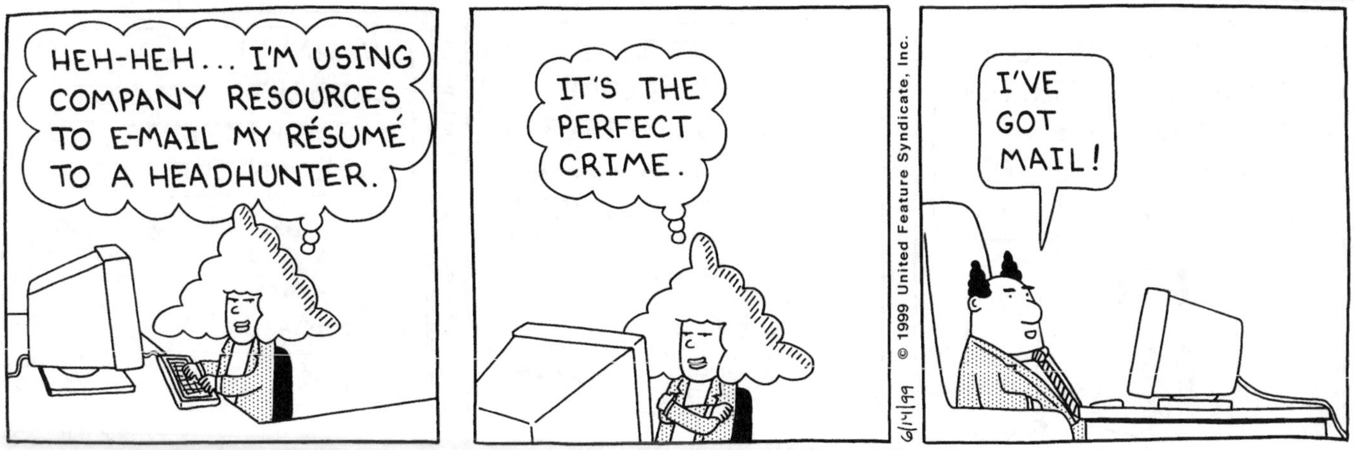
HEH-HEH... I'M USING COMPANY RESOURCES TO E-MAIL MY RÉSUMÉ TO A HEADHUNTER.
IT'S THE PERFECT CRIME.
6/14/99 © 1999 United Feature Syndicate, Inc.
I'VE GOT MAIL!

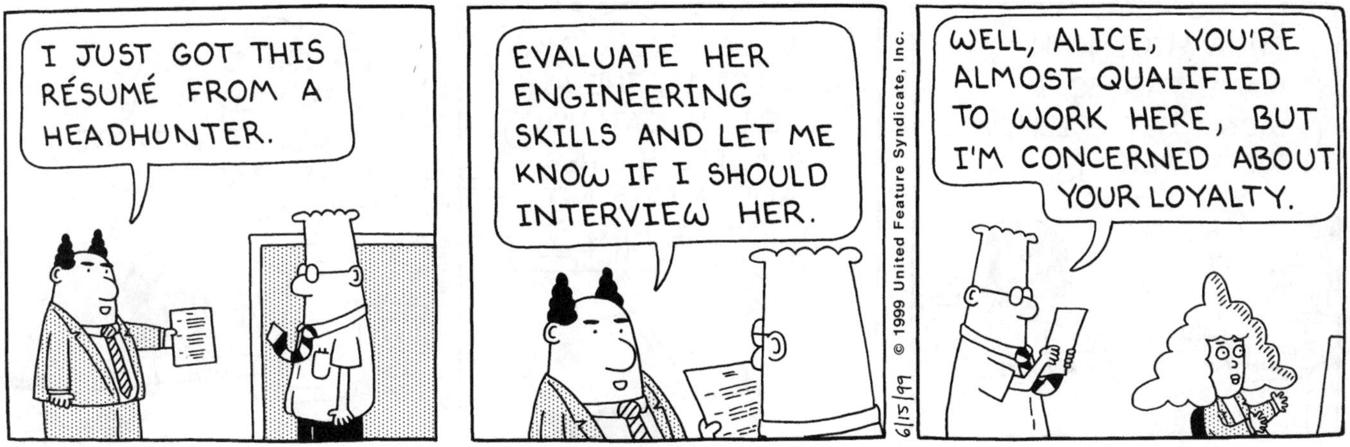
I JUST GOT THIS RÉSUMÉ FROM A HEADHUNTER.
EVALUATE HER ENGINEERING SKILLS AND LET ME KNOW IF I SHOULD INTERVIEW HER.
6/15/99 © 1999 United Feature Syndicate, Inc.
WELL, ALICE, YOU'RE ALMOST QUALIFIED TO WORK HERE, BUT I'M CONCERNED ABOUT YOUR LOYALTY.

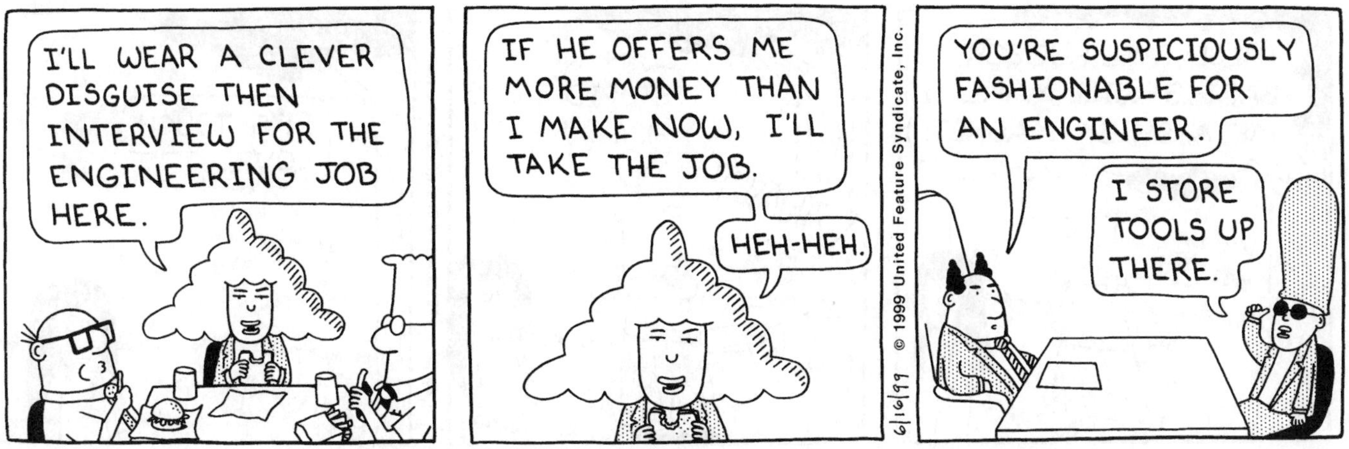
I'LL WEAR A CLEVER DISGUISE THEN INTERVIEW FOR THE ENGINEERING JOB HERE.
IF HE OFFERS ME MORE MONEY THAN I MAKE NOW, I'LL TAKE THE JOB.
HEH-HEH.
6/16/99 © 1999 United Feature Syndicate, Inc.
YOU'RE SUSPICIOUSLY FASHIONABLE FOR AN ENGINEER.
I STORE TOOLS UP THERE.

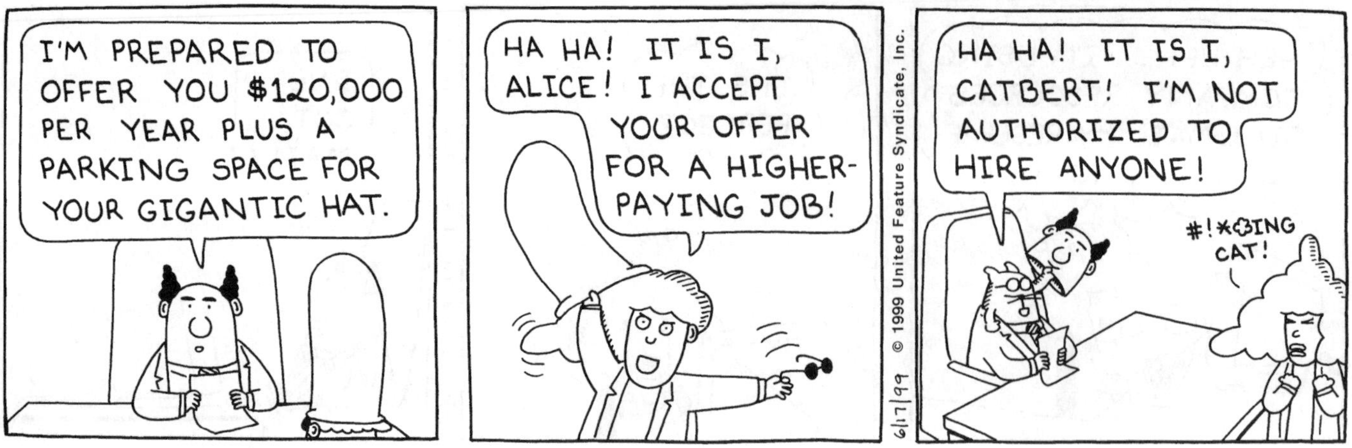
I'M PREPARED TO OFFER YOU $120,000 PER YEAR PLUS A PARKING SPACE FOR YOUR GIGANTIC HAT.
HA HA! IT IS I, ALICE! I ACCEPT YOUR OFFER FOR A HIGHER-PAYING JOB!
HA HA! IT IS I, CATBERT! I'M NOT AUTHORIZED TO HIRE ANYONE!
#!*✿ING CAT!
6/17/99 © 1999 United Feature Syndicate, Inc.

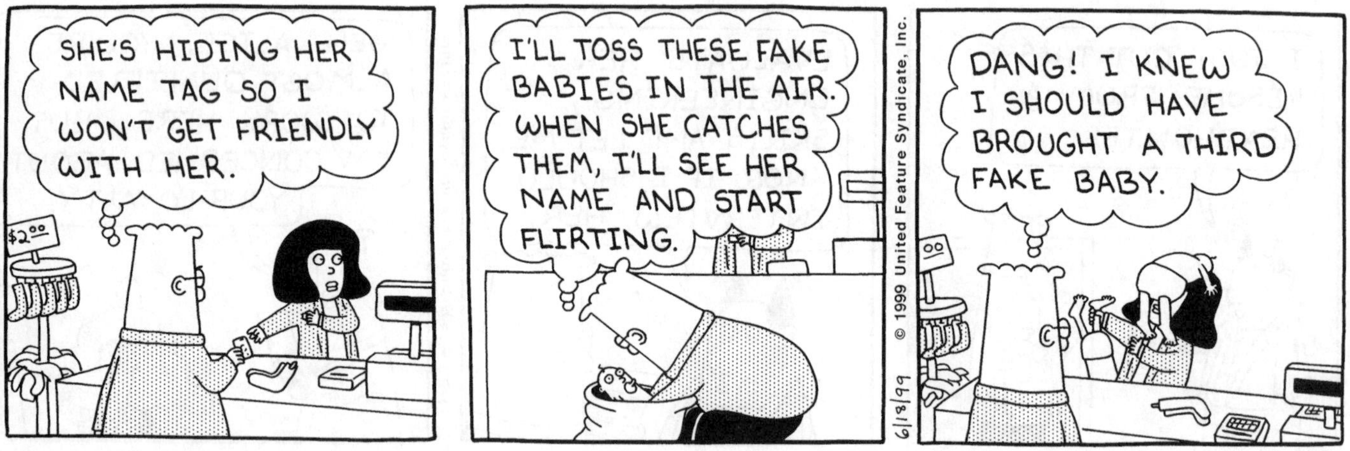
SHE'S HIDING HER NAME TAG SO I WON'T GET FRIENDLY WITH HER.
$2.00
I'LL TOSS THESE FAKE BABIES IN THE AIR. WHEN SHE CATCHES THEM, I'LL SEE HER NAME AND START FLIRTING.
DANG! I KNEW I SHOULD HAVE BROUGHT A THIRD FAKE BABY.
6/18/99 © 1999 United Feature Syndicate, Inc.

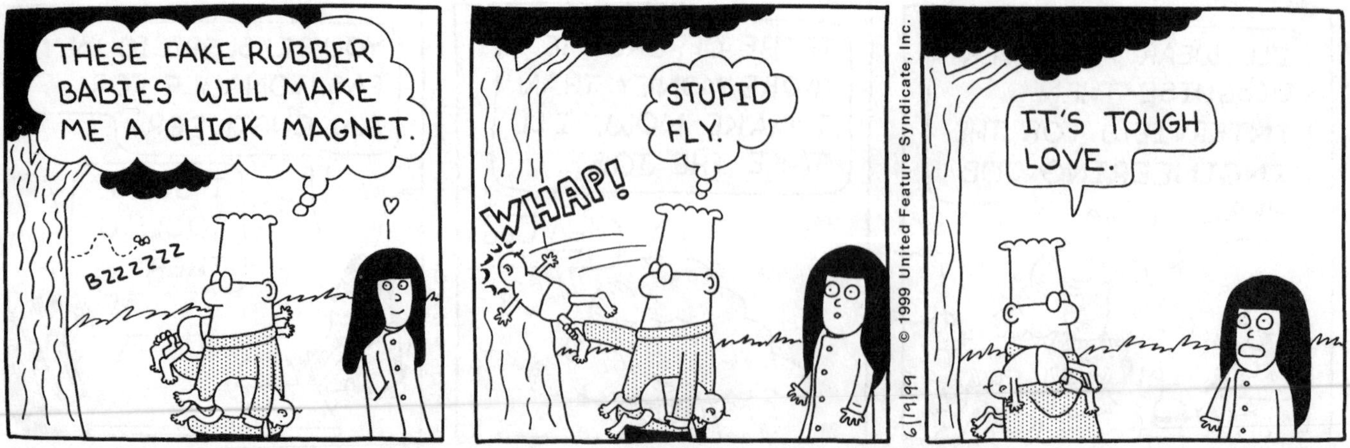
THESE FAKE RUBBER BABIES WILL MAKE ME A CHICK MAGNET.
BZZZZZZ
STUPID FLY.
WHAP!
IT'S TOUGH LOVE.
6/19/99 © 1999 United Feature Syndicate, Inc.

CATBERT: EVIL DIRECTOR OF HUMAN RESOURCES

I HIRED A NEW ENGINEER FOR YOUR PROJECT.

HE'S NEVER BEEN AN ENGINEER BEFORE.

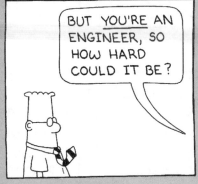

BUT YOU'RE AN ENGINEER, SO HOW HARD COULD IT BE?

AND HE'S CHEAP! I'LL GET A HUGE RAISE FOR BEING UNDER BUDGET.

AND YOUR PROJECT WILL FAIL! HA HA HA HA!

UH-OH. I LAUGHED MYSELF FULL OF STATIC ELECTRICITY.

FUZZY. CUTE.

ZAP!

HE'S DEAD. NOW WHAT?

I GUESS YOU'LL HAVE TO DRAG HIM TO MEETINGS.

© 1999 United Feature Syndicate, Inc.

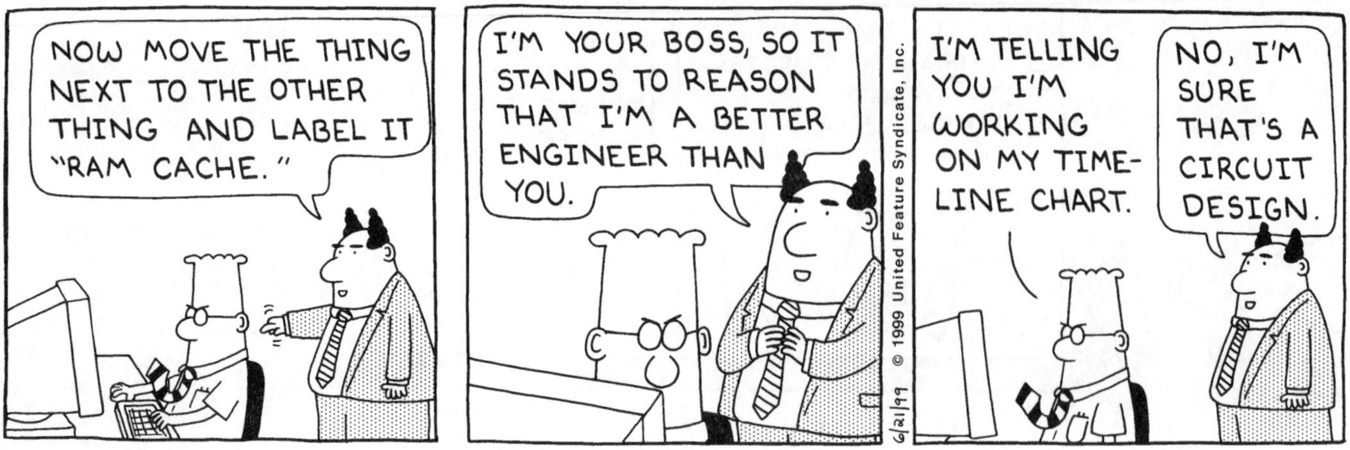
NOW MOVE THE THING NEXT TO THE OTHER THING AND LABEL IT "RAM CACHE."
I'M YOUR BOSS, SO IT STANDS TO REASON THAT I'M A BETTER ENGINEER THAN YOU.
6/21/99 © 1999 United Feature Syndicate, Inc.
I'M TELLING YOU I'M WORKING ON MY TIME-LINE CHART.
NO, I'M SURE THAT'S A CIRCUIT DESIGN.

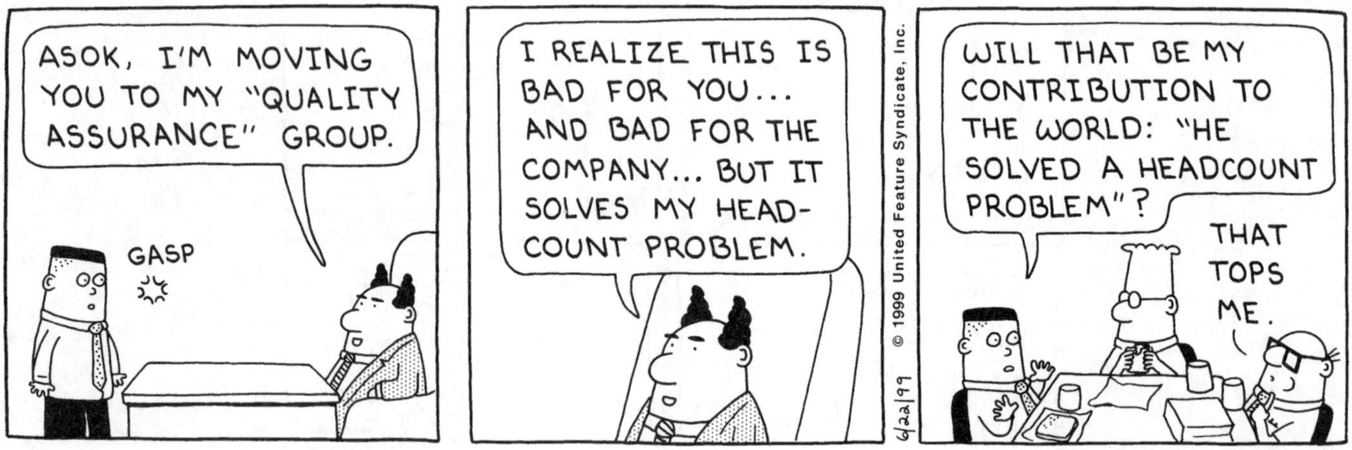
ASOK, I'M MOVING YOU TO MY "QUALITY ASSURANCE" GROUP.
GASP
I REALIZE THIS IS BAD FOR YOU... AND BAD FOR THE COMPANY... BUT IT SOLVES MY HEAD-COUNT PROBLEM.
6/22/99 © 1999 United Feature Syndicate, Inc.
WILL THAT BE MY CONTRIBUTION TO THE WORLD: "HE SOLVED A HEADCOUNT PROBLEM"?
THAT TOPS ME.

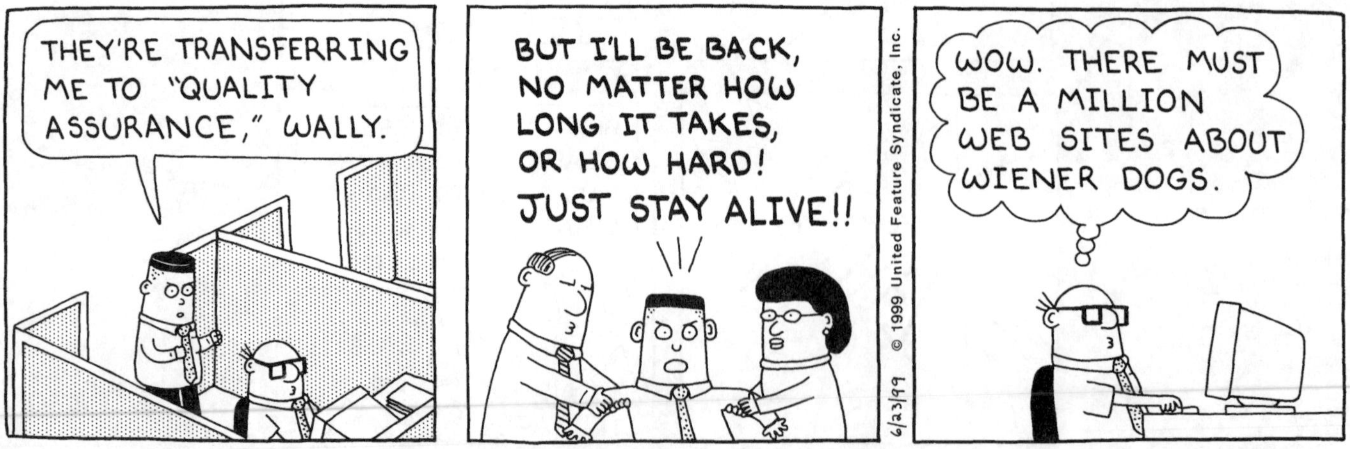
THEY'RE TRANSFERRING ME TO "QUALITY ASSURANCE," WALLY.
BUT I'LL BE BACK, NO MATTER HOW LONG IT TAKES, OR HOW HARD!
JUST STAY ALIVE!!
6/23/99 © 1999 United Feature Syndicate, Inc.
WOW. THERE MUST BE A MILLION WEB SITES ABOUT WIENER DOGS.

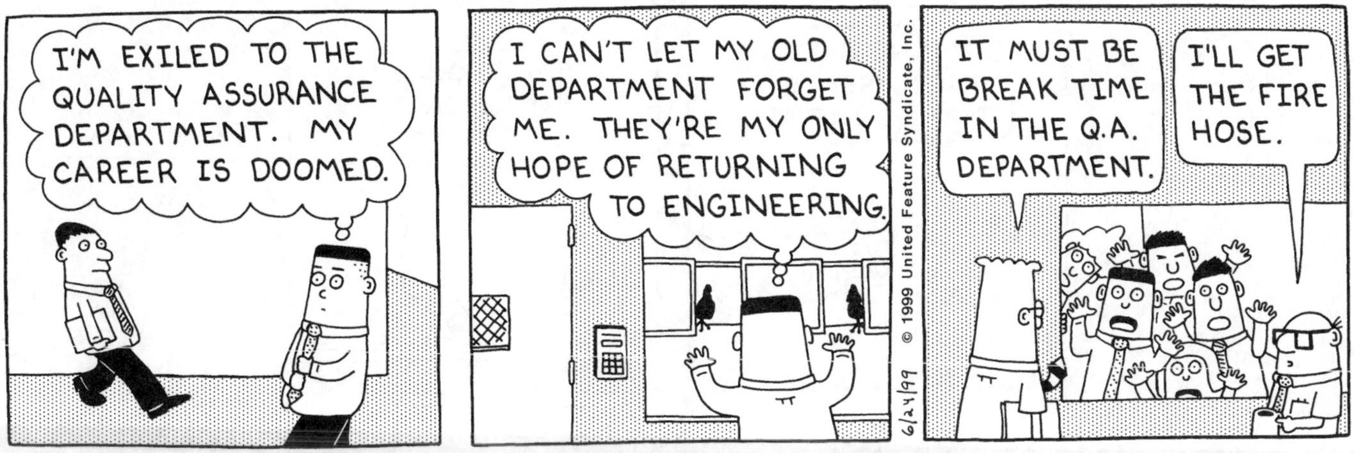
I'M EXILED TO THE QUALITY ASSURANCE DEPARTMENT. MY CAREER IS DOOMED.
I CAN'T LET MY OLD DEPARTMENT FORGET ME. THEY'RE MY ONLY HOPE OF RETURNING TO ENGINEERING.
6/24/99 © 1999 United Feature Syndicate, Inc.
IT MUST BE BREAK TIME IN THE Q.A. DEPARTMENT.
I'LL GET THE FIRE HOSE.

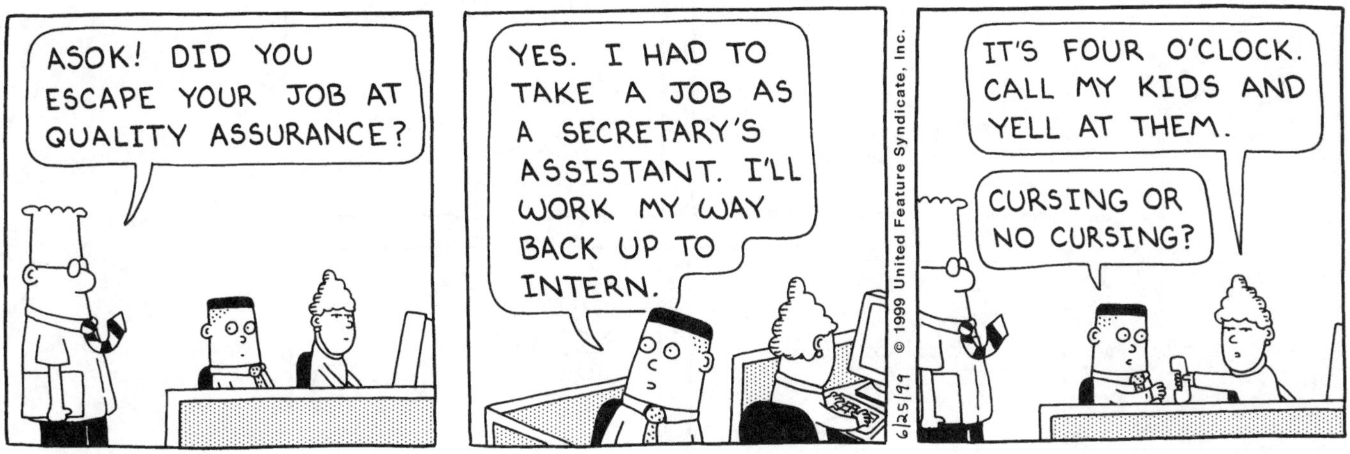
ASOK! DID YOU ESCAPE YOUR JOB AT QUALITY ASSURANCE?
YES. I HAD TO TAKE A JOB AS A SECRETARY'S ASSISTANT. I'LL WORK MY WAY BACK UP TO INTERN.
6/25/99 © 1999 United Feature Syndicate, Inc.
IT'S FOUR O'CLOCK. CALL MY KIDS AND YELL AT THEM.
CURSING OR NO CURSING?

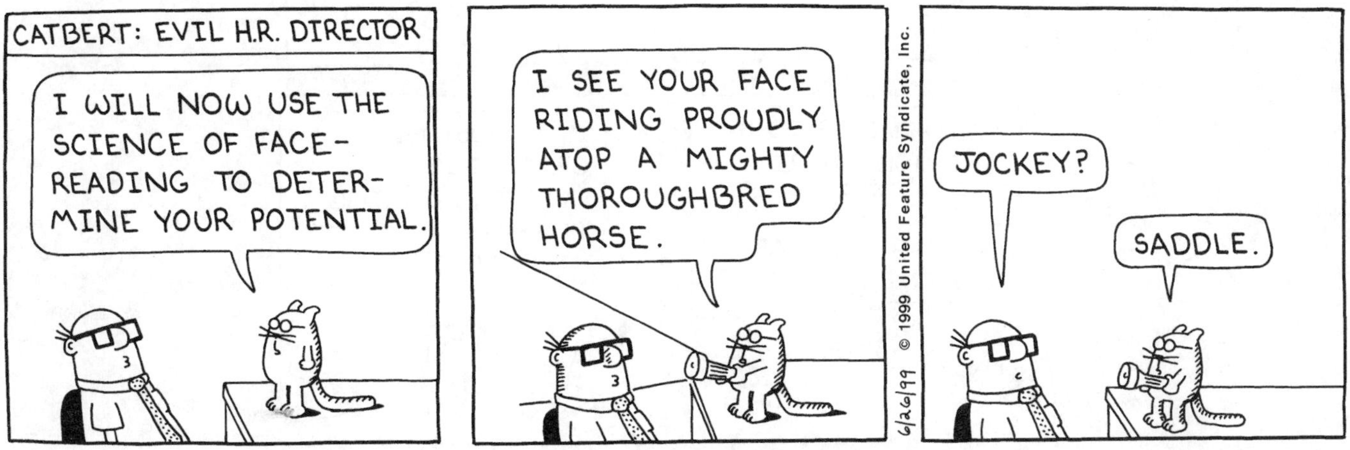
CATBERT: EVIL H.R. DIRECTOR
I WILL NOW USE THE SCIENCE OF FACE-READING TO DETERMINE YOUR POTENTIAL.
I SEE YOUR FACE RIDING PROUDLY ATOP A MIGHTY THOROUGHBRED HORSE.
6/26/99 © 1999 United Feature Syndicate, Inc.
JOCKEY?
SADDLE.

SOMEONE SHOULD TAKE CARE OF THAT PROBLEM!
YOU COULD TAKE CARE OF IT.
I CAN'T DO EVERYTHING.
YOU DON'T DO ANYTHING.
NOT A SINGLE THING.
IT'S MY JOB TO ANGRILY IDENTIFY PROBLEMS.
WALLY...
THAT IS NOT YOUR JOB!
WHAT?
EVERYTHING IS SO AMBIGUOUS HERE!
SOMEONE SHOULD TAKE CARE OF THAT PROBLEM!
IS IT JUST ME, OR IS THIS MEETING TAKING FOREVER?
6/27/99 © 1999 United Feature Syndicate, Inc.

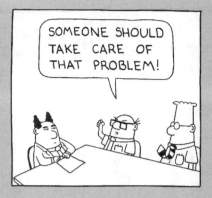

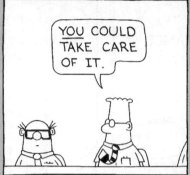

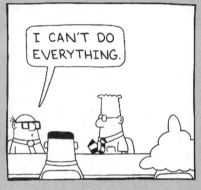

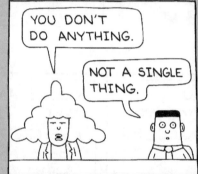

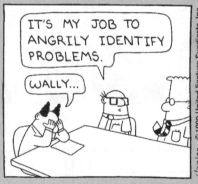

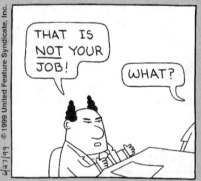

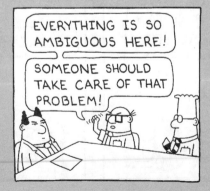

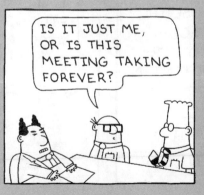

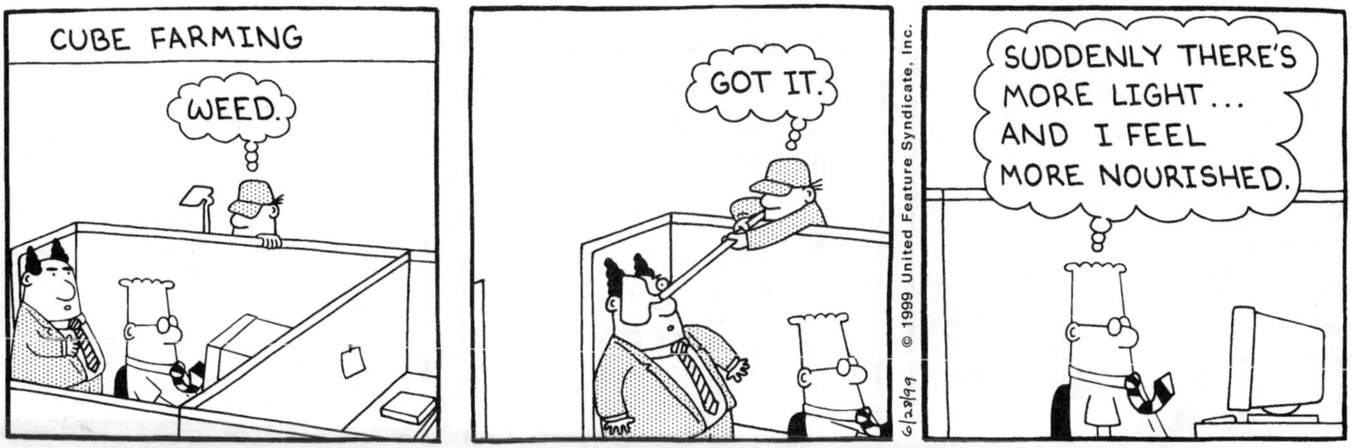
CUBE FARMING
WEED.
GOT IT.
6/28/99
© 1999 United Feature Syndicate, Inc.
SUDDENLY THERE'S MORE LIGHT... AND I FEEL MORE NOURISHED.

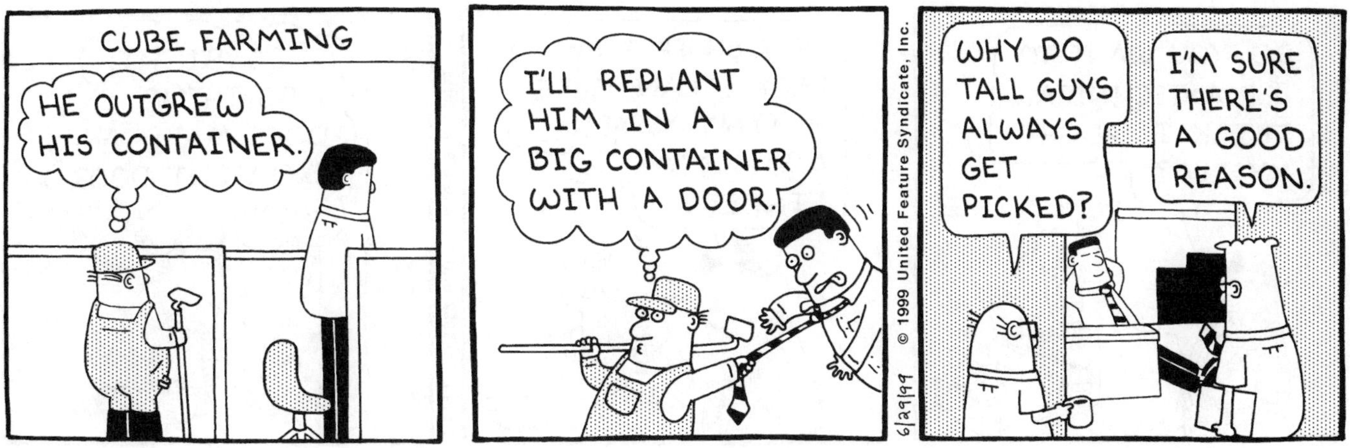
CUBE FARMING
HE OUTGREW HIS CONTAINER.
I'LL REPLANT HIM IN A BIG CONTAINER WITH A DOOR.
6/29/99
© 1999 United Feature Syndicate, Inc.
WHY DO TALL GUYS ALWAYS GET PICKED?
I'M SURE THERE'S A GOOD REASON.

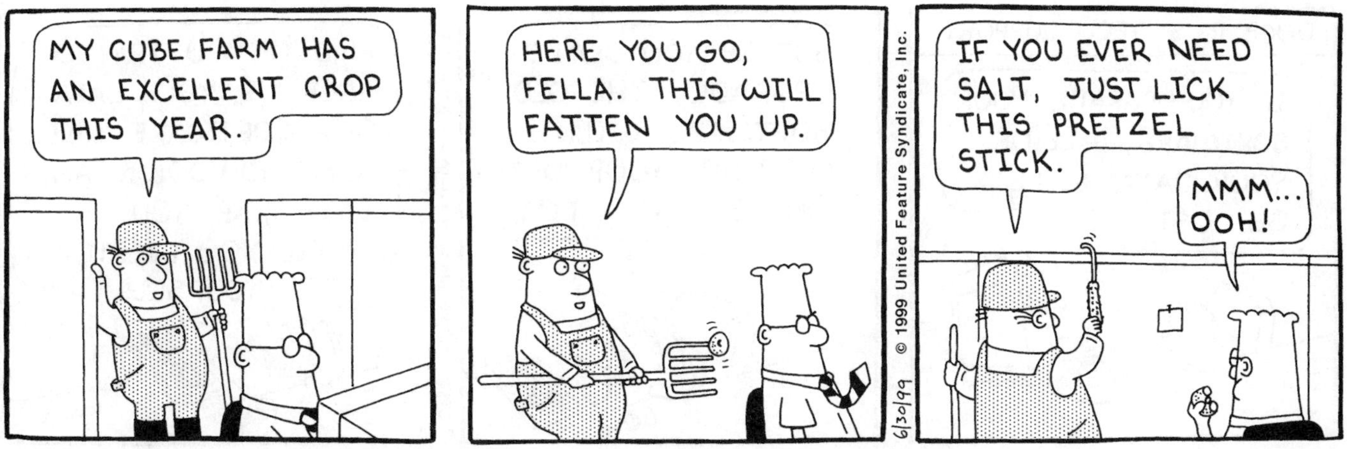
MY CUBE FARM HAS AN EXCELLENT CROP THIS YEAR.
HERE YOU GO, FELLA. THIS WILL FATTEN YOU UP.
6/30/99
© 1999 United Feature Syndicate, Inc.
IF YOU EVER NEED SALT, JUST LICK THIS PRETZEL STICK.
MMM... OOH!

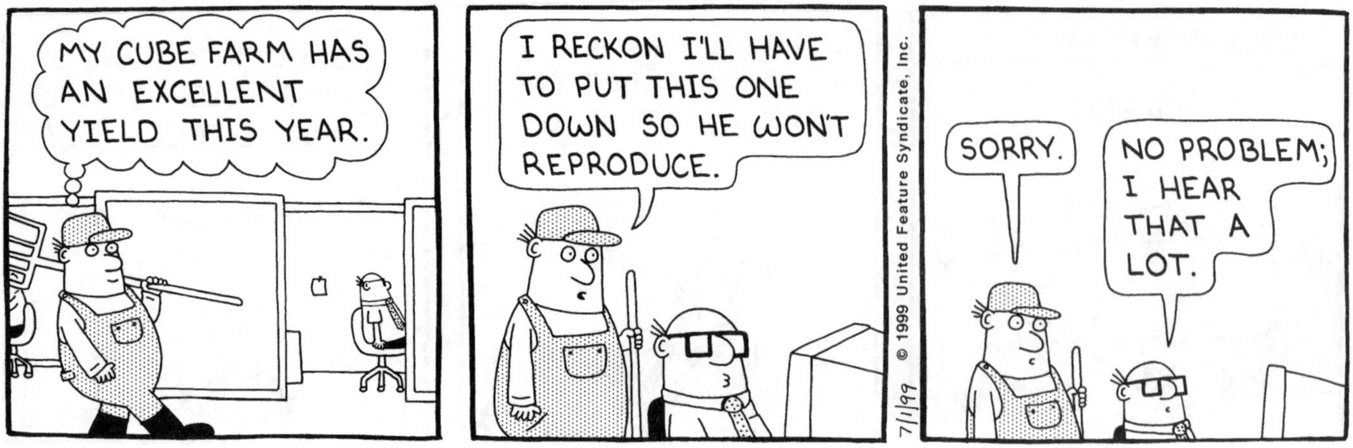
MY CUBE FARM HAS AN EXCELLENT YIELD THIS YEAR.
I RECKON I'LL HAVE TO PUT THIS ONE DOWN SO HE WON'T REPRODUCE.
7/1/99 © 1999 United Feature Syndicate, Inc.
SORRY.
NO PROBLEM; I HEAR THAT A LOT.

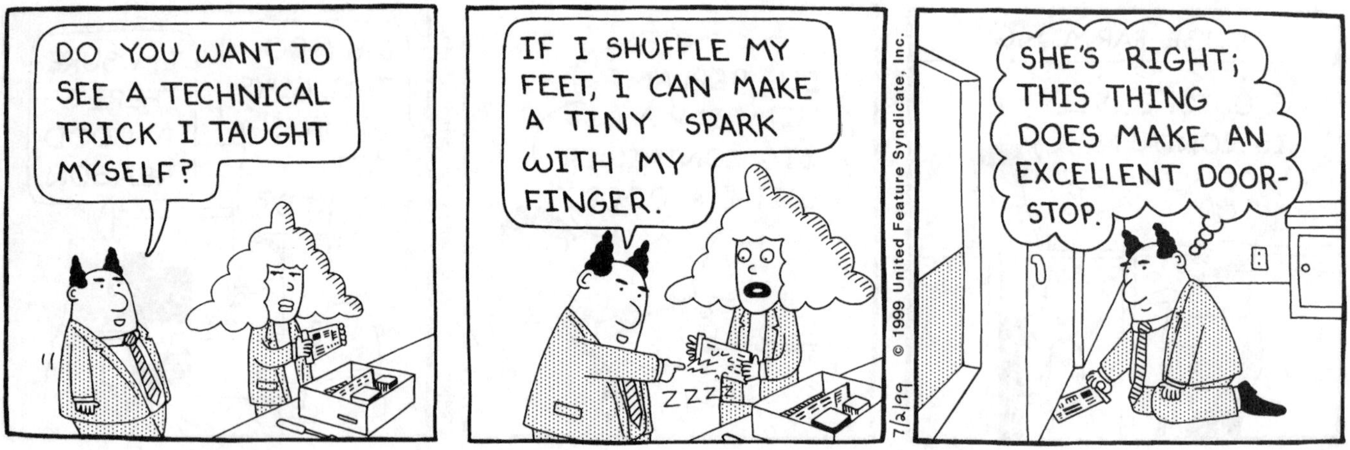
DO YOU WANT TO SEE A TECHNICAL TRICK I TAUGHT MYSELF?
IF I SHUFFLE MY FEET, I CAN MAKE A TINY SPARK WITH MY FINGER.
ZZZZ
7/2/99 © 1999 United Feature Syndicate, Inc.
SHE'S RIGHT; THIS THING DOES MAKE AN EXCELLENT DOOR-STOP.

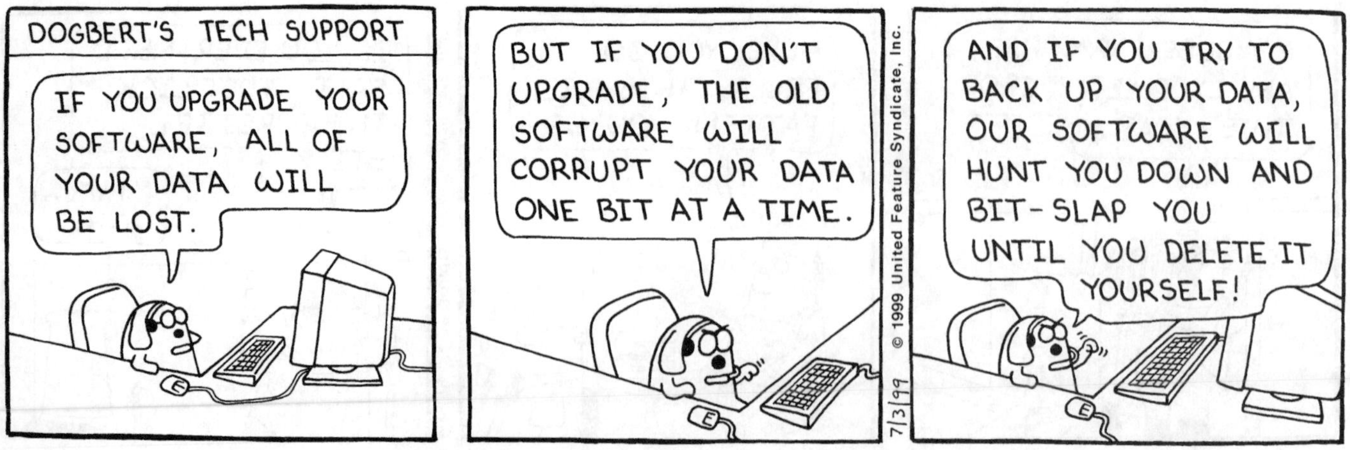
DOGBERT'S TECH SUPPORT
IF YOU UPGRADE YOUR SOFTWARE, ALL OF YOUR DATA WILL BE LOST.
BUT IF YOU DON'T UPGRADE, THE OLD SOFTWARE WILL CORRUPT YOUR DATA ONE BIT AT A TIME.
7/3/99 © 1999 United Feature Syndicate, Inc.
AND IF YOU TRY TO BACK UP YOUR DATA, OUR SOFTWARE WILL HUNT YOU DOWN AND BIT-SLAP YOU UNTIL YOU DELETE IT YOURSELF!

IF YOU DON'T FINISH THE PROJECT ON TIME, I'LL PROBABLY LOSE MY JOB.
WHAT WOULD HAPPEN TO US?
WE WOULD GET A BETTER BOSS.
WE MIGHT GET A BETTER PROJECT TOO!
THERE COULD BE WEEKS OF CONFUSION WITH NO WORK AT ALL!
YAY!!
IT'S ALL OURS IF WE SIMPLY DO LESS WORK!
WHOO! I'VE NEVER FELT MY MORALE GO UP BEFORE.
I'M DIZZY.
*!%
#
7/4/99
© 1999 United Feature Syndicate, Inc.

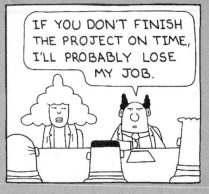

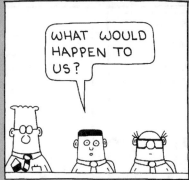

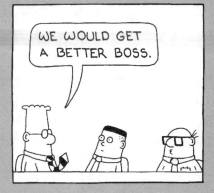

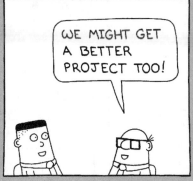

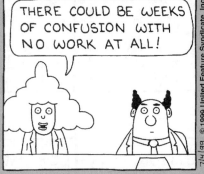

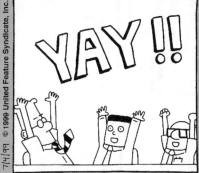

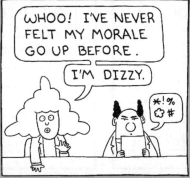

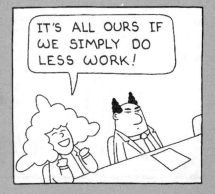

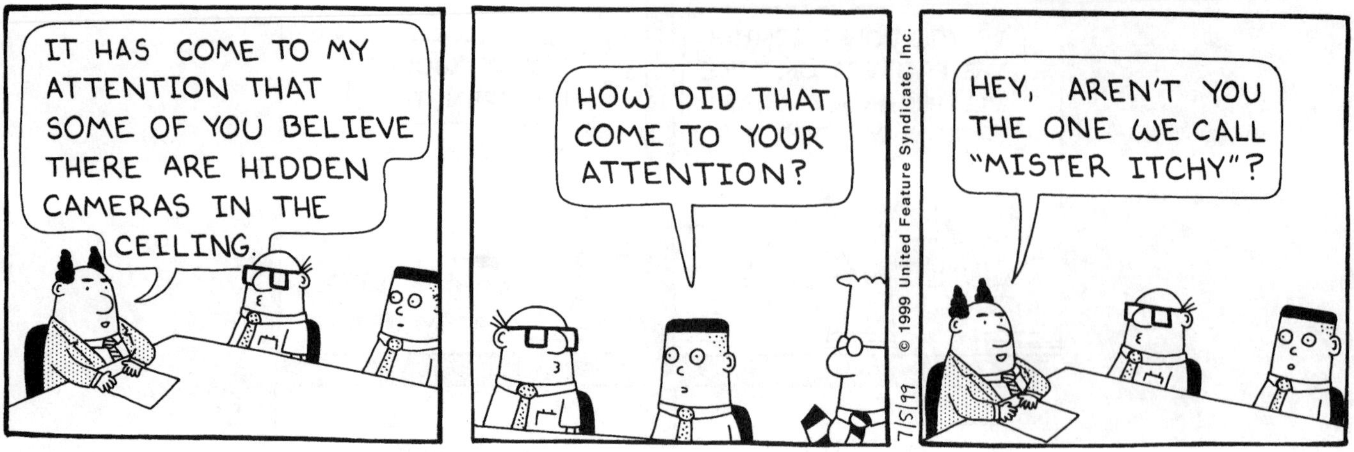
IT HAS COME TO MY ATTENTION THAT SOME OF YOU BELIEVE THERE ARE HIDDEN CAMERAS IN THE CEILING.
HOW DID THAT COME TO YOUR ATTENTION?
HEY, AREN'T YOU THE ONE WE CALL "MISTER ITCHY"?
© 1999 United Feature Syndicate, Inc.
7/5/99

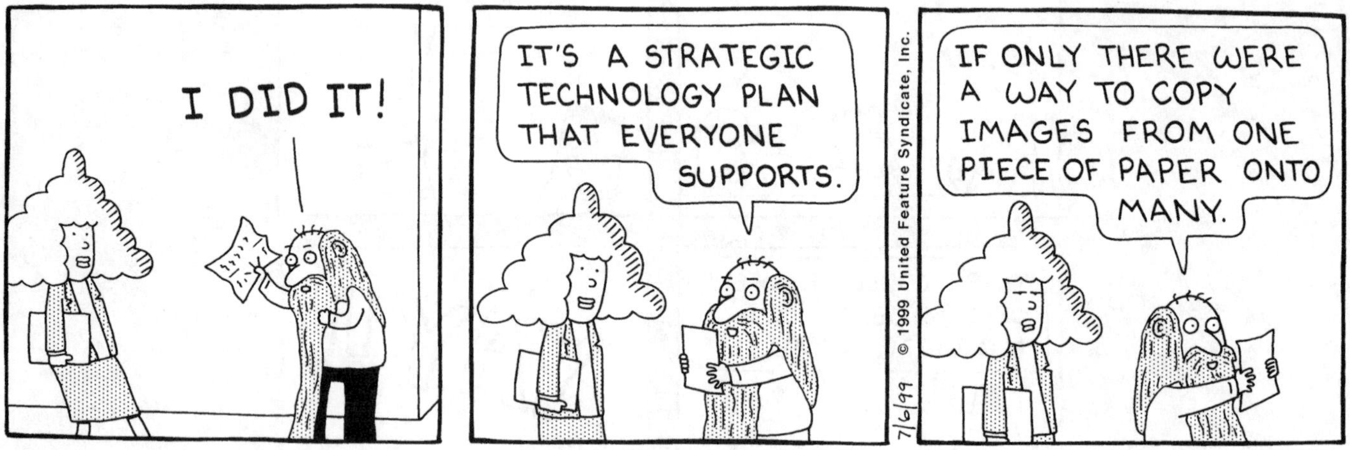
I DID IT!
IT'S A STRATEGIC TECHNOLOGY PLAN THAT EVERYONE SUPPORTS.
IF ONLY THERE WERE A WAY TO COPY IMAGES FROM ONE PIECE OF PAPER ONTO MANY.
© 1999 United Feature Syndicate, Inc.
7/6/99

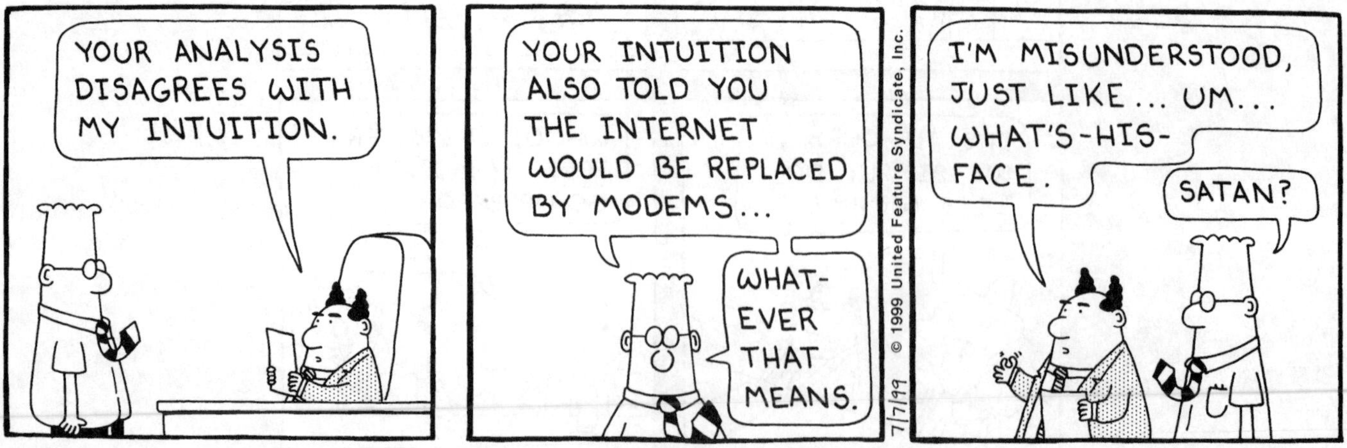
YOUR ANALYSIS DISAGREES WITH MY INTUITION.
YOUR INTUITION ALSO TOLD YOU THE INTERNET WOULD BE REPLACED BY MODEMS...
WHAT-EVER THAT MEANS.
I'M MISUNDERSTOOD, JUST LIKE ... UM... WHAT'S-HIS-FACE.
SATAN?
© 1999 United Feature Syndicate, Inc.
7/7/99

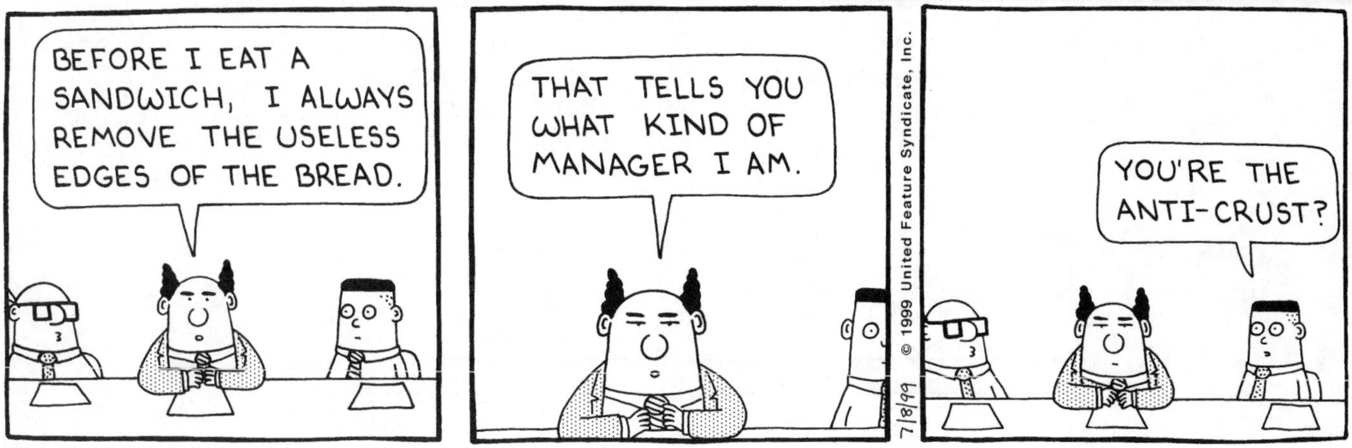
BEFORE I EAT A SANDWICH, I ALWAYS REMOVE THE USELESS EDGES OF THE BREAD.
THAT TELLS YOU WHAT KIND OF MANAGER I AM.
7/8/99 © 1999 United Feature Syndicate, Inc.
YOU'RE THE ANTI-CRUST?

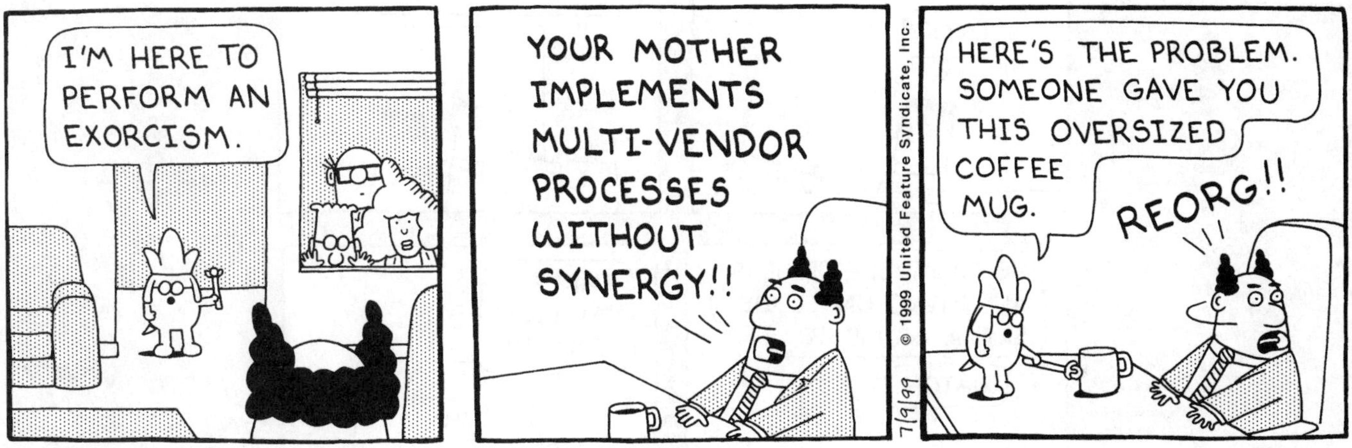
I'M HERE TO PERFORM AN EXORCISM.
YOUR MOTHER IMPLEMENTS MULTI-VENDOR PROCESSES WITHOUT SYNERGY!!
7/9/99 © 1999 United Feature Syndicate, Inc.
HERE'S THE PROBLEM. SOMEONE GAVE YOU THIS OVERSIZED COFFEE MUG.
REORG!!

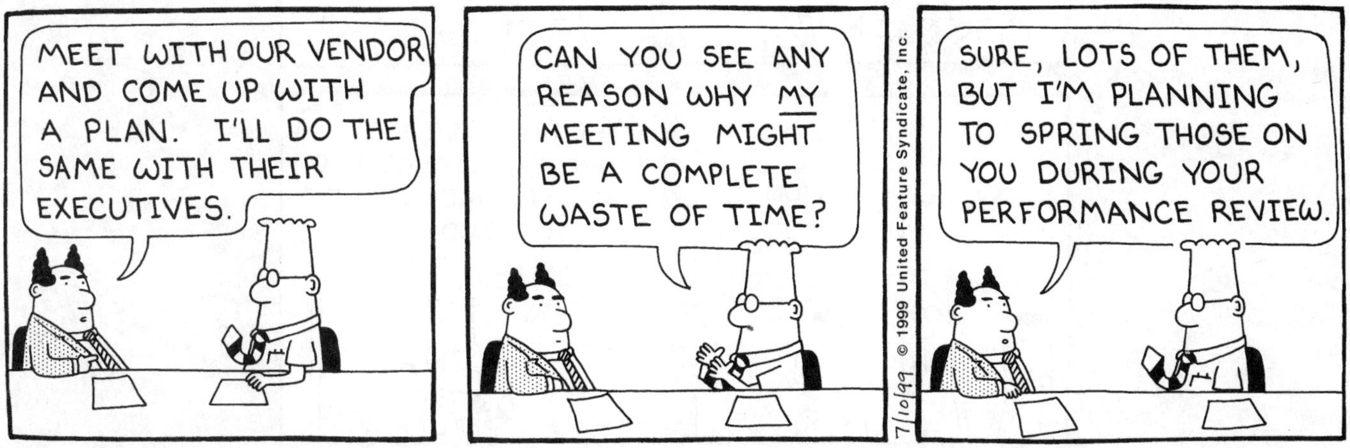
MEET WITH OUR VENDOR AND COME UP WITH A PLAN. I'LL DO THE SAME WITH THEIR EXECUTIVES.
CAN YOU SEE ANY REASON WHY MY MEETING MIGHT BE A COMPLETE WASTE OF TIME?
7/10/99 © 1999 United Feature Syndicate, Inc.
SURE, LOTS OF THEM, BUT I'M PLANNING TO SPRING THOSE ON YOU DURING YOUR PERFORMANCE REVIEW.

I NEED YOUR BUDGET ESTIMATE TODAY.
WE WON'T HAVE USEFUL NUMBERS UNTIL NEXT WEEK.
IT DOESN'T WORK THAT WAY, ASOK.
NO?
AS SOON AS HE ASKED THE QUESTION, HE WENT INTO "BOSS HIBERNATION."
HE CAN'T SEE OR HEAR ANYTHING UNTIL WE SAY A NUMBER.
WATCH.
THREE MILLION DOLLARS.
UHN!
THREE MILLION.
GOOD WORK.
THE FIRST TIME I SAW IT, I PANICKED AND ENDED UP WITH A BUDGET OF $911.
7/1/99

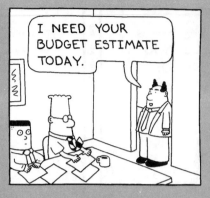

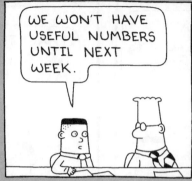

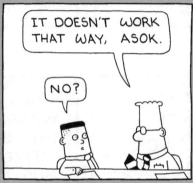

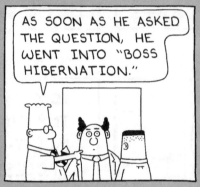

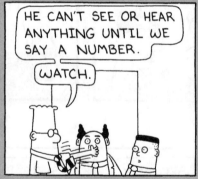

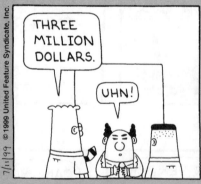

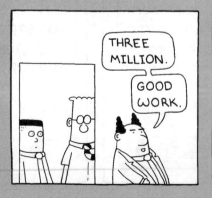

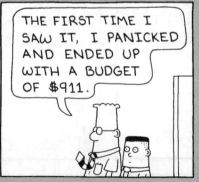

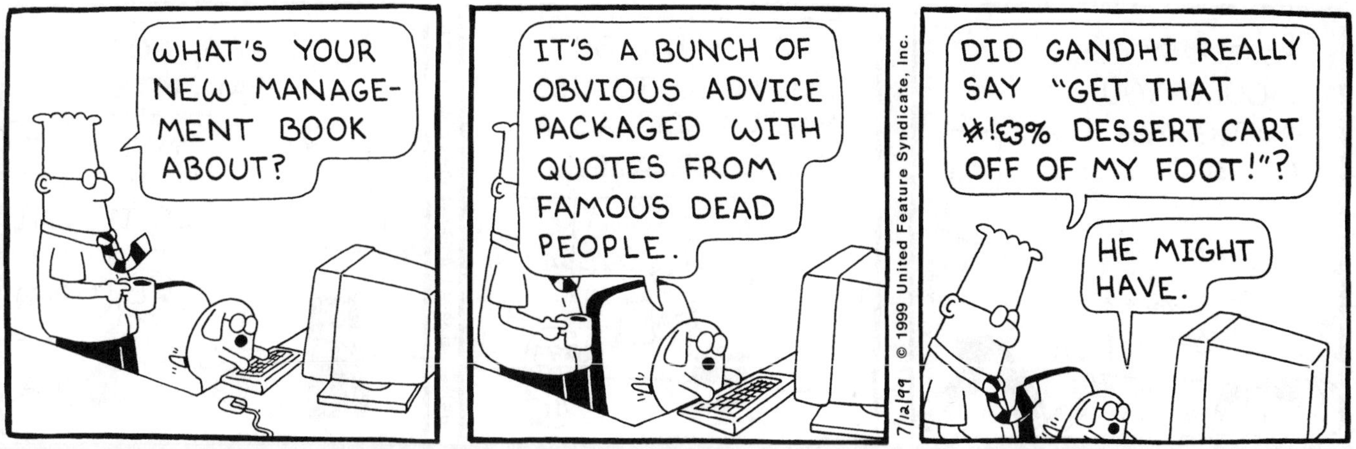
WHAT'S YOUR NEW MANAGEMENT BOOK ABOUT?
IT'S A BUNCH OF OBVIOUS ADVICE PACKAGED WITH QUOTES FROM FAMOUS DEAD PEOPLE.
DID GANDHI REALLY SAY "GET THAT #!✿% DESSERT CART OFF OF MY FOOT!"?
HE MIGHT HAVE.
7/2/99 © 1999 United Feature Syndicate, Inc.

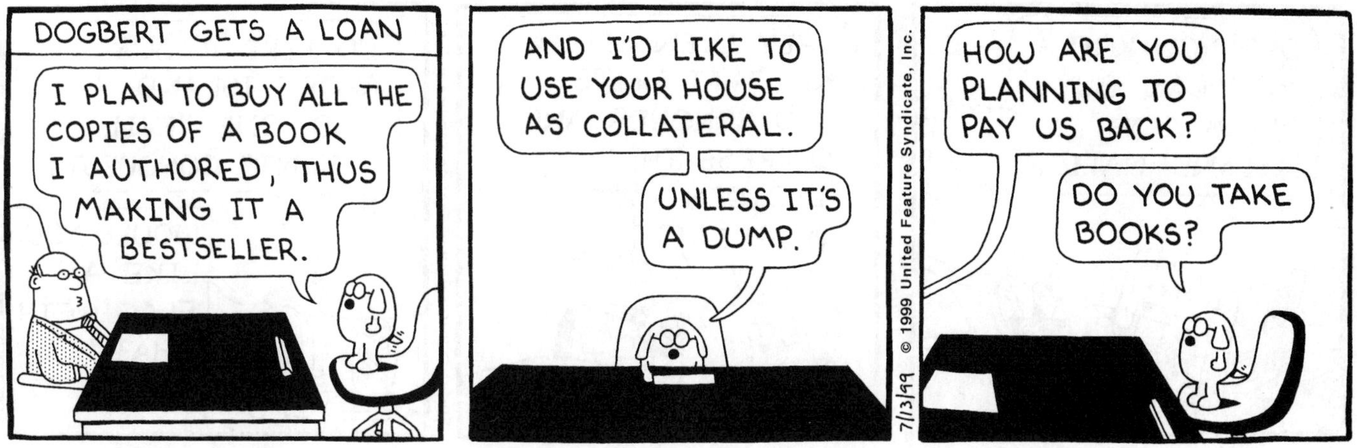
DOGBERT GETS A LOAN
I PLAN TO BUY ALL THE COPIES OF A BOOK I AUTHORED, THUS MAKING IT A BESTSELLER.
AND I'D LIKE TO USE YOUR HOUSE AS COLLATERAL.
UNLESS IT'S A DUMP.
HOW ARE YOU PLANNING TO PAY US BACK?
DO YOU TAKE BOOKS?
7/13/99 © 1999 United Feature Syndicate, Inc.

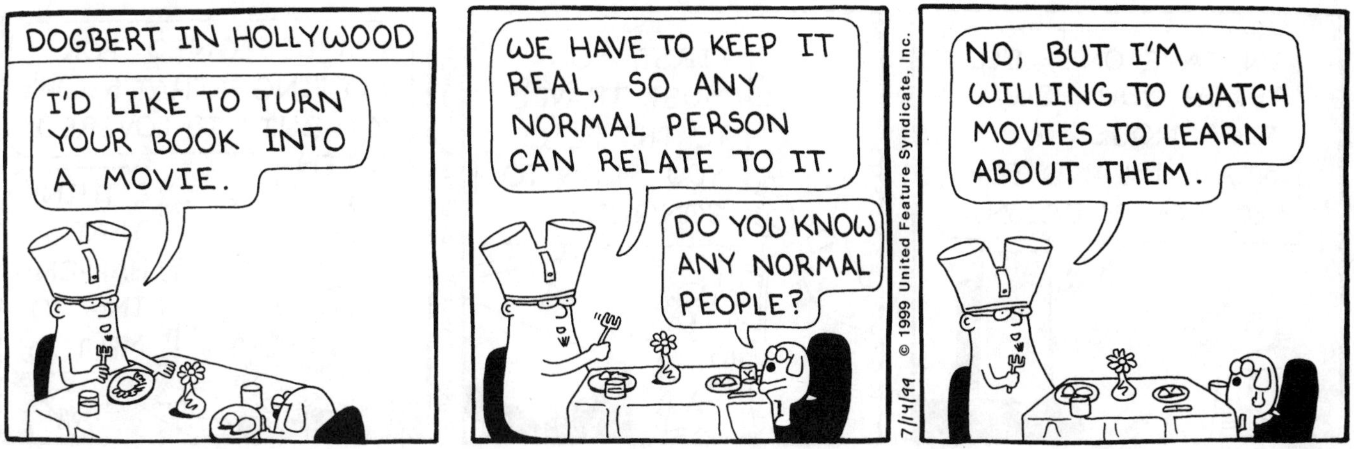
DOGBERT IN HOLLYWOOD
I'D LIKE TO TURN YOUR BOOK INTO A MOVIE.
WE HAVE TO KEEP IT REAL, SO ANY NORMAL PERSON CAN RELATE TO IT.
DO YOU KNOW ANY NORMAL PEOPLE?
NO, BUT I'M WILLING TO WATCH MOVIES TO LEARN ABOUT THEM.
7/14/99 © 1999 United Feature Syndicate, Inc.

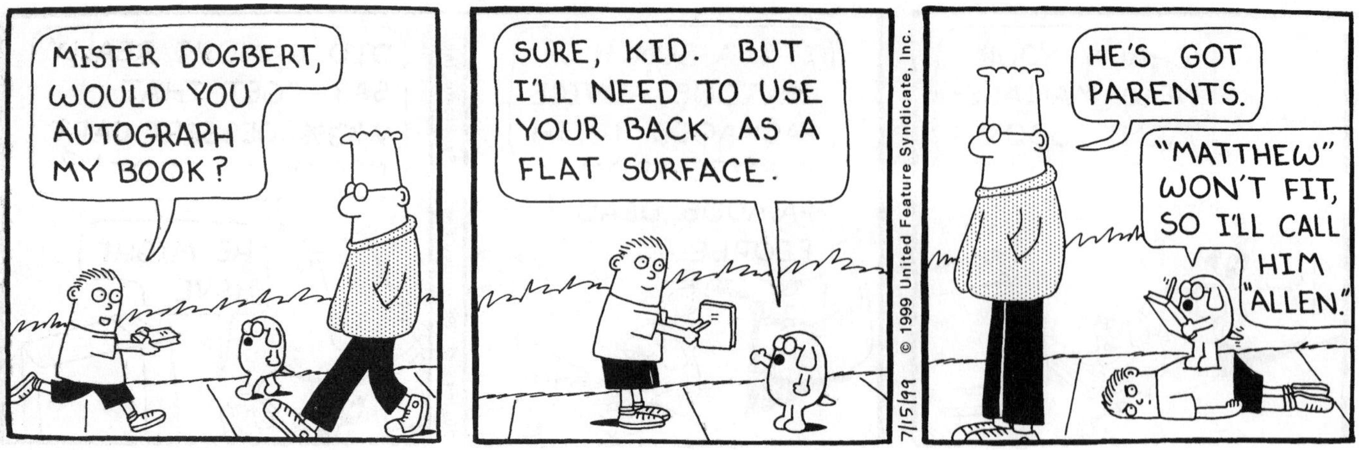
MISTER DOGBERT, WOULD YOU AUTOGRAPH MY BOOK?
SURE, KID. BUT I'LL NEED TO USE YOUR BACK AS A FLAT SURFACE.
7/15/99 © 1999 United Feature Syndicate, Inc.
HE'S GOT PARENTS.
"MATTHEW" WON'T FIT, SO I'LL CALL HIM "ALLEN."

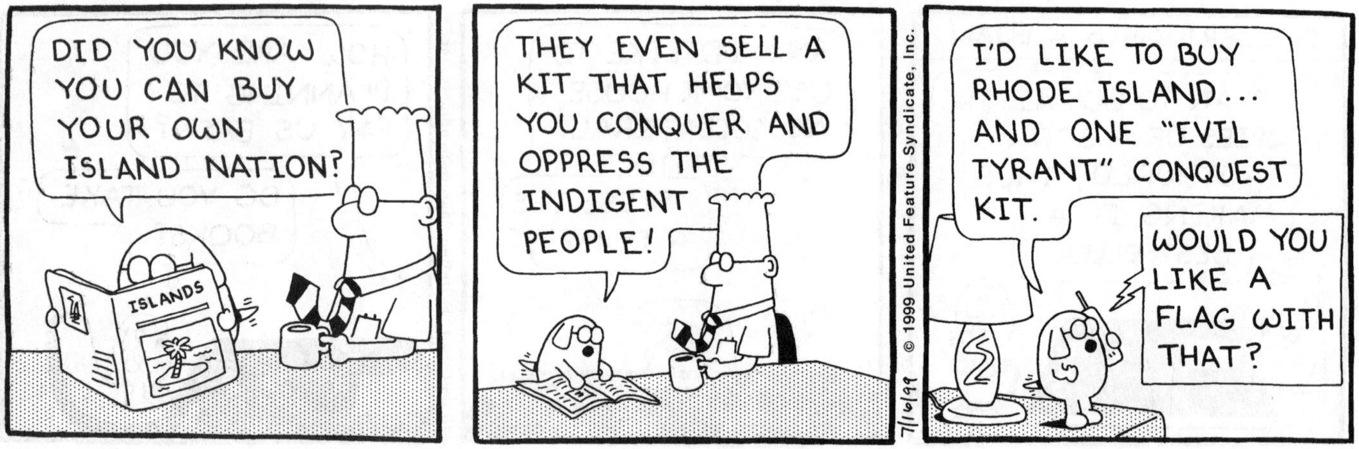
DID YOU KNOW YOU CAN BUY YOUR OWN ISLAND NATION?
ISLANDS
THEY EVEN SELL A KIT THAT HELPS YOU CONQUER AND OPPRESS THE INDIGENT PEOPLE!
7/16/99 © 1999 United Feature Syndicate, Inc.
I'D LIKE TO BUY RHODE ISLAND... AND ONE "EVIL TYRANT" CONQUEST KIT.
WOULD YOU LIKE A FLAG WITH THAT?

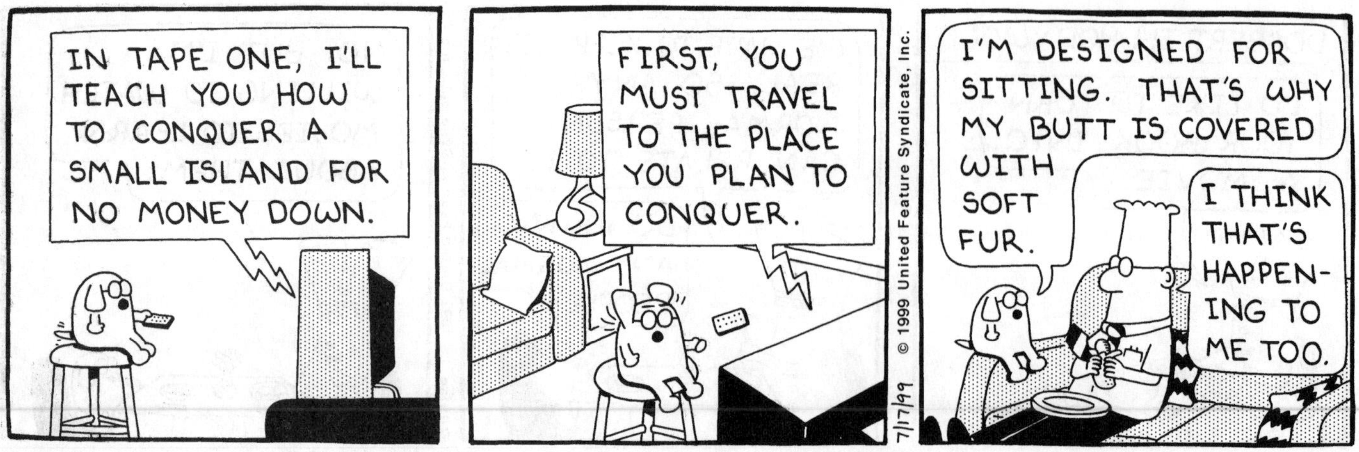
IN TAPE ONE, I'LL TEACH YOU HOW TO CONQUER A SMALL ISLAND FOR NO MONEY DOWN.
FIRST, YOU MUST TRAVEL TO THE PLACE YOU PLAN TO CONQUER.
7/17/99 © 1999 United Feature Syndicate, Inc.
I'M DESIGNED FOR SITTING. THAT'S WHY MY BUTT IS COVERED WITH SOFT FUR.
I THINK THAT'S HAPPENING TO ME TOO.

THE FENG SHUI CONSULTANT
THIS OFFICE IS SWARMING WITH EVIL SPIRITS.
IT IS?
THERE'S ONE IN YOUR VENT!
OOH – HE DUCKED BACK IN BEFORE YOU SAW HIM.
PUT RUBBER BANDS AROUND YOUR PANT LEGS TO KEEP THE SPIRITS OUT OF YOUR TROUSERS.
I FIGURE THE EVIL SPIRITS WILL MOUNT A REAR ASSAULT THROUGH THAT WINDOW.
AAAGH!
WHAT DID YOU SEE?!!
IT'S GONE NOW.
YOUR ONLY HOPE IS TO TURN YOUR SECRETARY'S CUBICLE INTO A KOI POND.
DO YOU FEEL ANY LUCKIER?
*#!

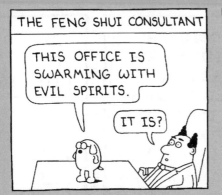

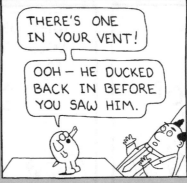

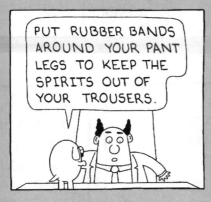

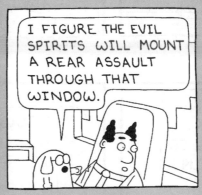

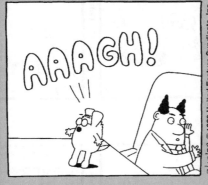

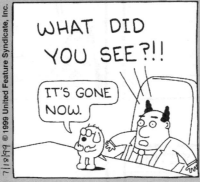

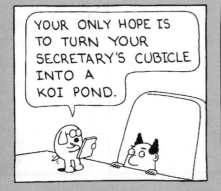

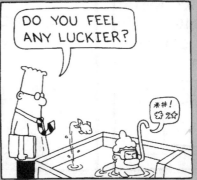

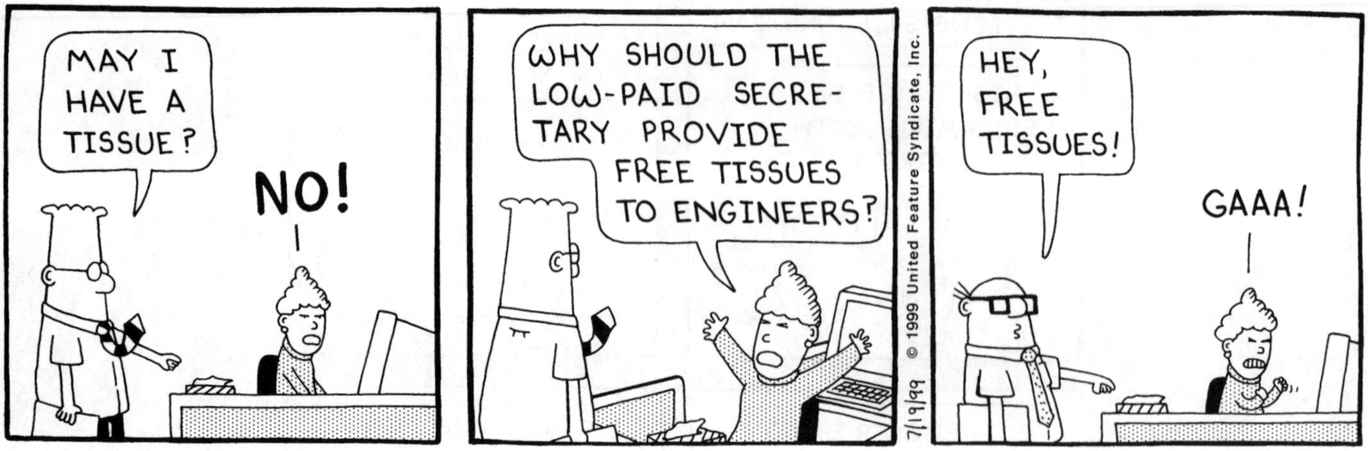
MAY I HAVE A TISSUE?
NO!
WHY SHOULD THE LOW-PAID SECRETARY PROVIDE FREE TISSUES TO ENGINEERS?
7/19/99 © 1999 United Feature Syndicate, Inc.
HEY, FREE TISSUES!
GAAA!

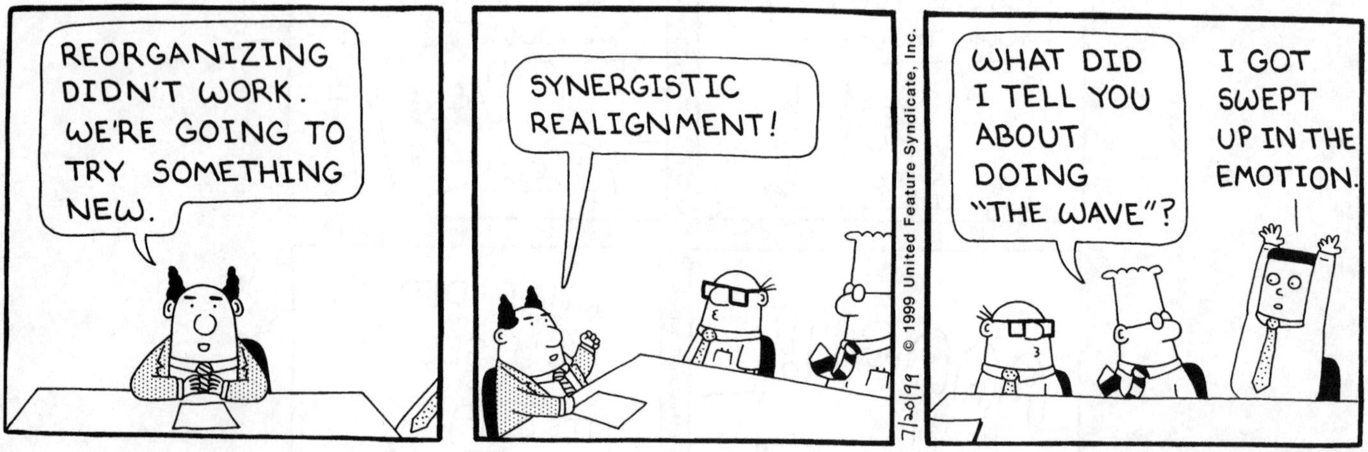
REORGANIZING DIDN'T WORK. WE'RE GOING TO TRY SOMETHING NEW.
SYNERGISTIC REALIGNMENT!
7/20/99 © 1999 United Feature Syndicate, Inc.
WHAT DID I TELL YOU ABOUT DOING "THE WAVE"?
I GOT SWEPT UP IN THE EMOTION.

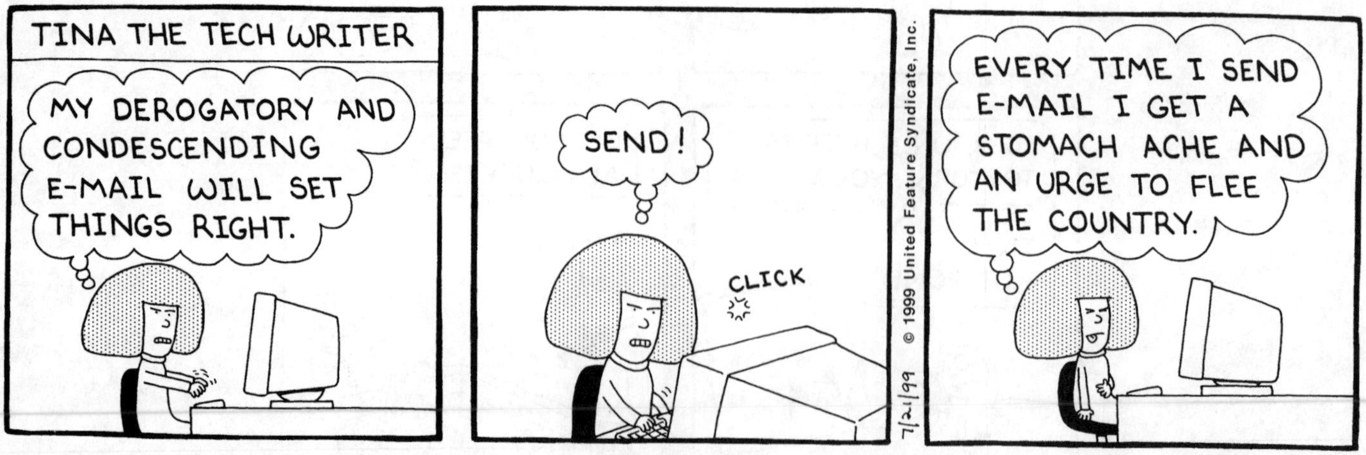
TINA THE TECH WRITER
MY DEROGATORY AND CONDESCENDING E-MAIL WILL SET THINGS RIGHT.
SEND!
CLICK
7/21/99 © 1999 United Feature Syndicate, Inc.
EVERY TIME I SEND E-MAIL I GET A STOMACH ACHE AND AN URGE TO FLEE THE COUNTRY.

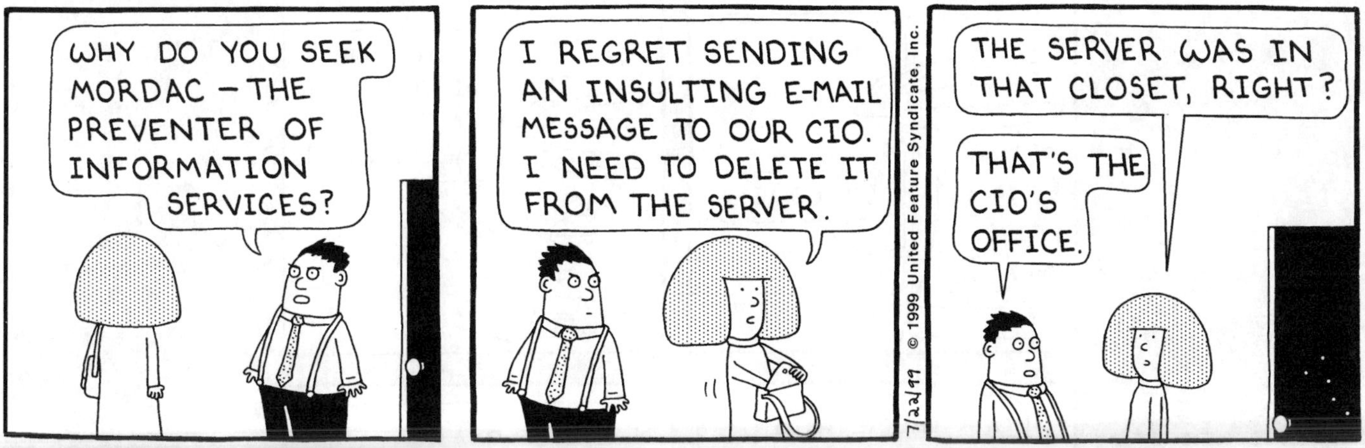
WHY DO YOU SEEK MORDAC – THE PREVENTER OF INFORMATION SERVICES?
I REGRET SENDING AN INSULTING E-MAIL MESSAGE TO OUR CIO. I NEED TO DELETE IT FROM THE SERVER.
7/22/99 © 1999 United Feature Syndicate, Inc.
THE SERVER WAS IN THAT CLOSET, RIGHT?
THAT'S THE CIO'S OFFICE.

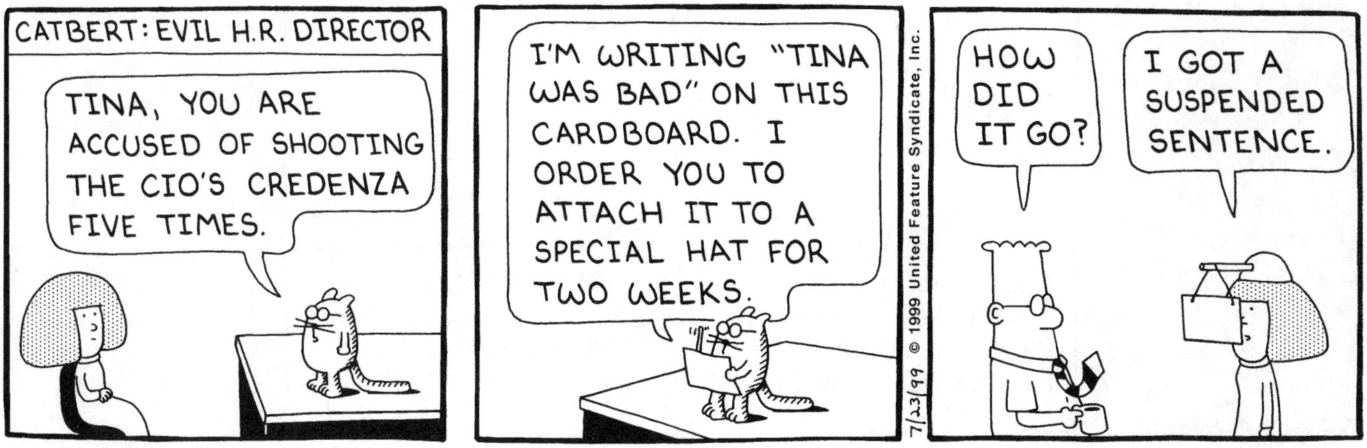
CATBERT: EVIL H.R. DIRECTOR
TINA, YOU ARE ACCUSED OF SHOOTING THE CIO'S CREDENZA FIVE TIMES.
I'M WRITING "TINA WAS BAD" ON THIS CARDBOARD. I ORDER YOU TO ATTACH IT TO A SPECIAL HAT FOR TWO WEEKS.
7/23/99 © 1999 United Feature Syndicate, Inc.
HOW DID IT GO?
I GOT A SUSPENDED SENTENCE.

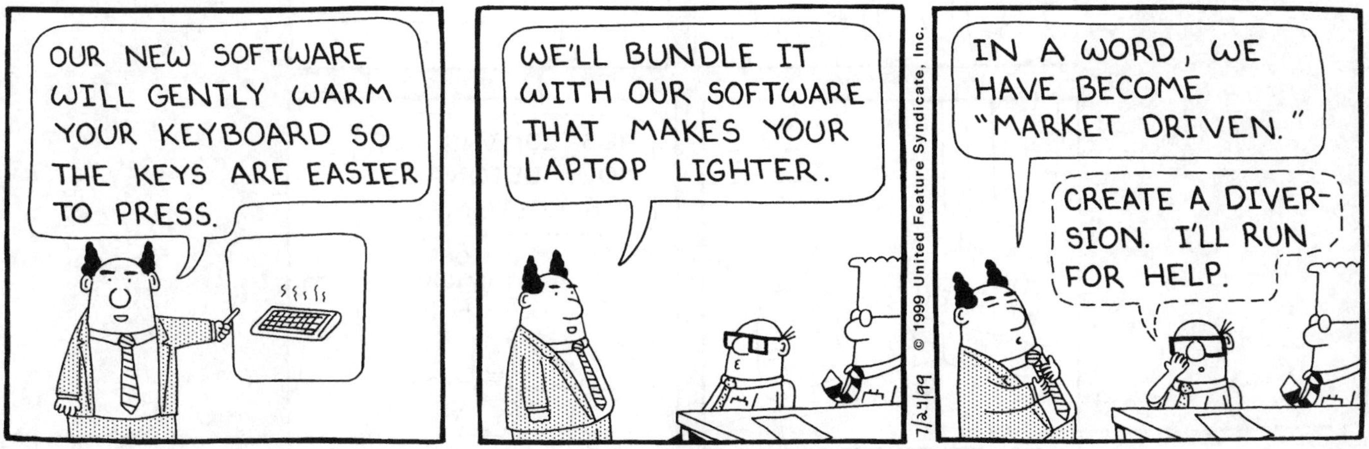
OUR NEW SOFTWARE WILL GENTLY WARM YOUR KEYBOARD SO THE KEYS ARE EASIER TO PRESS.
WE'LL BUNDLE IT WITH OUR SOFTWARE THAT MAKES YOUR LAPTOP LIGHTER.
7/24/99 © 1999 United Feature Syndicate, Inc.
IN A WORD, WE HAVE BECOME "MARKET DRIVEN."
CREATE A DIVERSION. I'LL RUN FOR HELP.

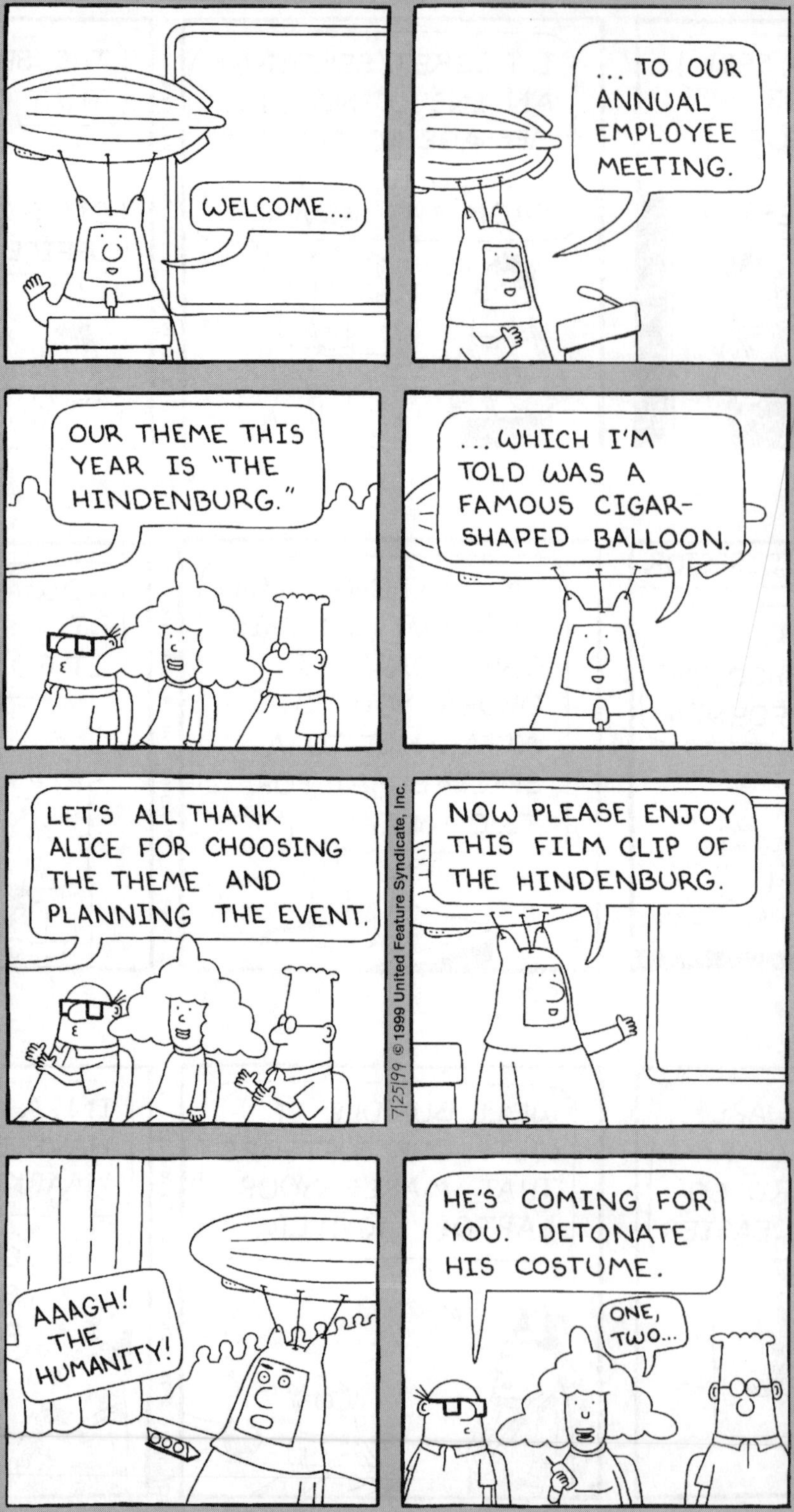
WELCOME...
... TO OUR ANNUAL EMPLOYEE MEETING.
OUR THEME THIS YEAR IS "THE HINDENBURG."
... WHICH I'M TOLD WAS A FAMOUS CIGAR-SHAPED BALLOON.
LET'S ALL THANK ALICE FOR CHOOSING THE THEME AND PLANNING THE EVENT.
7/25/99 © 1999 United Feature Syndicate, Inc.
NOW PLEASE ENJOY THIS FILM CLIP OF THE HINDENBURG.
AAAGH! THE HUMANITY!
HE'S COMING FOR YOU. DETONATE HIS COSTUME.
ONE, TWO...